Relax.

You've opened the right book.

Once upon a time, people were wrong. They thought the automobile was an electric death trap that would never replace the buggy, the internet was only for academic shut-ins, and people who used study guides were simply *cheaters*. Then cars stopped exploding every time you started the engine, people realized you could use computers for more than just calculating the digits of *pi*, and the "cheaters" with the study guides … well, they started getting it. They got better grades, got into better schools, and just plain ol' got better. Times change. Rules change. *You snooze, you lose, buggy drivers.*

SparkNotes is different. We've always been thinking ahead. We were the first study guides on the Internet back in 1999—you've been to SparkNotes.com haven't you? If not … why?! You'll find busy message boards, diagnostic test prep, and all kinds of tools you'll need to get your act together and your grades up. And if your act's already together, SparkNotes will help you brutalize the competition. Or work for peace. Your call.

We're inexpensive, not cheap. Not only are our books the best bang for the buck, they're the best bang, period. Our reputation is based on staying smart and trustworthy—one step ahead, making tough topics understandable. We explain, we strategize, we translate. We get you where you want to go: smarter, better, faster than anyone else.

If you've got something to say, tell us. Your input makes us better. Found a mistake? Check www.sparknotes.com/errors. Have a comment? Go to www.sparknotes.com/comments. Did you read all the way to the bottom? Awesome. We love you. You're gonna do just fine.

SPARKNOTES™

SPARKNOTES®

GUIDE TO THE

GRE®
TEST

by Eric Goodman

and David Younghans

SPARK PUBLISHING

Spark Publishing
A Division of Barnes & Noble, Inc.
120 Fifth Avenue
New York, NY 10011
www.sparknotes.com

Library of Congress Cataloging-in-Publication Data

Goodman, Eric (Eric Craig), 1966-
  SparkNotes guide to the GRE test / by Eric Goodman and David Younghans.
     p. cm.
  ISBN: 978-1-4114-9967-6 (alk. paper)
  1. Graduate Record Examination—Study guides. I. Younghans, David. II. SparkNotes
LLC. III. Title. IV. Title: SparkNotes guide to the GRE test. V. Title: Guide to the GRE test.
  LB2367.4.G57 2008
  378.1'662—dc22
                                    2007034027

Please submit changes or report errors to www.sparknotes.com/errors.

Printed and bound in Canada

10 9 8 7 6 5 4 3 2

ACKNOWLEDGMENTS

From Eric Goodman:

I wish to thank Jessica Allen and everyone at SparkNotes for their help and support. Special thanks to Laurie Barnett for the opportunity and her invaluable hands-on contributions to the manuscript.

From David Younghans:

The book in your hands is a collaborative effort, fine-tuned and improved over the course of more than a year. It has benefited greatly from the advice and expertise of many, including Laurie Barnett and Jessica Allen. Their editorial wisdom was invaluable at every stage of this book's production. Thanks also to Dr. Stefan Gunther for his expert guidance and review. Endless thanks to everyone else at SparkNotes for making this book possible. Finally, thank you to my fellow GRE teachers and students, whose suggestions helped make the explanations and problems in this book clearer and more realistic.

Contents

Meet the GRE

GRE test takers come from all walks of academic life and ultimately venture out into a wide variety of careers. Perhaps you're seeking a masters or doctoral degree in literature. Maybe oceanography is your game, or the socio-political dynamics of ancient Rome. The bottom line is that if you're planning to attend graduate school in any field other than business, law, or medicine, you'll need to take the Graduate Record Examinations General Test as part of the admissions process. If you find yourself overwhelmed by this prospect, a healthy dose of perspective is in order:

The GRE is a means to an end.

That's it. The GRE is not an IQ or personality test. It doesn't measure intelligence, creativity, or talent. Rather, the GRE is a test that you can study for, much like you would study for a biology or history test. That means you can learn what's being tested and how to answer the questions correctly. That's why we wrote this book: to help you face the GRE without fear and get into grad school.

In the following pages, you'll find a brief summary of the GRE to familiarize you with the basic components of the test. The chapters that follow will provide a much more detailed profile of each of the three sections on the test, along with the tips, strategies, explanations, and practice questions you'll need to raise your score on the GRE.

GRE X-RAY

The GRE is officially called a "CBT," which stands for "computer-based test." So while you're allowed to write stuff down on scratch paper provided by the testing center, all the questions and answers will be on the computer. This means you'll be clicking on the correct answers rather than filling in bubble sheets. But more important, the GRE is also a "CAT," which stands for "computer-*adaptive* test." This means that the GRE software adapts the test for each test taker, depending on his or her performance, and each test taker takes a unique test. Isn't that special? The GRE goes out of its way to create a personalized testing experience *just for you.*

Here's how it works: As each section begins, you'll be given several questions of medium-level difficulty (the test makers determine a question's level of difficulty through years of statistical analysis). If you answer the initial questions correctly, you'll continue to receive harder questions until you begin making mistakes. If you answer a question incorrectly, the software will give you a slightly easier question until you get one right, at which point you'll get slightly harder questions. Your score is determined using a complex mathematical formula that takes into account the total number of questions answered, the number of questions answered correctly, and the level of difficulty of those questions.

The GRE has three sections:

- **Analytical Writing,** which we'll call the Essay section

- **Quantitative,** which we'll call the Math section

- **Verbal,** which we'll (cleverly) call the Verbal section

Scoring

The GRE scores the Math and Verbal sections on a 200–800-point scale, in 10-point increments. Essays have the following scoring system: 0 (poor) to 6 (excellent), in half-point increments.

Note that you'll receive one score for the entire Math section, one score for the entire Verbal section, and one for the Essay section. You'll get your Math and Verbal scores immediately, right after you finish taking the test, and you'll get your Essay score about two weeks after you take the test.

Due to the adaptive nature of the exam, you won't know how you're doing on a question-by-question basis, but the computer will continue to track your answers, adjusting the questions' level of difficulty as the section goes on. So two test takers could get the same number of questions correct but still wind up with very different scores, because the software's mathematical algorithm awards test takers who answer tough questions correctly higher scores than those given to test takers who answer the same number of easy or medium questions correctly. The questions' level of difficulty resets when you begin a new section. We'll look more closely at scoring in the FAQ section of this chapter.

Structure

The GRE lasts about three hours, not including breaks, tutorials, or experimental sections. Here's the section-by-section breakdown of the official test:

Section	Structure	Time
Essay	1 Issue essay 1 Argument essay	45 minutes 30 minutes
Math	28 questions	45 minutes
Verbal	30 questions	30 minutes

On test day, you'll take one Essay, one Math, and one Verbal section. The Essay section will always come first, followed by either Math or Verbal. You might also be required to take an unidentified, unscored pretest section, which will be either another Verbal or Math section that appears at any point after the Essay section. You may also get an identified research section, also unscored. If they put you through this one, they'll at least tell you it's the research section, and it will always come at the end of the test. The purpose of these experimental sections is to allow the test makers to try out new questions. Since you may not know which Verbal and Math sections count toward your score, your best bet is to treat every section as if it counts.

Now let's take a look at the GRE sections in a little more detail.

The Essay Section

The Essay section measures your ability to analyze and reason logically, to express complex ideas coherently, and to use standard English. This section has two essays:

- **"Present Your Perspective on an Issue."** The test makers give you two broad statements about a general subject. You'll then choose one with which to agree or disagree in your essay.

- **"Analyze an Argument."** Here you'll be given a short argumentative passage, then asked to write an essay in which you evaluate that argument based on its logical structure and use of reason.

The Math Section

The GRE tests your ability to understand and answer questions involving basic math, including arithmetic, algebra, geometry, and data analysis. GRE Math has three types of questions:

- **Problem Solving.** You're asked to select the correct answer to a given mathematical problem.

- **Quantitative Comparison.** Here you are asked to determine the relationships between different quantities.

- **Data Interpretation.** These questions require you to read and analyze data in graphical form.

The Verbal Section

The GRE tests the strength of your vocabulary, as well as your ability to recognize the relationships between words. This section also measures your ability to analyze sentence structure and to understand and analyze written information. GRE Verbal has four types of questions:

- **Sentence Completions.** These questions require you to complete a sentence with the correct word or phrase.

- **Reading Comprehension.** You'll be asked questions about passages drawn from the humanities, social sciences, and natural sciences.

- **Antonyms.** Here you'll be given a word, then asked to correctly select its opposite.

- **Analogies.** These questions require you to determine parallel relationships between sets of words.

GRE FAQ

Still have questions about the test? We have answers. . . .

Registering

When should I take the GRE?

Different graduate programs have different deadlines, so be sure to check with the programs you're interested in to find out their specific requirements. If you're still in college, be sure to factor in your class assignments when deciding to take the test; you don't want to be taking the GRE the day before finals.

Also, try to time your study and preparation to culminate about a week before you take the test. This gives you enough time to go over any last minute weak spots, but it also gives you time to relax before test day.

How do I register?

You have three options for registering:

---

1. Visit www.gre.org and follow the online instructions. You'll need a credit card to register online.

2. Call 1-800-GRE-CALL. You'll need a credit card for this option too.

3. Complete a paper registration form, available at most colleges and universities.

When you register to take the test, you'll also have the opportunity to designate score recipients, or the graduate programs that you'd like to receive your GRE section scores.

When is it offered?

The GRE is offered year-round at various times throughout the day. Depending on demand, some locations may have more dates than others. Go to the GRE's website for specific dates: www.gre.org.

Where can I take it?

You may take the GRE at any of the approximately 3,500 GRE testing centers worldwide, including colleges, universities, and corporate conference centers. You and your fellow test takers will each have a computer on which to work. To find the location nearest you, visit www.gre.org.

Scoring

How is the GRE scored?

The Math and Verbal sections are scored in 10-point increments from 200 to 800. The test makers use a complicated algorithm to translate the number of questions you answer correctly into your official GRE score. This official score will also include a percentile ranking, which allows admission officers to compare your scores to those of other test takers. The Essay section is scored in half-point increments from 0 to 6. You'll receive a single score on this section, an average of the subscores of your two essays, rounded up to the nearest half point. In total, you'll receive three scores, one score for each of the three sections.

What's a "good score"?

Simply put, a good score is one that gets you into the graduate program of your choice. Since some programs have score cutoffs, you need to check with each individual program to see what it considers "good." Note too that some programs might not mind if you don't do so hot on a particular section of the test. For example, an English program probably wouldn't be concerned if you only got an average score of 500 on the Math section, because this type of program will be most interested in your Verbal score. Be safe, though, and do some research.

When will I get my score?

You—and the graduate programs you designated back when you registered for the GRE—should receive your official score report within three weeks of taking the test. You'll get your unofficial Verbal and Math scores immediately after taking the test, before you leave the testing center.

Is there a wrong-answer penalty?

Yes. Every question you answer incorrectly lowers your score. If you answer a question incorrectly, the GRE software will begin giving you easier questions. But while these easier questions might seem like a gift from the test makers, they're actually not. Easier questions translate into a lower score percentile, even if you get all the easy questions correct. Your goal as a test taker is to correctly answer the questions, especially those you get at the start of each section. These questions, which constitute about a third of the section, have the biggest overall effect on your GRE score, because the software makes the largest jumps in its assessment of your abilities during this early phase of the section and tends to merely fine-tune its assessment later on. So it pays to be especially careful on the first few questions to bump yourself into higher scoring territory as soon as possible.

Who grades my essays?

The Educational Testing Service (ETS), the company that develops and administers the GRE, hires college and university faculty to score the essays. Each essay is read and scored by two graders. If their scores match, that's the score you'll get. If their scores differ by a point, your score will be the average of those two scores. If the essay-graders differ by more than one point in their assessments, a third grader is brought in. Now, it may seem strange that someone who hasn't even graduated from elementary school would be brought in to judge your writing ability. . . . No, not *that kind* of third grader! An *additional* grader above and beyond the original two will read your essay to settle the score.

Your scores on the two essays will then also be averaged; this average, rounded to the nearest half point, will be the single score you receive on the Essay section.

Will graduate schools see my essays?

Yes. Your essays—and not just the scores—will be included in the score reports sent to your designated graduate schools. Many schools have begun using the

GRE Essays not only as factors in their decisions about admissions but also for funding, such as scholarships and grants.

How long are my scores valid?

GRE scores are valid for five years from the date you take the exam. This also means that if you take the exam more than once, graduate schools will see all of the scores you've received in the last five years.

What if I bomb the GRE? Can I take it again?

If you study the material in this book, you won't have to worry about bombing the exam. However, if you really don't get the score you want, you may retake the GRE. That said, you're only allowed to take it once in a single month and only five times in a twelve-month period. Graduate programs differ in how they treat multiple GRE scores. Some programs only look at the most recent scores, some only look at the highest scores, and some take all of your scores into consideration.

How do I cancel my scores?

You have the opportunity to cancel your scores before you leave the testing center. Think very, very carefully before deciding to cancel your scores. Neither you nor any graduate program will ever know how you did on a canceled test, but ETS will notify graduate schools that you once took a test and canceled the results, which means you might have some explaining to do on your applications.

Bottom line: Only cancel your scores if something goes horribly awry on test day.

GRE Minutiae

This section answers common questions often asked by those new to the GRE.

How long does the test take?

The whole test takes a little less than three hours: 75 minutes for the Essay section, 45 minutes for the Math section, and 30 minutes for the Verbal section. You'll also have to sit through a tutorial, and you'll probably also have to take an unscored pretest or research section. In all, you should allow around four hours for the test.

What should I bring to the test center?

You must bring a photo ID to the test center. Bring a pen or pencil and any vouchers or receipts from ETS as well. If you get cold easily, bring a sweater. You might also want to take a snack and some water with you, in addition to any good-luck charms. Hey, whatever works, right?

Do I need to know much about computers?

No. All you need is a basic understanding of how a computer mouse and keyboard work. The programs you'll use and screens you'll see on test day are very basic. Essentially, you click on the screen to enter your choices. After you click the bubble of your choice, you'll have to click the "next" button whereupon the program will give you even another chance to confirm your answer choice before the next question will appear. Rest assured that nothing about the programs or screens will distract you from your true purpose on test day: getting a good score.

Can I go back and change my answers within a section?

Unfortunately, no. Once you click on an answer, that question disappears forever. Same deal with the sections. You cannot go back and change or check your answers.

Will I get a tutorial before the test starts?

You'll get a tutorial before the test starts. But we suggest that you download and peruse all the sample software that ETS gives you when you register for the GRE. You should also get online and take our full-length practice test at http://www.sparknotes.com/testprep/gre/. Make sure you budget your time so that you have plenty of practice on the computer before test day!

During the test, you'll be given a set of general instructions at the start of every section. The GRE gives you a few minutes to read over the instructions; the section time starts after you leave the directions. You'll receive question-specific directions every time you begin a new group of questions within a section. We explain these directions throughout the book, so you can skip them and save time on test day.

How will I write the essays?

You'll use a rudimentary word-processing program to compose your two essays. The program does not include a grammar- or spell-checker, but you can cut, paste, undo, redo, delete, and backspace. Note: The GRE won't let you use keyboard shortcuts, so you'll have to use the cursor and mouse to make changes.

Can I choose my essay topic or write about whatever I want? Can I write the essay beforehand?

Only if you want to get a 0. Your essays must address the topics designed by the test makers. Writing about whatever you want or going off topic will result in no or a low score.

ETS makes potential Issue and Argument topics available online. Check them out at www.gre.org/pracmats.html. Making the topics available sounds counterintuitive, since ETS doesn't want test takers to memorize prewritten essays. But ETS also wants test takers to write the best essays possible on test day—hence the online topic pool.

May I use scratch paper?

Although you may not bring in your own scratch paper, the testing center will provide you with several pieces of 8½ × 11 paper. If you need more, the proctor will provide it for you, a few pages at a time. You won't be able to take the paper with you when you leave the test, and you'll have to hand in the used paper to get fresh sheets.

May I use a timer?

The official rule is that silent watches are allowed. Desktop clocks or any timer that makes a noise are not allowed. The testing software includes a timer right in the upper left-hand corner of the screen, which you can hide from view up until five minutes remaining in the section. From that point on, the timer remains on the screen and counts down by seconds until time is up. So you can bring a silent timepiece if you prefer, or use the one provided on the screen.

Do I need to know trigonometry or calculus?

The GRE tests basic math and only basic math. Advanced topics such as trig and calculus are not tested. Our Math 101 chapter explains every single topic, concept, term, and formula you'll need on test day. If it's not in our book, it's not on the test.

Do I need to memorize vocabulary words?

Having a great vocabulary will lead to more points on the exam, and memorizing words helps you increase your vocabulary. Our book includes a tear-out chart with 400 of the most commonly tested GRE words. This book also provides strategies to help you conquer the Verbal section.

How do I get a good score on the GRE?

You've come to the right place. Read on . . .

GENERAL GRE STRATEGIES

It's time to talk strategy, specifically study and test-taking strategies. It's no secret that getting a good score requires lots of time, energy, and preparation. We've included many strategies throughout this book, from general strategies to help you on test day to question-specific step methods that will ensure you have an effective plan of attack for very question type you face. So, without further ado, here are the general strategies designed to help you prepare for and beat the GRE:

- Unleash Your Inner Warrior

- Get Online

- Set a Target Score

- Pace Yourself

- Remember the Order of Difficulty

- Use the Process of Elimination

We'll spend the rest of this chapter looking at each strategy in detail.

Unleash Your Inner Warrior

You bought this book for a reason. You don't want to sweat through every question. You want to be an elegant, test-taking warrior, a destroyer of the GRE and all questions therein. The mistake many students make is taking the GRE cold—with no preparation, not even so much as a flip through the information booklet. By familiarizing yourself with every type of question, you can approach each one coolly and calmly, knowing in advance what needs to be done to get it right. It's about switching from survival mode to attack mode, and it's attack mode that will help you score high.

Everything tested on the GRE is covered in this book, so you can forget about digging out that algebra textbook or notes from Intro to English. Best of all, your confidence will continue to grow as you learn more about the exam and the specific techniques for each section.

Remember too that the test is predictable. The test makers announce in advance which concepts and skills will be covered by the GRE. A predictable test is a beatable test. We'll go into more detail during our review of each section, and you'll have a chance to practice on sample questions. Knowing what you'll see on test day means you can study and prepare.

Get Online

The GRE is a computer-based test, so you'll need to devote some time to familiarizing yourself with the mechanics of an online exam. We can't stress this enough: Taking a computer-based test is different from taking a pencil-and-paper test. You'll be using a mouse instead of a pencil, you'll be clicking from question to question, and you'll be reading a screen rather than a page.

At http://www.sparknotes.com/testprep/gre/, you'll find both a short mini-quiz (to provide a quick taste of what to expect) and two full-length practice tests.

You'll also want to head to the GRE's very own website, www.gre.org. There you'll be able to register for the test and download the test makers' PowerPrep software bundle, which includes sample questions. Last but not least, you can access the pool of Essay topics at www.gre.org/pracmats.html.

Set a Target Score

Concrete goals are better than vague hopes. Here's a vague hope: "I want to do really well on the GRE." Okay. Go study everything. In contrast, here's a concrete goal: "I want to score 600 or above on the Math section." Concrete goals allow you to come up with a specific plan. This will make the time you spend preparing for the GRE much more efficient, leaving you more time to enjoy your life.

When setting a target score, be honest and realistic. Do some research, and contact the graduate programs you want to apply to about their score requirements or cutoffs. Unlike the SAT, you don't necessarily have to do really well on all three sections of the GRE in order to get an acceptance letter. And lest you forget: A good score on the GRE is the score that gets you into the graduate program of your choice.

Base your target score on the range required by the schools you want to attend. Aim for a target score that's a few points higher than the average for those schools. You can also gauge your target score by the practice tests in this book and online. If you score a 500 on the Math section, don't set your target score at 700. You'll just get frustrated and you won't know where to focus your preparation time. Instead, your target should be about 50 points higher on each section than your score on the practice test. Use this new target score to set your expectations when you move on to other practice tests. You can download the official GRE PowerPrep software from ETS and take the two actual practice tests that they provide for free.

If You Reach Your Target Score . . .

Take yourself to a movie, eat some candy, go IM your friends for several hours, or do something else to celebrate. But just because you've hit your target score doesn't mean you should stop working. In fact, you should view reaching your target score as proof that you can do better than that score: Set a new target slightly higher than your original, pick up your pace a little bit, and kick some GRE butt.

Slow and steady wins the race and beats the test. By working to improve bit-by-bit, you'll integrate your knowledge of how to take the test and master the subjects the test covers without burning out. If you can handle working just a little faster without becoming careless and losing points, your score will certainly go up. If you meet your new target score again, rinse and repeat.

Pace Yourself

We advise you to pace yourself in all kinds of ways: as you're planning your application process, as you're studying, and as you're taking the test.

___

- **Pace yourself while you're planning.** Find out the due dates for your grad school applications. The GRE is offered year-round, so make sure you schedule to take it with enough time to meet any program deadlines. You'll also want to make sure you're not taking it while you're going through finals, switching jobs, getting married, adopting a cat, or doing anything that might detract from your study time.

- **Pace yourself while you're studying.** The GRE covers a lot of material, and it can seem overwhelming if you think about it as one huge block. That's why we've divided this book into parts, so that you can tackle the concepts and strategies when it's most convenient for you. To prevent cramming or burnout, structure your study time far in advance. Write up daily or weekly study goals—and meet them. Use e-mail reminders or calendar programs to your advantage.

- **Pace yourself while you're taking the test.** If the GRE were an untimed exam, scores would be much higher. The GRE challenges you to get the most right answers in a very short amount of time. As you begin studying, don't worry about time. Practice individual questions and problem sets without looking at the clock. When you feel comfortable with the strategies and start seeing some real improvement, then start timing yourself. Eventually, you'll want to take a timed full-length practice test to see how you're scoring within the time constraints.

___

In general, you can afford to spend an average of about 60 seconds per verbal question and about 95 seconds per math question. Remember the order of difficulty (more on that below). Work as quickly as you can without making mistakes on the initial questions so that you'll have time to carefully work through the hard questions. Don't feel like you should be timing yourself on every single question. Ultimately, what matters is that you complete the sections, answering as many questions correctly as you can, within the time allotted. How long you actually spend on each question is up to you.

The Essay section gives you 45 minutes to plan and draft the Issue essay and 30 minutes to do the same on the Argument essay. After you've mastered the Math and Verbal review, you should begin doing some timed writing to get used to writing strong essays within that time frame.

As mentioned above, on test day, you'll have an on-screen clock, which will count down the time you have to complete the sections. Although you'll be given the option to hide this clock, it will automatically alert you when you have just five minutes to go.

Remember the Order of Difficulty

The GRE software adapts to your skills as a test taker. At the start of each section, you'll be given a few questions of medium-level difficulty. If you answer the initial questions correctly, the GRE will automatically begin giving you harder questions. The more difficult questions you answer correctly, the higher your score. If you make mistakes on those initial questions, however, the GRE will begin giving you easier questions.

If you think you've got the answer to an easy question, don't second-guess yourself: You probably do. If you're looking at what you consider to be a difficult question, you might want to check your answer just to make sure you haven't made a careless mistake. No matter what, don't get hung up on trying to determine a question's level of difficulty. Do the best you can, but once you click the answer, forget about it—and concentrate on the next question.

Use the Process of Elimination

The GRE software won't let you skip or leave questions in the middle of the section blank, so you should always guess when you don't know the answer. But don't just randomly click the middle choice and move on. Instead, eliminate answers you know are wrong, and then guess from the remaining choices. If you're stuck on a nasty-looking question, work through it as best you can to try to eliminate any of the answers. As you're looking at the answer choices, remember to eliminate *distractors,* or choices that look temptingly correct but aren't.

- **Math distractors.** On Math questions, distractors will often be those numbers you'll come to in the process of solving a problem. They'll be the numbers you get when you're halfway done or when you make a careless error such as mistakenly making a negative number positive.

- **Verbal distractors.** On Verbal questions, *distractors* will be words that sound very similar to words in the question, or they'll be words that relate to a feeling or event discussed in the question.

Think of the process of elimination like this: If you don't know the answer to a standard multiple-choice question, you have a 20 percent chance of blindly guessing correctly. If you can eliminate just one choice, suddenly you have a 25 percent chance of getting the question right. And if you can eliminate three choices, you've upped your chances to 50 percent! Throughout the upcoming chapters, we'll show you how to spot—and dodge—distractors by reviewing common GRE answer traps.

No doubt, mastering the GRE is a considerable undertaking. As you'll soon see, however, the test is extremely systematic, coachable, and conquerable. Ready to get started? Okay, let's do it.

Part I

THE MATH SECTION

Gameplan

Here's how we organized this section to ensure your study time is efficient:

- **Meet GRE Math.** Here we'll provide a general overview of the Math section, sorting out all the particular math concepts you'll be tested on, explaining how the section is scored, and describing all the question types. We'll also present some general math strategies to anchor your approach to tackling all the questions you'll see in this section of the test.

- **Math 101.** The first step to succeeding on the Math section is getting a firm grasp of the concepts tested. This chapter contains every mathematical concept, term, figure, and equation you'll need to know for the big day—exponents, angles, 3-D shapes, word problems, probability—these topics are all here and then some. If it's not here, it's not on the GRE. Knowing how *to apply* those concepts is another matter. To that end, we devote a separate chapter with specific strategies for each question type.

- **Problem Solving.** Problem Solving is the most familiar of the three GRE math question types. These are standard multiple-choice questions, each containing five answer choices. We'll teach you how to apply the concepts you reviewed in Math 101 to solve the kinds of problems you'll see on test day. The chapter also includes a step method to guide your work and a practice set to assess where you stand.

- **Quantitative Comparisons.** This question type not only represents the majority of the math questions you'll see on the test but also is likely the most challenging. QCs ask you to determine the relationship between two quantities. We explain how to do that and also present a specific step method. The chapter ends with a practice set, so you can apply what you've learned.

- **Data Interpretation.** This question type contains two sets of graphs or charts, each accompanied by two multiple-choice questions. DI questions not only test your math skills but also your ability to interpret data. We'll take you through this question type with our step method and provide guided practice with sample questions.

Chapter 1

Meet GRE Math

AAAAAGGGHHHH!!!! If that's your general reaction to math, then you've come to the right place. If you're like many test takers, you might be dreading the math portion of the GRE, known officially as the "Quantitative Section." (No need for such formality—we'll just call it *Math*.) Many of the questions cover topics you may not have seen in a really long time, even if you majored in math. Plus, the test makers have a knack for wording questions in unfamiliar, unintuitive ways. That's the not-so-great news.

The great news is that the GRE Math section only tests *basic math*. Thankfully, the math content never goes beyond a junior high or early high school level, and advanced topics, such as trigonometry and calculus, are *never* tested. Calculations, when required, are basic enough to do by hand—you know this for a fact since you're not allowed to use a calculator. Brush up on the basics covered in "Math 101" and the specific techniques and methods presented in chapters 3–5, and you'll be good to go. If you're actually not too bad at math but haven't used any to speak of beyond occasionally balancing your checkbook by hand, then the refresher we provide will do you just fine too.

On test day, you'll have 45 minutes to get through 28 questions. This chapter introduces you to the types of questions you'll see and offers some general strategies that will help you to succeed. We'll get to all that in just a bit, but first let's take a quick look at scoring.

SCORING

As you learned in the introduction, you will receive a score between 200 and 800 on the Math section. The scores vary in 10-point increments, so all scores end in 0. Since the GRE is a computer-adaptive test, the computer calculates your score as you proceed through the section, taking into account not only right and wrong answers but also the level of difficulty of each question you answer. The way the computer actually arrives at your score is fairly complex. Suffice it to say that as the CAT program adjusts the questions it presents to you based on your performance, it homes in on your ability level until the end of the section when its assessment of your math prowess is complete. You will receive an unofficial score right there on the screen at the end of the test. Official scores will be mailed to you later.

SORTING IT ALL OUT

Some people find the GRE Math section to be an unmanageable mess because they have trouble keeping its many components straight. *Algebra, triangles, data interpretation, Pythagorean theorem, factoring, geometry* . . . the list of things to know seems to go on and on. Breaking down the components of the Math section into categories will help you wrap your mind around your task. So the first thing we'll do is sort out all this math terminology to give you a better understanding of what you need to do to raise your score.

The Math section can be broken down into three major elements: question types, math concepts, and subject areas. We'll introduce each one and tell you where we'll be discussing them.

- **Question Types.** Each GRE math question comes in one of three basic varieties: Problem Solving (PS), Quantitative Comparisons (QC), or Data Interpretation (DI). These represent how the test makers test your math knowledge; that is, the formats that the questions take. We briefly introduced you to these question types in the introduction. We discuss them further in the next section of this chapter, and then revisit each one individually and in great detail in chapters 3, 4, and 5.

- **Math Concepts.** Math concepts are the actual math facts and formulas tested throughout the Math section. The formula for calculating the probability of an event? The number of degrees in the angles of an isosceles triangle? The factors of a quadratic equation? These and many other essential concepts are the things you simply need to know to approach the math questions on the GRE. We cover them all in the next chapter, Math 101.

- **Subject Areas.** Many test takers get overwhelmed by the sheer number of concepts they're expected to know. And there *are* a lot of them, no doubt. These concepts, however, don't just fall from outer space—they're grouped into four main subject areas that you learned in junior high and high school: arithmetic, algebra, geometry, and data analysis. We group the essential concepts into these four categories in the Math 101 chapter to help you to organize your math knowledge. The order of the chapter is purposeful too, since algebra requires arithmetic, and geometry and data analysis build on arithmetic and algebra. The structure of the Math 101 chapter allows you to breeze by the stuff you know and focus your efforts on the concepts that are most difficult for you.

Hopefully the information above clarifies your conception of the Math section as a whole and in doing so begins to allay your anxiety about it. Let's continue with an introduction of the question types.

QUESTION TYPES

As mentioned, we treat each question type in depth in chapters 3–5, but it pays to introduce them now so they'll be lurking in the back of your mind as you make your way through the subject areas and concepts of Math 101. Statistically, your Math section will break down approximately like this:

Question Type	Number of Questions	Percent of Section
1. Problem Solving (PS)	10	36%
2. Quantitative Comparisons (QC)	14	50%
3. Data Interpretation (DI)	4	14%
Total	28	100%

To confuse matters, the question types are interspersed throughout the section; that is, you won't see all ten PS questions first, followed by fourteen QCs and then the four DIs. Instead, you may get a PS question to start the section, followed by two QCs, another few PS questions, a bloc of DI, another PS question, and so on until all 28 questions are present and accounted for. The DI questions *will* appear consecutively, since each question in a DI set relates to a particular chart or graph, but the order of the other questions will be fairly random. Each question type has a unique look, and after working through chapters 3–5 you'll have no trouble recognizing what kind of question you're up against.

Here's a brief glimpse of each question type.

1. Problem Solving

Problem Solving tests your understanding of basic mathematical concepts, including arithmetic, algebra, geometry, and data analysis. The questions appear in standard multiple-choice format: a question, followed by five answer choices. However, unlike those found on traditional paper-and-pencil tests, the choices will not be labeled **A** through **E** but rather will each come with a bubble to the left of it for you to click. For the questions we present in this book, we use the bubble format to get you used to what questions will actually look like on a GRE computer screen. For the sake of convenience and clarity, however, we'll stick to the **A** through **E** convention in our explanations, with **A** corresponding to the first choice, **B** the second, and so on.

2. Quantitative Comparisons

QC questions present a quantity in Column A and a quantity in Column B and ask you to ascertain the relationship between them. Any concept that we cover in Math 101 could theoretically be the basis of a QC question, but rather than answering a specific question, you'll need to compare the size of the two quantities presented. QCs have four—*not five*—answer choices:

- The quantity in Column A is greater.

- The quantity in Column B is greater.

- The two quantities are equal.

- The relationship cannot be determined from the information given.

As the fourth choice indicates, an important skill tested by this question type is the ability to recognize when not enough information is available to figure out how the two quantities stack up.

3. Data Interpretation

Each DI question set contains one or two graphs or charts, followed typically by two questions in standard five-choice, multiple-choice format. You'll see two of these sets on the Math section, for a total of four DI questions. These are presented in a split-screen layout, with the figure or figures on the left and the questions, presented one at a time, on the right. The two DI questions in each set come up consecutively, since they're both based on the same information on the left side of the screen. The chart or graph on the left and its accompanying description may not fit entirely on the screen, in which case you'll need to scroll, much like you will on some Reading Comprehension passages in the Verbal section.

The simplest DI questions merely test whether you understand the information presented and can eyeball relationships suggested by it. Most DI questions, however, also require that you perform some basic mathematical calculations, sometimes involving approximation when calculating a precise value is cumbersome and unnecessary. While all math concepts are fair game in PS and QC questions, due to their nature DI questions tend to favor certain concepts over others. For example, arithmetic concepts like percentages are common, while geometry concepts like lines and angles have no place. In chapter 5, we'll show you how to interpret the data in various kinds of charts and graphs and answer the questions based on them.

GENERAL MATH STRATEGIES

In this section we provide some general strategies to get you thinking in the right direction regarding GRE math. Here's a preview:

- Change Your Math Mindset

- Use Scratch Paper

- Avoid Careless Mistakes

Change Your Math Mindset

Earlier we told you the good news that the GRE tests only basic math from junior high or early high school. However, since the concepts tested are basic and predictable, those wily test makers have to resort to certain tricks and traps to throw you off; otherwise, most test takers would ace the section. This fact has one very important ramification:

You need to change the way you've typically approached math questions in the past.

Think about the typical math tests you took in high school. Many were accompanied by three dreaded and imposing words: SHOW YOUR WORK. This mandate implies a slogging mentality: You're taught to do a problem a certain way, and then required to spit back that exact method to get full credit.

GRE math, however, rewards cleverness to combat the traps the test makers set. It doesn't matter whether you answer the question using a traditional or untraditional method. It doesn't matter if you use algebra or don't use algebra, draw a diagram or don't draw a diagram, or simply get into the ballpark through approximation instead of calculating an answer precisely. All that matters is whether you answer the question correctly. Three elements of your new math mindset will be looking for shortcuts, approximating when possible, and keeping your eyes open for "common trap" and "left-field" answer choices. Let's have a look at each one.

Shortcuts

As discussed above, your high school math experience may have instilled in you an instinct to jump into math problems with your sleeves rolled up, ready to slog away. And yes, sometimes that is the only way, or at least the only way you can see at the moment. Unless you perform math calculations lightning fast, however, you'll probably need to sneak your way around at least some GRE Math problems to get to all 28 questions; that's simply how the section is constructed. If you find yourself up against a real monster calculation that you think you need to work through to get the right answer, think again: Chances are the question is testing your math reasoning skills—that is, your ability to spot a more *elegant*

solution that doesn't require hacking through the math. Consider, for example, the following problem:

> If $x = 33.87$, what is the value of $\dfrac{(x+1)(x-2)(3x+15)}{3x^2+18x+15}$?

Is it *really* likely that they expect you to plug such an unwieldy number such as 33.87 in for all those x's in the equation, especially given the fact that calculators aren't allowed on the test? No, of course not, although that's exactly what some people will attempt. Not you. Once you change your math mindset, you'd know instinctively that there must be some sort of shortcut here, and indeed there is.

If you multiply out the $(x + 1)$ and $(3x + 15)$ in the top part of the fraction (the "numerator"), you get $3x^2 + 18x + 15$, which cancels out the entire bottom part (the "denominator"), leaving the simplified value of the equation at $(x - 2)$. Alternatively, you may have factored the bottom into $(3x + 15)(x + 1)$ and then canceled out those terms from the numerator, again reducing the entire fraction to $(x - 2)$. No matter which shortcut you employ, all that's left is to substitute the given value for x into $(x - 2)$ to get $33.87 - 2 = 31.87$, and you're done.

FOIL, factoring quadratic equations, and canceling are the concepts in play here, and if you need to brush up on them, don't worry—we'll get to these and plenty more bits of math minutiae soon enough in the following chapter. The point is simply to understand that many GRE math questions are written with shortcuts in mind, so begin right now to look for shortcuts as part of your new GRE math mindset.

Approximating (When Possible)

Another habit that may be ingrained in you from your math background is to "get the right answer." *Well duh*, you may be saying; this *is* math, after all, so naturally you'll want to solve the problems. Well, yes and no: *yes* in Problem Solving and Data Interpretation, but *no* in Quantitative Comparison questions where your job is not necessarily to solve the problems but rather to learn enough about quantities A and B to compare them. So especially in QCs—but also in the other question types—approximating values may save time. (Some DI questions even ask flat out for an approximate answer.)

Let's see how we might use approximation on a sample QC question:

> | Column A | Column B |
> |----------|----------|
> | 48% of 54 | 11% of 273 |
>
> ○ The quantity in Column A is greater.
> ○ The quantity in Column B is greater.
> ○ The two quantities are equal.
> ○ The relationship cannot be determined from the information given.

There's no doubt that some test takers with an old-fashioned high school math mentality would wear down their pencils grinding out calculations to precisely determine the value of each quantity. Then they could say with complete confidence which column is greater, or if they're the same. (Note that with only numbers and no variables in the question, the answer cannot be **D**. More on that in chapter 4.) Will this method get the right answer? Maybe, if they don't botch the math—a not-so-unlikely prospect when dealing with awkward numbers like these. Even if this method *does* yield the right answer, it may take a good chunk of time.

Approximating is the way to go. Observe: 48% is pretty close to 50%, or one-half, so let's work with that figure instead. Half of 54 is 27, so *a little less than half* of 54 (remember, the real figure is 48%, not the full 50%) must be *a little less than 27*, which is a fine approximation for Column A. Similarly, 11% is awfully close to 10%, an extremely manageable percentage. To take 10% of anything, we simply move the decimal point one place to the left. The value in Column B is therefore a little more than 27.3, since 11% of a number is larger than 10% of that same number. Since the quantity in Column A is *less* than 27, and the quantity in Column B is *more* than 27.3, Column B must be larger than Column A, which means that choice **B** is correct.

It would actually take a quick test taker less time to approximate the two values and settle on choice **B** than it took us to explain the method above. And, needless to say, it would take way less time (with less risk of careless mistakes, to boot) than it would take to actually do the math.

Common Traps and Left-Field Choices

One more element of your new math mindset concerns how you interact with the answer choices. The test makers prefer that you don't stumble upon the right answer accidentally and therefore construct the choices accordingly. Let's first discuss "common trap" and "left-field" choices individually, and then we'll get to some examples.

Common Traps. Remember, the test makers often spice up what would otherwise be basic problems. That means that you should assume that they go out of their way to trap unwary test takers into selecting *appealing* wrong answer choices, sometimes called "distractors" since they're meant to distract you from the correct choice. What might make a wrong choice appealing? Three main things:

---

1. It repeats a number used in the problem itself.

2. It represents a number you derive along the way to the right answer choice.

3. It represents the answer that results from a common misunderstanding of the problem.

You'll see examples in just a bit, but first let's discuss another kind of answer choice you should keep on your radar.

Left-Field Choices. "Left-field" choices are just what they sound like—choices from way out in left field that simply make no sense in the context of the question. Say you get a complicated rate/time/distance problem in which you're given a whole bunch of information and need to calculate how long it would take someone to drive from New York to Chicago. (Don't worry—we'll cover this kind of problem in chapter 2 along with every other essential math concept you need to know.) Say you forgot to divide by 100 at some point along the way and ended up with an answer of 1,500 hours. It seems ludicrous, but some people take the test with blinders on, and if they get 1,500, they get 1,500—period. So if that answer appeared among the choices, they'd choose it. This despite the fact that traveling even at a reasonably slow rate of 40 miles per hour, *one could drive from New York to California twenty times in 1,500 hours.* The answer just doesn't make sense in the context of the question—it comes from left field. The test makers include some left-field choices to remind you that it's not just a math test; it's also a *reasoning* test, which means you can and should quickly eliminate choices that defy common sense.

Let's now take a look at some traps and left-field choices in action. See what you can make of the following question:

> Simone invests $10,000 in a bank account that pays 10% interest annually. If the interest is compounded quarterly, how much money will be in the account after two years assuming that no money is deducted from the account and no money other than interest and the initial investment is added to the account?
>
> ○ $10,000.00
> ○ $11,000.00
> ○ $12,000.00
> ○ $12,184.03
> ○ $21,435.89

If you understand the formula for compound interest and can get the answer that way, that's fine, although in this case we can eliminate choices to get there faster. Choice **A** repeats a number from the question, which makes it suspicious to begin with. Moreover, it contains shades of "left field" since it defies common sense. Does it sound reasonable that a bank account that receives interest will have the same amount it started with after two years, given that no deductions are made from it? No—it has to have more, so choice **A** bites the dust on this count as well. And speaking of left-field choices, we may as well cut **E** too: Does it seem logical that an account would *more than double* in two years at an interest rate of 10%? Any experience with an interest-bearing account should suggest that $21,000 is way out of the ballpark here, leaving only **B**, **C**, and **D** as contenders.

Ten percent of $10,000 is $1,000. If the problem were based on simple interest—which no doubt the test makers are hoping some people will think—then $11,000 would be in the account after one year, and $12,000 after two years. But neither of these takes into consideration that the interest is *compounded quarterly*. **B** and **C** are therefore traps, both written to tempt anyone who falls for this common misunderstanding. **C**, $12,000, is what results if you calculated simple instead of compound interest, while **B**, $11,000, represents a number on the way to that wrong answer. The correct answer is **D**, which is what we'd get if we plugged the numbers into the complicated equation for compound interest. In this case, we didn't have to.

INTELLIGENT GUESSING

Your familiarity with distractors will help lead you to some quick and easy points, but that's not the only use of this knowledge. Some questions are just downright tough, especially if you're doing well and land yourself in the deep end of the question pool. Since in the computer-adaptive format you can't move on to the next question until you answer the one in front of   can never leave an answer blank. If you get stuck, you still have to pull the trigger on some choice or another. In those cases, eliminating even a few common traps or left-field choices will put the odds in your favor and allow you to guess intelligently.

Use Scratch Paper

On test day, you'll receive at least three pieces of blank 8½ × 11 paper. Use them! Don't try to solve equations in your head—you get no extra points, and the risk of error is high when you're doing complex calculations or working with complicated strings of numbers. Some people even find it handy to jot down the letters **A** through **E** (or **A** through **D** for QC questions) on their scratch paper for each new question they face, allowing them to cross off choices they eliminate so they don't get confused with which ones they chopped and which ones are still in contention. Try out this strategy to see whether it works for you.

If you use up your batch of paper, ask for more during the break between sections. The test center's proctor will give you more, in batches of three sheets at a time. You'll have to hand in your used scratch paper to the test proctor to get more, and you won't be able to take the scratch paper with you when you leave the testing center.

Avoid Careless Mistakes

The bane of test takers at all levels is selecting the wrong answer to a question they know how to solve. Such mistakes are understandable, considering the pressure of the test and the timing restrictions which often force people to work faster than they'd like. But it doesn't have to be this way. To avoid careless mistakes, follow these tips:

- **Slow down.** Although rushing may allow you to answer more questions, a multitude of wrong answers, especially in the beginning of the test, could send your score plummeting. Think through the questions before jumping in to solve them. Taking the necessary time to select the proper approach will help you get off on the right foot before investing tons of time in a fruitless direction.

- **Read the question carefully.** The test makers have a knack for asking strange or unexpected questions, the kind not usually asked in math class. Make sure that you answer the question asked rather than the question you think they might ask. If you have time, reread the question one last time before making your final selection to make sure you're giving them what they want. For example, if they give you a question about boys and girls and ask for the number of boys, make sure you don't accidentally go with the number of girls or the total number of boys and girls, things you very well may determine along the way. As we noted earlier, the test makers like to scatter such traps among the choices to catch the careless. Also pay attention to the units given in the problems: If they give you information in terms of minutes but ask for the answer in hours, you better take notice. In addition, if the test makers want you to round an answer, they'll instruct you to do so, and when they're looking for an approximate value (as is sometimes the case in DI questions), they'll tell you that too. Listen for exactly what they want, and then give it to them.

- **Study your practice sets.** Don't gloss over careless errors in your practice problems. Study them! It's one thing to simply not know how to do a problem, and quite another to think you aced it only to find out otherwise. Figure out where you went wrong. Were you rushing? Did you mix up numbers or fall for a common trap? Perhaps you did all the right math but then selected something other than what they asked for? Determine where your mistake lies and figure out what you need to do to avoid making that same mistake again.

We've provided in this chapter an introduction to the GRE Math section and some general pointers to get you on your way. Now it's time for the specifics. By the end of the next four chapters, you'll have not only a solid grasp of the math concepts tested on the GRE but also effective techniques for applying those concepts to all three question types you'll face. First up, as promised, is a heaping helping of Math 101. Ready? Then let's get to it.

Chapter 2

Math 101

Don't say we didn't warn you. We told you in the previous chapter that we'd cover every math concept included on the GRE, and this chapter makes good on that promise. Yeah, Math 101 is long, very long, but you don't necessarily need to read it straight through—it's here as a *resource* to help you study any and all topics you need to review. If you're good with triangles, by all means skip 'em. If exponents have always baffled you, key in on that section. If you've never even heard of modes or frequency distributions—well, you'll know what to do when you get to that part. If you're a total super math genius, pass Go, collect $200, and proceed right to chapter 3. (That's just a *Monopoly* expression. No one's really going to give you $200.) Use as much or as little of what follows as you need, but make sure you have a good grasp of the concepts covered in this chapter if you want to ace GRE Math.

You'll see that we have highlighted all the math formulas, which are integral to solving any GRE Math question in this chapter. Additionally, in the subsequent chapters, we have bolded all the math concepts that turn up in our explanations to the practice questions. That way, if anything seems difficult or particularly confusing, you can easily reference that particular math concept and come back here to get some targeted study.

As we discussed in chapter 1, GRE Math questions take many forms, but they all test one or more of four main subject areas:

---

1. Arithmetic

2. Algebra

3. Geometry

4. Data Analysis

We begin with one of the so-called three R's of education, which for some reason doesn't even begin with the letter "R". . .

ARITHMETIC

Arithmetic is the fundamental building block of math. The other three subject areas tested in GRE Math are all pretty much unthinkable without arithmetic. You'll certainly need to know your arithmetic to power through algebra, geometry, and data analysis problems, but the Math section also includes some pure arithmetic problems as well. So it makes sense to start Math 101 with a discussion of numbers and the typical things we do with them.

Common Math Symbols

You may remember these from way back when, but in case you need a quick refresher, here's a list of some of the most commonly used math symbols you should know for the GRE. We'll discuss some of them in this arithmetic section and others later in the chapter.

Symbol	Name	Meaning
<	Less than	The quantity to the left of the symbol is less than the quantity to the right.
>	Greater than	The quantity to the left of the symbol is greater than the quantity to the right.
≤	Less than or equal to	The quantity to the left of the symbol is less than or equal to the quantity to the right.
≥	Greater than or equal to	The quantity to the left of the symbol is greater than or equal to the quantity to the right.
√	Square root	A number which when multiplied by itself equals the value under the square root symbol.
$\lvert x \rvert$	Absolute value	The positive distance a number enclosed between two vertical bars is from 0.
!	Factorial	The product of all the numbers up to and including a given number.
‖	Parallel	In geometry, two lines separated by this symbol have the same slope (go in exactly the same direction).
⊥	Perpendicular	In geometry, two lines separated by this symbol meet at right angles.
°	Degrees	A measure of the size of an angle. There are 360 degrees in a circle.
π	Pi	The ratio of the circumference of any circle to its diameter; approximately equal to 3.14.

Number Terms

The test makers assume that you know your numbers. Make sure you do by comparing your knowledge to our definitions below.

Number	Definition	Example
Whole numbers	The set of counting numbers, including zero	0, 1, 2, 3
Natural numbers	The set of whole positive numbers except zero	1, 2, 3, 4
Integers	The set of all positive and negative whole numbers, including zero, not including fractions and decimals. Integers in a sequence, such as those in the example to the right, are called consecutive integers.	–3, –2, –1, 0, 1, 2, 3
Rational numbers	The set of all numbers that can be expressed as integers in fractions—that is, any number that can be expressed in the form $\frac{m}{n}$, where m and n are integers	$\frac{9}{10}, \frac{7}{8}, \frac{1}{2}$
Irrational numbers	The set of all numbers that cannot be expressed as integers in a fraction	π, $\sqrt{3}$, 1.010100001000110000
Real numbers	Every number on the number line, including all rational and irrational numbers	Every number you can think of

Even and Odd Numbers

An even number is an integer that is divisible by 2 with no remainder, including zero.

Even numbers: –10, –4, 0, 4, 10

An odd number is an integer that leaves a remainder of 1 when divided by 2.

Odd numbers: –9, –3, –1, 1, 3, 9

Even and odd numbers act differently when they are added, subtracted, multiplied, and divided. The following chart shows the rules for addition, subtraction, and multiplication (multiplication and division are the same in terms of even and odd).

Addition	Subtraction	Multiplication/Division
even + even = even	even – even = even	even × even = even
even + odd = odd	even – odd = odd	even × odd = even
odd + odd = even	odd – odd = even	odd × odd = odd

Zero, as we've mentioned, is even, but it has its own special properties when used in calculations. Anything multiplied by 0 is 0, and 0 divided by anything is 0. However, anything divided by 0 is undefined, so you won't see that on the GRE.

Positive and Negative Numbers

A positive number is greater than 0. Examples include $\frac{1}{2}$, 15, and 83.4. A negative number is less than 0. Examples include –0.2, –1, and –100. One tip-off is the negative sign (–) that precedes negative numbers. Zero is neither positive nor negative. On a number line, positive numbers appear to the right of zero, and negative numbers appear to the left:

–5, –4, –3, –2, –1, 0, 1, 2, 3, 4, 5

Positive and negative numbers act differently when you add, subtract, multiply, or divide them. Adding a negative number is the same as *subtracting* a positive number:

5 + (–3) = 2, just as 5 – 3 = 2

Subtracting a negative number is the same as *adding* a positive number:

7 – (–2) = 9, just as 7 + 2 = 9

To determine the sign of a number that results from multiplication or division of positive and negative numbers, memorize the following rules.

Multiplication	Division
positive × positive = positive	positive ÷ positive = positive
positive × negative = negative	positive ÷ negative = negative
negative × negative = positive	negative ÷ negative = positive

Here's a helpful trick when dealing with a series of multiplied or divided positive and negative numbers: If there's an even number of negative numbers in the series, the outcome will be positive. If there's an odd number, the outcome will be negative.

When negative signs and parentheses collide, it can get pretty ugly. However, the principle is simple: A negative sign outside parentheses is distributed across the parentheses. Take this question:

$$3 + 4 - (3 + 1 - 8) = ?$$

You'll see a little later on when we discuss order of operations that in complex equations we first work out the parentheses, which gives us:

$$3 + 4 - (4 - 8)$$

This can be simplified to:

$$3 + 4 - (- 4)$$

As discussed earlier, subtracting a negative number is the same as adding a positive number, so our equation further simplifies to:

$$3 + 4 + 4 = 11$$

An awareness of the properties of positive and negative numbers is particularly helpful when comparing values in Quantitative Comparison questions, as you'll see later in chapter 4.

Remainders

A remainder is the integer left over after one number has been divided by another. Take, for example, $92 \div 6$. Performing the division we see that 6 goes into 92 a total of 15 times, but $6 \times 15 = 90$, so there's 2 left over. In other words, the remainder is 2.

Divisibility

Integer x is said to be divisible by integer y when x divided by y yields a remainder of zero. The GRE sometimes tests whether you can determine if one number is divisible by another. You could take the time to do the division by hand to see if the result is a whole number, or you could simply memorize the shortcuts in the table below. Your choice. We recommend the table.

DIVISIBILITY RULES

1	All whole numbers are divisible by 1.
2	A number is divisible by 2 if it's even.
3	A number is divisible by 3 if the sum of its digits is divisible by 3. This means you add up all the digits of the original number. If that total is divisible by 3, then so is the number. For example, to see whether 83,503 is divisible by 3, we calculate $8 + 3 + 5 + 0 + 3 = 19$. 19 is not divisible by 3, so neither is 83,503.
4	A number is divisible by 4 if its last two digits, taken as a single number, are divisible by 4. For example, 179,316 is divisible by 4 because 16 is divisible by 4.
5	A number is divisible by 5 if its last digit is 0 or 5. Examples include 0, 430, and −20.
6	A number is divisible by 6 if it's divisible by both 2 and 3. For example, 663 is not divisible by 6 because it's not divisible by 2. But 570 is divisible by 6 because it's divisible by both 2 and 3 ($5 + 7 + 0 = 12$, and 12 is divisible by 3).
7	7 may be a lucky number in general, but it's unlucky when it comes to divisibility. Although a divisibility rule for 7 does exist, it's much harder than dividing the original number by 7 and seeing if the result is an integer. So if the GRE happens to throw a "divisible by 7" question at you, you'll just have to suck it up and do the math.
8	A number is divisible by 8 if its last three digits, taken as a single number, are divisible by 8. For example, 179,128 is divisible by 8 because 128 is divisible by 8.
9	A number is divisible by 9 if the sum of its digits is divisible by 9. This means you add up all the digits of the original number. If that total is divisible by 9, then so is the number. For example, to see whether 531 is divisible by 9, we calculate $5 + 3 + 1 = 9$. Since 9 is divisible by 9, 531 is as well.
10	A number is divisible by 10 if the units digit is a 0. For example, 0, 490, and −20 are all divisible by 10.
11	This one's a bit involved but worth knowing. (Even if it doesn't come up on the test, you can still impress your friends at parties.) Here's how to tell if a number is divisible by 11: Add every other digit starting with the leftmost digit and write their sum. Then add all the numbers that you *didn't* add in the first step and write their sum. If the difference between the two sums is divisible by 11, then so is the original number. For example, to test whether 803,715 is divisible by 11, we first add $8 + 3 + 1 = 12$. To do this, we just started with the leftmost digit and added alternating digits. Now we add the numbers that we didn't add in the first step: $0 + 7 + 5 = 12$. Finally, we take the difference between these two sums: $12 − 12 = 0$. Zero is divisible by all numbers, including 11, so 803,715 is divisible by 11.
12	A number is divisible by 12 if it's divisible by both 3 and 4. For example, 663 is not divisible by 12 because it's not divisible by 4. 162,480 is divisible by 12 because it's divisible by both 4 (the last two digits, 80, are divisible by 4) and 3 ($1 + 6 + 2 + 4 + 8 + 0 = 21$, and 21 is divisible by 3).

Factors

A factor is an integer that divides into another integer evenly, with no remainder. In other words, if $\frac{a}{b}$ is an integer, then b is a factor of a. For example, 1, 2, 4, 7, 14, and 28 are all factors of 28, because they go into 28 without having anything left over. Likewise, 3 is *not* a factor of 28 since dividing 28 by 3 yields a remainder of 1. The number 1 is a factor of every number.

Some GRE problems may require you to determine the factors of a number. To do this, write down all the factors of the given number in pairs, beginning with 1 and the number you're factoring. For example, to factor 24:

- 1 and 24 ($1 \times 24 = 24$)

- 2 and 12 ($2 \times 12 = 24$)

- 3 and 8 ($3 \times 8 = 24$)

- 4 and 6 ($4 \times 6 = 24$)

Five doesn't go into 24, so you'd move on to 6. But we've already included 6 as part of the 4×6 equation, and there's no need to repeat. If you find yourself beginning to repeat numbers, then the factorization's complete. The factors of 24 are therefore 1, 2, 3, 4, 6, 8, 12, and 24.

Prime Numbers

Everyone's always insisting on how unique they are. Punks wear leather. Goths wear black. But prime numbers actually *are* unique. They are the only numbers whose sole factors are 1 and themselves. More precisely, a prime number is a number that has exactly two positive factors, 1 and itself. For example, 3, 5, and 13 are all prime, because each is only divisible by 1 and itself. In contrast, 6 is *not* prime, because, in addition to being divisible by 1 and itself, 6 is also divisible by 2 and 3. Here are a couple of points about primes that are worth memorizing:

- All prime numbers are positive. This is because every negative number has −1 as a factor in addition to 1 and itself.

- The number 1 is *not* prime. Prime numbers must have two positive factors, and 1 has only one positive factor, itself.

- The number 2 is prime. It is the only even prime number. All prime numbers besides 2 are odd.

Here's a list of the prime numbers less than 100:

2, 3, 5, 7, 11, 13, 17, 19, 23, 29, 31, 37, 41,
43, 47, 53, 59, 61, 67, 71, 73, 79, 83, 89, and 97

It wouldn't hurt to memorize this list. In addition, you can determine whether a number is prime by using the divisibility rules listed earlier. If the number is divisible by anything other than 1 and itself, it's not prime.

If a number under consideration is larger than the ones in the list above, or if you've gone and ignored our advice to memorize that list, here's a quick way to figure out whether a number is prime:

1. Estimate the square root of the number.

2. Check all the prime numbers that fall below your estimate to see if they are factors of the number. If no prime below your estimate is a factor of the number, then the number is prime.

Let's see how this works using the number 97.

1. Estimate the square root of the number: $\sqrt{97} \approx 10$

2. Check all the prime numbers that fall below 10 to see if they are factors of 97:

Is 97 divisible by 2? No, it does not end with an even number.

Is 97 divisible by 3? No, 9 + 7 = 16, and 16 is not divisible by 3.

Is 97 divisible by 5? No, 97 does not end with 0 or 5.

Is 97 divisible by 7? No, 97 ÷ 7 = 13, with a remainder of 6.

Therefore, 97 is prime. (Of course, you knew that already from familiarizing yourself with the prime numbers less than 100. . . .)

Prime Factorization

Come on, say it aloud with us: "prime factorization." Now imagine Arnold Schwarzenegger saying it. Then imagine if he knew how to do it. Holy Moly. He would probably be governor of the entire United States!

A math problem may ask you to directly calculate the prime factorization of a number. Other problems, such as those involving greatest common factors or least common multiples (which we'll discuss soon), are easier to solve if you know how to calculate the prime factorization. Either way, it's good to know how to do it.

To find the prime factorization of a number, divide it and all its factors until every remaining integer is prime. The resulting group of prime numbers is the prime factorization of the original integer. Want to find the prime factorization of 36? We thought so:

$$36 = 2 \times 18 = 2 \times 2 \times 9 = 2 \times 2 \times 3 \times 3$$

That's two prime 2s, and two prime 3s, for those of you keeping track at home.

It can be helpful to think of prime factorization in the form of a tree:

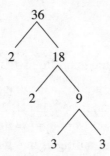

As you may already have noticed, there's more than one way to find the prime factorization of a number. Instead of cutting 36 into 2 and 18, you could have factored it into 6 × 6, and then continued from there. As long as you don't screw up the math, there's no wrong path—you'll always get the same result.

Let's try one more example. The prime factorization of 220 could be found like so:

$$220 = 10 \times 22$$

10 is not prime, so we replace it with 5 × 2:

$$10 \times 22 = 2 \times 5 \times 22$$

22 is not prime, so we replace it with 2 × 11:

$$2 \times 5 \times 22 = 2 \times 2 \times 5 \times 11$$

2, 5, and 11 are all prime, so we're done. The prime factorization of 220 is thus $2 \times 2 \times 5 \times 11$.

Greatest Common Factor

The greatest common factor (GCF) of two numbers is the largest number that is a factor of both numbers—that is, the GCF is the largest factor that both numbers have in common. For example, the GCF of 12 and 18 is 6, because 6 is the largest number that divides evenly into 12 and 18. Put another way, 6 is the largest number that is a factor of both 12 and 18.

To find the GCF of two numbers, you can use their prime factorizations. The GCF is the product of all the numbers that appear in both prime factorizations. In other words, the GCF is the overlap of the two factorizations.

For example, let's calculate the GCF of 24 and 150. First, we figure out their prime factorizations:

$$24 = 2 \times 2 \times 2 \times 3$$

$$150 = 2 \times 3 \times 5 \times 5$$

Both factorizations contain 2 × 3. The overlap of the two factorizations is 2 and 3. The product of the overlap is the GCF. Therefore, the GCF of 24 and 150 is 2 × 3 = 6.

Multiples

A multiple can be thought of as the opposite of a factor: If $\frac{x}{y}$ is an integer, then x is a multiple of y. Less formally, a multiple is what you get when you multiply an integer by another integer. For example, 7, 14, 21, 28, 70, and 700 are all multiples of 7, because they each result from multiplying 7 by an integer. Similarly, the numbers 12, 20, and 96 are all multiples of 4 because 12 = 4 × 3, 20 = 4 × 5, and 96 = 4 × 24. Keep in mind that zero is a multiple of every number. Also, note that any integer, n, is a multiple of 1 and n, because 1 × n = n.

Least Common Multiple

The least common multiple (LCM) of two integers is the smallest number that is divisible by the two original integers. As with the GCF, you can use prime factorization as a shortcut to find the LCM. For example, to find the least common multiple of 10 and 15, we begin with their prime factorizations:

$$10 = 5 \times 2$$

$$15 = 5 \times 3$$

The LCM is equal to the product of each factor by the maximum number of times it appears in either number. Since 5 appears once in both factorizations, we need to include it once in our final product. The same goes for the 2 and the 3, since each of these numbers appears one time in each factorization. The LCM of 10 and 15, then, is 5 × 3 × 2 = 30. In other words, 30 is the smallest number that is divisible by both 10 and 15. Remember that the LCM is the *least* common multiple—you have to choose the smallest number that is a multiple of each original number. So, even though 60 is a multiple of both 10 and 15, 60 is not the LCM, because it's not the smallest multiple of those two numbers.

This is a bit tricky, so let's try it again with two more numbers. What's the LCM of 60 and 100?

First, find the prime factorizations:

$$60 = 2 \times 2 \times 3 \times 5$$

$$100 = 2 \times 2 \times 5 \times 5$$

So, 2 occurs twice in each of these factorizations, so we'll need to include two 2s in our final product. We have one 5 in our factorization of 60, but *two* 5s in our factorization of 100. Since we're looking to include the *maximum* number of appearances of each factor, we'll include two 5s in our product. There's also one 3 in the first factorization, and no 3s in the second, so we have to add one 3 to the mix. This results in an LCM of $2 \times 2 \times 3 \times 5 \times 5 = 300$.

Order of Operations

What if you see something like this on the test:

$$\frac{(18-3) \times 2^2}{5} - 7 + (6 \times 3 - 1) =$$

You basically have two choices. You can (a) run screaming from the testing site yelling "I'll never, ever, EVER get into graduate school!!!" or (b) use PEMDAS.

PEMDAS is an acronym for the order in which mathematical operations should be performed as you move from left to right through an expression or equation. It stands for:

- **P**arentheses

- **E**xponents

- **M**ultiplication

- **D**ivision

- **A**ddition

- **S**ubtraction

You may have had PEMDAS introduced to you as "Please Excuse My Dear Aunt Sally." Excuse us, but that's a supremely lame 1950s-style acronym. We prefer, Picking Eminem Made Dre A Star. Whatever. Come up with one of your own if you want. Just remember PEMDAS.

If an equation contains any or all of these PEMDAS elements, first carry out the math within the parentheses, then work out the exponents, then the multiplication, and the division. Addition and subtraction are actually a bit more complicated. When you have an equation to the point that it only contains addition and subtraction, perform each operation moving from left to right across the equation. Let's see how this all plays out in the context of the example above:

$$\frac{(18-3) \times 2^2}{5} - 7 + (6 \times 3 - 1) =$$

First work out the math in the parentheses, following PEMDAS even *within* the parentheses. So here we focus on the second parentheses and do the multiplication before the subtraction:

$$\frac{(18-3)\times 2^2}{5} - 7 + (18-1)$$

Now taking care of the subtraction in both sets of parentheses:

$$\frac{15 \times 2^2}{5} - 7 + 17$$

Now work out the exponent (more on those later):

$$\frac{15 \times 4}{5} - 7 + 17$$

Then do the multiplication:

$$\frac{60}{5} - 7 + 17$$

Then the division:

$$12 - 7 + 17$$

We're left with just addition and subtraction, so we simply work from left to right:

$$5 + 17$$

And finally:

$$22$$

Piece of cake! Well, not exactly, but it beats fleeing the room in hysterics. PEMDAS is the way to crunch down the most difficult-looking equations or expressions. Take it one step at a time, and you'll do just fine.

Fractions

Much of what we've covered so far concerns whole numbers. Now we enter the vast universe that exists *between* those nice round numbers: the world of fractions. The GRE *loves* fractions. The number of questions on the Math section that involve fractions in some way or another is nothing short of stupefying. This means you must know fractions inside and out. Know how to compare them, reduce them, add them, and multiply them. Know how to divide them, subtract them, and convert them to mixed numbers. Know them. Love them like the GRE does. Make them your friend on the test, not your enemy.

To begin, here are the basics: A fraction is a part of a whole. It's composed of two expressions, a numerator and a denominator. The numerator of a fraction is the quantity above the fraction bar, and the denominator is the quantity below the fraction bar. For example, in the fraction $\frac{1}{2}$, 1 is the numerator and

2 is the denominator. The denominator tells us how many units there are in all, while the numerator tells us how many units out of that total are specified in a given instance. For example, if your friend has five cookies and offers you two of them, you'd be entitled to eat $\frac{2}{5}$ of her cookies. How many you sneak when she's not looking is up to you.

The general concept of fractions isn't difficult, but things can get dicey when you have to do things with them. Hence, the following subtopics that you need to have under your belt.

Fraction Equivalencies

Fractions represent a part of a whole, so if you increase both the part and whole by the same multiple, you will not change the relationship between the part and the whole.

To determine if two fractions are equivalent, multiply the denominator and numerator of one fraction so that the denominators of the two fractions are equal (this is one place where knowing how to calculate LCM and GCF comes in handy). For example, $\frac{1}{2} = \frac{3}{6}$ because if you multiply the numerator and denominator of $\frac{1}{2}$ by 3, you get: $\frac{1 \times 3}{2 \times 3} = \frac{3}{6}$. As long as you multiply or divide both the numerator and denominator of a fraction by the same nonzero number, you will not change the overall value of the fraction.

Reducing Fractions

Reducing fractions makes life simpler, and we all know life is complicated enough without crazy fractions weighing us down. Reducing takes unwieldy monsters like $\frac{450}{600}$ and makes them into smaller, friendlier critters. To reduce a fraction to its lowest terms, divide the numerator and denominator by their GCF. For example, for $\frac{450}{600}$, the GCF of 450 and 600 is 150. So the fraction reduces down to $\frac{3}{4}$, since $450 \div 150 = 3$ and $600 \div 150 = 4$.

A fraction is in its simplest, totally reduced form when the GCF of its numerator and denominator is 1. There is no number but 1, for instance, that can divide into both 3 and 4, so $\frac{3}{4}$ is a fraction in its lowest form, reduced as far as it can go. The same goes for the fraction $\frac{3}{5}$, but $\frac{3}{6}$ is a different story because 3 is a common factor of both the numerator and denominator. Dividing each by this common factor yields $\frac{1}{2}$, the fraction in its most reduced form.

Adding, Subtracting, and Comparing Fractions

To add fractions with the same denominators, all you have to do is add up the numerators and keep the denominator the same:

$$\frac{1}{20} + \frac{3}{20} + \frac{13}{20} = \frac{17}{20}$$

Subtraction works similarly. If the denominators of the fractions are equal, just subtract one numerator from the other and keep the denominator the same:

$$\frac{13}{20} - \frac{2}{20} = \frac{11}{20}$$

Remember that fractions can be negative too:

$$\frac{2}{20} - \frac{13}{20} = \frac{-11}{20}$$

Some questions require you to compare fractions. Again, this is relatively straightforward when the denominators are the same. The fraction with the greater numerator will be the larger fraction. For example, $\frac{13}{27}$ is greater than $\frac{5}{27}$, while $\frac{-5}{27}$ is greater than $\frac{-13}{27}$. (Be careful of those negative numbers! Since –5 is less *negative* than –13, –5 is greater than –13.)

Working with fractions with the same denominators is one thing, but working with fractions with different denominators is quite another. So we came up with an easy alternative: the Magic X. For adding, subtracting, and comparing fractions with different denominators, the Magic X is a lifesaver. Sure, you can go ahead and find the least common denominator, a typical way of tackling such problems, but we don't call our trick the "Magic X" for nothing. Here's how it works in each situation.

Adding. Consider the following equation:

$$\frac{3}{7} + \frac{2}{9} = ?$$

You could try to find the common denominator by multiplying $\frac{3}{7}$ by 9 and $\frac{2}{9}$ by 7, but then you'd be working with some pretty big numbers. Keep things simple, and use the Magic X. The key is to multiply *diagonally and up*, which in this case means from the 9 to the 3 and also from the 7 to the 2:

$$9 \times 3 = 27 \qquad 7 \times 2 = 14$$

In an addition problem, we add the products to get our numerator: 27 + 14 = 41. For the denominator, we simply multiply the two denominators to get:

$$7 \times 9 = 63$$

Believe it or not, we're already done! The numerator is 41, and the denominator is 63, which results in a final answer of $\frac{41}{63}$.

Subtracting. Same basic deal, except this time we subtract the products that we get when we multiply diagonally and up. See if you can feel the magic in this one:

$$\frac{4}{5} - \frac{5}{6} = ?$$

Multiplying diagonally and up gives:

$$6 \times 4 = 24 \qquad 5 \times 5 = 25$$

$$\frac{4}{5} \diagdown \frac{5}{6}$$

The problem asks us to subtract fractions, so this means we need to *subtract* these numbers to get our numerator: 24 – 25 = –1. Just like in the case of addition, we multiply across the denominators to get the denominator of our answer:

$$\frac{4}{5} \longrightarrow \frac{5}{6}$$

$$5 \times 6 = 30$$

That's it! The numerator is –1 and the denominator is 30, giving us an answer of $\frac{-1}{30}$. Not the prettiest number you'll ever see, but it'll do.

Comparing. The Magic X is so magical that it can also be used to compare two fractions, with just a slight modification: omitting the step where we multiply the denominators. Say you're given the following Quantitative Comparison problem. We'll explain much more about QCs in chapter 4, but for now remember that the basic idea is to compare the quantity in Column A with the quantity in Column B to see which, if either, is bigger. (In some cases, the answer will be that you *can't determine* which is bigger, but as you'll learn, when the two quantities are pure numbers with no variables, that option is impossible.) See what you can make of this sample QC:

Column A	Column B
$\frac{5}{23}$	$\frac{7}{30}$

Now, if you were a mere mortal with no magic at your fingertips, this would be quite a drag. But the Magic X makes it a pleasure. Again, begin by multiplying diagonally and up:

$$30 \times 5 = 150 \qquad 23 \times 7 = 161$$

$$\frac{5}{23} \diagdown \frac{7}{30}$$

Now compare the numbers you get: 161 is larger than 150, so $\frac{7}{30}$ is greater than $\frac{5}{23}$. Done.

Why does this work? Who knows? Who cares? It just does. (Actually, the rationale isn't too complex, but it doesn't add anything to your GRE repertoire, so let's skip it.) Learn how to employ the Magic X in these three circumstances, and you're likely to save yourself some time and effort.

Multiplying Fractions

Multiplying fractions is a breeze, whether the denominators are equal or not. The product of two fractions is merely the product of their numerators over the product of their denominators:

$$\frac{a}{b} \times \frac{c}{d} = \frac{ac}{bd}$$

Want an example with numbers? You got one:

$$\frac{3}{7} \times \frac{2}{5} = \frac{3 \times 2}{7 \times 5} = \frac{6}{35}$$

Canceling Out. You can make multiplying fractions even easier by canceling out. If the numerator and denominator of any of the fractions you need to multiply share a common factor, you can divide by the common factor to reduce both numerator and denominator before multiplying. For example, consider this fraction multiplication problem:

$$\frac{4}{5} \times \frac{1}{8} \times \frac{10}{11}$$

You could simply multiply the numerators and denominators and then reduce, but that would take some time. Canceling out provides a shortcut. We can cancel out the numerator 4 with the denominator 8 and the numerator 10 with the denominator 5, like this:

$$\frac{\cancel{4}^{1}}{\cancel{5}^{1}} \times \frac{1}{\cancel{8}^{2}} \times \frac{\cancel{10}^{2}}{11} = \frac{1}{1} \times \frac{1}{2} \times \frac{2}{11}$$

Then, canceling the 2s, you get:

$$\frac{1}{1} \times \frac{1}{\cancel{2}^{1}} \times \frac{\cancel{2}^{1}}{11} = \frac{1}{1} \times \frac{1}{1} \times \frac{1}{11} = \frac{1}{11}$$

Canceling out can dramatically cut the amount of time you need to spend working with big numbers. When dealing with fractions, whether they're filled with numbers or variables, always be on the lookout for chances to cancel out.

Dividing Fractions

Multiplication and division are inverse operations. It makes sense, then, that to perform division with fractions, all you have to do is flip the second fraction and then multiply. Check it out:

$$\frac{a}{b} \div \frac{c}{d} = \frac{a}{b} \times \frac{d}{c} = \frac{ad}{bc}$$

Here's a numerical example:

$$\frac{1}{2} \div \frac{4}{5} = \frac{1}{2} \times \frac{5}{4} = \frac{5}{8}$$

Compound Fractions. Compound fractions are nothing more than division problems in disguise. Here's an example of a compound fraction:

$$\frac{\frac{9}{5}}{\frac{3}{10}}$$

It looks intimidating, sure, but it's really only another way of writing $\frac{9}{5} \div \frac{3}{10}$, which now looks just like the previous example. Again, the rule is to invert and multiply. Take whichever fraction appears on the bottom of the compound fraction, or whichever fraction appears second if they're written in a single line, and flip it over. Then multiply by the other fraction. In this case, we get $\frac{9}{5} \times \frac{10}{3}$. Now we can use our trusty canceling technique to reduce this to $\frac{3}{1} \times \frac{2}{1}$, or plain old 6. A far cry from the original!

Mixed Numbers

Sick of fractions yet? We don't blame you. But there's one topic left to cover, and it concerns fractions mixed with integers. Specifically, a mixed number is an integer followed by a fraction, like $1\frac{2}{3}$. But operations such as addition, subtraction, multiplication, and division can't be performed on mixed numbers, so you have to know how to convert them into standard fraction form.

Since we already mentioned $1\frac{2}{3}$, it seems only right to convert it.

The method is easy: Multiply the integer (the 1) of the mixed number by the denominator of the fraction part, and add that product to the numerator: $1 \times 3 + 2 = 5$. This will be the numerator. Now, put that over the original denominator, 3, to finalize the converted fraction: $\frac{5}{3}$.

Let's try a more complicated example:

$$3\frac{2}{13} = \frac{(3 \times 13) + 2}{13} = \frac{39 + 2}{13} = \frac{41}{13}$$

Pretty ugly as far as fractions go, but definitely something we can work with.

Decimals

A decimal is any number with a nonzero digit to the right of the decimal point. Like fractions, decimals are a way of writing parts of wholes. Some GRE questions ask you to identify specific digits in a decimal, so you need to know the names of these different digits. In this case, a picture is worth a thousand (that is, 1000.00) words:

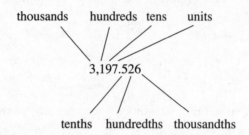

Notice that all of the digits to the right of the decimal point have a *th* in their names.

In the number 839.401, for example, here are the values of the different digits.

Left of the decimal point	Right of the decimal point
Units: 9	Tenths: 4
Tens: 3	Hundredths: 0
Hundreds: 8	Thousandths: 1

Converting Fractions to Decimals

So, what if a problem contains fractions, but the answer choices are all decimals? In that case, you'll have to convert whatever fractional answer you get to a decimal. A fraction is really just shorthand for division. For example, $\frac{6}{15}$ is exactly the same as 6 ÷ 15. Dividing this out on your scratch paper results in its decimal equivalent, .4.

Converting Decimals to Fractions

What comes around goes around. If we can convert fractions to decimals, it stands to reason that we can also convert decimals to fractions. Here's how:

1. Remove the decimal point and make the decimal number the numerator.

2. Let the denominator be the number 1 followed by as many zeros as there are decimal places in the original decimal number.

3. Reduce this fraction if possible.

Let's see this in action. To convert .3875 into a fraction, first eliminate the decimal point and place 3875 as the numerator:

$$.3875 = \frac{3,875}{?}$$

Since .3875 has four digits after the decimal point, put four zeros in the denominator following the number 1:

$$.3875 = \frac{3,875}{10,000}$$

We can reduce this fraction by dividing the numerator and denominator by the GCF, which is 125, or, if it's too difficult to find the GCF right off the bat, we can divide the numerator and denominator by common factors such as 5 until no more reduction is possible. Either way, our final answer in reduced form comes out to $\frac{31}{80}$.

Ratios

Ratios look like fractions and are related to fractions, but they don't quack like fractions. Whereas a fraction describes a part of a whole, a ratio compares one part to another part.

A ratio can be written in a variety of ways. Mathematically, it can appear as $\frac{3}{1}$ or as 3:1. In words, it would be written out as "the ratio of 3 to 1." Each of these three forms of the ratio 3:1 means the same thing: that there are three of one thing for every one of another. For example, if you have three red alligators and one blue alligator, then your ratio of red alligators to blue alligators would be 3:1. For the GRE, you must remember that ratios compare parts to parts rather than parts to a whole. Why do you have to remember that? Because of questions like this:

For every 40 games a baseball team plays, it loses 12 games. What is the ratio of the team's losses to wins?

○ 3:10
○ 7:10
○ 3:7
○ 7:3
○ 10:3

The question says that the team loses 12 of every 40 games, but it asks you for the ratio of losses to *wins*, not losses to *games*. So the first thing you have to do is find out how many games the team wins per 40 games played: 40 – 12 = 28. So for every 12 losses, the team wins 28 games, for a ratio of 12:28. You can reduce this ratio by dividing both sides by 4 to get 3 losses for every 7 wins, or 3:7. Choice **C** is therefore correct. If you instead calculated the ratio of losses to games played (part to whole), you might have just reduced the ratio 12:40 to 3:10, and then selected choice **A**. For good measure, the test makers include 10:3 to entice anyone who went with 40:12 before reducing. There's little doubt that on ratio problems, you'll see an incorrect *part : whole* choice and possibly these other kinds of traps that try to trip you up.

Proportions

Just because you have a ratio of three red alligators to one blue alligator doesn't mean that you can only have three red alligators and one blue one. It could also mean that you have six red and two blue alligators or that you have 240 red and 80 blue alligators. (Not that we have any idea where you'd keep all those beasts, but you get the point.) Ratios compare only relative magnitude. To know how many of each color alligator you actually have, in addition to knowing the ratio, you also need to know how many *total* alligators there are. This concept forms the basis of another kind of ratio problem you may see on the GRE, a problem that provides you with the ratio among items and the total number of items, and then asks you to determine the number of one particular item in the group. Sounds confusing, but as always, an example should clear things up:

> Egbert has red, blue, and green marbles in the ratio of 5:4:3, and he has a total of 36 marbles. How many blue marbles does Egbert have?

First let's clarify what this means. For each *group* of 5 red marbles, Egbert (who does sound like a marble collector, doesn't he?) has a *group* of 4 blue marbles and a *group* of 3 green marbles. If he has one group of each, then he'd simply have 5 red, 4 blue, and 3 green marbles for a total of 12. But he doesn't have 12—we're told he has 36. The key to this kind of problem is determining how many groups of each item must be included to reach the total. We have to multiply the total we'd get from having one group of each item by a certain factor that would give us the total given in the problem. Here, as we just saw, having one group of each color marble would give Egbert 12 marbles total, but since he has 36 marbles, we have to multiply by a factor of 3 (since 36 ÷ 12 = 3). That means Egbert has 3 groups of red marbles with 5 marbles in each group, for a total of 3 × 5 = 15 red marbles. Multiplying the other marbles by our factor of 3 gives us 3 × 4 = 12 blue marbles, and 3 × 3 = 9 green marbles. Notice that the numbers work out, because 15 + 12 + 9 does add up to 36 marbles total. The answer to the question is therefore 12 blue marbles.

So here's the general approach: Add up the numbers given in the ratio. Divide the total items given by this number to get the factor by which you need to multiply each group. Then find the item type you're looking for and multiply its ratio number by the factor you determined. In the example above, that would look like this:

$$5 \text{ (red)} + 4 \text{ (blue)} + 3 \text{ (green)} = 12$$

$$36 \div 12 = 3 \text{ (factor)}$$

$$4 \text{ (blue ratio \#)} \times 3 \text{ (factor)} = 12 \text{ (answer)}$$

For the algebraic-minded among you, you can also let x equal the factor, and work the problem out this way:

$$5x + 4x + 3x = 36$$

$$12x = 36$$

$$x = 3$$

$$\text{blue} = (4)(3) = 12$$

Percents

Percents occur frequently in Data Interpretation questions but are also known to appear in Problem Solving and Quantitative Comparison questions as well. The basic concept behind percents is pretty simple: *Percent* means *divide by 100*. This is true whether you see the word *percent* or you see the percentage symbol, %.

For example, 45% is the same as $\dfrac{45}{100}$ or .45.

Here's one way percent may be tested:

4 is what percent of 20?

The first thing you have to know how to do is translate the question into an equation. It's actually pretty straightforward as long as you see that "is" is the same as "equals," and "what" is the same as "x." So we can rewrite the problem as 4 equals x percent of 20, or:

$$4 = x\% \left(20\right)$$

Since a percent is actually a number out of 100, this means:

$$4 = \frac{x}{100}(20)$$

Now just work out the math:

$$4 = \frac{20x}{100}$$

$$400 = 20x$$

$$x = 20$$

Therefore, 4 is 20% of 20.

Percent problems can get tricky, because some seem to be phrased as if the person who wrote them doesn't speak English. The GRE test makers do this purposefully because they think that verbal tricks are a good way to test your math skills. And who knows—they may even be right. Here's an example of the kind of linguistic trickery we're talking about:

What percent of 2 is 5?

Because the 2 is the smaller number and because it appears first in the question, your first instinct may be to calculate what percent 2 is of 5. But as long as you remember that "is" means "equals" and "what" means "x" you'll be able to correctly translate the word problem into math:

$$x\%(2) = 5$$
$$\frac{x}{100}(2) = 5$$
$$\frac{2x}{100} = 5$$
$$2x = 500$$
$$x = 250$$

So 5 is 250% of 2.

You may also be asked to figure out a percentage based on a specific occurrence. For example, if there are 200 cars at a car dealership, and 40 of those are used cars, then we can divide 40 by 200 to find the percentage of used cars at the dealership: $\frac{40}{200} = \frac{4}{20} = \frac{1}{5} = 20\%$. The general formula for this kind of calculation is:

$$\text{Percent of a specific occurrence} = \frac{\text{the number of specific occurences}}{\text{the total number}} \times 100\%$$

Converting Percents into Fractions or Decimals

Converting percents into fractions or decimals is an important GRE skill that may come into play in a variety of situations.

- To convert from a percent to a fraction, take the percentage number and place it as a numerator over the denominator 100. If you have 88 percent of something, then you can quickly convert it into the fraction $\frac{88}{100}$.

- To convert from a percent to a decimal, you must take a decimal point and insert it into the percent number two spaces from the right: 79% equals .79, while 350% equals 3.5.

Percent Increase and Decrease

One of the most common ways the GRE tests percent is through the concept of percent increase and decrease. There are two main varieties: problems that give you one value and ask you to calculate another, and problems that give you two values and ask you to calculate the percent increase or decrease between them. Let's have a look at both.

ONE VALUE GIVEN

In this kind of problem, they give you a single number to start, throw some percentage increases or decreases at you, and then ask you to come up with a new number that reflects these changes. For example, if the price of a $10 shirt increases 10%, the new price is the original $10 plus 10% of the $10 original. If the price of a $10 shirt decreases 10%, the new price is the original $10 minus 10% of the $10 original.

One of the classic blunders test takers make on this type of question is to forget to carry out the necessary addition or subtraction after figuring out the percent increase or decrease. Perhaps their joy or relief at accomplishing the first part distracts them from finishing the problem. In the problem above, since 10% of $10 is $1, some might be tempted to choose $1 as the final answer, when in fact the answer to the percent increase question is $11, and the answer to the percent decrease question is $9.

Try the following example on your own. Beware of the kind of distractor we've just discussed.

> A vintage bowling league shirt that cost $20 in 1990 cost 15% less in 1970. What was the price of the shirt in 1970?
>
> ○ $3
> ○ $17
> ○ $23
> ○ $35
> ○ $280

First find the price decrease (remember that 15% = .15):

$$\$20 \times .15 = \$3$$

Now, since the price of the shirt was less back in 1970, subtract $3 from the $20 1990 price to get the actual amount this classic would have set you back way back in 1970 (presumably before it achieved "vintage" status):

$$\$20 - \$3 = \$17$$

Seventeen bucks for a bowling shirt!? We can see that . . . If you finished only the first part of the question and looked at the choices, you might have seen $3 in choice **A** and forgotten to finish the problem. **B** is the choice that gets the point.

Want a harder example? Sure you do! This one involves a double-percent maneuver, which should be handled by only the most experienced of percent mavens. Do not attempt this at home! Oh, wait . . . *Do* attempt this at home, or wherever you're reading this book.

> The original price of a banana in a store is $2.00. During a sale, the store reduces the price by 25% and Joe buys the banana. Joe then raises the price of the banana 10% from the price at which he bought it and sells it to Sam. How much does Sam pay for the banana?

This question asks you to determine the cumulative effect of two successive percent changes. The key to solving it is realizing that each percentage change is dependent on the last. You have to work out the effect of the first percentage change, come up with a value, and then use that value to determine the effect of the second percentage change.

We begin by finding 25% of the original price:

$$\frac{25}{100} \times \$2 = \frac{\$50}{100} = \$.50$$

Now subtract that $.50 from the original price:

$$\$2 - \$.50 = \$1.50$$

That's Joe's cost. Then increase $1.50 by 10%:

$$\frac{10}{100} \times \$1.50 = \frac{\$15}{100} = \$.15$$

Sam buys the banana for $1.50 + $.15 = $1.65. A total rip-off, but still 35 cents less than the original price.

Some test takers, sensing a shortcut, are tempted to just combine the two percentage changes on double-percent problems. This is not a real shortcut. It's more like a dark alley filled with cruel and nasty people who want you to do badly on the GRE. Here, if we reasoned that the first percentage change lowered the price 25%, and the second raised the price 10%, meaning that the total change was a reduction of 15%, then we'd get:

$$\frac{15}{100} \times \$2 = \frac{\$30}{100} = \$.30$$

Subtract that $.30 from the original price:

$$\$2 - \$.30 = \$1.70 = \text{WRONG!}$$

We promise you that if you see a double-percent problem on the GRE, it will include this sort of wrong answer as a trap.

TWO VALUES GIVEN

In the other kind of percent increase/decrease problem, they give you both a first value and a second value, and then ask for the percent by which the value changed from one to the other. If the value goes up, that's a percent increase problem. If it goes down, then it's a percent decrease problem. Luckily, we have a handy formula for both:

$$\text{percent increase} = \frac{\text{difference between the two numbers}}{\text{smaller of the two numbers}} \times 100\%$$

$$\text{percent decrease} = \frac{\text{difference between the two numbers}}{\text{greater of the two numbers}} \times 100\%$$

To borrow some numbers from the banana example, Sam pays $1.65 for a banana that was originally priced at $2.00. The percent decrease in the banana's price would look like this:

$$\text{percent decrease} = \frac{\$2.00 - \$1.65}{\$2.00} \times 100\% = \frac{\$.35}{\$2.00} \times 100\% = .175 \times 100\% = 17.5\%$$

So Sam comes out with a 17.5% discount from the original price, despite lining Joe's pockets in the process.

A basic question of this type would simply provide the two numbers for you to plug into the percent decrease formula. A more difficult question might start with the original banana question above, first requiring you to calculate Sam's price of $1.65 and then asking you to calculate the percent decrease from the original price on top of that. If you find yourself in the deep end of the GRE's question pool, that's what a complicated question might look like.

Common Fractions, Decimals, and Percents

Some fractions, decimals, and percents appear frequently on the GRE. Being able to quickly convert these into each other will save time on the exam, so it pays to memorize the following table.

Fraction	Decimal	Percent
$\dfrac{1}{8}$	0.125	12.5%
$\dfrac{1}{6}$	$0.16\overline{6}$ (the little line above the 6 means that the 6 repeats indefinitely, so $0.16\overline{6} = .1666666666\ldots$)	$16\dfrac{2}{3}\%$
$\dfrac{1}{5}$	0.2	20%
$\dfrac{1}{4}$	0.25	25%
$\dfrac{1}{3}$	$0.33\overline{3}$	$33\dfrac{1}{3}\%$
$\dfrac{3}{8}$	0.375	37.5%
$\dfrac{2}{5}$	0.4	40%
$\dfrac{1}{2}$	0.5	50%
$\dfrac{5}{8}$	0.625	62.5%
$\dfrac{2}{3}$	$0.66\overline{6}$	$66\dfrac{2}{3}\%$
$\dfrac{3}{4}$	0.75	75%
$\dfrac{4}{5}$	0.8	80%
$\dfrac{7}{8}$	0.875	87.5%

Exponents

An exponent is a shorthand way of saying, "Multiply this number by itself this number of times." In a^b, a is multiplied by itself b times. Here's a numerical example: $2^5 = 2 \times 2 \times 2 \times 2 \times 2$. An exponent can also be referred to as a power: 2^5 is "two to the fifth power." Before jumping into the exponent nitty-gritty, learn these five terms:

- **Base.** The base refers to the 3 in 3^5. In other words, the base is the number multiplied by itself however many times specified by the exponent.

- **Exponent.** The exponent is the 5 in 3^5. The exponent tells how many times the base is to be multiplied by itself.

- **Squared.** Saying that a number is squared is a common code word to indicate that it has an exponent of 2. In the expression 6^2, 6 has been squared.

- **Cubed.** Saying that a number is cubed means it has an exponent of 3. In the expression 4^3, 4 has been cubed.

- **Power.** The term power is another way to talk about a number being raised to an exponent. A number raised to the third power has an exponent of 3. So 6 raised to the third power is 6^3.

Common Exponents

It can be very helpful and a real time saver on the GRE if you can easily translate back and forth between a number and its exponential form. For instance, if you can easily see that $36 = 6^2$, it can really come in handy when you're dealing with binomials, quadratic equations, and a number of other algebraic topics we'll cover later in this chapter. Below are some lists of common exponents.

Squares	Cubes	Powers of 2
We'll start with the squares of the first ten integers:	Here are the first five cubes:	Finally, the powers of 2 up to 2^{10} are useful to know for various applications:
$1^2 = 1$	$1^3 = 1$	$2^0 = 1$
$2^2 = 4$	$2^3 = 8$	$2^1 = 2$
$3^2 = 9$	$3^3 = 27$	$2^2 = 4$
$4^2 = 16$	$4^3 = 64$	$2^3 = 8$
$5^2 = 25$	$5^3 = 125$	$2^4 = 16$
$6^2 = 36$		$2^5 = 32$
$7^2 = 49$		$2^6 = 64$
$8^2 = 64$		$2^7 = 128$
$9^2 = 81$		$2^8 = 256$
$10^2 = 100$		$2^9 = 512$
		$2^{10} = 1,024$

Adding and Subtracting Exponents

The rule for adding and subtracting values with exponents is pretty simple, and you can remember it as the inverse of the Nike slogan:

Just *Don't* Do It.

This doesn't mean that you won't see such addition and subtraction problems; it just means that you can't simplify them. For example, the expression $2^{15} + 2^7$ does *not* equal 2^{22}. The expression $2^{15} + 2^7$ is written as simply as possible, so don't make the mistake of trying to simplify it further. If the problem is simple enough, then work out each exponent to find its value, then add the two numbers. For example, to add $3^3 + 4^2$, work out the exponents to get $(3 \times 3 \times 3) + (4 \times 4) = 27 + 16 = 43$.

However, if you're dealing with algebraic expressions that have the same base variable and exponents, then you can add or subtract them. For example, $3x^4 + 5x^4 = 8x^4$. The base variables are both x, and the exponents are both 4, so we can add them. Just remember that expressions that have different bases or exponents cannot be added or subtracted.

Multiplying and Dividing Exponents with Equal Bases

Multiplying or dividing exponential numbers or terms that have the same base is so quick and easy it's like a little math oasis. When multiplying, just add the exponents together. This is known as the Product Rule:

$$3^6 \times 3^2 = 3^{(6+2)} = 3^8$$
$$x^4 \times x^3 = x^{(4+3)} = x^7$$

To divide two same-base exponential numbers or terms, subtract the exponents. This is known as the Quotient Rule:

$$\frac{3^6}{3^2} = 3^{(6-2)} = 3^4$$

$$\frac{x^4}{x^3} = x^{(4-3)} = x^1$$

Quick and easy, right?

Multiplying and Dividing Exponents with Unequal Bases

You want the bad news or the bad news? The same isn't true if you need to multiply or divide two exponential numbers that *don't* have the same base, such as, say, $3^3 \times 4^2$. When two exponents have different bases, you just have to do your work the old-fashioned way: Multiply the numbers out and multiply or divide the result accordingly: $3^3 \times 4^2 = 27 \times 16 = 432$.

There is, however, one trick you should know. Sometimes when the bases aren't the same, it's still possible to simplify an expression or equation if one base can be expressed in terms of the other. For example:

$$2^5 \times 8^9$$

Even though 2 and 8 are different bases, 8 can be rewritten as a power of 2; namely, $8 = 2^3$. This means that we can replace 8 with 2^3 in the original expression:

$$2^5 \times (2^3)^9$$

Since the base is the same for both values, we can simplify this further, but first we're going to need another rule to deal with the $(2^3)^9$ term. This is called . . .

Raising an Exponent to an Exponent

This one may sound like it comes from the Office of Redundancy Office, but it doesn't. To raise one exponent to another exponent (also called taking the power of a power), simply multiply the exponents. This is known as the Power Rule:

$$\left(3^2\right)^4 = 3^{(2\times4)} = 3^8$$
$$\left(x^4\right)^3 = x^{(4\times3)} = x^{12}$$

Let's use the Power Rule to simplify the expression that we were just working on:

$$2^5 \times (2^3)^9 = 2^5 \times 2^{3\times9} = 2^5 \times 2^{27}$$

Our "multiplication with equal bases rule" tells us to now add the exponents, which yields:

$$2^5 \times 2^{27} = 2^{32}$$

2^{32} is a pretty huge number, and the GRE would *never* have you calculate out something this large. This means that you can leave it as 2^{32}, because that's how it would appear in the answer choices.

To Recap: Multiply the exponents when raising one exponent to another, and add the exponents when multiplying two identical bases with exponents. The test makers expect lots of people to mix these operations up, and they're usually not disappointed.

Fractions Raised to an Exponent

To raise a fraction to an exponent, raise both the numerator and denominator to that exponent:

$$\left(\frac{1}{3}\right)^3 = \frac{1^3}{3^3} = \frac{1\times1\times1}{3\times3\times3} = \frac{1}{27}$$

That's it; nothing fancy.

Negative Numbers Raised to an Exponent

When you multiply a negative number by another negative number, you get a positive number, and when you multiply a negative number by a positive number, you get a negative number. Since exponents result in multiplication, a negative number raised to an exponent follows these rules:

- A negative number raised to an even exponent will be positive. For example, $(-2)^4 = 16$. Why? Because $(-2)^4$ means $-2 \times -2 \times -2 \times -2$. When you multiply the first two -2s together, you get positive 4 because you're multiplying two negative numbers. When you multiply the $+4$ by the next -2, you get -8, since you're multiplying a positive number by a negative number. Finally, you multiply the -8 by the last -2 and get $+16$, since you're once again multiplying two negative numbers. The negatives cancel themselves out and vanish.

- A negative number raised to an odd exponent will be negative. To see why, just look at the example above, but stop the process at -2^3, which equals -8.

Special Exponents

It's helpful to know a few special types of exponents for the GRE.

ZERO

Any base raised to the power of zero is equal to 1. Strange, but true:

$$123^0 = 1$$

$$0.8775^0 = 1$$

$$\text{a million trillion gazillion}^0 = 1$$

Like we said: strange, but true. You should also know that 0 raised to any positive power is 0. For example:

$$0^1 = 0$$

$$0^{73} = 0$$

ONE

Any base raised to the power of 1 is equal to itself: $2^1 = 2$, $-67^1 = -67$, and $x^1 = x$. This fact is important to know when you have to multiply or divide exponential terms with the same base:

$$3x^6 \times x = 3x^6 \times x^1 = 3x^{(6+1)} = 3x^7$$

The number 1 raised to any power is 1:

$$1^2 = 1$$

$$1^{4,000} = 1$$

NEGATIVE EXPONENTS

Any number or term raised to a negative power is equal to the reciprocal of that base raised to the opposite power. Got that? Didn't think so. An example will make it clearer:

$$x^{-5} = \frac{1}{x^5}$$

Here's a more complicated example:

$$\left(\frac{2}{3}\right)^{-3} = \left(\frac{1}{\frac{2}{3}}\right)^3 = \left(\frac{3}{2}\right)^3 = \frac{27}{8}$$

Here's an English translation of the rule: If you see a base raised to a negative exponent, put the base as the denominator under a numerator of 1 and then drop the negative from the exponent. From there, just simplify.

FRACTIONAL EXPONENTS

Exponents can be fractions too. When a number or term is raised to a fractional power, it is called taking the root of that number or term. This expression can be converted into a more convenient form:

$$x^{\left(\frac{a}{b}\right)} = \sqrt[b]{x^a}$$

The $\sqrt{\ }$ symbol is known as the *radical sign*, and anything under the radical is called the radicand. We've got a whole section devoted to roots and radicals coming right up. But first let's look at an example with real numbers:

$8^{\left(\frac{2}{3}\right)} = \sqrt[3]{8^2} = \sqrt[3]{64} = 4$, because $4 \times 4 \times 4 = 64$. Here we treated the 2 as an ordinary exponent and wrote the 3 outside the radical.

Roots and Radicals

The only roots that appear with any regularity on the GRE are square roots, designated by a fancier-looking long division symbol, like this: $\sqrt{25}$. Usually the test makers will ask you to simplify roots and radicals.

As with exponents, though, you'll also need to know when such expressions *can't* be simplified.

Square roots require you to find the number that, when multiplied by itself, equals the number under the radical sign. A few examples:

$$\sqrt{25} = 5, \text{ because } 5 \times 5 = 25$$

$$\sqrt{100} = 10, \text{ because } 10 \times 10 = 100$$

$$\sqrt{1} = 1, \text{ because } 1 \times 1 = 1$$

$$\sqrt{\frac{1}{4}} = \frac{1}{2}, \text{ because } \frac{1}{2} \times \frac{1}{2} = \frac{1}{4}$$

Here's another way to think about square roots:

$$\text{if } x^n = y, \text{ then } \sqrt[n]{y} = x$$

When the GRE gives you a number under a square root sign, that number is always going to be positive. For example, $\sqrt{25}$ is just 5, even though in real life it could be –5. If you take the square root of a variable, however, the answer could be positive or negative. For example, if you solve $x^2 = 100$ by taking the square root of both sides, x could be 10 or –10. Both values work because $10 \times 10 = 100$ and $-10 \times -10 = 100$ (recall that a negative times a negative is a positive).

Very rarely, you may see cube and higher roots on the GRE. These are similar to square roots, but the number of times the final answer must be multiplied by itself will be three or more. You'll always be able to determine the number of multiplications required from the little number outside the radical, as in this example:

$$\sqrt[3]{8} = 2, \text{ because } 2 \times 2 \times 2 = 8$$

Here the little 3 indicates that the correct answer must be multiplied by itself a total of three times to equal 8.

A few more examples:

$$\sqrt[3]{27} = 3, \text{ because } 3 \times 3 \times 3 = 27$$
$$\sqrt[4]{625} = 5, \text{ because } 5 \times 5 \times 5 \times 5 = 625$$
$$\sqrt[4]{1} = 1, \text{ because } 1 \times 1 \times 1 \times 1 = 1$$

Simplifying Roots

Roots can only be simplified when you're multiplying or dividing them. Equations that add or subtract roots cannot be simplified. That is, you can't add or subtract roots. You have to work out each root separately and then perform the operation. For example, to solve $\sqrt{9} + \sqrt{4} = ?$, do not add the 9 and 4 together to get $\sqrt{13}$. Instead, $\sqrt{9} + \sqrt{4} = 3 + 2 = 5$.

You can multiply or divide the numbers under the radical sign as long as the roots are of the same degree—that is, both square roots, both cube roots, etc. You cannot multiply, for example, a square root by a cube root. Here's the rule in general form:

$$\sqrt[n]{x} \times \sqrt[n]{y} = \sqrt[n]{x \times y}$$

Here are some examples with actual numbers. We can simplify the expressions below because every term in them is a square root. To simplify multiplication or division of square roots, combine everything under a single radical sign.

$$\sqrt{12} \times \sqrt{3} = \sqrt{12 \times 3} = \sqrt{36} = 6$$
$$\sqrt{50} \times \sqrt{2} = \sqrt{50 \times 2} = \sqrt{100} = 10$$
$$\frac{\sqrt{32}}{\sqrt{2}} = \sqrt{\frac{32}{2}} = \sqrt{16} = 4$$

You can also use this rule in reverse. That is, a single number under a radical sign can be split into two numbers whose product is the original number. For example:

$$\sqrt{200} = \sqrt{100 \times 2} = \sqrt{100} \times \sqrt{2} = 10\sqrt{2}$$

The reason we chose to split 200 into 100 × 2 is because it's easy to take the square root of 100, since the result is an integer, 10. The goal in simplifying radicals is to get as much as possible out from under the radical sign. When splitting up square roots this way, try to think of the largest perfect square that divides evenly into the original number. Here's another example:

$$\sqrt{75} = \sqrt{25 \times 3} = \sqrt{25} \times \sqrt{3} = 5\sqrt{3}$$

It's important to remember that as you've seen earlier, you can't add or subtract roots. You have to work out each root separately and then add (or subtract). For example, to solve $\sqrt{25} + \sqrt{9}$, you cannot add 25 + 9 and put 34 under a radical sign. Instead, $\sqrt{25} + \sqrt{9} = 5 + 3 = 8$.

Absolute Value

The absolute value of a number is the distance that number is from zero, and it's indicated with vertical bars, like this: |8|. Absolute values are always positive or zero—never negative. So, the absolute value of a positive number is that number: |8| = 8. The absolute value of a negative number is the number without the negative sign: |–12| = 12. Here are some other examples:

$$|5| = 5$$
$$|-4.234| = 4.234$$
$$\left|\frac{3}{7}\right| = \frac{3}{7}$$
$$\left|\frac{-1}{4}\right| = \frac{1}{4}$$
$$|0| = 0$$

It is also possible to have expressions within absolute value bars:

$$3 - 2 + |3 - 7|$$

Think of absolute value bars as parentheses. Do what's inside them first, then tackle the rest of the problem. You can't just make that –7 positive because it's sitting between absolute value bars. You have to work out the math first:

$$3 - 2 + |-4|$$

Now you can get rid of the bars and the negative sign from that 4.

$$3 - 2 + 4 = 5$$

You'll see more of absolute value in the algebra section of this Math 101 chapter. And speaking of which, it's time to head there now.

ALGEBRA

See if you can notice the difference between most of the math problems we've considered so far, and these:

$$16 = \frac{2}{a}$$

$$27 + m = 184$$

$$6 + \frac{4x}{3} + 10x - 8 = 2x + 4$$

Eek! There are *letters* in there! As you no doubt know, the letters are called *variables*, and they make possible the wonderful world of algebra. Whoever thought of adding variables into math certainly made tens of millions of school kids' lives harder, because without algebra, there would be no geometry, no trigonometry, no calculus, and possibly no misery at all in the world. *Thanks a lot, Mr. or Mrs. Math Genius* . . . Of course, there would probably be no microwave ovens or iPods either, so it's not all bad.

Since the variables represent unspecified quantities, algebra brings arithmetic into the world of the unknown. Of course, much of algebra deals with making that unknown known; that is, solving equations so that variables can be replaced by good old-fashioned numbers. We'll get to all that soon enough, but first a little vocabulary is in order.

Algebra Terms

There are six main terms that describe the world of algebra. The GRE won't ask you to define them but will nonetheless give you questions that require you to work with them.

---

1. **Constant.** A numerical quantity that does not change.

2. **Variable.** An unknown quantity written as a letter. A variable can be represented by any letter in the English alphabet; x or y are common on the GRE, but you'll see others as well. Variables may be associated with specific things, like x number of apples or y dollars. Other times, variables have no specific association, but you'll need to manipulate them to show that you understand basic algebraic principles.

3. **Coefficient.** A coefficient is a number that appears next to a variable and tells how many of that variable there are. For example, in the term $4x$, 4 is the coefficient and tells us there are four xs. In the term $3x^3$, 3 is the coefficient and tells us there are three x^3s.

4. **Term.** The product of a constant and a variable. Or, a quantity separated from other quantities by addition or subtraction. For example, in the equation $3x^3 + 2x^2 - 7x + 4 = x - 1$, the side to the left of the equal sign contains four terms $(3x^3, 2x^2, -7x, 4)$, while the right side contains two terms $(x, -1)$. The constants, 4 and –1, are considered terms because they are coefficients of variables raised to the zero power: $4 = 4x^0$. So technically, every algebraic term is the product of a constant and a variable raised to some power.

5. **Expression.** A funny look on your face. Or in math, any combination of terms. An expression can be as simple as a single constant term, like 5, or as complicated as the sum or difference of many terms, each of which is a combination of constants and variables, such as $\dfrac{\left\{\left(x^2+2\right)^3 - 6x\right\}}{7x^5}$. Expressions don't include an equal sign—this is what differentiates expressions from equations. If you're given the value of every variable in the expression, then you can calculate the numerical value of the expression. Lacking those values, expressions can't be solved, although they can often be simplified.

6. **Equation.** Two expressions linked by an equal sign. Much of the algebra on the GRE consists of solving equations.

Inputs and Outputs: Simple Substitutions

We mentioned above that we can calculate the numerical value of an expression if we're given the value of every variable in it. In this case, the expression itself is like a machine that takes an input (the variable value) and outputs a solution.

One of the simplest kinds of algebraic problems on the GRE operates like this, as in the following example:

$$\text{If } x = 2, \text{ what is the value of } \frac{3x^2 + 6}{3} \text{ ?}$$

There's nothing to do but simply input 2 into the expression in place of x and do the math:

$$\frac{3(2)^2 + 6}{3} = \frac{(3)(4) + 6}{3} = \frac{12 + 6}{3} = \frac{18}{3} = 6$$

So here, an input of 2 yields an output of 6.

You may see something like this in the beginning of the Math section, but things will most likely get more complicated after that. For example, the inputs themselves may be a bit more complex than a single number; in fact, an input may itself contain variables:

$$\text{If } 2y + 8x = 11, \text{ what is the value of } 3(2y + 8x)?$$

You might see this equation bubbling over with variables and panic. Don't. Since the expression $2y + 8x$ appears in both parts of the question, and we're told this expression equals 11, we can simply substitute that figure in place of the expression on the right to get $3(11) = 33$.

A question may also involve multiple substitutions. For instance:

$$z = \frac{4y}{x^2}, y = 3x, \text{ and } x = 2, \text{ then what is the value of } z?$$

To approach this problem, you just have to input 2 for x to find y, and then input those values into the equation for z. Substituting 2 for x into $y = 3x$ gives $y = 3(2) = 6$. Inputting $x = 2$ and $y = 6$ into the equation for z gives:

$$z = \frac{4y}{x^2} = \frac{4(6)}{2^2} = \frac{24}{4} = 6$$

Simplifying Algebraic Expressions

Before we move on to solving more complicated equations, we need to cover a few simplification tools that allow us to change algebraic expressions into simpler but equivalent forms.

Distributing

The rule of distribution states:

$$a(b + c) = (a \times b) + (a \times c)$$

The a in this expression can be any kind of term, meaning it could be a variable, a constant, or a combination of the two. When you distribute a factor into an expression within parentheses, multiply each term inside the parentheses by the factor outside the parentheses. $4(x + 2)$, for example, would become $4x + (4)(2)$, or $4x + 8$. Let's try a harder one: $3y(y^2 - 6)$. Distributing the $3y$ term across the terms in the parentheses yields:

$$3y(y^2 - 6) = 3y^3 - 18y$$

Seems logical enough. But the true value of distributing becomes clear when you see a distributable expression in an equation. We'll see an example of this later in the section on linear equations.

Factoring

Factoring an expression is the opposite of distributing. $4x^3 - 8x^2$ is one mean-looking expression, right? Or so it seems, until you realize that both terms share the greatest common factor $4x^2$, which you can factor out:

$$4x^3 - 8x^2 = 4x^2(x - 2)$$

By distributing and factoring, you can group or ungroup quantities in an equation to make your calculations simpler, depending on what the other terms in the equation look like. Sometimes distributing will help; other times, factoring will be the way to go. Here are a few more examples of both techniques:

$3(x + y + 4) = 3x + 3y + 12$	3 is distributed.
$2x + 4x + 6x + 8x = 2x(1 + 2 + 3 + 4)$	$2x$ is factored out.
$x^2(x - 1) = x^3 - x^2$	x^2 is distributed.
$xy^2(xy^2 + x^2y) = x^2y^4 + x^3y^3$	xy^2 is distributed.
$14xy^2 - 4xy + 22y = 2y(7xy - 2x + 11)$	$2y$ is factored out.

Combining Like Terms

After factoring and distributing, you can take additional steps to simplify expressions or equations. Combining like terms is one of the simplest techniques you can use. It involves adding or subtracting the coefficients of variables that are raised to the same power. For example, by combining like terms, the expression

$$x^2 - x^3 + 4x^2 + 3x^3$$

can be simplified by adding the coefficients of the variable x^3 (–1 and 3) together and the coefficients of x^2 (1 and 4) together to get:

$$2x^3 + 5x^2$$

Variables that have different exponential values are not like terms and can't be combined. Two terms that do not share a variable are also not like terms and cannot be combined regardless of their exponential value. For example, you can't combine:

$$x^4 + x^2$$

or

$$y^2 + x^2$$

You can, however, factor the first expression to get $x^2(x^2 + 1)$, which you should do if it helps you answer the question.

Linear Equations with One Variable

Simplifying is nice, and helpful to boot, but solving is really where it's at. To solve an equation, you have to isolate the variable you're solving for. That is, you have to "manipulate" the equation until you get the variable alone on one side of the equal sign. By definition, the variable is then equal to everything on the other side of the equal sign. You can't manipulate an equation the way you used to manipulate your little brother or sister. When manipulating equations, there are rules. Here's the first and most fundamental. In fact, it's so important we're going to bold it:

Whatever you do to one side of an equation, you must do to the other side.

If you divide one side of an equation by 3, divide the other side by 3. If you take the square root of one side of an equation, take the square root of the other. If you fall in love with one side of the equation, fall in love with the other. Neither side will think you're a two-timer. They'll think you're a highly skilled mathematician.

By treating the two sides of the equation in the same way, you don't change what the equation means. You change the *form* of the equation into something easier to work with—that's the point of manipulating it—but the equation remains true since both sides stay equal.

Take, for instance, the equation $3x + 2 = 5$. You can do anything you want to it as long as you do the same thing to both sides. Here, since we're trying to get the variable x alone on the left, the thing to do is subtract 2 from that side of the equation. But we can only do that if we subtract 2 from the other side as well:

$$3x + 2 - 2 = 5 - 2$$
$$3x = 3$$

Ah, that's better. Now we can just divide both sides by 3 to get $x = 1$, and we're done.

You should use the simplification techniques you learned above (distributing, factoring, and combining like terms) to help you solve equations. For example:

$$3y(y^2 + 6) = 3y^3 + 36$$

That seems fairly nasty, since there aren't any like terms to combine. But wait a sec . . . what if you distribute that $3y$ on the left side of the equation? That would give:

$$3y^3 + 18y = 3y^3 + 36$$

Shiver our timbers! Now we can subtract $3y^3$ from both sides to get

$$18y = 36$$

and then simply divide both sides by 18 to get $y = 2$.

Reverse PEMDAS

Many equations include a combination of elements you learned about in our arithmetic discussion. Remember PEMDAS, the acronym you learned to help you remember the order of operations? Well, what do you get if you do PEMDAS in reverse? SADMEP, of course. Or, using the old corny mnemonic device, Sally Aunt Dear My Excuse Please. Wait, scratch that—mnemonics don't work in reverse.

Why do we want to reverse our trusty order of operations, anyway? The idea is to *undo* everything that has been done to the variable so that it will be isolated in the end. So you should first subtract or add any extra terms on the same side as the variable. Then divide and multiply anything on the same side as the variable. Next, raise both sides of the equation to a power or take their roots according to any exponent attached to the variable. Finally, work out anything inside parentheses. In other words, do the order of operations backward: SADMEP!

We'll need to demonstrate with an example. Here's a little monstrosity that at first glance might make you reconsider your decision to go to grad school:

$$2 + \frac{3(2\sqrt{x} + 3)}{2} = 17$$

At second glance you might feel the same way. But at third glance you'd know what to do.

In this equation, poor little x is being square rooted, multiplied by 2, added to 3, and encased in parentheses—all in the numerator of a fraction. That's hardly what we'd call "alone time." You've got to get him out of there! Undo all of these operations to liberate x and solve the equation.

Let SADMEP be your guide: First, subtract 2 from both sides of the equation:

$$\frac{3(2\sqrt{x} + 3)}{2} = 15$$

There's no addition or division possible at this point, but we can multiply both sides by 2 to get rid of the fraction:

$$3(2\sqrt{x} + 3) = 30$$

Now divide both sides by 3 (see you later, parentheses!):

$$2\sqrt{x} + 3 = 10$$

Now we're in position to subtract 3 from each side:

$$2\sqrt{x} = 7$$

Divide both sides by 2:

$$\sqrt{x} = \frac{7}{2}$$

Finally, square each side to get rid of the square root:

$$x = \frac{49}{4}$$

Success! You've freed poor x from all of those bullying operations.

Variables in the Denominator

Remember, the key to solving equations is to isolate the variable, but how to do this depends on where the variable is located. A variable in the numerator of a fraction is usually pretty easy to isolate. But if the variable is in the denominator, things get more complicated. See what you can make of this one:

$$\frac{1}{x+2} + 3 = 7$$

Following SADMEP, start by subtracting the 3:

$$\frac{1}{x+2} = 4$$

But now you have to get the x out of the denominator, and the only way to do that is to multiply both sides of the equation by that denominator, $x + 2$:

$$1 = 4(x+2)$$

Divide both sides by 4:

$$\frac{1}{4} = x + 2$$

Subtract 2 from each side:

$$-\frac{7}{4} = x$$

Equations with Absolute Value

To solve an equation in which the variable is within absolute value bars, you have to follow a two-step process:

1. Isolate the expression within the absolute value bars.

2. Divide the equation in two.

Divide the equation in two? What is this, a magic trick? Kind of. Watch:

If $|x + 3| = 5$, then $x =$

Since both 5 and –5 within absolute value bars equal 5, the expression inside the bars can equal 5 or –5 and the equation will work out. That's why we have to work through both scenarios. So we're actually dealing with two equations:

$$x + 3 = 5$$

$$x + 3 = -5$$

For a complete solution, we need to solve both. In the first equation, $x = 2$. In the second equation, $x = -8$. So the solutions to the equation $|x + 3| = 5$ are $x = \{-8, 2\}$. Both work. Substitute them back into the equation if you have any doubts and to reinforce why we need to solve two equations to get a full answer to the question.

Equations with Exponents and Radicals

Absolute value equations aren't the only ones with more than one possible answer. Exponents and radicals can also have devilish effects on algebraic equations that are similar to those caused by absolute value. Consider the equation $x^2 = 25$. Seems pretty simple, right? Just take the square root of both sides, and you end up with $x = 5$. But remember the rule of multiplying negative numbers? When two negative numbers are multiplied together the result is positive. In other words, –5 squared *also* results in 25: $-5 \times -5 = 25$. This means that whenever you have to take the square root to simplify a variable brought to the second power, the result will be two solutions, one positive and one negative: $\sqrt{x^2} = \pm x$. (The only exception is if $x = 0$.) You'll see what we mean by working through this question:

If $2x^2 = 72$, what is the value of x?

To solve this problem, we first divide both sides by 2 to get $x^2 = 36$. Now we need to take the square root of both sides: $x = \pm 6$.

Recognizing when algebraic equations can have more than one possible answer is especially important in Quantitative Comparison questions. Sometimes it may appear that the relationship between columns A and B leans in a definite direction, until you notice that one of the columns can actually have more than one possible value. Keep your eyes peeled for this common nuance.

Linear Equations with Two or More Variables

So you're kicking butt and taking names on those old one-variable equations, huh? Good. But some GRE questions contain *two* variables. Lucky for you, those questions also contain two equations, and you can use the two equations in conjunction to solve for the variables. These two equations together are called a *system of equations* or *simultaneous equations*. We said earlier that manipulating equations isn't like manipulating your younger brother or sister. Actually, that's not entirely true: Solving simultaneous equations is like manipulating your younger brother and sister. You use one equation against the other, and in the end you get whatever you want.

There are two ways to solve simultaneous equations. The first method involves substitution, and the second involves adding or subtracting one equation from the other. Let's look at both techniques.

Solving by Substitution

You've already seen examples of substitution in the Input/Output discussion earlier in the chapter, so you should be familiar with the mechanics of plugging values or variables from one place into another place to find what you're looking for. In these next examples, both pieces of the puzzle are equations. Our method will be to find the value of one variable in one equation and then plug that into a second equation to solve for a different variable. Here's an example:

If $x - 4 = y - 3$ and $2y = 6$, what is x?

You've got two equations, and you have to find x. The first equation contains both x and y. The second equation contains only y. To solve for x, you first have to solve for y in the second equation and substitute that value into the first equation. If $2y = 6$, then dividing both sides by 2, $y = 3$. Now, substitute 3 for y in the equation $x - 4 = y - 3$:

$$x - 4 = 3 - 3$$
$$x - 4 = 0$$
$$x = 4$$

That's all there is to it. But here's one that's more likely to give you trouble:

If $3x = y + 5$ and $2y - 2 = 12k$, what is x in terms of k?

Notice anything interesting? There are *three* variables in this one. To solve for x in terms of k, we have to first get x and k into the same equation. To make this happen, we can solve for y in terms of k in the second equation and then substitute that value into the first equation to solve for x:

$$2y - 2 = 12k$$
$$2y = 12k + 2$$
$$y = 6k + 1$$

Then substitute $6k + 1$ for y in the equation $3x = y + 5$:

$$3x = y + 5$$
$$3x = (6k + 1) + 5$$
$$3x = 6k + 6$$
$$x = 2k + 2$$

This is our answer, since x is now expressed in terms of k. Note that you could also solve this problem by solving for y in terms of x in the first equation and substituting that expression in for y in the second equation. Either way works.

Solving by Adding or Subtracting

The amazing thing about simultaneous equations is that you can actually add or subtract the entire equations from each other. Here's an example:

If $6x + 2y = 11$ and $5x + y = 10$, what is $x + y$?

Look what happens if we subtract the second equation from the first:

$$\begin{aligned} 6x + 2y &= 11 \\ -(5x + y &= 10) \\ \hline x + y &= 1 \end{aligned}$$

To add or subtract simultaneous equations, you need to know what variable or expression you want to solve for, and then add or subtract accordingly. We made the example above purposely easy to show how the method works. But you won't always be given two equations that you can immediately add or subtract from each other to isolate the exact variable or expression you seek, as evidenced by this next example:

If $2x + 3y = -6$ and $-4x + 16y = 13$, what is the value of y?

We're asked to solve for y, which means we've got to get rid of x. But one equation has $2x$ and the other has $-4x$, which means the x terms won't disappear by simply adding or subtracting them. Don't despair; our Golden Rule of Algebra comes to the rescue: If you do the same thing to both sides of an equation, you don't change the meaning of the equation. That means that in this case, we could multiply both sides of $2x + 3y = -6$ by 2, which would give us $2(2x +3y) = 2(-6)$. Using the trusty distributive law, and multiplying out the second part, gives us $4x +6y = -12$. Now we're in a position to get rid of those pesky x terms by adding this new (but equivalent) form of equation 1 to equation 2:

$$\begin{aligned} 4x + 6y &= -12 \\ +(-4x + 16y &= 13) \\ \hline 22y &= 1 \\ y &= \frac{1}{22} \end{aligned}$$

On the GRE, you will almost always be able to manipulate one of the two equations in a pair of simultaneous equations so that they can be added and subtracted to isolate the variable or expression you want. If you can't see how to do this, or for questions with easy numbers, go ahead and solve by using substitution instead. As you practice with these types of problems, you'll get a sense for which method works best for you.

Binomial and Quadratic Equations

A binomial is an expression containing two terms. The terms $(x + 5)$ and $(x - 6)$ are both binomials. A quadratic expression takes the form $ax^2 + bx + c$, where $a \neq 0$. Quadratics closely resemble the products formed when binomials are multiplied. Coincidence? Fat chance. That's why we treat these topics together. We'll start off with binomials, and work our way to quadratics.

Multiplying Binomials

The best acronym ever invented (other than SCUBA: "self-contained underwater breathing apparatus") will help you remember how to multiply binomials. This acronym is FOIL, and it stands for First + Outer + Inner + Last. The acronym describes the order in which we multiply the terms of two binomials to get the correct product.

$$(x + 1)(x + 3)$$

For example, let's say you were kidnapped by wretched fork-tongued lizard-men whose only weakness was binomials. Now what if the lizard-king asked you to multiply these binomials:

$$(x + 1)(x + 3)$$

What would you do? Follow FOIL, of course. First, multiply the first (F) terms of each binomial:

$$x \times x = x^2$$

Next, multiply the outer (O) terms of the binomials:

$$x \times 3 = 3x$$

Then, multiply the inner (I) terms:

$$1 \times x = x$$

And then multiply the last (L) terms:

$$1 \times 3 = 3$$

Add all these terms together:

$$x^2 + 3x + x + 3$$

Finally, combine like terms, and you get:

$$x^2 + 4x + 3$$

Here are a few more examples of multiplied binomials to test your FOILing faculties:

$$(y + 3)(y - 7) = y^2 - 7y + 3y - 21 = y^2 - 4y - 21$$
$$(-x + 2)(4x + 6) = -4x^2 - 6x + 8x + 12 = -4x^2 + 2x + 12$$
$$(3a + 2b)(6c - d) = 18ac - 3ad + 12bc - 2bd$$

Note that the last one doesn't form a quadratic equation, and that none of the terms can be combined. That's okay. When presented with binomials, follow FOIL wherever it leads.

Working with Quadratic Equations

A quadratic equation will always have a variable raised to the power of 2, like this:

$$x^2 = 10x - 25$$

Your job will be to solve for the given variable, as we've done with other algebraic equations throughout this section. The basic approach, however, is significantly different from what you've done so far. Instead of isolating the variable on the left, you'll want to get everything on the left side of the quadratic equation, leaving 0 on the right. In the example above, that means moving the $10x$ and -25 to the left side of the equation:

$$x^2 - 10x + 25 = 0$$

Now it's looking like most of the products of binomials we saw in the previous section, except instead of being just a quadratic expression, it's a quadratic equation because it's set equal to 0.

To solve the equation, we need to factor it. Factoring a quadratic equation means rewriting it as a product of two terms in parentheses, like this:

$$x^2 - 10x + 25 = (x - 5)(x - 5)$$

How did we know to factor the equation into these binomials? Here's the secret: Factoring quadratic equations on the GRE always fits the following pattern:

$$(x \pm m)(x \pm n)$$

Essentially, we perform FOIL in reverse. When we approach a quadratic like $x^2 - 10x + 25$, the two numbers we're looking for as our m and n terms need to *multiply to give the last number* in the equation. The last number in the equation is 25, so we need to find two numbers whose product is 25. Some pairs of numbers that work are:

1 and 25

−1 and −25

5 and 5

−5 and −5

Further, the sum of the two numbers needs *to give the middle number* in the equation. Be very careful that you don't ignore the sign of the middle number:

$$x^2 - 10x + 25$$

Since you're subtracting $10x$, the middle number is −10. That means the m and n numbers we seek not only need to multiply to 25 but also need to add to −10. Going back to our factor list above, −5 and −5 is the only pair that works. Substituting this into the pattern gives:

$$(x - 5)(x - 5)$$

And since we originally set the equation equal to 0, we now have:

$$(x - 5)(x - 5) = 0$$

For the product of two terms to equal 0, that means that either one could be 0. Here both terms are $(x - 5)$, so $x - 5$ must equal 0.

$$x - 5 = 0$$

$$x = 5$$

The final answer is $x = 5$.

In this example, m and n are equal, which is why we end up with only one answer. But that's usually not the case. Let's look at another example, using different numbers:

$$x^2 = -10x - 21$$

To solve for x, first move everything to the left to set the equation equal to 0:

$$x^2 + 10x + 21 = 0$$

Now we need to figure out what numbers fit our pattern:

$$(x \pm m)(x \pm n)$$

We know from our equation that $m \times n$ needs to equal 21, and $m + n$ needs to equal 10. So, which numbers work? Let's look at $m \times n = 21$ first:

1 and 21

−1 and −21

3 and 7

−3 and −7

We can eliminate (1 and 21) and (−1 and −21), since neither of these pairs add up to 10. The third pair, 3 and 7, adds to 10, so we can stop right there and plug these numbers into our pattern:

$$(x + 3)(x + 7) = 0$$

If you need to double-check your factoring, just FOIL the resulting binomials, which should bring you right back to the original quadratic. Since we now have the product of two different binomials sets equal to 0, one of the two terms needs to be 0. So, either $(x + 3) = 0$ or $(x + 7) = 0$, which means x could be equal to −3 or −7. There's no way to determine for sure, since both values work.

QUADRATIC FACTORING PATTERNS

There are three patterns of quadratics that commonly appear on the GRE. Learn them now, and you'll work faster on test day.

Pattern 1: $x^2 + 2xy + y^2 = (x + y)(x + y) = (x + y)^2$

   Example: $x^2 + 6xy + 9 = (x + 3)^2$

Pattern 2: $x^2 - 2xy + y^2 = (x - y)(x - y) = (x - y)^2$

   Example: $x^2 - 10xy + 25 = (x - 5)^2$

Pattern 3: $(x + y)(x - y) = x^2 - y^2$

   Example: $(x + 4)(x - 4) = x^2 - 16$

You may be wondering why we wrote the last pattern with the factored form first. We wrote it this way because this is the way it often appears on the GRE: You'll be given an expression that fits the pattern on the left of the equal sign $[(x + y)(x - y)]$, and you'll need to recognize its equivalent form of $(x^2 - y^2)$.

Here's an example of how you can use this pattern on test day:

$$\text{What is the value of } (\sqrt{85} + \sqrt{72})(\sqrt{85} - \sqrt{72})?$$

This looks horrific, and, well, it is if you attempt to perform a full FOIL treatment on it. Who wants to multiply 72 by 85 and deal with all those radical signs? Not us. Not you. Not anyone. Luckily, quadratic pattern 3 helps us avoid all that work. That pattern states that whenever we have the sum of two values multiplied by the difference of those same values, the whole messy expression is equal to $x^2 - y^2$. Here, if we let $x = \sqrt{85}$ and $y = \sqrt{72}$, then $x^2 - y^2 = \sqrt{85}^2 - \sqrt{72}^2$. If this doesn't look any better to you, then you're not realizing that the squared symbol (the little 2) and the square root symbol (the $\sqrt{}$) cancel each other out. This gives the much simpler expression $85 - 72$, which equals 13.

This is an excellent example of how changing your math mindset, something we implored you to do in the previous chapter, will help you on the GRE. In the difficult-looking problem we just tackled, your first instinct may have been to hack your way through the numbers. However, if you instead suspected that the GRE test makers probably wouldn't present a problem like this if there wasn't a more elegant solution, then you might have searched for an easy way in. Quadratic factoring pattern 3 does the trick.

Inequalities

Life isn't always fair. That's why there are inequalities. An inequality is like an equation, but instead of relating equal quantities, it specifies exactly how two quantities are *not* equal. There are four types of inequalities:

---

1. $x > y$ x is greater than y.

2. $x < y$ x is less than y.

3. $x \geq y$ x is greater than or equal to y.

4. $x \leq y$ x is less than or equal to y.

So, for example, $x + 3 \leq 2x$ may be read as "$x + 3$ is less than or equal to $2x$." Similarly, $y > 0$ is another way of saying "y is greater than 0." Inequalities may also be written in compound form, such as $4 < y - 7 < 3y - 10$. This is really just two separate inequalities: $4 < y - 7$ and $y - 7 < 3y - 10$. Another way to think about this compound inequality is that $y - 7$, the expression stuck in the middle, is between 4 and $3y - 10$.

Solving Inequalities

Solving inequalities is a lot like solving equations: Get the variable on one side of the inequality and all the numbers on the other, using the algebraic rules you've already learned. The one exception to this, and it's a *crucial* exception, is that multiplying or dividing both sides of an inequality by a negative number requires that you flip the direction of the inequality.

This exception is crucial, so we'll repeat it:

> **THE INEQUALITY EXCEPTION**
>
> Multiplying or dividing both sides of an inequality by a
> negative number requires you to flip the direction of the inequality.

Let's try some examples.

Solve for x in the inequality $\dfrac{x}{2} - 3 < 2y$.

First we knock that 3 away from the x by adding 3 to both sides:

$$\frac{x}{2} < 2y + 3$$

That 2 in the denominator is quite annoying, but by now you should know the fix for that—just multiply both sides by 2 and it will disappear from the left side of the inequality:

$$x < 2(2y + 3)$$

Almost there. We can simplify the right side with our handy distributive law, multiplying the 2 by both terms in the parentheses to get a final answer of:

$$x < 4y + 6$$

We're done. The x stands alone, and we know that it's less than the expression $4y + 6$. Now try this one:

Solve for x in the inequality $\dfrac{4}{x} \geq -2$.

Here are the steps, all at once:

$$\frac{4}{x} \geq -2$$
$$4 \geq -2x$$
$$-2 \leq x$$

Notice that in this example the inequality had to be flipped, since both sides had to be divided by –2 to isolate the variable in the end.

To help remember that multiplication or division by a negative number reverses the direction of the inequality, remember that if $x > y$, then $-x < -y$. Just as 5 is greater than 4, –5 is less than –4. The larger the number, the smaller it becomes when you make it negative. That's why multiplying or dividing inequalities by negatives requires switching the direction of the inequality sign.

Inequalities with Two Variables

Another type of inequality problem involves two variables. For these, you'll be given a range of values for each of the two variables. For example:

$$-8 \leq a \leq 0$$

$$5 \leq b \leq 25$$

This is just another way of saying that a is between –8 and 0, inclusive, and that b is between 5 and 25, inclusive. *Inclusive* means that we include the values at each end, which is what's meant by the *greater than or equal to* and *less than or equal to* signs. If the test makers didn't want –8 and 0 to be possible values for a, for example, they would have to use simple greater-than and less-than signs (> and <). That scenario corresponds to the word *exclusive*, which means you should exclude the values at each end.

Once the range of the two variables has been established, the problem will then ask you to determine the range of values for some expression involving the two variables. For example, you could be asked for the range of values of $a - b$. This is really just asking for the smallest and largest possible values of $a - b$.

One good way to tackle these problems is to whip up a handy Inequality Table, a table with columns for each of the two variables and one column for the expression whose range you're trying to determine. First write in the largest and smallest values for a and b from the original inequalities. In this example, the extreme values for a are –8 and 0, and for b are 5 and 25. Write these values in the table so that each combination of a and b is represented. There will be four combinations total: the smallest value of a with the smallest value of b; the smallest value of a with the largest value of b; the largest value of a with the smallest value of b; and the largest value of a with the largest value of b:

a	b	$a - b$
-8	5	
-8	25	
0	5	
0	25	

Now simply evaluate the expression you're asked about for each of the four combinations in the table—in this case, $a - b$:

a	b	$a - b$
-8	5	$-8 - 5 = -13$
-8	25	$-8 - 25 = -33$
0	5	$0 - 5 = -5$
0	25	$0 - 25 = -25$

The Inequality Table shows us that the smallest possible value of $a - b$ is -33 and the largest is -5. Writing this as a compound inequality gives our final answer:

$$-33 \le a - b \le -5$$

Inequality Ranges

The previous question demonstrated how inequalities can be used to express the range of values that a variable can take. There are a few ways that inequality problems may involve ranges. We consider three scenarios below.

OPERATIONS ON RANGES

Ranges can be added, subtracted, or multiplied. Consider the following:

If $4 < x < 7$, what is the range of $2x + 3$?

To solve this problem, manipulate the range like an inequality until you have a solution. Begin with the original range:

$$4 < x < 7$$

Since the range we're ultimately looking for contains $2x$, we need to turn the x in the inequality above into that. We can do this by multiplying the whole inequality by 2:

$$8 < 2x < 14$$

Since we're doing the same thing to all parts of the inequality, this manipulation doesn't change its value or meaning. In other words, we're simply invoking the Golden Rule: Do unto one part what we do unto the other part. But we're not there yet, because the range we seek is $2x + 3$, not plain old $2x$. No problem: Just add 3 to the inequality across the board, and you have the final answer:

$$11 < 2x + 3 < 17$$

Always remember the crucial rule about multiplying inequalities: If you multiply or divide a range by a negative number, you must flip the greater-than or less-than signs. For example, if you multiply the range $2 < x < 8$ by -1, the new range will be $-2 > -x > -8$.

ABSOLUTE VALUE AND SINGLE RANGES

Absolute values do the same thing to inequalities that they do to equations. You have to split the inequality into two parts, one reflecting the positive value of the inequality and one reflecting the negative value. You'll see an example just below. If the absolute value is less than a given quantity, then the solution will be a single range with a lower and an upper bound. An example of a single range would be the numbers between -5 and 5, as seen in the following number line:

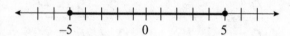

A single range question will look something like this:

Solve for x in the inequality $|2x - 4| \leq 6$.

First, split the inequality into two. In keeping with the rule for negative numbers, you'll have to flip around the inequality sign when you write out the inequality for the negative scenario:

$$2x - 4 \leq 6$$
$$2x - 4 \geq -6$$

Solve the first:

$$2x - 4 \leq 6$$
$$2x \leq 10$$
$$x \leq 5$$

Then solve the second:

$$2x - 4 \geq -6$$
$$2x \geq -2$$
$$x \geq -1$$

So x is greater than or equal to -1 and less than or equal to 5. In other words, x lies between those two values. So you can write out the value of x in a single range, $-1 \leq x \leq 5$.

ABSOLUTE VALUE AND DISJOINTED RANGES

You won't always find that the value of the variable lies between two numbers. Instead, you may find that the solution is actually two separate ranges: one whose lower bound is negative infinity and whose upper bound is a real number, and one whose lower bound is a real number and whose upper bound is infinity. Yeah, words make it sound confusing. A number line will make it clearer. An example of a disjointed range would be all the numbers smaller than –5 and larger than 5, as shown below:

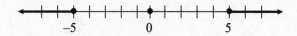

On the GRE, disjointed ranges come up in problems in which the absolute value is greater than a given quantity, such as the following:

Solve for x in the inequality $|3x + 4| > 16$.

You know the drill. Split 'er up, then solve each inequality:

$$3x + 4 > 16$$

$$3x + 4 < -16$$

Again, notice that we have to switch the inequality sign in the second case because of the negative-number rule.

Solving the first:

$$3x + 4 > 16$$

$$3x > 12$$

$$x > 4$$

And the second:

$$3x + 4 < -16$$

$$3x < -20$$

$$x < -\frac{20}{3}$$

Notice that x is greater than the positive number and smaller than the negative number. In other words, the possible values of x don't lie *between* the two numbers; they lie outside the two numbers. So you need two separate ranges to show the possible values of x: $-\infty < x < -\frac{20}{3}$ and $4 < x < \infty$. There are two distinct ranges for the possible values of x in this case, which is why the ranges are called *disjointed*. It doesn't mean they can bend their fingers back all the way— that's *double-jointed*.

Made-up Symbols

As if there aren't enough real math symbols in the world, the GRE test makers occasionally feel the need to make up their own. You may see a made-up symbol problem on the GRE involving little graphics you've never seen before in a math context. Sure, they look weird, but they often involve variables and equations, which is why we thought we'd cover them here in the algebra section. Anyway, there's a silver lining to this weirdness: Made-up symbol problems *always* give you exact instructions of what to do. Follow the instructions precisely, and you'll do just fine. Let's see how this works with an example:

$$\text{If } x \, \Omega \, y = 5x + 2y - 10, \text{ what is } 3 \, \Omega \, 4?$$

Some test takers will see a problem like this and think, "Ω is one of those symbols that only math geniuses learned. I never learned this symbol. I'm not a math genius. I majored in Spanish. AAAAGGGHHHH!!!!"

Relax: The fact is, no one learned what this symbol means, because the test makers made it up. Fortunately, the test makers have also made up a definition for it—that is, they tell us exactly what do to when we see a Ω. All it requires is some simple calculating.

Look at the first part of the problem again: $x \, \Omega \, y = 5x + 2y - 10$. All that's really saying is that whenever we have two numbers separated by a Ω, we need to take 5 times the first number and 2 times the second number, add them together, and subtract 10. That's it—these are the only instructions we need to follow.

For the expression $3 \, \Omega \, 4$, then, x is 3, which we multiply by 5 to get 15. Similarly, y is 4, which we're told to multiply by 2, which gives us 8. Adding these together gives us 23, and subtracting 10 brings us to 13 and a quick and easy point. Quick and easy, that is, if you don't panic and just follow the directions to a T.

Try one more example to get the hang of this symbol business:

$$\text{If } j@k = \frac{k}{2} - 13j, \text{ what is } 5@-1?$$

Forget the actual variables for a moment and focus on the instructions given: Whenever we have two numbers separated by an @, we need to divide the second number by 2, multiply the first number by 13 and subtract the two numbers. So, substituting 5 for j and -1 for k:

$$5@-1 = \frac{-1}{2} - (13 \times 5) = \frac{-1}{2} - 65 = -65\frac{1}{2}$$

The test makers may keep the choices as fractions, or they may decide to write them in decimal form, in which case -65.5 will be correct.

Geometry-Algebra Hybrids: Coordinate Geometry

Once upon a time, geometry and algebra hooked up after a drunken night. The result was coordinate geometry: a geometry-algebra hybrid. Coordinate geometry combines the graphical figures found in geometry with the variables used in algebra. So where does it belong, in algebra or geometry? Geometry wins on the name front, since it appears in the title and algebra doesn't. But the GRE Official Guide includes this as an algebra topic, so we'll defer to that and cover it here.

The Coordinate Plane

The coordinate plane is where all the magic happens. It's the space in which coordinate geometry exists. Pretty snazzy.

Every point on a coordinate plane can be mapped by using two perpendicular number lines. The horizontal x-axis defines the space from left to right. The vertical y-axis defines the space up and down. And the two meet at a point called the origin.

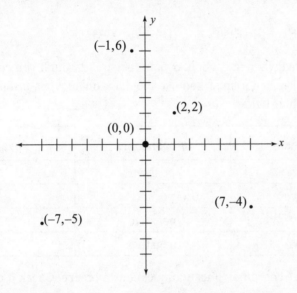

Every point on the plane has two coordinates. Because it's the center of the plane, the origin gets the coordinates (0,0). The coordinates of all other points indicate how far they are from the origin. These coordinates are written in the form (x, y). The x-coordinate is the point's location along the x-axis (its distance either to the left or right of the origin). If a point is to the right of the origin, its x-coordinate is positive. If a point is to the left of the origin, its x-coordinate is negative. If a point is anywhere on the y-axis, its x-coordinate is 0.

The y-coordinate of a point is its location along the y-axis (either up or down from the origin). If a point is above the origin, its y-coordinate is positive, and if a point is below the origin, its y-coordinate is negative. If a point is anywhere on the x-axis, its y-coordinate is 0.

So the point labeled (2, 2) is 2 units to the right and 2 units above the origin. The point labeled (–7, –5) is 7 units to the left and 5 units below the origin.

Quadrants

Each graph has four quadrants, or sections. The upper-right quadrant is quadrant I, and the numbering continues counterclockwise. At the exact center of the graph, the origin is not in any of the four quadrants. Similarly, the *x*-axis and *y*-axis are not in any quadrant, either.

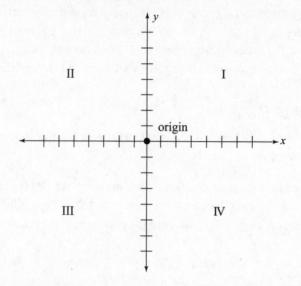

You may be asked where a particular point exists. Although you could graph the point on a sketched graph, then use the diagram above, a faster method is to memorize the chart below:

x-coordinate	*y*-coordinate	quadrant
positive	positive	I
negative	positive	II
negative	negative	III
positive	negative	IV

This chart makes coordinate-location questions a breeze. Check it out:

In which quadrant is coordinate pair (–8.4, –2) located?

Sure, you could draw the coordinate plane and plot the pair. Or you could simply note that both the *x*-coordinate and the *y*-coordinate are negative, which means that (–8.4, –2) lives in quadrant III.

Distance on the Coordinate Plane

You may come across a GRE math question that asks you to find the distance between two points on the coordinate plane or to find the midpoint between two points. This news should make you happy. Why? Because these are fairly easy as long as you know the necessary formulas. There are two methods for finding distance and a formula for finding midpoints. We'll tackle distance first.

FINDING DISTANCE USING THE DISTANCE FORMULA

If you know the coordinates of any two points—we'll call them (x_1, y_1) and (x_2, y_2)—you can find their distance from each other with the aptly named distance formula:

$$\text{distance} = \sqrt{\left(x_2 - x_1\right)^2 + \left(y_2 - y_1\right)^2}$$

Let's say you were suddenly overcome by the desire to calculate the distance between the points (4,–3) and (–3, 8). Just plug the coordinates into the formula:

$$\text{distance} = \sqrt{(-3-4)^2 + (8-(-3))^2}$$
$$= \sqrt{(-7)^2 + (11)^2}$$
$$= \sqrt{49+121}$$
$$= \sqrt{170}$$

FINDING DISTANCE USING RIGHT TRIANGLES

You can also solve distance questions using right triangles. Consider this one:

What is the distance between the points (2, 4) and (5, 0)?

Plot the two points on a graph and connect them with a straight line:

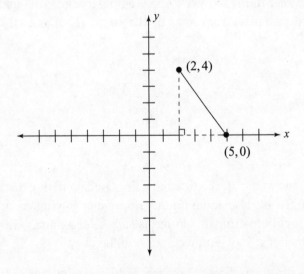

The distance between these two points is the length of the dark line connecting them. To calculate this length, let the dark line be the longest side of a right triangle. Then draw two perpendicular lines to construct the short sides, as indicated by the slashed lines in the diagram.

Since the horizontal side went from an x-coordinate of 2 to an x-coordinate of 5, its length is 5 – 2 = 3.

Since the vertical side went from a y-coordinate of 0 to a y-coordinate of 4, its length is 4 – 0 = 4.

These two sides fit the {3, 4, 5} right-triangle pattern, and so the long side must be 5. And that's the distance between the two points. (No doubt you've learned about right triangles, but don't worry, we'll review them extensively in the upcoming geometry section.)

So which method for calculating distance should you use? If you're given the two points, there's no reason why you shouldn't be able to plug them into the distance formula and get the answer without bothering to sketch out a picture. The reason we also teach you the right-triangle method is because, hey, you may just like it better, but more important, a question may present you with a diagram to start, in which case the triangle method may be easier.

FINDING MIDPOINTS

To find the midpoint between points (x_1, y_1) and (x_2, y_2) in the coordinate plane, use this formula:

$$\text{midpoint} = \left(\frac{x_1 + x_2}{2}, \frac{y_1 + y_2}{2} \right)$$

In other words, the x- and y-coordinates of the midpoint are simply the averages of the x- and y-coordinates of the endpoints. (Again, we know you've heard of and worked with averages before, but we'll review the concept in the data analysis section later in the chapter.) Applying the formula, the midpoint of the line in the coordinate plane connected by the points (6, 0) and (3, 7) is:

$$\text{Midpoint} = \left(\frac{6+3}{2}, \frac{0+7}{2} \right)$$
$$= \left(\frac{9}{2}, \frac{7}{2} \right)$$
$$= (4.5, \ 3.5)$$

Slope

Coordinate geometry isn't all the fun and games of calculating distances and naming quadrants—it's also about finding slopes and solving equations. What follows isn't particularly difficult, but terms such as *slope* and *y-intercept* rarely evoke positive feelings. Stay with us, and you'll be okay.

A line's slope is a measurement of how steeply that line climbs or falls as it moves from left to right. The slopes of some lines are positive; the slopes of others are negative. Whether a line has a positive or negative slope is easy to tell just by looking at a graph of the line. If the line slopes uphill as you trace it from left to right, the slope is positive. If a line slopes downhill as you trace it from left to right, the slope is negative. Uphill = positive. Downhill = negative.

You can get a sense of the magnitude of the slope of a line by looking at the line's steepness. The steeper the line, the greater the slope; the flatter the line, the smaller the slope. Note that an extremely positive slope is larger than a moderately positive slope, while an extremely negative slope is smaller than a moderately negative slope.

Check out the lines below and try to determine whether the slope of each line is negative or positive and which has the greatest slope:

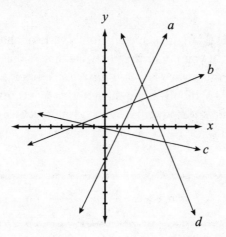

Lines *a* and *b* have positive slopes, and lines *c* and *d* have negative slopes. In terms of slope magnitude, line *a* > *b* > *c* > *d*.

SLOPES YOU SHOULD KNOW BY SIGHT
There are certain easy-to-recognize slopes that it pays to recognize by sight:

- A horizontal line has a slope of zero.

- A vertical line has an undefined slope.

- A line that makes a 45° angle with a horizontal line has a slope of either 1 or –1, depending on whether it's going up or down from left to right.

Of the four lines pictured below, which has a slope of 0, which has a slope of 1, which has a slope of –1, and which has an undefined slope?

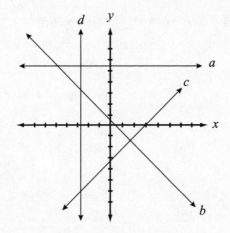

Line a has slope 0 because it's horizontal. Line b has slope –1 because it slopes downward at 45° as you move from left to right. Line c has slope 1 because it slopes upward at 45° as you move from left to right. The slope of line d is undefined because it is vertical.

CALCULATING SLOPE

If you want the technical jargon, slope is a line's vertical change divided by its horizontal change. Or, if you prefer the poetic version, slope is "the rise over run." Okay, it's not Hemingway (*The Sun Also Rises*), but it'll do. For some strange reason, slope is symbolized by the letter m. We think s would be a better choice. *Hello* . . . Maybe s was taken. Anyway, you have two points on a line—once again (x_1, y_1) and (x_2, y_2)—the slope of that line can be calculated using the following formula:

$$\text{slope} = m = \frac{\text{rise}}{\text{run}} = \frac{y_2 - y_1}{x_2 - x_1}$$

Rise is how far the line goes up between two points. *Run* is how far the line goes to the right between two points. The formula is just shorthand for the difference between the two y-coordinates divided by the difference between the two x-coordinates. Let's work out an example:

Calculate the slope of the line passing through (–4, 1) and (3, 4).

The difference in y-coordinates, $y_2 - y_1$, is $4 - 1 = 3$. The difference in x-coordinates, $x_2 - x_1$, is $3 - (-4) = 7$. The slope is simply the ratio of these two differences, $\frac{3}{7}$.

SLOPES OF PARALLEL AND PERPENDICULAR LINES

The slopes of parallel and perpendicular lines exhibit the following relationships:

- **The slopes of parallel lines are always the same.** If one line has a slope of m, any line parallel to it will also have a slope of m.

- **The slopes of perpendicular lines are always the opposite reciprocals of each other.** A line with slope m is perpendicular to a line with a slope of $-\frac{1}{m}$.

In the figure below, lines q and r both have a slope of 2, so they are parallel. Line s is perpendicular to both lines q and r, so it has a slope of $-\frac{1}{2}$.

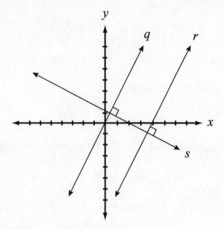

Finding the Equation of a Line

Now that you've mastered slope, you're ready to determine the entire equation for a line that passes through two points. There are two ways to do this, and we'll cover both.

THE POINT-SLOPE FORMULA

The equation of a line passing through two points in the coordinate plane can be expressed by the point-slope formula:

$$(y - y_1) = m(x - x_1)$$

You already know how to calculate the slope, m. And x and y are just variables. You don't have to do anything special with them in the formula other than write them down, unchanged.

As for x_1 and y_1, these are just the x- and y-coordinates of one of the points given. You can use whichever point you like; just make sure you use the same point for both the x_1 and y_1 values.

Let's use the formula to work through an example, using the same points we used in the previous question:

What is the equation of the line passing through $(-4, 1)$ and $(3, 4)$?

We already calculated $m = \frac{3}{7}$. Now we have to decide which of the two points to use in the equation. Again, either point will do. Maybe $(3, 4)$ in this case would be a little easier, since it doesn't have a negative sign. Letting $x_1 = 3$ and $y_1 = 4$ gives:

$$y - 4 = \frac{3}{7}(x - 3)$$

Believe it or not, we're almost done! We've actually written the equation of the line passing between the two points; all that's left is to simplify it. First, eliminate the fraction by multiplying both sides by 7:

$$7(y - 4) = 7\left(\frac{3}{7}\right)(x - 3)$$
$$7y - 28 = 3(x - 3)$$

Then distribute the 3 on the right side:

$$7y - 28 = 3x - 9$$

Finally, move the $3x$ to the left and the -28 to the right to isolate the variables:

$$-3x + 7y = 19$$

This is the final equation of the line passing through $(-4, 1)$ and $(3, 4)$, written in simplest form.

X-INTERCEPT AND Y-INTERCEPT

The x- and y-intercepts are the points at which the graph intersects the x-axis and the y-axis, respectively. A useful way to think about this is that at the x-intercept, $y = 0$, and at the y-intercept, $x = 0$.

Graphically, this is what the x- and y-intercepts look like for the equation we derived above:

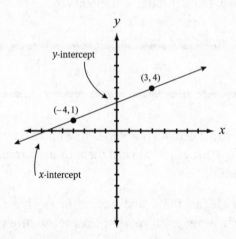

To calculate the precise values of these intercepts, recall the equation of this line, which we figured out earlier: $-3x + 7y = 19$. Since $x = 0$ at the y-intercept, you can calculate it simply by setting $x = 0$ in the equation, like this:

$$0 + 7y = 19$$

$$y = \frac{19}{7}$$

So $\frac{19}{7}$ is where the graph intersects the y-axis. Since the x-coordinate at this point is 0, the coordinate pair for the y-intercept is $\left(0, \frac{19}{7}\right)$. Following the same mysterious naming conventions that cause slope to be named m, the point where the graph intersects the y-axis is called b.

For the x-intercept, let $y = 0$ in the equation $-3x + 7y = 19$. This gives:

$$-3x + 0 = 19$$

$$x = -\frac{19}{3}$$

So $-\frac{19}{3}$ is where the graph intersects the x-axis. Since the y-coordinate at this point is 0, the coordinate pair for the x-intercept is $\left(-\frac{19}{3}, 0\right)$.

THE SLOPE-INTERCEPT EQUATION

The second method for calculating the equation of a line designated by two points in the coordinate plane is the slope-intercept equation. It looks like this:

$$y = mx + b$$

It's likely that you had this one drilled into your head in high school, and you therefore recall the sound of it while having absolutely no idea what it means. Relearning it now is like being reacquainted with an old friend. Aren't you glad you're taking the GRE?

You're now familiar with each part of this equation:

- x and y are variables, which you don't need to change.

- m is the slope, calculated by $\frac{y_2 - y_1}{x_2 - x_1}$.

- b is the y-intercept, the point where the graph intersects the y-axis.

For the line we've been working with, the slope, m, is $\frac{3}{7}$. The y-intercept, b, is $\frac{19}{7}$. Plugging these values into the slope-intercept equation gives:

$$y = \frac{3}{7}x + \frac{19}{7}$$

This is the equation in slope-intercept format. You could simplify it by multiplying both sides by 7, then moving the variables to the left and the numbers to the right. As you may or may not expect, this gives exactly the same result as the point-slope format above:

$$-3x + 7y = 19$$

This actually makes a lot of sense: The equation for the line should be the same, regardless of the method you use to calculate it.

WHICH EQUATION RULES?

You might be wondering when you should use each of the two equations, $(y - y_1) = m(x - x_1)$ and $y = mx + b$. Decisions, decisions. Although slope-intercept is more commonly taught (most of us have at least heard of $y = mx + b$), the point-slope format is actually more useful when it comes to certain problems on the GRE. Both equations require the slope, so they're similar in that respect. The slope-intercept formula requires a very specific point, the y-intercept, but the point-slope formula can be calculated with any point. Since it's less restrictive, you may therefore find more uses for point-slope. But if they flat-out give you the slope and the y-intercept, then $y = mx + b$ may be the way to go. The bottom line: Know both, and decide which to use depending on the question's parameters.

Word Problems

Perhaps you've had nightmares in high school, certainly around SAT time, involving two trains, traveling in opposite directions, at different speeds, over different distances . . . That might be the point where you woke up screaming, or your dream morphed into Aunt Mabel offering you a piece of cheesecake.

Well, relax. Word problems are nothing more than algebra problems, complicated by one small inconvenience: You have to come up with your own equations. Word problems present particular scenarios; the trick is to translate the information into math. The good news is that once you have your equations, they usually aren't hard to solve.

Pretty much any math concept is fair game for a word problem, but there are certain types that show up with some regularity. We'll work through a few examples here, and you'll see more later in the book.

Using Simultaneous Equations

Try this:

> In a sack of 50 marbles, there are 20 more red marbles than blue marbles. All of the marbles in the sack are either red or blue. How many blue marbles are in the sack?

Well, these are very nice words and all, but talk is cheap—we want equations to crunch. And to get equations, we're going to need to round ourselves up some variables. We don't need a variable for total marbles, since that's given: 50. However, we do need variables for the red and blue marbles, since those are unknown quantities. Unlike those nutty folks who come up with things like m for slope and b for y-intercept, we'll be reasonable and just use r for red and b for blue. Since there's no y-intercept for miles around in this one, we doubt anyone will mind if we borrow that b.

Now for some translating: Is there a math expression that means the same thing as "there are 20 more red marbles than blue marbles"? You bet:

$$r = b + 20$$

Since both *r* and *b* are unknown, we can't solve the problem from this equation alone, so we'll need to squeeze another equation out of this scenario. The only other facts are that there are 50 marbles total, and only red and blue ones in the sack. So it must also be true that:

$$r + b = 50$$

Eureka! Why so excited? Because we have two different equations, each containing two variables, which means we have enough information to solve the problem. And if you remember from earlier in the chapter, we even have a choice of how to solve such simultaneous equations. We'll go with substitution. Since the first equation tells us that $r = b + 20$, we can go ahead and substitute $b + 20$ for *r* in the second equation, giving us:

$$b + 20 + b = 50$$
$$2b + 20 = 50$$
$$2b = 30$$
$$b = 15$$

Done.

Now perhaps the CAT software would present you with the problem in the form we just solved. Or, perhaps, if you answered one or two more questions correctly before this one, that wily CAT would up the ante and make the question a tad harder by requiring an additional step. For example, instead of merely asking you to find the number of blue marbles in the sack, the question could ask you to find the ratio of blue to red marbles. No problem; it requires a few more steps, but it's not so difficult.

First, use either equation to find the number of red marbles. We'll just plug 15 for *b* into $r = b + 20$, to get 35 reds. Then set up the ratio as 15:35 and simplify to 3:7.

Ratios

And speaking of ratios, here's another kind of word problem based on this concept.

> In a certain class, the ratio of boys to girls is 4 to 5. If the class has 12 boys, what is the total number of boys and girls in the class?

Again, the first step is to translate the English into algebra. Since ratios are part-to-part fractions, the ratio of boys to girls in the class is really just the fraction $\frac{boys}{girls}$. A common careless mistake is to write the fraction upside down— that is, as $\frac{girls}{boys}$. A great way to avoid making this mistake is to remember $\frac{of}{to}$. In other words, whatever quantity appears after the word *of* in the problem goes in the numerator, and whatever quantity appears after the word *to* goes in the denominator.

So, the ratio of boys to girls is 4 to 5, which, in math terms, can be written like this:

$$\frac{\text{boys}}{\text{girls}} = \frac{4}{5}$$

We're also told that the class has 12 boys. Substituting this into our equation gives:

$$\frac{12}{\text{girls}} = \frac{4}{5}$$

We'll now use the Magic X to cross-multiply diagonally and up:

$$5 \times 12 = \text{girls} \times 4$$

$$60 = \text{girls} \times 4$$

$$\frac{60}{4} = \text{girls}$$

$$15 = \text{girls}$$

Think 15 is the answer? Think again. The question didn't ask for the number of girls, but for the *total* number of boys and girls in the class. Easy: Total = 12 + 15 = 27, and we're done.

Distance

Since practically everyone who ever attended high school has had that nightmare about the trains traveling in different directions, the GRE test makers figure it's a good problem to torment people with. Of course, they don't always use trains. But these problems are really not that bad if you learn how to handle them; in fact, distance problems require only one fairly basic formula:

$$\text{rate} \times \text{time} = \text{distance}$$

The concept is fairly intuitive: If you bike at a rate of 10 miles per hour, and you bike for 2 hours, you're going to cover 10 × 2 = 20 miles. What gets confusing is the various ways they state these problems, but rest assured they always give you enough information to set up an equation and solve for the variable you seek. Here's an example:

> Jim roller-skates 6 miles per hour. One morning, Jim roller-skates continuously for 60 miles. How many hours did Jim spend roller-skating?

One thing that makes word problems annoying is that they sometimes include unnecessary facts. Here, for example, we're told such exciting things as *how* Jim is traveling (by roller skates) and when he started (in the morning). Heck, it doesn't even matter that his name is *Jim*—he could be Egbert the marble collector for all we care. You have to ignore the nonessentials and focus on the facts you need to solve the problem. Begin with the trusty distance formula:

$$\text{rate} \times \text{time} = \text{distance}$$

Then fill in the values you know:

$$6 \text{ miles per hour} \times \text{time} = 60 \text{ miles}$$

Divide both sides by 6 miles per hour to calculate the time spent as 10 hours.

This next distance problem is a bit more difficult because it requires one extra step. Instead of being given two variables and simply setting up an equation to solve for the third, you need to first calculate one of the variables before getting to that point. Try it out:

> A traveler begins driving from California and heads east across the United States. If she drives at a rate of 528,000 feet per hour, and drives 4.8 hours without stopping, how many miles has she traveled? (1 mile = 5,280 feet)

The reason you need to go the extra mile (so to speak) is because the rate is given in feet per hour but the distance traveled is given in miles. The units must jibe for the problem to work, so a conversion is necessary. Luckily, the numbers are easy to work with: The driver drives 528,000 feet per hour, and 5,280 feet equal one mile. So to change her rate into miles per hour, simply divide:

$$\frac{528,000 \text{ feet per hour}}{5,280 \text{ feet per mile}} = 100 \text{ miles per hour}$$

That's some fast traveler. Now plug the values from the problem, including this new one, into the formula:

$$100 \text{ miles per hour} \times 4.8 \text{ hours} = \text{distance}$$

The distance traveled is 480 miles.

Work

Work sucks. You're there from at least 9 to 5, get two weeks off per year (at best), and you've got a boss constantly checking up on you. Work word problems on the GRE are a breeze in comparison. Work word problems are very similar to distance word problems, except the final outcome is units of something produced instead of distance covered. The other two variables are analogous to those in distance problems: the rate at which the units are produced, and the time someone spends producing them. If you knit 2 sweaters per hour, and knit for 8 hours, then you'll knit 2 × 8 = 16 sweaters. This generalizes to the same basic formula we saw earlier:

$$\boxed{\text{rate} \times \text{time} = \text{units produced}}$$

Since you've seen this basic mechanism in action in the previous section, we'll jump right to a difficult work word problem:

Four workers can dig a 40-foot well in 4 days. How long would it take for 8 workers working at the same rate to dig a 60-foot well?

Sure, it's complicated, but the three parameters are the same: rate, time worked, and amount of work completed. We know the latter: 60 feet dug. The middle amount, time, is what we're looking for, so we'll just leave that as our unknown variable for now. The question then hinges on the rate, which we need to calculate ourselves. Well, since 4 workers dig 40 feet in 4 days, we can divide by 4 to determine that those 4 workers can dig 10 feet in one day. The 8 workers that we're interested in dig at the same rate, and since they represent twice as many people, they'll be able to dig twice as many feet in a day: 20. Now we have the variables to plug into our formula:

20 feet per day × time = 60 units produced (in this case, feet dug)

Divide both sides by 20 to get a time of 3 days of work for the 8 workers to dig the 60-foot well.

Many other word problems follow the same basic form as the examples above. For example, in a price word problem, the price of an item times the number of items bought will equal the total cost. The particulars are slightly different, but the concept is basically the same. Use the information given in the problem to get two of the values, and you'll always be able to calculate the third. And you'll never have a word problem nightmare again.

That wraps it up for algebra. Now we move on to triangles, circles, and all of the other fun shapes of our next math subject, geometry.

GEOMETRY

Geometry has a long and storied history that goes back thousands of years, which we're sure you're dying to hear about. But unless you're taking the GRE to go for your masters in math history, this has no possible relevance to your life. So we'll skip the history lesson and get right to the facts.

Lines and Angles

An angle is composed of two lines and is a measure of the spread between them. The point where the two lines meet is called the *vertex*. On the GRE, angles are measured in degrees. Here's an example:

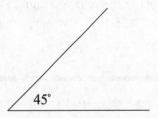

The ° after the 45 is a degree symbol. This angle measures 45 degrees.

Acute, Obtuse, and Right Angles

Angles that measure less than 90° are called *acute angles*. Angles that measure more than 90° are called *obtuse angles*. A special angle that the GRE test makers love is called a *right angle*. Right angles always measure exactly 90° and are indicated by a little square where the angle measure would normally be, like this:

Straight Angles

Multiple angles that meet at a single point on a line are called straight angles. The sum of the angles meeting at a single point on a straight line is always equal to 180°. You may see something like this, asking you to solve for *n*:

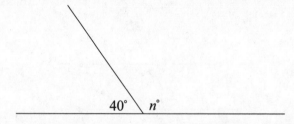

The two angles (one marked by 40° and the one marked by *n*°) meet at the same point on the line. Since the sum of the angles on the line must be 180°, you can plug 40° and *n*° into a formula like this:

$$40° + n° = 180°$$

Subtracting 40° from both sides gives *n*° = 140°, or *n* = 140.

Vertical Angles

When two lines intersect, the angles that lie opposite each other, called *vertical angles*, are always equal.

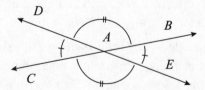

Angles ∠*DAC* and ∠*BAE* are vertical angles and are therefore equal. Angles ∠*DAB* and ∠*CAE* are also vertical, equal angles.

Parallel Lines

A more complicated version of this figure that you may see on the GRE involves two parallel lines intersected by a third line, called a *transversal*. *Parallel* means that the lines run in exactly the same direction and never intersect. Here's an example:

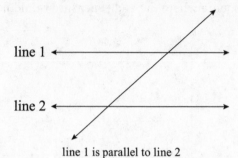

line 1 is parallel to line 2

Don't assume lines are parallel just because they look like they are—the question will always tell you if two lines are meant to be parallel. Even though this figure contains many angles, it turns out that it only has two *kinds* of angles: big angles (obtuse) and little angles (acute). All the big angles are equal to each other, and all the little angles are equal to each other. Furthermore, *any big angle + any little angle = 180°*. This is true for any figure with two parallel lines intersected by a third line. In the following figure, we label every angle to show you what we mean:

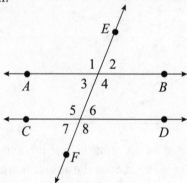

As described above, the eight angles created by these two intersections have special relationships to each other:

- Angles 1, 4, 5, and 8 are equal to one another. Angle 1 is vertical to angle 4, and angle 5 is vertical to angle 8.

- Angles 2, 3, 6, and 7 are equal to one another. Angle 2 is vertical to angle 3, and angle 6 is vertical to angle 7.

- The sum of any two adjacent angles, such as 1 and 2 or 7 and 8, equals 180° because they form a straight angle lying on a line.

- The sum of *any big angle + any little angle = 180°*, since the big and little angles in this figure combine into straight lines and all the big angles are equal and all the little angles are equal. So a big and little angle don't need to be next to each other to add to 180°; *any* big plus *any* little will add to 180°. For example, since angles 1 and 2 sum to 180°, and since angles 2 and 7 are equal, the sum of angles 1 and 7 also equals 180°.

By using these rules, you can figure out the degrees of angles that may seem unrelated. For example:

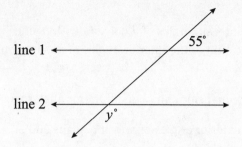

If line 1 is parallel to line 2, what is the value of y in the figure above?

Again, this figure has only two kinds of angles: big angles (obtuse) and little angles (acute). We know that 55° is a little angle, so y must be a big angle. Since *big angle* + *little angle* = 180°, you can write:

$$y° + 55° = 180°$$

Solving for y:

$$y° = 180° - 55°$$

$$y = 125$$

Perpendicular Lines

Two lines that meet at a right angle are called *perpendicular lines*. If you're told two lines are perpendicular, just think 90°. We'd love to tell you more about these beauties, but there's really not much else to say.

Polygon Basics

A polygon is a two-dimensional figure with three or more straight sides. Polygons are named according to the number of sides they have.

Number of Sides	Name
3	triangle
4	quadrilateral
5	pentagon
6	hexagon
7	heptagon
8	octagon
9	nonagon
10	decagon
12	dodecagon
n	n-gon

All polygons, no matter how many sides they possess, share certain characteristics:

- The sum of the interior angles of a polygon with n sides is $(n - 2)180°$. For instance, the sum of the interior angles of an octagon is $(8 - 2)180° = 6(180°) = 1080°$.

- A polygon with equal sides and equal interior angles is a regular polygon.

- The sum of the exterior angles of any polygon is 360°.

- The perimeter of a polygon is the sum of the lengths of its sides.

- The area of a polygon is the measure of the area of the region enclosed by the polygon. Each polygon tested on the GRE has its own unique area formula, which we'll cover below.

For the most part, the polygons tested in GRE math include triangles and quadrilaterals. All triangles have three sides, but there are special types of triangles that we'll cover next. Then we'll move on to four common quadrilaterals (four-sided figures) that appear on the test: rectangles, squares, parallelograms, and trapezoids.

We'll then leave the world of polygons and make our way to circles and then conclude this geometry section with a discussion of the three-dimensional solids you may see on your test: rectangular solids, cubes, and right circular cylinders.

Triangles

Of all the geometric shapes, triangles are among the most commonly tested on the GRE. But since the GRE tends to test the same triangles over and over, you just need to master a few rules and a few diagrams. We'll look at some special triangles shortly, but first we'll explain four very special rules.

The Four Rules of Triangles

Commit these four rules to memory.

1. The Rule of Interior Angles. *The sum of the interior angles of a triangle always equals 180°.* Interior angles are those on the inside. Whenever you're given two angles of a triangle, you can use this formula to calculate the third angle. For example:

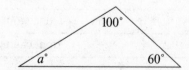

What is the value of a in the figure above?

Since the sum of the angles of a triangle equals 180°, you can set up an equation:

$$a° + 100° + 60° = 180°$$

Isolating the variable and solving for a gives $a = 20$.

2. The Rule of Exterior Angles. An exterior angle of a triangle is the angle formed by extending one of the sides of the triangle past a vertex (or the intersection of two sides of a figure). In the figure below, d is the exterior angle.

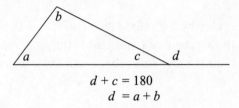

$$d + c = 180$$
$$d = a + b$$

Since, together, d and c form a straight angle, they add up to 180°: $d + c = 180°$. According to the first rule of triangles, the three angles of a triangle always add up to 180°, so $a + b + c = 180°$. Since $d + c = 180°$ and $a + b + c = 180°$, d must be equal to $a + b$ (the remote interior angles). This generalizes to all triangles as the following rules: *The exterior angle of a triangle plus the interior angle with which it shares a vertex is always 180°. The exterior angle is also equal to the sum of the measures of the remote interior angles.*

3. The Rule of the Sides. The length of any side of a triangle must be greater than the difference and less than the sum of the other two sides. In other words:

difference of other two sides < one side < sum of other two sides

Although this rule won't allow you to determine a precise length of the missing side, it will allow you to determine a range of values for the missing side, which is exactly what the test makers would ask for in such a problem. Here's an example:

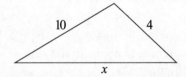

What is the range of values for x in the triangle above?

Since the difference of 10 and 4 is 6, and the sum of 10 and 4 is 14, we can determine the range of values of x:

$$6 < x < 14$$

Keep in mind that x must be *inside* this range. That is, x could *not* be 6 or 14.

4. The Rule of Proportion. *In every triangle, the longest side is opposite the largest angle and the shortest side is opposite the smallest angle.* Take a look at the following figure and try to guess which angle is largest.

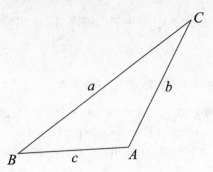

In this figure, side *a* is clearly the longest side and ∠*A* is the largest angle. Meanwhile, side *c* is the shortest side and ∠*C* is the smallest angle.

So *c* < *b* < *a* and ∠*C* < ∠*B* < ∠*A* This proportionality of side lengths and angles holds true for all triangles.

Use this rule to solve the question below:

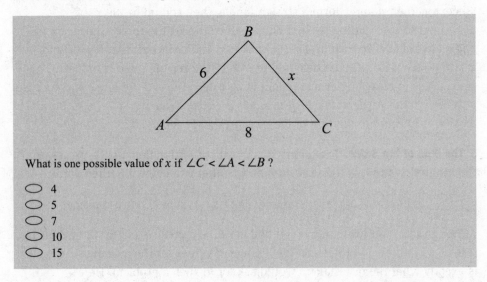

What is one possible value of *x* if ∠*C* < ∠*A* < ∠*B* ?

  ⬭ 4
  ⬭ 5
  ⬭ 7
  ⬭ 10
  ⬭ 15

According to the rule of proportion, the longest side of a triangle is opposite the largest angle, and the shortest side of a triangle is opposite the smallest angle. The question tells us that angle *C* < angle *A* < angle *B*. So, the largest angle in triangle *ABC* is angle *B*, which is opposite the side of length 8. We know too that the smallest angle is angle *C*, since angle *C* < angle *A*. This means that the third side, with a length of *x*, measures between 6 and 8 units in length. The only choice that fits this criterion is 7, choice **C**.

Isosceles Triangles

An isosceles triangle has two equal sides and two equal angles, like this:

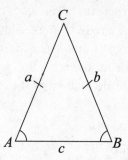

The tick marks indicate that sides a and b are equal, and the curved lines inside the triangle indicate that angle A equals angle B. Notice that the two equal angles are the ones opposite the two equal sides. Let's see how we might put this knowledge to use on the test. Check out this next triangle:

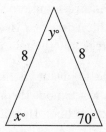

With two equal sides, this is an isosceles triangle. Even though you're not explicitly told that it has two equal angles, any triangle with two equal sides must also have two equal angles. This means that x must be 70°, because angles opposite equal sides are equal. Knowing that the sum of the angles of any triangle is 180°, we can also calculate y: $y + 70 + 70 = 180$, or $y = 40$.

Equilateral Triangles

An equilateral triangle has three equal sides and three equal angles, like this:

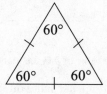

The tick marks tip us off that the three sides are equal. We can precisely calculate the angles because the 180° of an equilateral triangle broken into three equal angles yields 60° for each. As soon as you're given one side of an equilateral triangle, you'll immediately know the other two sides, because all three have the same measure. If you ever see a triangle with three equal sides, you'll immediately know its angles measure 60°. Conversely, if you see that a triangle's three interior angles all measure 60°, then you'll know its sides must all be equal.

Right Triangles

A right triangle is any triangle that contains a right angle. The side opposite the right angle is called the *hypotenuse.* The other two sides are called *legs.* The angles opposite the legs of a right triangle add up to 90°. That makes sense, because the right angle itself is 90° and every triangle contains 180° total, so the other two angles must combine for the other 90°. Right triangles are so special that they even have their own rule, known as the Pythagorean theorem.

THE PYTHAGOREAN THEOREM

The ancient Greeks spent a lot of time philosophizing, eating grapes, and riding around on donkeys. They also enjoyed the occasional mathematical epiphany. One day, Pythagoras discovered that the sum of the squares of the two legs of a right triangle is equal to the square of the hypotenuse. "Eureka!" he shouted, and the GRE had a new topic to test. And the Greek police had a new person to arrest, since Pythagoras had this epiphany while sitting in the bath and immediately jumped out to run down the street and proclaim it to the world, *entirely in the buff.* Or maybe that was Archimedes . . . ? Hey, it was a long time ago. Suffice it to say that some naked Greek guy thought up something cool.

Since Pythagoras took the trouble to invent his theorem, the least we can do is learn it. Besides, it's one of the most famous theorems in all of math, and it is tested with regularity on the GRE, to boot. Here it is:

In a right triangle, $a^2 + b^2 = c^2$, where c is the length of the hypotenuse and a and b are the lengths of the two legs.

And here's a simple application:

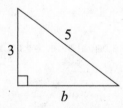

What is the value of b in the triangle above?

The little square in the lower left corner lets you know that this is a right triangle, so you're clear to use the Pythagorean theorem. Substituting the known lengths into the formula gives:

$$3^2 + b^2 = 5^2$$

$$9 + b^2 = 25$$

$$b^2 = 16$$

$$b = 4$$

This is therefore the world-famous 3-4-5 right triangle. Thanks to the Pythagorean theorem, if you know the measures of any two sides of a right triangle, you can always find the third. "Eureka!" indeed.

Pythagorean Triples. Because right triangles obey the Pythagorean theorem, only a specific few have side lengths that are all integers. For example, a right triangle with legs of length 3 and 5 has a hypotenuse of length $\sqrt{3^2 + 5^2} = \sqrt{9 + 25} = \sqrt{34} = 5.83$. Positive integers that obey the Pythagorean theorem are called Pythagorean triples, and these are the ones you're likely to see on your test as the lengths of the sides of right triangles. Here are some common ones:

{3, 4, 5}

{5, 12, 13}

{7, 24, 25}

{8, 15, 17}

In addition to these Pythagorean triples, you should also watch out for their multiples. For example, {6, 8, 10} is a Pythagorean triple, since it is a multiple of {3, 4, 5}, derived from simply doubling each value. This knowledge can significantly shorten your work in a problem like this:

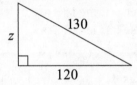

What is the value of *z* in the triangle above?

Sure, you could calculate it out using the Pythagorean theorem, but who wants to square 120 *and* 130 and then work the results into the formula? Pythagoras himself would probably say, "Ah, screw it . . ." and head off for a chat with Socrates. (Actually, Pythagoras died about twenty years before Socrates was born, but you get the point.)

But armed with our Pythagorean triples, it's no problem for us. The hypotenuse is 130, and one of the legs is 120. The ratio between these sides is 130:120, or 13:12. This exactly matches the {5, 12, 13} Pythagorean triple. So we're missing the 5 part of the triple for the other leg. However, since the sides of the triangle in the question are 10 times longer than those in the {5, 12, 13} triple, the missing side must be 5 × 10 = 50.

30-60-90 RIGHT TRIANGLES
As you can see, right triangles are pretty darn special. But there are two extra-special ones that appear with astounding frequency on the GRE. They are 30-60-90 right triangles and 45-45-90 right triangles. When you see one of these, instead of working out the Pythagorean theorem, you'll be able to apply standard ratios that exist between the length of the sides of these triangles.

The guy who named 30-60-90 triangles didn't have much of an imagination—or maybe he just didn't have a cool name like "Pythagoras." The name derives from the fact that these triangles have angles of 30°, 60°, and 90°. So, what's so special about that? This: The side lengths of 30-60-90 triangles always follow a specific pattern. If the short leg opposite the 30° angle has length x, then the hypotenuse has length $2x$, and the long leg, opposite the 60° angle, has length $x\sqrt{3}$. Therefore:

> The sides of every 30-60-90 triangle will follow the ratio $1 : \sqrt{3} : 2$

Thanks to this constant ratio, if you know the length of just one side of the triangle, you'll immediately be able to calculate the lengths of the other two. If, for example, you know that the side opposite the 30° angle is 2 meters, then by using the ratio you can determine that the hypotenuse is 4 meters, and the leg opposite the 60° angle is $2\sqrt{3}$ meters.

45-45-90 RIGHT TRIANGLES

A 45-45-90 right triangle is a triangle with two angles of 45° and one right angle. It's sometimes called an *isosceles right triangle*, since it's both isosceles and right. Like the 30-60-90 triangle, the lengths of the sides of a 45-45-90 triangle also follow a specific pattern. If the legs are of length x (the legs will always be equal), then the hypotenuse has length $x\sqrt{2}$.

> The sides of every 45-45-90 triangle will follow the ration of $1 : 1 : \sqrt{2}$

This ratio will help you when faced with triangles like this:

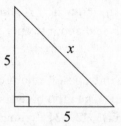

This right triangle has two equal sides, which means the two angles other than the right angle must be 45° each. So we have a 45-45-90 right triangle, which means we can employ the $1 : 1 : \sqrt{2}$ ratio. But instead of being 1 and 1, the lengths of the legs are 5 and 5. Since the lengths of the sides in the triangle above are five times the lengths in the $\{1, 1, \sqrt{2}\}$ right triangle, the hypotenuse must be $5 \times \sqrt{2}$, or $5\sqrt{2}$.

Area of a Triangle

The formula for the area of a triangle is:

$$\text{area} = \frac{1}{2} \times \text{base} \times \text{height} \ \text{ or } \ a = \frac{1}{2}bh$$

Keep in mind that the base and height of a triangle are *not* just any two sides of a triangle. The base and height must be perpendicular, which means they must meet at a right angle.

Let's try an example. What's the area of this triangle?

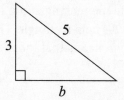

Note that the area is not $\frac{1}{2} \times 3 \times 5$, because those two sides do not meet at a right angle. To calculate the area, you must first determine b. You'll probably notice that this is the 3-4-5 right triangle you saw earlier, so $b = 4$. Now you have two perpendicular sides, so you can correctly calculate the area as follows:

$$\text{area} = \frac{1}{2}bh = \frac{1}{2}(3 \times 4) = 6$$

Triangles are surely important, but they aren't the only geometric figures you'll come across on the GRE. We move now to quadrilaterals, which are four-sided figures. The first two we cover you're no doubt familiar with, no matter how long you've been out of high school. The other two you may have forgotten about long ago.

Rectangles

A rectangle is a quadrilateral in which the opposite sides are parallel and the interior angles are all right angles. The opposite sides of a rectangle are equal, as indicated in the figure below:

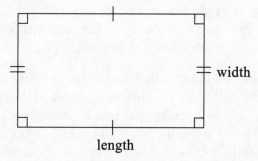

Area of a Rectangle

The formula for the area of a rectangle is:

$$\text{area} = \text{base} \times \text{height or simply } a = bh$$

Since the base is the length of the rectangle and the height is the width, just multiply the length by the width to get the area of a rectangle.

Diagonals of a Rectangle

The two diagonals of a rectangle are always equal to each other, and either diagonal through the rectangle cuts the rectangle into two equal right triangles. In the figure below, the diagonal BD cuts rectangle $ABCD$ into congruent right triangles BAD and BCD. *Congruent* means that those triangles are exactly identical.

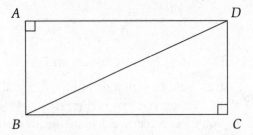

Since the diagonal of the rectangle forms right triangles that include the diagonal and two sides of the rectangle, if you know two of these values, you can always calculate the third with the Pythagorean theorem. For example, if you know the side lengths of the rectangle, you can calculate the length of the diagonal. If you know the diagonal and one side length, you can calculate the other side length. Also, keep in mind that the diagonal might cut the rectangle into a 30-60-90 triangle, in which case you could use the $1 : \sqrt{3} : 2$ ratio to make your calculating job even easier.

Squares

> "Hey, buddy, don't you be no square . . ."
> Elvis Presley, *Jailhouse Rock*

We don't know why, but sometime around the 1950s the word *square* became synonymous with "uncool." Of course, that's the same decade that brought us words like *daddy-O* and dances called "The Hand Jive."

We think that squares are in fact nifty little geometric creatures. They, along with circles, are perhaps the most symmetrical shapes in the universe—nothing to sneeze at. A square is so symmetrical because its angles are all 90° and all four of its sides are equal in length. Rectangles are fairly common, but a perfect square is something to behold. Like a rectangle, a square's opposite sides are parallel and it contains four right angles. But squares one-up rectangles by virtue of their equal sides.

As if you've never seen one of these in your life, here's what a square looks like:

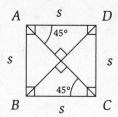

Area of a Square

The formula for the area of a square is:

$$\text{area} = s^2$$

In this formula, s is the length of a side. Since the sides of a square are all equal, all you need is one side to figure out a square's area.

Diagonals of a Square

The square has two more special qualities:

- Diagonals bisect each other at right angles and are equal in length.

- Diagonals bisect the vertex angles to create 45° angles. (This means that one diagonal will cut the square into two 45-45-90 triangles, while *two* diagonals break the square into *four* 45-45-90 triangles.)

Because a diagonal drawn into the square forms two congruent 45-45-90 triangles, if you know the length of one side of the square, you can always calculate the length of the diagonal:

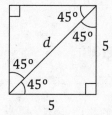

Since d is the hypotenuse of the 45-45-90 triangle that has legs of length 5, according to the ratio $1:1:\sqrt{2}$, you know that $d = 5\sqrt{2}$. Similarly, if you know only the length of the diagonal, you can use the same ratio to work backward to calculate the length of the sides.

Parallelograms

A parallelogram is a quadrilateral whose opposite sides are parallel. That means that rectangles and squares qualify as parallelograms, but so do four-sided figures that don't contain right angles.

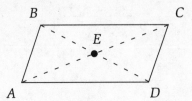

In a parallelogram, opposite sides are equal in length. That means that in the figure above, $BC = AD$ and $AB = DC$. Opposite angles are equal: $\angle ABC = \angle ADC$ and $\angle BAD = \angle BCD$. Adjacent angles are supplementary, which means they add up to 180°. Here, an example is $\angle ABC + \angle BCD = 180°$.

Area of a Parallelogram

The area of a parallelogram is given by the formula:

$$\text{area} = bh$$

In this formula, b is the length of the base, and h is the height. As shown in the figure below, the height of a parallelogram is represented by a perpendicular line dropped from one side of the figure to the side designated as the base.

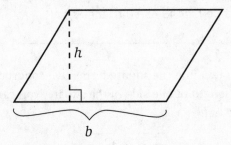

Diagonals of a Parallelogram

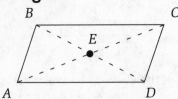

- The diagonals of a parallelogram bisect (split) each other: $BE = ED$ and $AE = EC$

- One diagonal splits a parallelogram into two congruent triangles: $\triangle ABD = \triangle BCD$

- Two diagonals split a parallelogram into two pairs of congruent triangles: $\triangle AEB = \triangle DEC$ and $\triangle BEC = \triangle AED$

Trapezoids

A trapezoid may sound like a new *Star Wars* character, but it's actually the name of a quadrilateral with one pair of parallel sides and one pair of nonparallel sides. Here's an example:

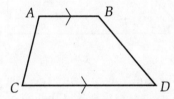

In this trapezoid, AB is parallel to CD (shown by the arrow marks), whereas AC and BD are not parallel.

Area of a Trapezoid

The formula for the area of a trapezoid is a bit more complex than the area formulas you've seen for the other quadrilaterals in this section. We'll set it off so you can take a good look at it:

$$\text{area} = \frac{s_1 + s_2}{2}\, h$$

In this formula, s_1 and s_2 are the lengths of the parallel sides (also called the bases of the trapezoid), and h is the height. In a trapezoid, the height is the perpendicular distance from one base to the other.

If you come across a trapezoid question on the GRE, you may need to use your knowledge of triangles to solve it. Here's an example of what we mean:

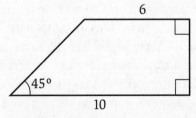

Find the area of the figure above.

First of all, we're not told that the figure is a trapezoid, but we can infer as much from the information given. Since both the line labeled 6 and the line labeled 10 form right angles with the line connecting them, the 6 and 10 lines must be parallel. Meanwhile, the other two lines (the left and right sides of the figure) cannot be parallel because one connects to the bottom line at a right angle, while the other connects with that line at a 45° angle. So we can deduce that the figure is a trapezoid, which means the trapezoid area formula is in play.

The bases of the trapezoid are the parallel sides, and we're told their lengths are 6 and 10. So far so good, but to find the area, we also need to find the trapezoid's height, which isn't given.

To do that, split the trapezoid into a rectangle and a 45-45-90 triangle by drawing in the height.

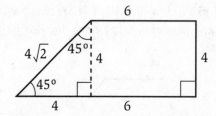

Once you've drawn in the height, you can split the base that's equal to 10 into two parts: The base of the rectangle is 6, and the leg of the triangle is 4. Since the triangle is 45-45-90, the two legs must be equal. This leg, though, is also the height of the trapezoid. So the height of the trapezoid is 4. Now you can plug the numbers into the formula:

$$\text{area} = \frac{6+10}{2}(4) = 8(4) = 32$$

Another way to find the area of the trapezoid is to find the areas of the triangle and the rectangle, then add them together:

$$\text{area} = \frac{1}{2}(4 \times 4) + (6 \times 4)$$

$$\frac{1}{2}(16) + 24$$

$$8 + 24 = 32$$

Circles

A circle is the collection of points equidistant from a given point, called the *center*. Circles are named after their center points—that's just easier than giving them names like Ralph and Betty. All circles contain 360°. The distance from the center to any point on the circle is called the *radius* (*r*). Radius is the most important measurement in a circle, because if you know a circle's radius, you can figure out all its other characteristics, such as its area, diameter, and circumference. We'll cover all that in the next few pages. The diameter (*d*) of a circle stretches between endpoints on the circle, passing through the center. A chord also extends from endpoint to endpoint on the circle, but it does not necessarily pass through the center. In the following figure, point *C* is the center of the circle, *r* is the radius, and *AB* is a chord.

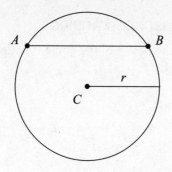

Tangent Lines

Tangents are lines that intersect a circle at only one point. Just like everything else in geometry, tangent lines are defined by certain fixed rules.

Here's the first: A radius whose endpoint is the intersection point of the tangent line and the circle is always perpendicular to the tangent line, as shown in the following figure:

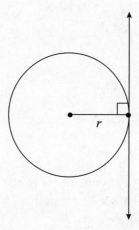

And the second rule: Every point in space outside the circle can extend exactly two tangent lines to the circle. The distances from the origin of the two tangents to the points of tangency are always equal. In the figure below, $XY = XZ$.

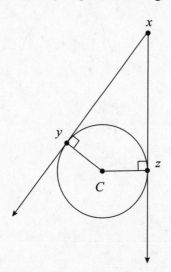

Central Angles and Inscribed Angles

An angle whose vertex is the center of the circle is called a *central angle*.

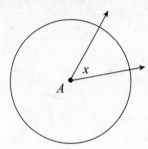

The degree of the circle (the slice of pie) cut by a central angle is equal to the measure of the angle. If a central angle is 25°, then it cuts a 25° arc in the circle.

An *inscribed angle* is an angle formed by two chords originating from a single point.

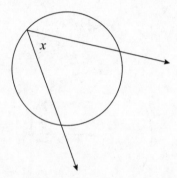

An inscribed angle will always cut out an arc in the circle that is *twice* the size of the degree of the inscribed angle. For example, if an inscribed angle is 40°, it will cut an arc of 80° in the circle.

If an inscribed angle and a central angle cut out the same arc in a circle, the central angle will be twice as large as the inscribed angle.

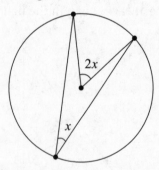

Circumference of a Circle

The circumference is the perimeter of the circle—that is, the total distance around the circle. The formula for circumference of a circle is:

$$\text{circumference} = 2\pi r$$

In this formula, r is the radius. Since a circle's diameter is always twice its radius, the formula can also be written $c = \pi d$, where d is the diameter. Let's find the circumference of the circle below:

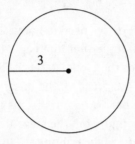

Plugging the radius into the formula, $c = 2\pi r = 2\pi\,(3) = 6\pi$.

Arc Length

An arc is a part of a circle's circumference. An arc contains two endpoints and all the points on the circle between the endpoints. By picking any two points on a circle, two arcs are created: a major arc, which is by definition the longer arc, and a minor arc, the shorter one.

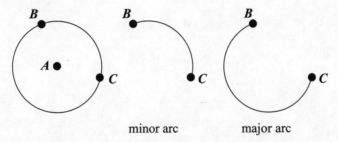

minor arc   major arc

Since the degree of an arc is defined by the central or inscribed angle that intercepts the arc's endpoints, you can calculate the arc length as long as you know the circle's radius and the measure of either the central or inscribed angle.

The arc length formula is:

$$\text{arc length} = \frac{n}{360} \times 2\pi r$$

In this formula, n is the measure of the degree of the arc, and r is the radius. This makes sense, if you think about it: There are 360° in a circle, so the degree of an arc divided by 360 gives us the fraction of the total circumference that arc represents. Multiplying that by the total circumference ($2\pi r$) gives us the length of the arc.

Here's the sort of arc length question you might see on the test:

Circle *D* has radius 9. What is the length of arc *AB*?

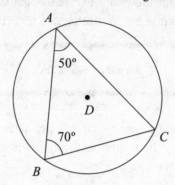

To figure out the length of arc *AB*, we need to know the radius of the circle and the measure of ∠*C*, the inscribed angle that intercepts the endpoints of arc *AB*. The question provides the radius of the circle, 9, but it throws us a little curveball by not providing the measure of ∠*C*. Instead, the question puts ∠*C* in a triangle and tells us the measures of the other two angles in the triangle. Like we said, only a little curveball: You can easily figure out the measure of ∠*C* because, as you know by now, the three angles of a triangle add up to 180°:

$$\angle c = 180° - (50° + 70°)$$

$$\angle c = 180° - 120°$$

$$\angle c = 60°$$

Since ∠*c* is an inscribed angle, arc *AB* must be twice its measure, or 120°. Now we can plug these values into the formula for arc length:

$$\text{arc } ab = \frac{120}{360} \times 2\pi(9)$$

$$= \frac{1}{3} \times 18\pi$$

$$= 6\pi$$

Area of a Circle

If you know the radius of a circle, you can figure out its area. The formula for area is:

$$\text{area} = \pi r^2$$

In this formula, *r* is the radius. So when you need to find the area of a circle, your real goal is to figure out the radius. In easier questions the radius will be given. In harder questions, they'll give you the diameter or circumference and you'll have to use the formulas for those to calculate the radius, which you'll then plug into the area formula.

Area of a Sector

A sector of a circle is the area enclosed by a central angle and the circle itself. It's shaped like a slice of pizza. The shaded region in the figure on the left below is a sector. The figure on the right is a slice of pepperoni pizza. See the resemblance?

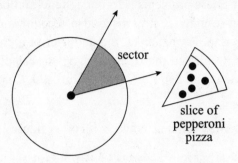

sector

slice of
pepperoni
pizza

The area of a sector is related to the area of a circle just as the length of an arc is related to the circumference. To find the area of a sector, find what fraction of 360° the sector makes up and multiply this fraction by the total area of the circle. In formula form:

$$\text{area of a sector} = \frac{n}{360} \times \pi r^2$$

In this formula, n is the measure of the central angle that forms the boundary of the sector, and r is the radius. An example will help. Find the area of the sector in the figure below:

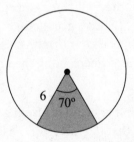

6   70°

The sector is bounded by a 70° central angle in a circle whose radius is 6. Using the formula, the area of the sector is:

$$\frac{70}{360} \times \pi(6)^2 = \frac{7}{36} \times 36\pi = 7\pi$$

Mish-Mashes: Figures with Multiple Shapes

The GRE test makers evidently feel it would be no fun if all of these geometric shapes you're learning appeared in isolation, so sometimes they mash them together. The trick in these problems is to understand and be able to manipulate the rules of each figure individually, while also recognizing which elements of the mish-mashes overlap. For example, the diameter of a circle may also be the side of a square, so if you use the rules of circles to calculate that length, you can then use that answer to determine something about the square, such as its area or perimeter.

Mish-mash problems often combine circles with other figures. Here's an example:

What is the length of minor arc *BE* in circle A if the area of rectangle *ABCD* is 18?

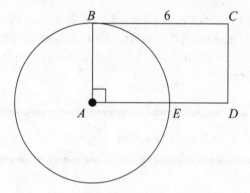

To find the length of minor arc *BE*, you have to know two things: the radius of the circle and the measure of the central angle that intersects the circle at points *B* and *E*. Because *ABCD* is a rectangle, and rectangles only have right angles, ∠*BAD* is 90°. In this question, they tell you as much by including the right-angle sign. But in a harder question, they'd leave the right-angle sign out and expect you to deduce that ∠*BAD* is 90° on your own. And since that angle also happens to be the central angle of circle *A* intercepting the arc in question, we can determine that arc *BE* measures 90°.

Finding the radius requires a bit of creative visualization as well, but it's not so hard. The key is to realize that the radius of the circle is equal to the width of the rectangle. So let's work backward from the rectangle to give us what we need to know about the circle. The area of the rectangle is 18, and its length is 6. Since the area of a rectangle is simply its length multiplied by its width, we can divide 18 by 6 to get a width of 3. As we've seen, this rectangle width doubles as the circle's radius, so we're in business: radius = 3. All we have to do is plug in the values we found into the arc length formula, and we're done.

$$\text{length of minor arc } BE = \frac{90}{360} \times 2\pi(3)$$

$$= \frac{1}{4} \times 6\pi$$

$$= \frac{6\pi}{4}$$

$$= \frac{3\pi}{2}$$

That covers the two-dimensional figures you should know, but there are also some three-dimensional figures you may be asked about as well. We'll finish up this geometry section with a look at those.

Rectangular Solids

A rectangular solid is a prism with a rectangular base and edges that are perpendicular to its base. In English, it looks a lot like a cardboard box.

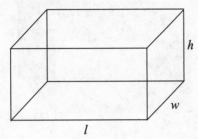

A rectangular solid has three important dimensions: length (l), width (w), and height (h). If you know these three measurements, you can find the solid's volume, surface area, and diagonal length.

Volume of a Rectangular Solid

The formula for the volume of a rectangular solid builds on the formula for the area of a rectangle. As discussed earlier, the area of a rectangle is equal to its length times its width. The formula for the volume of a rectangular solid adds the third dimension, height, to get:

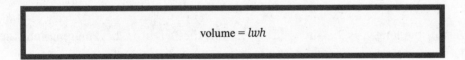

$$\text{volume} = lwh$$

Here's a good old-fashioned example:

What is the volume of the figure presented below?

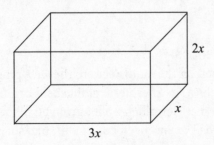

The length is $3x$, the width is x, and the height is $2x$. Just plug the values into the volume formula and you're good to go: $v = (3x)(x)(2x) = 6x^3$.

Surface Area of a Rectangular Solid

The surface area of a solid is the area of its outermost skin. In the case of rectangular solids, imagine a cardboard box all closed up. The surface of that closed box is made of six rectangles: The sum of the areas of the six rectangles is the surface area of the box. To make things even easier, the six rectangles come in three congruent pairs. We've marked the congruent pairs by shades of gray in the image below: One pair is clear, one pair is light gray, and one pair is dark gray.

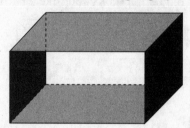

Two faces have areas of $l \times w$, two faces have areas of $l \times h$, and two faces have areas of $w \times h$. The surface area of the entire solid is the sum of the areas of the congruent pairs: surface area = $2lw + 2lh + 2wh$.

Let's try the formula out on the same solid we saw above. Find the surface area of this:

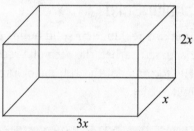

Again, the length is $3x$, the width is x, and the height is $2x$. Plugging into the formula, we get:

$$\text{surface area} = 2(3x)(x) + 2(3x)(2x) + 2(x)(2x)$$

$$= 6x^2 + 12x^2 + 4x^2$$

$$= 22x^2$$

DIVIDING RECTANGULAR SOLIDS

If you're doing really well on the Math section, the CAT program will begin scrounging for the toughest, most esoteric problems it can find to throw your way. One such problem may describe a solid, give you all of its measurements, and then tell you that the box has been cut in half, like so:

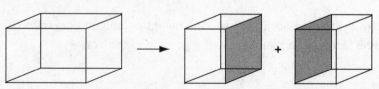

A number of possible questions could be created from this scenario. For example, you may be asked to find the combined surface area of the two new boxes.

Or maybe a Quantitative Comparison question would ask you to compare the volume of the original solid with that of the two new ones. Actually, the volume remains unchanged, but the surface area increases because two new sides (shaded in the diagram) emerge when the box is cut in half. You may need to employ a bit of reasoning along with the formulas you're learning to answer a difficult question like this, but it helps to know this general rule: *Whenever a solid is cut into smaller pieces, its surface area increases, but its volume is unchanged.*

Diagonal Length of a Rectangular Solid

The diagonal of a rectangular solid, *d*, is the line segment whose endpoints are opposite corners of the solid. Every rectangular solid has four diagonals, each with the same length, that connect each pair of opposite vertices. Here's one diagonal drawn in:

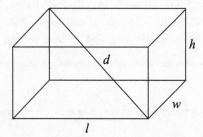

It's possible that a question will test to see if you can find the length of a diagonal. Here's the formula:

$$d = \sqrt{l^2 + w^2 + h^2}$$

Again, *l* is the length, *w* is the width, and *h* is the height. The formula is like a pumped-up version of the Pythagorean theorem. Check it out in action:

What is the length of diagonal *AH* in the
rectangular solid below if *AC* = 5, *GH* = 6, and *CG* = 3?

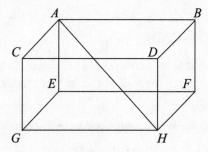

The question gives the length, width, and height of the rectangular solid, so you can just plug those numbers into the formula:

$$AH = \sqrt{5^2 + 6^2 + 3^2} = \sqrt{25 + 36 + 9} = \sqrt{70}$$

The problem could be made more difficult if it forced you to first calculate some of the dimensions before plugging them into the formula.

Cubes

A cube is a three-dimensional square. The length, width, and height of a cube are equal, and each of its six faces is a square. Here's what it looks like—pretty basic:

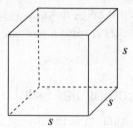

Volume of a Cube

The formula for finding the volume of a cube is essentially the same as the formula for the volume of a rectangular solid: We just need to multiply the length, width, and height. However, since a cube's length, width, and height are all equal, the formula for the volume of a cube is even easier:

$$volume = s^3$$

In this formula, s is the length of one edge of the cube.

Surface Area of a Cube

Since a cube is just a rectangular solid whose sides are all equal, the formula for finding the surface area of a cube is the same as the formula for finding the surface area of a rectangular solid, except with s substituted in for l, w, and h. This boils down to:

$$volume = 6s^2$$

Diagonal Length of a Cube

The formula for the diagonal of a cube is also adapted from the formula for the diagonal length of a rectangular solid, with s substituted for l, w, and h. This yields $\sqrt{3s^2}$, which simplifies to:

$$volume = s\sqrt{3}$$

Right Circular Cylinders

A right circular cylinder looks like one of those cardboard things that toilet paper comes on, except it isn't hollow. It has two congruent circular bases and looks like this:

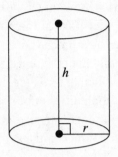

The height, h, is the length of the line segment whose endpoints are the centers of the circular bases. The radius, r, is the radius of its base. For the GRE, all you need to know about a right circular cylinder is how to calculate its volume.

Volume of a Right Circular Cylinder

The volume of this kind of solid is the product of the area of its base and its height. Because a right circular cylinder has a circular base, its volume is equal to the area of the circular base times the height or:

$$\text{volume} = \pi r^2 h$$

Find the volume of the cylinder below:

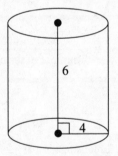

This cylinder has a radius of 4 and a height of 6. Using the volume formula, its volume = $\pi(4)^2(6) = 96\pi$.

We've covered a lot of ground so far in this Math 101 chapter, working our way through arithmetic, algebra, and now geometry. We'll bring it on home with our final subject, data analysis.

DATA ANALYSIS

If there's one thing we can say about modern society, it's that we love our data. If you spend just a few minutes on the Internet, you can find out roughly how many people there are in America; how much, on average, they earn; how long they're expected to live; what percentage of them marry; what percentage have kids; how many kids they have; how much those kids weigh; and so on and so forth until every aspect of daily life is reduced to numerical form. Perhaps expressing everything numerically makes us feel in control of our fate, or perhaps it helps us cope with the ambiguities of our complex technological lives. Whatever the reason, we love our data, we surround ourselves with it, and we have invented all sorts of statistical mechanisms to express what all this information means.

The GRE test makers have taken our numerical fetish to heart. In this final Math 101 section, you'll find more than you ever wanted to know about statistical concepts such as mean, median, mode, probability, and every other data analysis topic tested on the GRE.

Mean

On the GRE, *mean* and *arithmetic mean* both represent the concept that you may recognize by its more common name, *average*. No matter what we call it, the calculation is the same: Add up all the terms and divide by the number of terms. You've no doubt seen this in school: If you get scores of 90, 95, and 100 on three tests, then 95 is the average of the three test scores. In this basic example you can probably see at a glance that 95 is the average, but technically you can calculate it by taking the sum of the scores (90 + 95 + 100) and dividing it by the number of scores (3). The formula, in general terms, is:

$$\text{mean} = \frac{\text{sum of terms}}{\text{number of terms}}$$

Let's try one out:

What's the arithmetic mean of 3, −5, 7, and 0?

Solve by using the formula:

$$\frac{3-5+7+0}{4} = \frac{5}{4} = 1.25$$

Some mean problems may be straightforward like the one above, but the more complicated ones may give you two values and ask you to solve for a third. For example, the test makers might give you the mean and the number of terms and ask you to solve for the sum of the terms. Your job will still be to plug the known values into the formula and solve from there. Here's an example:

The average height of five people is 54 inches. One of the people leaves the group, and the average height of those remaining is 52 inches. How tall is the person who left?

In the first sentence, we're given the number of people, five, and their average height, 54. We can use the mean formula to calculate the sum of the heights of these five people:

$$\text{mean} = \frac{\text{sum of terms}}{\text{number of terms}}$$

$$54 = \frac{\text{sum of terms}}{5}$$

$$\text{sum} = 54 \times 5 = 270$$

In the second sentence, we're told that the average height of the remaining people is 52. Since one person left the group, four people remain. Plugging 4 and 52 into the mean formula gives:

$$\text{mean} = \frac{\text{sum of terms}}{\text{number of terms}}$$

$$52 = \frac{\text{sum of terms}}{4}$$

$$\text{sum} = 52 \times 4 = 208$$

The difference between the sum of the heights of the original five people and the sum of the heights of the remaining four must be equal to the height of the person who left. Subtract the second sum from the first to get the height of the person who left: 270 – 208 = 62 inches, the final answer.

Median

The *median* of a group of numbers is the middle term when the numbers are written in either ascending or descending order. That means that before you can calculate a median, you must first rewrite the terms of the group in ascending or descending order. For example, to calculate the median of 0.3, 7, 0, 9, and 10, you can't choose 0 simply because it appears in the middle. You must first write the numbers in order: 0, 0.3, 7, 9, 10. Since 7 appears in the middle of this *ordered* list, 7 is the median.

If two numbers appear in the middle, which will happen whenever the total number of terms is even, take the *mean of the two middle numbers* to determine the median. For example, the median of 1, 2, 4, and 8 is 3, since 3 is the mean of 2 and 4.

One wrinkle you may come across in a median problem is a *description* of a list of consecutive numbers, instead of a list of the *actual* numbers, as in this example:

> What is the median of all the integers between 210 and 260, inclusive?

You certainly don't want to write out all the numbers from 210 to 260, and then try to find the one in the middle. It's better to use the following formula:

$$\text{median of sequence of consecutive numbers} = \frac{\text{first number} + \text{last number}}{2}$$

In our example, the median would be:

$$\frac{210 + 260}{2} = 235$$

Remember, *inclusive* means "including," which is why we used 210 and 260. Had the question said *exclusive*, we would have used 211 and 259, divided by 2, and also gotten a median of 235.

Mode

The *mode* of a group of numbers is the number that occurs most frequently. If multiple numbers are tied for first place in the race to occur the most, then the group will have more than one mode. For example, the modes of the set of numbers {6, 6, 1, 3, 4, 1} are 6 and 1, since both 6 and 1 occur twice, and all the other numbers occur only once.

Range

The *range* of a group of numbers is the difference between the largest term and the smallest term. For example, the range of 10, –25, 3, 2, and 4 is 10 – (–25) = 35. One would need to travel 35 units on a number line to get from the smallest value, –25, to the largest value, 10.

Standard Deviation

Standard deviation is one of the most difficult statistical concepts, but thankfully you'll only need a very general understanding of it for the GRE. The test makers won't ask you to actually calculate standard deviation, as the formula for doing so is pretty difficult. You will, however, be expected to know that *standard deviation* is a measure of how spread out a group of numbers is. The more spread out a group of numbers, the larger its standard deviation. Let's look at an example:

Which of the following groups of numbers has the greater standard deviation?

Group A: 11, 12, 13, 14, 15

Group B: 50, 51, 51, 52, 53

Even though the numbers in Group B are larger than those in Group A, they're closer together thanks to the double occurrence of number 51. No such overlapping occurs in Group A. Group A exhibits a slightly greater spread and therefore has the greater standard deviation.

The 34-14-2 Rule

Standard deviation also lets you know how likely it is that a value will differ from the mean by a certain amount. In general, the farther a value is from the mean, the less likely it is to occur. The following graph, called a Normal Distribution, shows this in more detail:

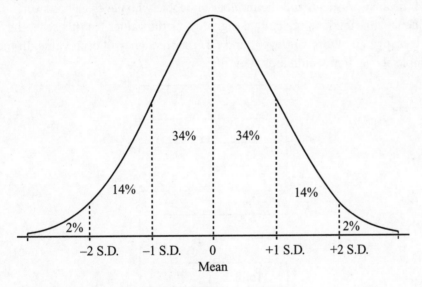

This graph is the basis for the 34-14-2 Rule:

34%, 14%, and 2% represent the likelihood that a value will fall into each given region. For example, there is a 34% chance that a value will be between the mean and one standard deviation to the right or left of the mean. Similarly, there is a 14% chance that a value will be between one and two standard deviations to the right or left of the mean.

Here's how to use the numbers. Say that the mean for some group of values is 10, and the standard deviation is 2. One standard deviation to the right of the mean will therefore be 10 + 2 = 12. The Normal Distribution graph states that there is a 34% chance that a value from the group will fall between 10 (the mean) and 12 (one standard deviation up from the mean). Based on this kind of analysis, you may be asked something like this:

> What is the likelihood that a value within a group of values with a mean of 10 and a standard deviation of 2 equals 5?

If the mean is 10, then one standard deviation below the mean is 10 – 2 = 8, which creates a 34% chance that a value from the group falls between 10 and 8.

A second standard deviation to the left would be 8 – 2 = 6, meaning that there's a 14% chance that a particular value would fall between 8 and 6. More than two standard deviations to the left of the mean would be all values below 6. The graph tells us that these values have a 2% likelihood. The number 5 falls into this group, so 2% would be the answer.

Frequency Distribution

Say, for example, that fifteen college graduates were asked how many different jobs they had in their first five years following college, and the responses came back like so:

2, 4, 2, 1, 0, 1, 3, 2, 2, 5, 3, 4, 1, 2, 1

Not very pleasing to the eye, is it? One way to organize this information is to express it in the form of a *frequency distribution*: a chart that shows at a glance all of the answers given and the number of people who gave each answer. Frequency distributions typically designate x as the values (in this case, the answers given by those surveyed) and f as the frequency of each value. In the example above, that would look like this:

x	*f*
0	1
1	4
2	5
3	2
4	2
5	1
Total	15

We can see from the chart that one person surveyed had no jobs in the first five years after college (slacker!), four people had one job, five people had two jobs, and so on. So what's so great about this? Well, the best thing about it is that it allows us to quickly determine many of the other statistical features we've been discussing so far. For example, eyeing only the left-hand column tells us that the range of responses is 5 – 0 = 5. A quick scan of the right-hand column indicates that 5 is the largest frequency corresponding to any one answer, and it corresponds to the answer 2, which therefore qualifies 2 as the mode. The chart already lists the responses in ascending order, so the median will be the eighth value from the beginning—eighth because with fifteen values total, the eighth value is right in the middle with seven values below it and seven above it. The first value is 0, the next four values are 1, bringing us to the fifth value, and the next five values are 2, bringing us to the tenth value. The eighth value is therefore a 2, so 2 is the median of this group of values.

You may also be asked to calculate the mean from a frequency distribution. Recall the formula for mean:

$$\text{mean} = \frac{\text{sum of terms}}{\text{number of terms}}$$

Using the frequency distribution, we can quickly calculate the sum of the terms by finding the sum of each term multiplied by its frequency. The number of terms will be either given in the table (such as "total = 15" in our chart), or you can just add up the frequency numbers in the right-hand column to calculate the number of terms. In this case, the mean is:

$$\text{mean} = \frac{(0)(1) + (1)(4) + (2)(5) + (3)(2) + (4)(2) + (5)(1)}{15}$$

$$= \frac{0 + 4 + 10 + 6 + 8 + 5}{15}$$

$$= \frac{33}{15}$$

$$= \frac{11}{5}$$

If you learn the basics of frequency distributions, it should be a welcome sight if one of these appears on your test.

Probability

Probability is the measure of how often something is expected to occur, expressed as a fraction or decimal between 0 and 1. A probability of 0 means there's no chance that the event under consideration will take place. A probability of 1 means it *definitely* will happen. Most probabilities tested on the GRE fall somewhere in between. We'll use the common scenario of selecting colored marbles from a bag to illustrate the various kinds of probability questions you might see on your test.

Single Trials

The most basic kind of probability question involves a single selection from a given group of elements. Here's an example:

In a bag containing 12 red, 13 white, and 15 black marbles, what is the probability of selecting a red marble on a single draw?

To tackle probability problems, use the following formula:

$$\text{probability of an event} = \frac{\text{number of favorable outcomes}}{\text{total number of possible outcomes}}$$

The *number of favorable outcomes* is math lingo for the number of ways you can get what the problem is asking you to get. Here, *red marble* is the favorable outcome, so the numerator of the fraction is 12, the number of red marbles in the bag. The *total number of possible outcomes* is the total number of possibilities, or, in our problem, the total number of marbles. Make sure to include *all* of the marbles, including those already counted as favorable outcomes. The total number of marbles is 12 + 13 + 15 = 40. Plugging 12 and 40 into the formula gives:

$$\text{probability of a red marble} = \frac{12}{40}$$

Simplifying this gives $\frac{3}{10}$, the final answer.

Independent Events

If one event does not influence the occurrence or nonoccurrence of another event, the two events are *independent*. To find the probability of two independent events occurring, simply multiply their individual probabilities. For example, if there's a 1 in 4 chance that Mary will be selected for a committee, and a 1 in 3 chance that Bill will be kicked out of college, and the events are independent (that is, Mary isn't angling to join the committee with the purpose in mind of booting Bill), then there's a $\frac{1}{4} \times \frac{1}{3} = \frac{1}{12}$ chance that both Mary will be selected for the committee and Bill will be given his college walking papers.

We mention independent events at this point because this concept affects our next topic, multiple trials.

Multiple Trials

Frequently, probability questions on the GRE won't be limited to a single draw, or trial, but will instead involve repeated draws. When a question involves drawing multiple times from the same group of entities, you need to distinguish between draws *with replacement* and draws *without replacement*. Let's illustrate the difference using our marble example:

---

1. You select a marble, note its color, and put it back in the bag. You then select a marble again. This is called *drawing with replacement*.

2. You select a marble and put it aside. Then you draw another marble from those remaining. This is called *drawing without replacement*.

The GRE will always make it clear which method is being used either by including the actual phrase *with replacement* or *without replacement* or by explicitly describing the method of selection in a way that makes it obvious which mechanism is in play. Let's look at an example of each type.

DRAWING WITH REPLACEMENT

Try your hand at this one:

> A bag contains 12 red, 13 white, and 15 black marbles. What is the
> probability of selecting two black marbles in a row if the selection is
> made with replacement?

The number of black marbles, or favorable outcomes, is 15. The total number of
marbles is 40. First, use the probability formula to find the probability of selecting a black marble on the first draw:

$$\frac{\text{number of favorable outcomes}}{\text{total number of possible outcomes}} = \frac{15}{40} = \frac{3}{8}$$

Since this problem involves drawing with replacement, we'll need to put the black
marble selected on the first draw back into the bag before selecting again. So the
bag will still contain 15 black marbles out of 40 total for the second draw. The
probability of drawing a black marble on the second draw is thus the same $\frac{3}{8}$.

Now, even though the marbles are coming from the same bag, these two
events—a black marble on the first draw and a black marble on the second—are
independent; that is, what happens on one draw doesn't affect what happens on
the other. To get the probability of two black marbles in a row, we can therefore
multiply the individual probabilities:

$$\frac{3}{8} \times \frac{3}{8} = \frac{9}{64}$$

DRAWING WITHOUT REPLACEMENT

Now let's see what happens when we *don't* put the first marble back into the bag
after selecting it:

> A bag contains 12 red, 13 white, and 15 black marbles. What is the
> probability of selecting two black marbles in a row if the selection is
> made without replacement?

The probability of the first marble being black is $\frac{3}{8}$, just as before. For the
second draw, however, only 14 black marbles remain out of 39 total. (Remember,
we took a black marble out of the bag and *did not* put it back.) This means that
the probability of the second marble being black is $\frac{14}{39}$. By assuming the first
draw was favorable (a black marble selected), we adjusted the figures for our
second probability. Since these figures are already adjusted to account for the
first favorable outcome, the second drawing is independent from the first, so we
can still multiply the individual probabilities to get the chances of selecting two
black marbles in a row:

$$\frac{3}{8} \times \frac{14}{39}$$

We can cancel the 3 and 39 before multiplying and also cancel a factor of 2 from the 8 and 14 to make our lives easier:

$$\frac{1}{4} \times \frac{7}{13} = \frac{7}{52}$$

This can't be reduced any further, so it's the final answer.

The Probability of Something NOT Happening

You're probably familiar with the phrase *not happening*, as in when you ask your boss for three weeks off in the summer and he tells you "that is *so not happening*." But do you know that there's an actual math formula for "not happening"? You probably do, without even realizing it. For example, if you're told that the chance of snow tomorrow is 25%, it's likely you recognize without much thought that the chance that it will *not* snow is 75%. Here's the formula you used, whether you were aware of it or not:

---

the probability of an event NOT happening = 1 – the probability of that event

---

This formula can turn very hard probability questions into easier ones. Consider this next one:

> A bag contains 12 red, 13 white, and 15 black marbles. What is the probability of selecting at least one red or one white marble in two draws if the selection is made with replacement?

This is harder than the previous problems, because it's not altogether clear what must happen on any individual draw for a favorable outcome. For instance, the first draw might be black, and you still could have a favorable outcome if the second draw is red or white. Similarly, the second draw could be black, and you'd still have a favorable outcome if the first draw is red or white. And of course, a first *and* a second draw of red or white would also count as a favorable outcome. So how do we deal with this ambiguity?

Simple: Use the formula for "NOT happening." It's far easier in this case to calculate the probability of *not* getting at least one red or white marble in two draws because this is actually the same thing as drawing two black marbles, with replacement. We already calculated this earlier as $\frac{9}{64}$. The probability of drawing at least one red or white in two draws is 1 minus the probability of that NOT happening, which is simply the probability of drawing two black marbles. The answer is therefore:

$$1 - \frac{9}{64} = \frac{55}{64}$$

Still no piece of cake, but doable.

"Or" Questions

A difficult question may ask you for the probability of event A *or* event B occurring, which is different from the probability of A *and* B occurring. If you see one of these, use the formula:

> probability of A or B = probability of A + probability of B – probability of A and B

For example, say the probability of Marcie passing a test is 70%, and the probability of Jerome passing the same test is 30%. The events in this problem are independent: Neither person passing the test influences whether the other person does so (unless of course they cheat from each other, which we'll assume is not the case). So the final term of the expression, the probability of Marcie *and* Jerome passing, is equal to the product of the individual probabilities of those events, as we've seen all along. We'll convert the percentages to fractions, since working with those may be easier. Then we'll plug 'em into the formula:

$$\frac{7}{10} + \frac{3}{10} - \left(\frac{7}{10}\right)\left(\frac{3}{10}\right) = 1 - \frac{21}{100} = \frac{79}{100}$$

The probability of Marcie *or* Jerome passing the test is therefore equal to 79%.

In some cases, two events may be *mutually exclusive*, meaning that the probability of both occurring is 0. For example, in choosing a single dog from a kennel, the chances of choosing a black Labrador and a white schnauzer are zero—you can't have both. If these represented the A and B elements of the "or" formula, the final term would be 0, and you wouldn't have to subtract anything.

Sequences

A sequence is a list of numbers that follows a particular pattern. If you get a sequence problem, you'll probably be given at least one of the terms in the sequence, along with the rule that defines the pattern. You probably won't have to figure out the pattern on your own; that's more like the kind of thing you'd see on an IQ test.

However, what could make sequence problems tough is the notation. Each term in a sequence has the same variable, but each has a different subscript. This subscript indicates a particular term. For example:

$$a_1 = \text{the first term}$$

$$a_2 = \text{the second term}$$

$$a_{10} = \text{the tenth term}$$

$$a_n = \text{the nth term}$$

$$a_{n+1} = \text{the term immediately after the } n\text{th term}$$

For example, to indicate that the second term of a sequence is 5 and that the third term is 7, the test makers might write:

$$a_2 = 5$$

$$a_3 = 7$$

This subscript notation can also be used to indicate how each term relates to the others. For example:

$$a_{n+1} = a_n - 3$$

This just means that each successive term is three less than the previous term. Here's an example, using the notation we just discussed:

If a_n = the nth term in a sequence, and $a_1 = 3$ and $a_{n+1} = a_n + 2$, what is the value of a_{10}?

Let's use 1 as n to keep things simple:

$$a_1 = a_n = 3$$

So a_{n+1} is the same as saying a_{1+1} or a_2. This second term we're told is equal to the first term, a_n, plus 2, which means that the second term will be 3 + 2, or 5. So the notation, which looks intimidating, is really a shorthand way of saying that each successive term is two more than the previous term. Writing out this sequence from the first to the tenth terms gives 3, 5, 7, 9, 11, 13, 15, 17, 19, 21. The tenth term is 21, and so $a_{10} = 21$.

Arithmetic Sequences

In an arithmetic sequence, the difference between each term and the next is constant. This is the kind of sequence we saw in the previous example. In addition to understanding the notation and concepts for sequences, you should know the formula for arithmetic sequences:

$$a_n = a_1 + (n - 1)d$$

where

a_n = the nth term

a_1 = the first term

d = the difference between consecutive terms

This formula is useful if you need to determine the value of some very high term and don't want to write down a long sequence of numbers. In our previous example, the first term (a_1) is 3 and the difference between consecutive terms is 2. If you plug these numbers into the equation above looking for a_{10}, you'll get the same answer, 21, that we got earlier. In this example, it's just as easy to write out the terms. But to determine the *100th* term in that sequence, we'll need to plug the numbers into the formula:

$$a_{100} = 3 + (100 - 1)2 = 3 + 99 \times 2 = 201$$

Geometric Sequences and Exponential Growth

In a geometric sequence, the *ratio* between one term and the next is constant, not the actual difference between the terms. For example, in the sequence 3, 9, 27, 81, each successive term is three times greater than the preceding one, but the actual difference between the terms changes: 9 – 3 = 6, 27 – 9 = 18, and so on. Geometric sequences exhibit *exponential growth*, as opposed to the constant growth of arithmetic sequences. Here's an example of the kind of geometric sequence that the test makers might toss at you:

$$g_1 = 4$$

$$g_n = 2g_{n-1}$$

Trying out some terms, this means that $g_2 = (2)g_1$, $g_3 = (2)g_2$, and so on. In other words, the first term is 4, and each successive term is twice the value of the preceding term. Writing out the first few terms lets us see that the ratio between terms is constant and thus confirms that this is a geometric sequence:

$$4, 8, 16, 32, \ldots$$

The ratio between consecutive terms is always 2, even though the differences between the terms increase as you move to the right.

As with arithmetic sequences, you should learn the special formula for geometric sequences, just in case it's not convenient to list out all of the terms up to the one you're looking for:

$$g_n = g_1 r^{n-1}$$

where

g_n = the nth term

g_1 = the first term

r = the ratio between consecutive terms

Let's use the formula to calculate the value of the tenth term in the geometric sequence defined by $g_1 = 4$ and $g_n = 2g_{n-1}$. We already know $r = 2$:

$$g_{10} = 4 \times (2)^{10-1} = 4 \times 2^9 = 4 \times 512 = 2{,}048$$

Digit Counting

Here's an interesting kind of problem that appears with some regularity on the GRE. In digit counting problems, you're asked how many times a particular digit appears in a defined group of numbers, or how many numbers within such a group *don't* contain a certain digit. An example will make this clearer:

> How many three-digit positive even integers contain at least one digit that is a 7?
>
> ◯ 45
> ◯ 60
> ◯ 90
> ◯ 140
> ◯ 210

First make sure you understand the range of numbers under consideration. Positive three-digit numbers begin with 100 and go to 999. Moreover, we're only interested in the even ones. The question is looking for how many numbers fit this description and contain at least one 7.

Well, we're not going to go and count them all—that would take too long. But we *will* list a few examples that fit the criteria and then see if we can discern a pattern. Beginning with the 100s, the first number that has a 7 is 107, but since that's not an even number, it doesn't count. In fact, the next one, 117, doesn't count either, nor does 127, 137, and so on. So we begin to see a pattern. The first even number we get to that has a 7 is 170, followed by 172, 174, 176, and 178. No number from 179 to 200 fits the bill, so in the entire 100s we have a total of 5 numbers that satisfy the question's requirements.

Now we can generalize from what we've learned: The 200s will be no different, nor the 300s, nor the 400s, and so on. So if there are 5 cases in each of the nine groups of 100 numbers from 100 to 999, we can multiply 5 instances per each group of hundreds by nine groups of hundreds (100s, 200s, etc.) to get 45, choice **A**.

However, we'd be wrong. Naturally, **A** is a trap for people who forget that the 700s contain plenty of numbers that work, so we need to consider the numbers from 700 to 800 separately. The other eight groups of hundreds follow our pattern, so we'll go with 5 × 8 = 40 to represent the instances that make the cut among those. But we also have to consider all of the numbers in the 700s, since every number in the 700s contains at least one 7. How many are even? There are 100 numbers between 700 and 799, and half are even, so we need to add 50 more cases to the 40 we've found already. The correct answer is 40 + 50 = 90, choice **C**.

Digit counting questions can be difficult, and if you see one, chances are the GRE software is throwing you more difficult questions because you're doing pretty well. Understand the range, find a pattern and generalize it to as many cases as you can, and then check for special cases. If you're careful, you'll find them all.

Factorials

You may see some problems on your exam in which a number is followed by an exclamation point, like this: 5!. This does not mean you should loudly exclaim, "Five!" Nor does it mean that the test makers are extra-specially enthusiastic about a particular problem. The exclamation point makes it look like there's something really exciting going on! But there's not.

An exclamation point used in math symbolizes a *factorial*. A factorial stands for the product of all the numbers up to and including the given number.
So $5! = 5 \times 4 \times 3 \times 2 \times 1 = 120$.

Some more examples:

$3! = 3 \times 2 \times 1 = 6$

$4! = 4 \times 3 \times 2 \times 1 = 24$

$55! = 55 \times 54 \times 53 \times \ldots \times 3 \times 2 \times 1 =$ a really huge number you would never be expected to solve for

$0! = 1$

The proof of this last example is beyond the scope of what you need to know for the GRE. Just remember that $0! = 1$ by definition. Consider it another bit of math trivia picked up on your way to GRE mastery.

The factorial of n also signifies the number of ways that the n elements of a group can be ordered. So, if you decide to ditch grad school and become a wedding planner instead, and need to figure out how many different ways six people can sit at a table with six chairs, 6! is the way to go: $6 \times 5 \times 4 \times 3 \times 2 \times 1 = 720$ possible seating arrangements. You'll astound the other wedding planners with this quick calculation, never revealing the true source of your knowledge.

As you might guess from the name, factorials have many factors. Recall that a factor is a number that divides into another number with no remainder. Whenever you take the factorial of a number, the result will be divisible by all of the integers up to and including the original number. For example, 6! is divisible by 6, 5, 4, 3, 2, and 1, and all of those numbers are factors of 6!. This is all inherent in the definition of factorial, but it's good to understand it in these terms too.

Simplifying Factorials

The test makers may ask you to work out a problem that involves factorials in fractions, and as you'll soon see, this becomes downright necessary in permutation and combination problems. The trick is to cancel before calculating. As you've seen in earlier examples, canceling with fractions means dividing the numerator and denominator by the same number. A little cancellation makes complicated-looking factorial problems much easier to solve. Check it out:

$$\text{What is } \frac{100!}{98!}?$$

This expression looks like it might be a huge number. And, in fact, trying to calculate 98! or 100! would be near impossible without a computer or ultra-fancy calculator. Fortunately, we can simplify this equation significantly:

$$\frac{100!}{98!} = \frac{100 \times 99 \times 98 \times 97 \times \dots}{98 \times 97 \times 96 \times \dots} = 100 \times 99 = 9{,}900$$

This works, because everything after and including the 98 cancels out in both the numerator and the denominator, leaving 100 × 99 in the numerator and 1 in the denominator. Here's another way to think about this:

$$\frac{100!}{98!} = \frac{100 \times 99 \times 98!}{98!}$$

The 98! in the numerator cancels out with the 98! in the denominator, leaving only 100 × 99 = 9,900.

Truth be told, even factorial problems involving smaller numbers benefit from canceling out. For example:

$$\frac{11!}{10!} = \frac{11 \times 10!}{10!} = 11$$

$$\frac{6!}{3!} = \frac{6 \times 5 \times 4 \times 3!}{3!} = 6 \times 5 \times 4 = 120$$

Before you get sucked into multiplying out the factorials in the top and bottom parts of the fraction and then dividing the results, first cancel out what you can.

Permutations and Combinations

Knowing how to calculate and simplify factorials is especially useful for problems involving permutations and combinations. These types of questions ask you to determine how many ways something can be done. They're similar to the simple wedding planner example above, except that they involve choosing a certain number of entities from a larger group. For example, "In a race of eight horses, how many ways can the horses finish first, second, and third?" and "How many ways can two students be selected for a Grammar Jamboree out of a class of 20 students?" In this section, we'll explain not only how to answer both of these questions but also the very important difference between them.

Permutations

In a permutation, *order matters*—that is, being first in a group is different from being second, third, or in any other position. The easiest way to tell that a question is a permutation is if it includes the word *order* or the word *arrange*. Even if it doesn't contain these words, the question might describe some kind of ranking or race. Our horse race question above, for instance, is a permutation since finishing first is certainly different from finishing second or third in a horse race. If, for example, three of the horses are A, B, and C, then ABC is one possible finish, CAB is another, and BCA is a third. They all involve the same three horses, but switching them around yields additional arrangements that we need to add to our tally. In a combination problem, however, we're not concerned with order, so BCA would be considered the same as CAB, and we wouldn't count those twice. We'll get to combinations in just a bit, but let's continue with the permutation problem at hand.

Here's the permutation formula:

$$_nP_r = \frac{n!}{(n-r)!}$$

In this case, $_nP_r$ is the number of subgroups of size r that can be taken from within a set with n elements.

Here's the horse race question again, and this time we'll work through it using the formula:

> In a race of eight horses, how many ways can the
> horses finish first, second, and third?

In this problem, $n = 8$, because that's the total number of horses racing, and $r = 3$, because that's the number of winners we're interested in (first, second, and third place). Plugging into the formula gives:

$$_8P_3 = \frac{8!}{(8-3)!} = \frac{8!}{5!}$$

Now we'll solve, using our knowledge of factorials and canceling out:

$$\frac{8!}{5!} = \frac{8 \times 7 \times 6 \times 5!}{5!} = 8 \times 7 \times 6 = 336$$

Notice how the 5!s cancel out, leaving us with some basic multiplication to get our final answer.

Combinations

As we mentioned earlier, in a combination, *order does not matter*. For example, if you're trying to *buy* three horses instead of ordering them first through third in a race, then it really doesn't matter if you come away from the horse farm with horses ABC or horses CBA—they're all the same horses. You wouldn't shuffle them around and then say, "Look, a whole new group of horses! Lucky me!" Well, you *could* say that, but people would think you're nuts.

You'll be able to recognize a combination problem because it will involve selecting a small group from a larger group, with no regard to order. An example is the Grammar Jamboree problem introduced earlier:

> How many ways can two students be selected for a Grammar
> Jamboree out of a class of 20 students?

Two students are to be selected from a class of 20, and no mention of order is made. This is common for situations involving teams: A team consisting of Jonathan and Gloria is the same as a team consisting of Gloria and Jonathan. Unless some specific mention is made of an ordering element, assume you're dealing with a combination problem. Here's the combination formula:

$$_nC_r = \frac{n!}{(n-r)!r!}$$

Here, unordered subgroups of size r are selected from a set of size n. Notice that this is the same as the permutation formula, except that it tacks on an extra r! term in the denominator. This means that we divide by a larger number in combination problems, resulting in a smaller number of final orderings. And that makes sense too: We'd expect fewer total orderings in combinations, since order doesn't matter and we therefore count the shuffled orderings (ABC, CAB, BCA, etc.) as one.

Use the formula to solve our Grammar Jamboree problem:

$$_{20}C_2 = \frac{20!}{(20-2)!2!}$$
$$= \frac{20!}{18!2!}$$
$$= \frac{20 \times 19 \times 18!}{18!2!}$$

Cancel the 18!s:

$$\frac{20 \times 19}{2!} = \frac{20 \times 19}{2 \times 1} = \frac{10 \times 19}{1 \times 1} = 190$$

So, there are 190 possible two-person teams of jamboree-ers to choose from the class of 20. Let the jamboree begin!

Multiple Permutations and Combinations

If the CAT software is really impressed by your math acumen, it might throw you a problem involving *multiple* permutations, combinations, or both. The key is to break the problem down into parts, solving each independently using the formulas discussed above. To obtain a final answer, multiply all of the individual results. Here's an example:

> How many ways can Suzanne order an ice cream cone if she is to select three different flavors out of fifteen available flavors and three different toppings out of five available toppings? The order in which the flavors are stacked is significant, but the order in which the toppings are added is not.

We admit it—this looks hard. However, it helps to think of this as two completely separate problems:

1. Selecting ice cream flavors

2. Selecting toppings

Don't worry, we'll combine them in the end, much as the flavors and toppings will be combined in Suzanne's cone. But first things first.

Since the order of flavors matters, this part of the problem is a permutation. Suzanne must select three different flavors out of a total of fifteen. Let's use the P formula:

$$_nP_r = \frac{n!}{(n-r)!}$$

As per the problem, $n = 15$ and $r = 3$:

$$_{15}P_3 = \frac{15!}{(15-3)!} = \frac{15!}{12!} = \frac{15 \times 14 \times 13 \times 12!}{12!} = 15 \times 14 \times 13 = 2,730$$

So Suzanne has 2,730 choices of flavors. Delicious! But back to the problem: Since the order of toppings does not matter, this part is a combination. Suzanne must select three different toppings out of a total of five. Let's use the C formula:

$$_nC_r = \frac{n!}{(n-r)!r!}$$

Now $n = 5$ and $r = 3$:

$$_5C_3 = \frac{5!}{(5-3)!3!}$$

$$= \frac{5!}{2!3!}$$

$$= \frac{5 \times 4 \times 3!}{2!3!}$$

Cancel the 3!s, and restate 2! as 2×1:

$$\frac{5 \times 4}{2 \times 1} = \frac{20}{2} = 10$$

Now we know that there are 10 possible combinations of toppings. The last step is to multiply the two results: $2,730 \times 10 = 27,300$. And there we go: Suzanne has an unbelievable 27,300 choices for her ice cream cone. It's a wonder people don't have anxiety attacks in ice cream stores—just one cone but more than 27,000 varieties to choose from!

Groups

This topic sounds innocuous enough, but problems involving groups can drive test takers batty. The basic idea is that some people or things belong to one group, others belong to another group, and still others belong to *both* groups or *neither* group. For example, at a certain country club, some members play golf, some play tennis, others play both sports, and still others prefer reading to playing. You'll be given some of the specific numbers in such a problem and then asked to determine the missing values.

The approach you should use depends on whether the problem concerns two or three groups. We'll cover the most effective techniques for both cases. You won't see problems with more than three groups.

Problems with Two Groups

All you need for two-group problems is this formula:

> *group 1 + group 2 − both + neither = total*
>
> where
>
> *group 1* = the number of entities in one of the two groups
>
> *group 2* = the number of entities in the other group
>
> *both* = the number of entities in both groups
>
> *neither* = the number of entities in neither group
>
> *total* = the total number of entities

You'll most likely be given values for all of the parts of this formula except for one. You'll then have to determine the value of the missing part. Let's see how this works in the following example.

> At a certain animal refuge, 180 animals have four legs, 240 are warm-blooded, and 85 both have four legs and are warm-blooded. If the animal refuge has 500 animals in total, how many animals at the refuge have neither four legs nor are warm-blooded?

If you don't know the formula above, this question could be a nightmare. But the formula makes it very doable. We'll let *group 1* be the 180 animals that have four legs and *group 2* be the 240 animals that are warm-blooded. Since we're also given the number of animals that belong to *both* groups and the *total* number of animals, the missing value is the number of animals that belong to neither group. Not surprisingly, that's what the question is after. Plugging the values into the formula gives:

$$180 + 240 - 85 + neither = 500$$

Solving for *neither* is a simple matter of solving this linear equation with one variable, something we discussed way back in the algebra section. Here goes:

$$180 + 240 - 85 + n = 500$$

$$335 + n = 500$$

$$n = 165$$

Voila! (That's genuine excitement—not a factorial.) But things get a bit more difficult if they throw in an extra group.

Problems with Three Groups

The formula for three-group problems is really long and complicated (it involves nine unique terms!). So, we'll skip it in favor of an easier approach: Venn diagrams. Remember these from junior high? Venn diagrams consist of intersecting circles, in which each circle represents the number of entities in a particular group. For example:

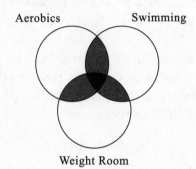

You'll notice that the circles overlap. The upside-down triangular section in the middle, with the darker shading, represents the number of entities that belongs to all three groups. Sections in which only two circles overlap, indicated with the lighter shading, represent the number of entities that belongs to two overlapping groups. The outermost section of each circle, the part that doesn't overlap with any of the other circles, represents the number of entities that belongs to each group alone. For example, in the swimming circle, the outermost section represents the number of swimmers who neither lift weights nor do aerobics.

The key to three-group problems is to work *from the inside out*. Begin with the entities that belong to all three groups, then address the entities that belong to two groups, and finally deal with the entities that belong to only one group.

Here's an example of a three-group problem that conveniently makes use of the diagram above:

> At the Get Fit Athletic Club, every member swims, lifts weights, does aerobics, or participates in some combination of these three activities. Sixty members swim, 75 lift weights, and 100 do aerobics. If 34 members both lift weights and swim, 25 members both do aerobics and swim, 44 members both use the weight room and do aerobics, and 10 participate in all three activities, how many members belong to the Get Fit Athletic Club?

We'll start by filling in values, *working from the inside out*. Since 10 people belong to all three groups, we'll write 10 in the middle section:

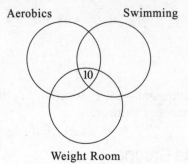

Next, we'll fill in the values for people who belong to two groups. We're told that 25 members participate in aerobics and in swimming, and it would be very tempting to write 25 in the section above the 10. Keep in mind, however, that 10 of these 25 people *have already been accounted for*: The 10 people who participate in all three activities are included among those who participate in aerobics and swimming. That leaves 25 – 10 = 15 people for the aerobics/swimming overlap section above the 10 in the middle. Similarly, 44 people do aerobics and use the weight room. Since 10 of these people have already been accounted for in the middle section, that leaves 44 – 10 = 34 people in the section that overlaps aerobics and weight room. Also, 34 people swim and use the weight room, so we'll write 34 – 10 = 24 in the section overlapping those categories. That brings us to here:

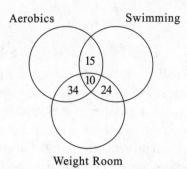

Next we need to fill in values for people who belong to only one group. As with the previous step, we have to be very careful not to count anyone more than once. For example, we're told that 60 members swim. That means that the total of *all* the numbers in the swimming circle must be 60. We already have 10 + 15 + 24 = 49 members in the swimming circle. That leaves 60 – 49 = 11 members for the outermost section of the swimming circle. Similarly, since 75 members use the weight room, that leaves 75 – 10 – 34 – 24 = 7 members for the outermost section of the weight room circle. Finally, since the total of the aerobics circle must be 100, the number in the remaining section must be 100 – 10 – 34 – 15 = 41. Filling these numbers in the appropriate sections of our Venn diagram yields the following:

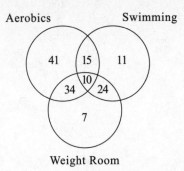

Aerobics   Swimming

41   15   11

10

34   24

7

Weight Room

The problem asks for the total number of club members, and we're told specifically that every member participates in at least one of these activities. That means that no member exists outside of our three circles. We can therefore add all of the values in our diagram to arrive at the total number of club members. This gives us a final answer of 41 + 15 + 11 + 34 + 10 + 24 + 7 = 142.

We realize that this was a bit of work, but Venn diagrams are the only way to go on three-group problems. And the good news is that you'd have to be doing something right on the Math section for the CAT software to throw something *this* nasty your way, since the questions increase in difficulty the better you do.

That finishes up our discussion of data analysis. Keep in mind that the GRE also requires you to analyze data presented in the form of graphs and charts, but we have a whole chapter called Data Interpretation devoted to that. In fact, we have a special chapter devoted specifically to each of the three question types you'll see. It's high time we got to those, where you'll learn how the concepts covered here in Math 101 play out in GRE math questions, as well as effective ways to go about tackling them.

Problem Solving is the first question type we'll cover, and it's up next.

Problem Solving

Now that you've got all those math concepts under your belt, no doubt you're itching to use them. Here's your first chance. As you learned back in chapter 1, Problem Solving (PS) questions are in standard multiple-choice format: a single question, followed by five answer choices. You should be pretty familiar with this type of problem from years of school and standardized tests. So without further ado, let's jump right in and see what they're all about.

PS X-RAY

Here is what a typical Problem Solving question looks like:

<u>Directions:</u> The following question has five answer choices. Select the best of the answer choices given.

Which of the following numbers is prime?

- ○ 1
- ○ 2
- ○ 15
- ○ 32
- ○ 56

Note that the answer choices on the computer screen are preceded by ovals, not letters. We use ovals in the questions in this book to replicate that format, although we stick to letters **A** through **E** in the explanations for the sake of clarity.

Nothing fancy here—you're given a question, then asked to choose the correct answer. You'll choose the answer by clicking on the oval that precedes the choices you want. If you change your mind, you can de-select an answer by clicking on it again or by simply selecting another answer. If you're wondering, the correct answer is **B**, 2. As you may recall from the previous chapter, 1 is not prime because it has only one positive factor, and 15, 32, and 56 all have factors besides 1 and themselves.

PS FUNDAMENTALS

Later in the chapter we'll present a step method that you should employ on every Problem Solving question you face. However, since different problems call for different approaches, one of the steps, "Plan the Attack," is open-ended and calls for you to choose the most effective approach to the problem at hand. So before we get to the step method itself, we'll first demonstrate a standard approach, as well as a few alternative approaches that may come in handy in particular situations. Each approach discussed in this section represents a different way to use the math concepts you reviewed in the previous chapter. We'll cover the following:

- Standard Applications of Math Concepts
- Alternative Approaches for Special Cases

Standard Applications of Math Concepts

There's no need to make things more complicated than they need to be; some questions require nothing more than straightforward applications of the concepts you learned in chapter 2. This doesn't necessarily mean that such questions will be easy, since some of the concepts themselves can be complex, and the test makers occasionally complicate matters by sprinkling traps among the choices. Easier questions often require the application of a single concept, while harder questions may involve multiple concepts. Some may even require you to draw your own diagram when none is given. Regardless of the difficulty level, the standard application approach is the same: Scope out the situation, decide on what concept or concepts are being tested, and then use what you know about those concepts to answer the question before looking at the choices. If you've done your work well, the answer you get will be among the choices on the screen, and you'll click it and move on.

Let's look at a few examples spanning various difficulty levels. We'll take a look at single-concept questions based around one particular math concept, and multiple-concept questions that require you to make use of numerous bits of math knowledge to arrive at the answer. As you'll see, we've bolded all our Math 101 concepts as they come up to make it easier for you to navigate through our explanations.

Single-Concept Questions

Here's an example of the most basic kind of Problem Solving question you'll see:

> What is the value of x if $3x - 27 = 33$?
>
> ○ 2
> ○ 11
> ○ 20
> ○ 27
> ○ 35

The math concept in play here is **equations with one variable**, something you likely remember from junior high school. There's nothing to do here but apply the concept: First isolate the variable by adding 27 to both sides to get $3x = 60$, and then divide both sides by 3 to get $x = 20$, choice **C**. No doubt the test makers include 2 among the answer choices to trap people who accidentally subtracted 27 from both sides, yielding $3x = 6$ and $x = 2$. 11, choice **B**, is what you get if you divide one number in the problem (33) by another (3), and 27, choice **D**, appears in the problem itself. Assuming you didn't fall for any of these traps, there's not much to it: Just apply a single, fairly basic concept directly to the problem to pick up the point.

Not all single-concept questions are necessarily so straightforward, however, especially as you get on in the section. Try this one on for size:

> At a local golf club, 75 members attend weekday lessons, 12 members attend weekend lessons, and 4 members attend both weekday and weekend lessons. If 10 members of the club do not attend any lessons, how many members are in the club?
>
> ○ 65
> ○ 75
> ○ 82
> ○ 93
> ○ 101

There's only one concept in play here, but if you don't know it, you're in for a very tough time. You need the formula for **group problems with two groups:** *group 1 + group 2 – both + neither = total.* This is a formula you probably didn't learn in junior high or high school, or most likely forgot even if you did. You probably won't see a question like this early in the section, but if you're doing well, the CAT's going to challenge you and start spitting out questions from the harder end of the question pool. In any case, it's really only testing whether you've done your homework and memorized the formula.

If you did, then you'd be in great shape, since the math itself is not particularly difficult: If we let *group 1* be the 75 members who attend weekday lessons and let *group 2* be the 12 members who attend weekend lessons, we get: $75 + 12 - 4 + 10 = total$. Solving for total gives 93, choice **D**. Notice how choice **B**, 75, is a number contained in the problem, while choice **E**, 101, is what you get if you mistakenly add 4 instead of subtract it.

Multiple-Concept Questions

Some Problem Solving questions require you to pull together two or more choice tidbits from your arsenal of essential math concepts. One of the most common examples of a multiple-concept question involves geometric formulas that generate equations that need to be solved arithmetically and/or algebraically. Here's an example:

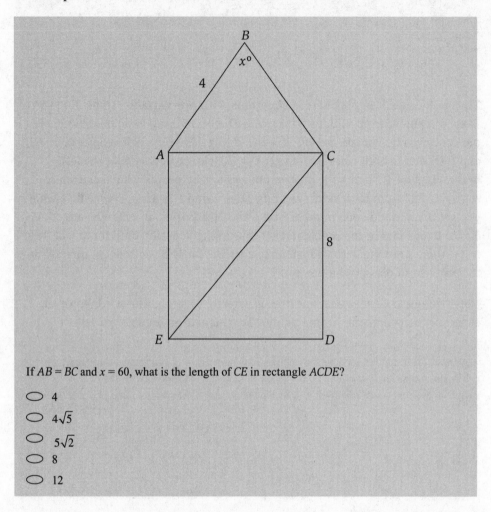

If $AB = BC$ and $x = 60$, what is the length of CE in rectangle $ACDE$?

- 4
- $4\sqrt{5}$
- $5\sqrt{2}$
- 8
- 12

This is a bit more involved than a typical single-concept question because there are a number of geometry concepts you need to know and some genuine opportunities to slip up on the arithmetic end too. It's a mish-mash problem to boot, involving three triangles and a rectangle, so if you don't know the special and exciting properties of these geometric figures, you're pretty much sunk right there. If you do, then you should be able to at least formulate the correct equation for line EC, but then you still have to crunch the numbers to solve it. Let's see what a solid effort on this question might look like.

First, you're best off redrawing the diagram on your scratch paper, since you wouldn't want to keep all the information you're going to add to it in your head. Since AB and BC are equal, $\angle BAC$ and $\angle BCA$ must be equal since the **angles in a triangle opposite from equal sides are equal** (*concept 1*). Since the third angle labeled x equals 60°, $\angle BAC$ and $\angle BCA$ together must total 120° because the **three angles of a triangle add up to 180°** (*concept 2*). Since we determined that

∠*BAC* and ∠*BCA* are equal, they both must be 60°. Notice anything now? **A triangle with three equal angles is an equilateral triangle** (*concept 3*). Since **all three sides in an equilateral triangle are equal** (*concept 4*), *AB* = *BC* = *AC* = 4. Since *ACDE* is a rectangle, and **opposite sides of a rectangle are equal** (*concept 5*), *AC* = *ED* = 4. By now your sketch should look like this:

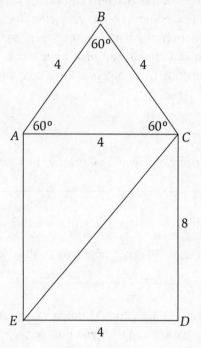

Now that we have two sides of right triangle *ECD*, we have everything we need to figure out the length of *EC*, thanks to the **Pythagorean theorem:** $x^2 + y^2 = z^2$ where *x* and *y* are the sides and *z* is the hypotenuse (*concept 6*). Substituting 4 and 8 as the sides and *EC* as the hypotenuse gives us:

$$(EC)^2 = 4^2 + 8^2$$

For convenience, we'll denote all of the ensuing **arithmetic**, including **simplifying the radical**, as *concept 7*:

$$(EC)^2 = 4^2 + 8^2$$
$$(EC)^2 = 16 + 64$$
$$(EC)^2 = 80$$
$$EC = \sqrt{80}$$
$$EC = \sqrt{16}\sqrt{5}$$
$$EC = 4\sqrt{5}$$

Voila!—choice **B**. Check out the traps: 4 (**A**) is a number calculated along the way; 8 (**D**) is a number given in the problem; and 12 (**E**) is what you get if you add the two known sides of triangle *ECD* together.

Notice that no fewer than seven math concepts made their way into this problem—none of them particularly earth-shattering or treacherous, mind you, but still adding up to a medium-level challenge with plenty of potential pitfalls.

Alternative Approaches for Special Cases

The standard "do question, look for answer" approach is all well and good in many cases, but some questions call out for alternative approaches. When the question contains variables in the answer choices, making up numbers and substituting them into the problem is often very effective. Conversely, when the answer choices contain actual numbers, you may benefit from simply plugging them into the given situation to see which one works, instead of hacking through some difficult arithmetic or algebra. Let's take a look at each of these strategies, one by one.

Making Up Numbers

Which of the following problems would you rather be faced with on test day?

- Question 1: If x apples cost y cents, how much will z apples cost in dollars?

- Question 2: If 5 apples cost 50 cents, how much will 10 apples cost in dollars?

If you're like most people, question 2 looks much easier, and you probably wouldn't have much trouble solving it: If you double the number of apples, you double the number of cents. One hundred cents equals one dollar. Done.

The difference between question 1 and question 2 is simple. We replaced the variables in question 1 with some made-up numbers, thus creating the easier question 2. So, if you see x, y, m, n, or any other variables in both the question and the answer choices, see if you can avoid using complicated algebra by making up numbers and inserting them into the problem. You don't want to just make up any old numbers, however—you want numbers that will simplify the problem. Use the following guidelines:

- **Pick easy numbers.** Although you could choose 582.97 as a value, you definitely wouldn't be making the problem any easier. Stick to relatively small, whole numbers whenever possible.

- **Avoid 0, 1, and any numbers used in the problem.** The numbers 0 and 1 have unique properties that may skew the results when used for this technique, so don't substitute either of those into the problem. (We'll give you the exact opposite advice in the Quantitative Comparisons chapter, since in those questions the special properties of 0 and 1 come in handy.) Also, since the test makers sometimes use numbers from the question to construct distractors, you may get yourself into trouble by selecting those as well. If, for example, the problem contains the expression $3a + 5$, don't use 3 or 5. You shouldn't have any trouble avoiding the few numbers used in the question itself, just for good measure.

- **Choose different numbers for different variables.** For example, if the problem contains the variables m and n, you wouldn't want to choose 2 for both. Instead, you might choose 2 for m and 3 for n.

- **Pay attention to units.** If a problem involves a change in units (such as minutes to hours, pennies to dollars, feet to yards, and so on), choose a number that works well for both units. For example, 120 would be a good choice for a variable representing minutes, since 120 minutes is easily converted into 2 hours.

- **Obey the rules of the problem.** Occasionally, the problem may include specific requirements for variables. For example, if the problem says that x must be negative, you can't make up a positive value for x.

- **Save dependent variables for last.** If the value of one variable is determined by the value of one or more other variables, make up numbers for those other variables first. That will automatically determine the value of the variable that depends on the value of the others. For example, if the problem states that $a = b + c$, a is dependent on b and c. Choose values for b and c first, and the value of a will then simply emerge as the sum of b and c.

Once you've selected your values, an actual number will emerge when you work the problem out with the numbers you've selected. All you need to do then is check which answer choice contains an expression that yields the same value when you make the same substitutions. This will make more sense in the context of an example, so let's apply the strategy to the following question.

> A gear makes r rotations in m minutes. If it rotates at a constant speed, how many rotations will the gear make in h hours?
>
> ○ $\dfrac{60r}{m}$
>
> ○ $\dfrac{60rh}{m}$
>
> ○ $\dfrac{60rm}{h}$
>
> ○ $\dfrac{rh}{m}$
>
> ○ $\dfrac{mrh}{60}$

Sure, you could crunch through this algebraically, and if that floats your boat, great. However, if you're among those who get a headache from just looking at questions like this, making up numbers may be just the way to go. Here's how.

The variables in this problem are r, m, and h. We can make up whatever values we'd like for these, as long as the values we choose make it easy to work the problem. For r, the number of rotations, let's choose something small, like 3. For m, the number of minutes, we should choose a value that will make it easy to convert to hours: 120 works well, since 120 minutes is the same as 2 hours.

Finally, for *h*, we should choose something small again. Remember that we need to choose a different value for each variable, so let's use 4. Now that we have our numbers, simply plug them into the situation:

A gear makes **3** rotations in **120** minutes. If it rotates at a constant speed, how many rotations will the gear make in **4** hours?

Okay, much better—that's something we can sink our teeth into. 120 minutes is the same as 2 hours, during which time the gear rotates 3 times. If it rotates 3 times in 2 hours, how many times will it rotate in 4 hours? That's just twice as much time, so it will make twice as many rotations: 2 × 3 = 6, and so 6 is what we get when we substitute our values into the problem. Now we have to find the answer choice that's equal to 6 when the same values are substituted for its variables. Just work your way down the list, using 3 for *r*, 120 for *m*, and 4 for *h*:

A: $\frac{60r}{m} = \frac{(60)(3)}{120} = \frac{180}{120} = \frac{3}{2}$ That's not 6, the answer we seek, so move on.

B: $\frac{60rh}{m} = \frac{(60)(3)(4)}{120} = \frac{720}{120} = 6$ Yup—this is exactly what we're looking for, so **B** is correct. If you're sure of your work, there's no need to even continue with the choices; you'd just click **B** and move on to the next question. For practice, though, let's see how the other three pan out:

C: $\frac{60rm}{h} = \frac{(60)(3)(120)}{4} = 5,400$ Way too big.

D: $\frac{rh}{m} = \frac{(3)(4)}{120} = \frac{1}{10}$ Way too small.

E: $\frac{mrh}{60} = \frac{(120)(3)(4)}{60} = 24$ Four times bigger than what we're after. Just what we thought: **B** is the only choice that matches the number we derived from our made-up numbers, so **B** gets the point.

You'll get more practice with this strategy as we go forward. Let's now move on to our other specialty technique, an exercise in role reversal that we call . . .

Working Backward

When the question includes an equation (or a word problem that can be translated into an equation), and the answer choices contain relatively simple numbers, then it may be possible to plug the choices into the equation to see which one works. Working backward from the choices in this manner may help you avoid setting up or solving complicated equations and can save you time as well because of a neat wrinkle of this technique: Since the choices in math questions are usually written in either ascending or descending order, you can start with the middle choice, choice **C**, and either get the answer immediately or at least eliminate three choices for the price of one. Here's how.

Let's say the answer choices are in ascending order. If you start by plugging in **C**, then even if that choice doesn't work, you can use the outcome to determine whether you need to plug in a smaller or larger number. If you need a smaller number, then **D** and **E** are out of the question, and you can go right to test choice **A** or **B**. If instead you need a larger number, chop **A** and **B** and try **D** or **E**. Notice another nice feature: When you plug in for the second time, that choice will either work or leave only one choice standing. If you follow this alternative approach, you shouldn't ever have to check more than two choices.

As always, math strategies make the most sense in the context of examples, so we'll demonstrate using the following question.

A classroom contains 31 chairs, each of which has either a cushion or a hard back. If the room has five more cushion chairs than hard-backed chairs, how many cushion chairs does it contain?

○ 10
○ 13
○ 16
○ 18
○ 21

Now if you happen to be an algebra whiz, you'd go ahead and use the information to set up a pair of simultaneous equations to solve the problem. However, you may find it easier to work backward instead. Since the choices are in ascending order, we'll start with the middle one and pretend it's correct. If it really *is* correct, then plugging it into the problem's scenario will cause all the numbers to work out, so let's see if it does.

The question is looking for the number of cushion chairs, which for the moment we're assuming to be 16. We can bounce that number off the information in the beginning of the second sentence (5 more cushion chairs than hard chairs) to determine that with 16 cushion chairs, there would have to be 11 hard chairs. Now all we have to do is check whether this scenario matches the information in the first sentence. Would that give us 31 chairs total? Nope: $16 + 11 = 27$, so the numbers don't jibe. That tells us three things: Choice **C** isn't correct, choice **B** isn't correct, and choice **A** isn't correct. We can knock out **A** and **B** along with **C** because they're both smaller than **C**, and if the number in **C** isn't big enough to get us to our required 31 chairs, **A** and **B** ain't gonna cut it either.

Now let's try **D**—if it works, it's correct, and if it doesn't, we can select **E** without even trying it out: 18 cushion chairs means $18 - 5 = 13$ hard chairs and $18 + 13 = 31$ chairs total. That matches the information in the question, so **D** is correct. Note that you could have worked the numbers the other way: If there are 31 chairs total, and we assume there are 18 cushion chairs, then there would have to be 13 hard chairs. That matches the information in the second sentence that requires 5 more cushion chairs than hard ones. Either way you slice it, the number 18 fits the bill when plugged back into the situation, and we didn't have to bother with creating and solving simultaneous equations.

Use your judgment as to when to work backward. If there are numbers in the answer choices, then consider it, but don't do it if the numbers are unwieldy, such as complex fractions. One of the skills that the best math test takers possess is the ability to determine the most effective way to work through the problems. We've shown you standard applications and a few powerful alternatives. Now let's assimilate what you've learned into the general step method you'll use for all Problem Solving questions.

PS STEP METHOD

Here are the four steps to Problem Solving success:

Step 1: Get the Specs.

Step 2: Plan the Attack.

Step 3: Mine the Math.

Step 4: Power Through.

Let's have a closer look.

Step 1: Get the Specs. Step 1 puts you in the right frame of mind to successfully work through a PS question. The main specifications that should interest you include the following:

- What general subject area—arithmetic, algebra, geometry, or data analysis—is tested?

- What relevant features does the question contain? For example, is it amenable to a straightforward standard application of one or more math concepts? Is it a word problem that requires English-to-math translation? Does it contain variables or manageable numbers in the answer choices that suggest you may want to try an alternative approach? The answers to these questions will help you to plan your attack in Step 2.

- What specific math concepts does the question concern? This will be your catalyst for mining the math in Step 3 and doing the work in Step 4.

Step 2: Plan the Attack. While knowing math concepts cold is necessary to succeed on GRE math, you still need to apply them effectively to solve the problems. In Step 2, you'll determine how you'll use what you know to answer the questions; that is, whether you'll apply math concepts in a standard way and then search the choices for the answer you get, or whether it's better to make up numbers or work backward. Use the information you discover as you scope out the problem in Step 1 to help you decide how to proceed.

Step 3: Mine the Math. With a solid plan in mind, you'll then dig through your storehouse of Math 101 concepts to pick out the ones you'll need to solve the problem. If the question concerns a right triangle, for example, then the Pythagorean theorem and rules for the length of the sides of right triangles should pop into your head. If you're up against exponents, or an arithmetic mean situation, or a quadratic equation, then you'd pull concepts related to those topics from your reservoir of math knowledge. Don't think you have to gather every single concept you'll need at this stage; some necessary concepts will emerge as you proceed through the problem in Step 4. In Step 3, simply dig out the essential math concept or concepts you need to get started. Note that for easy reference, we've bolded all these math concepts whenever they appear in the explanations to our practice questions.

Step 4: Power Through. With relevant math concepts and a plan for how to use them firmly in mind, you'll now be able to power through the question. "Power Through," however, doesn't necessarily imply using brute force, since in many cases clever or elegant solutions may be possible. How you do the work will depend on the method you choose in Step 2, and in many cases the standard approach works fine (hence, we call it "standard"). But in other cases you may settle on one of the alternative approaches we've shown you. Either way, Step 4 is the time to solve the problem and make your selection.

Guided Practice

It's time to test drive the method, so when you feel you have a good sense of the steps, sink your teeth into this:

If $a \neq 0$, then $a^2(a^3)^3 a^{-2} =$

- ○ a^{-36}
- ○ a^{-9}
- ○ a^9
- ○ a^{18}
- ○ a^{36}

Step 1: Get the Specs. The little raised 2s and 3s in the equation tell you you're dealing with exponents, an arithmetic concept, and the huge powers that the as are raised to in the choices suggest it would be insane to try to make up numbers in this case.

Step 2: Plan the Attack. Nothing particularly fancy here—either you know the rules of exponents, or you don't. (If you still don't after our lengthy Math 101 chapter, back to chapter 2 for you!) Our analysis from Step 1 indicates that this problem is best approached via a standard application of the rules of exponents—precisely our concern in the next step.

Step 3: Mine the Math. **The rule of negative exponents states that** $x^{-y} = \dfrac{1}{x^y}$, something you need to know to deal with the a^{-2} part of the expression. Beyond that, **when multiplying terms with exponents containing the same base, we add the exponents, and something raised to a power and then taken to another power requires multiplying those exponents.** These are the relevant math concepts you may need to call upon to simplify the expression.

Step 4: Power Through. Based on the concepts discussed above, $a^{-2} = \dfrac{1}{a^2}$. That means we can rewrite the expression as $\dfrac{a^2(a^3)^3}{a^2}$, and cancel out the a^2 from the top and bottom, leaving $(a^3)^3$. Multiplying the exponents gives us our final answer, a^9, choice **C**.

PRACTICE PROBLEMS

This question type is called Problem Solving, after all, so you may as well get some practice solving some problems. There may be more than one effective way to solve any given problem, so remember to use Step 2 of the PS step method and give some thought as to the approach that might work best for you before jumping in. See how you make out with the problems in the set, and then review the guided explanations that follow.

Directions: The following questions have five answer choices. Select the best of the answer choices given.

1. Working together at a constant rate, machines L, M, and N can produce a total of 200 bolts in 4 hours. If machine L can produce 20 bolts in 30 minutes, and machines M and N work at the same constant rate as each other, how many bolts can machine M produce in 1 hour?

    ○ 5
    ○ 10
    ○ 20
    ○ 30
    ○ 50

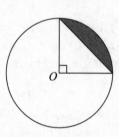

2. If the area of the circle above with center O is 36π, what is the area of the shaded region?

    ○ $6\sqrt{2}$
    ○ $9\pi - 18$
    ○ $3\pi + 6\sqrt{2}$
    ○ 9π
    ○ $36\pi - 18$

3. The average (arithmetic mean) of the first five numbers in a group of ten positive integers is 110. The sum of the remaining numbers in the group is 250. What is the average (arithmetic mean) of all ten numbers?

○ 22
○ 36
○ 50
○ 80
○ 180

4. What is .5 percent of 55?

○ .275
○ 2.75
○ 27.5
○ 50
○ 110

5. A coin flipped a number of times landed on heads y more times than twice the number of times it landed on tails. If h is the number of times the coin landed on heads, how many times was the coin flipped, expressed in terms of h and y?

○ $h + y$

○ $y + \dfrac{h}{2}$

○ $\dfrac{h - y}{2}$

○ $\dfrac{3h - y}{2}$

○ $\dfrac{3h - y}{2}$

Guided Explanations

1. **A**

Step 1: Get the Specs. That's sure an awful lot of words for a math question, which tells us we've entered word problem territory. Specifically, we're asked to determine the number of bolts that can be made in an hour, so it's a *work* kind of word problem. (It doesn't hurt that the first word of the question is *working*, another clue as to what kind of problem we're up against.) The numbers in the choices seem fairly manageable, so we'll take that into account as we move on to Step 2.

Step 2: Plan the Attack. Since there are straightforward numbers in the choices, you may have been tempted to work backward. But since there's really only one basic formula for work problems, we'll go for the standard approach and see how that pans out.

Step 3: Mine the Math. The only real piece of math we need is the **work formula: rate × time = amount.** We will, however, need to be careful to keep the units straight, since time in the problem is expressed both in minutes and in hours.

Step 4: Power Through. Applying the work formula from Step 3 to the first sentence of the problem gives rate × 4 hours = 200 bolts for all three machines working together. We can then solve for rate by dividing both sides of the equation by 4, yielding rate = 50 bolts per hour for all three machines working together. The next most concrete piece of information concerns machine L: It alone can produce 20 bolts in 30 minutes. Since we've been dealing with hours so far, let's keep it that way and multiply both sides by 2 to convert L's rate to 40 bolts per hour. Now we're getting somewhere: If all three machines can turn out 50 bolts in an hour, and machine L alone can turn out 40 in one hour, then machines M and N together must account for 50 − 40 = 10 bolts per hour. Since we're told that machines M and N have identical rates, each must produce 10 ÷ 2 = 5 bolts per hour, choice **A**.

2. **B**

Step 1: Get the Specs. The diagram pretty much gives it away: Geometry is the name of this game, and a mish-mash challenge at that given the overlap between the circle, right triangle, and shaded region. The choices are pretty intimidating, so it doesn't appear as if it will be helpful to work backward from them.

Step 2: Plan the Attack. Looks like we'll just go the traditional route and work our way through the question, keeping in mind that mish-mash problems often require us to recognize which pieces of which geometric figures overlap with the other figures.

Step 3: Mine the Math. Area is the key element here, so at the very least
circle area $= \pi r^2$ and **triangle area** $= \frac{1}{2}$ **base** $\times$ **height** should spring to mind
to get you heading in the right direction. Since this is a multiple-concept ques-
tion, a few other bits and pieces of math knowledge may be needed, but we'll
cross those bridges when we come to them.

Step 4: Power Through. We're asked for the area of the shaded region, but as is
often the case in mish-mashes, we have to step back and consider how the
shaded area might be the result of simpler shapes. Even though it looks like a
complicated shape, the right angle at the center tells us the shaded region is
really just a quarter circle with a right triangle subtracted from it. Since the area
of the whole circle is 36π, the area of the quarter circle must be $\frac{36\pi}{4} = 9\pi$.

Now we need the area of the right triangle. Since the area of the whole circle is
36π, we can use the trusty area formula recalled in Step 3 above to solve for r:

$$\pi r^2 = 36\pi$$

$$r^2 = 36$$

$$r = 6$$

Both of the lines that intersect O are radii, so each must have a length of 6. Since
the base and height of the right triangle are 6, its area is $\frac{1}{2} \times 6 \times 6 = 18$. Subtracting this area from the area of the quarter circle yields the area of the shaded
region, $9\pi - 18$, which is choice **B**.

Before we leave this one, we'd like to make a quick point about approximating.
We discussed the importance of approximating answers in our chapter 1 introduction to GRE math. If you were stuck for a guess in this problem, estimating
the answer would have been an excellent approach. The area of the entire circle
is 36π, or about 120 (recall that π **is roughly equal to 3.14**). The shaded region
is just a small portion of that, and it looks to be less than one-tenth of the whole
figure. That means that the correct answer should be less than 12, eliminating
C, **D**, and **E**. To decide between **A** and **B**, keep in mind that the correct answer to
a problem involving a circle often contains π. This makes **B** the best guess, even
if you blanked on the problem otherwise.

---

3.   **D**

Step 1: Get the Specs. The problem clearly concerns averages and contains basic
numbers in the choices. We'll get to the specifics soon enough, but there's not
much more to notice at this point.

Step 2: Plan the Attack. You can certainly go with a straightforward application
of the arithmetic mean formula, but let's, for the sake of practice, use our alternative working-backward approach.

Step 3: Mine the Math. The problem involves averages, so we'll need to call to mind the standard formula $\textbf{average} = \dfrac{\textbf{sum of terms}}{\textbf{\# of terms}}$.

Step 4: Power Through. Since the choices are in ascending order, we'll start with **C**, the middle one. This, as we demonstrated earlier, allows us to knock off three choices by testing just one—or, of course, get the answer straightaway if **C** happens to be correct. Let's work with the info in the first two sentences of the problem and then see whether 50 works as the final answer.

Manipulating the formula from Step 3 results in *sum of terms = (average) × (# of terms)*. If five numbers average out to 110, then the sum of those five numbers is 110 × 5 = 550. We're told that the sum of the remaining five numbers is 250, which means the sum of all ten numbers must be 550 + 250 = 800. Now let's see if choice **C** fits with this calculation. If the average of all ten numbers is 50, then the sum of all ten would be 50 × 10 = 500, which doesn't match the 800 figure we just calculated. So not only is **C** incorrect, but we can also see that it's too small, which means choices **A** and **B**, containing even smaller values, must be incorrect as well. All we have to do now is try one of the two remaining choices; either it will work, or the other choice will be correct. **D** works. An average of 80 for all ten numbers yields a sum of 80 × 10 = 800, which does match the total of 800 we calculated initially. **D** is therefore correct.

You may have gone with a traditional application of the arithmetic mean formula all the way through, instead of stopping to work backward from the choices. That's fine if it worked for you. Still, give some thought to the working-backward strategy demonstrated above to see if you may have been able to get the answer faster and with less risk.

---

4.   **A**

Step 1: Get the Specs. Not much to it, is there? Straight arithmetic, nothing too crazy.

Step 2: Plan the Attack. A straightforward approach is the way to go. We'll dig out the math concept we need, and use it to do the math.

Step 3: Mine the Math. Adding the word *percent* to a number means taking that number two places to the left when converting it to a decimal. For example, 20 percent = .2. In this example, .5 percent = .005. The other thing you need to know is that the word *of* means multiplication; whenever we take a certain percent of something, we multiply the figures.

Step 4: Power Through. Let's do the math: .005 × 55 = .275, which is choice **A**. Maybe you just multiplied it out by hand, or instead used approximations to get into the ballpark. Here's one way you can work through it without actually multiplying: 10 percent of 55 is 5.5, so to get 1 percent of 55, we just move the decimal place back one more place, giving us .55. Now, .5 percent is half of 1 percent, so we have to divide .55 by 2, which gives us .275.

As for the distractors, 2.75 (**B**) is what you get if you ignore the decimal point and take 5 percent of 55. 27.5 (**C**) is what you get if you ignore the word *percent* and simply take .5 of 55. 50 (**D**) is what you get if you subtract 5 from 55, and 110 (**E**) is what you get if you double 55, perhaps by mistakenly translating the problem into 55 ÷ .5. So while the question is a straightforward test of your arithmetic knowledge, there are still a few concepts you need to know, some steps you need to perform, and some traps that could potentially trip you up.

---

5. **E**

Step 1: Get the Specs. The presence of a coin in the problem might initially suggest a data analysis probability problem, but that's not how it plays out—it's actually an algebra question. We're given a word problem that requires some English-to-math translation, and some scary-looking expressions containing variables in the choices. These are the basic aspects of the problem that should catch your eye.

Step 2: Plan the Attack. Word problems containing variables lend themselves naturally to algebraic solutions, so if you're comfortable with algebra, you could power through this one by setting up and solving some basic equations. Alternatively, the variables scattered across the answer choices suggest that this problem may also lend itself well to our making-up-numbers strategy, so you may have chosen that route instead. Tell you what—for practice, we'll do both.

Step 3: Mine the Math. For the algebraic approach, you'll need to draw on your knowledge of **constructing and solving multiple equations.** For both approaches, you'll need to correctly **translate the English into math.**

Step 4: Power Through, *Algebra Style*. First, the English-to-math translation: If we designate tails as t, then "twice the number of times it landed on tails" is $2t$. y more times than "twice the number of times it landed on tails" is therefore $2t + y$. Using h for heads as instructed, our equation becomes $h = 2t + y$. The question is looking for the total number of flips, which is the number of heads plus the number of tails, or $h + t$. However, the question asks for the total expressed in terms of h and y. No problem—we can solve for t in terms of y in our first equation and substitute that into the equation representing the total:

$$h = 2t + y$$
$$2t = h - y$$
$$t = \frac{h - y}{2}$$

Now replace t with this new value in the total equation:

$$\text{total flips} = h + t$$
$$= h + \frac{h - y}{2}$$

Now some basic arithmetic is in order, making this a multiple-concept question. We can use the Magic X to simplify our equation to

$$\text{total flips} = \frac{2h + h - y}{2} \text{ or } \frac{3h - y}{2} \text{, choice } \mathbf{E}$$

Step 5: Power Through by Making Up Numbers. Okay, so what if all those equations in the previous solution look like Egyptian hieroglyphics to you? Then the "make up numbers" alternative approach is the way to go. We start the same way by translating the wording of the question into the expression $h = 2t + y$. Variable h is the dependent variable because its value is determined by the values of t and y, so when it comes to picking numbers, we'll want to save h for last. In this case, we'll only need to use our imagination for t and y, since h will follow from those. And remember to go with simple numbers—why make your life more difficult than it needs to be? $t = 2$ is friendly enough; a nice small number that's easy to double. $2t$ is 4, so if we set $y = 6$, then h will be an even 10, giving us:

$$t = 2$$
$$y = 6$$
$$h = 10$$

With all the variables set, we can focus on what the question is after. The total number of flips equals the number of heads plus the number of tails. In our imaginary world, that's $10 + 2 = 12$. Now we simply need to determine which combination of hs and ys in the choices calculates to 12. Let's try them out.

A: $h + y = 10 + 6 = 16$ No good.

B: $y + \dfrac{h}{2} = 6 + 5 = 11$ Nope.

C: $\dfrac{h - y}{2} - \dfrac{4}{2} = 2$ Uh-uh.

D: $\dfrac{3y - h}{3} = \dfrac{8}{3}$ Not even close.

E: $\dfrac{3h - y}{2} = \dfrac{24}{2} = 12$ That's the one. **E** is correct, no matter which approach we take.

We presented two solutions to this final problem, both to give you extra practice and to remind you of the old, somewhat sadistic saying "There are many ways to skin a cat"—not that we can figure out why anyone would want to. While there are definite math concepts to know and specific options for applying them, you should always attempt to determine the approach that works best *for you* in each situation.

You'll get more practice with Problem Solving in the practice test at the end of the book. For now, let's move on to our next, slightly more complicated math question type, Quantitative Comparisons.

Chapter 4

Quantitative Comparisons

So, how does this math question grab you?

$$144^6 = ?$$

D'oh! Not fun, huh? It would take a heavy-duty calculator, something you have no access to on the GRE, to come up with the correct answer of just under 9 trillion. That's *trillion*, with a *tr*, with the "just under" clocking in at around *100 billion*—numbers you'll thankfully never see on the GRE. But what about this question:

What is larger, 144^6 or 11^{12}?

Well, that's more like it—something definitely GRE-worthy. But how, you may wonder, can you figure out which of these two quantities is bigger if you can't even figure out the value of the first one? That's the beauty of it—you don't *have to* figure out the actual values; you just have to figure out how to *compare* them. We can make this much easier by using a technique called "mirroring," which we'll cover later in this chapter: Since 144 is the same as 12×12, 144 multiplied by itself 6 times (which is what 144^6 means) is the same thing as 12×12 multiplied by itself 6 times, which is the same as 12 multiplied by itself 12 times, or 12^{12}. Now we can see that 12^{12} is greater than 11^{12}, so 144^6 must be greater than 11^{12}, and we have our answer. No fuss, no muss, and certainly no calculating into the trillions involved. (If the exponents in this example are making your head spin, go back and review that section in chapter 2 on pages 53–58).

As the name implies, Quantitative Comparison questions (QCs) ask you to compare the sizes of two given quantities. That's not to say that some QCs won't benefit from some actual computation—they do rely on the same basic concepts as other GRE math questions, and sometimes, when the calculations aren't difficult, crunching the numbers *will* be the way to go. However, the QCs that usually throw people are the ones requiring math *reasoning*, not number-crunching, so we'll show you how to find the shortcuts you need—such as the one described above—to cut these down to size.

QCs have an unusual format that you've probably never dealt with before, so let's first clear up the mechanics of the question type. The following X-ray should do the trick.

QC X-RAY

Here's a typical QC, complete with directions. Don't attempt the question just yet—we'll get to it in just a bit.

Directions: Each of the following questions consists of two quantities, one in Column A and one in Column B. You are to compare the quantity in Column A with the quantity in Column B and decide whether:

(A) The quantity in Column A is greater.
(B) The quantity in Column B is greater.
(C) The two quantities are equal.
(D) The relationship cannot be determined from the information given.

In a question, there may be additional information, centered above the two columns, that concerns one or both of the quantities to be compared. A symbol that appears in both columns represents the same thing in Column A as it does in Column B.

A certain bread recipe calls for water, flour, and yeast to be mixed in a ratio of 4:5:2 ounces, respectively.

Column A	Column B
The amount of flour needed to make 220 ounces of bread according to the recipe	100 ounces

○ The quantity in Column A is greater.
○ The quantity in Column B is greater.
○ The two quantities are equal.
○ The relationship cannot be determined from the information given.

The directions are fairly self-explanatory: You're given two quantities and asked to figure out whether one is definitely bigger than the other, if they're equal, or if you don't have enough information to tell. The quantities may be absolute numbers or may include variables—a difference of no small importance when it comes to strategy, as you'll soon see. Sometimes the test makers will provide additional information above the columns as part of the question, sometimes not. In this case, the additional information is the sentence describing the ingredient ratios for the bread recipe. Any additional symbols or variables provided mean the same thing for both quantities.

QC answer choices are always the same, so it pays to memorize them right now. And notice the major difference between these questions and all of the other math questions on the GRE: *There are only four choices.* Hey, that improves your odds right there, even if you have to take a blind guess. Of course, the purpose of this chapter is to help you keep blind guessing to a minimum.

QC FUNDAMENTALS

Here's a rundown of the QC fundamentals, the main things you need to know about this question type before you solidify your approach with the step method presented later in the chapter. Just like in Problem Solving, we'll present you with multiple approaches, which you'll choose from, depending on the specifics of each question you face. Here's what we'll cover:

- Disguised Problem Solving

- Math Logic

- Shortcuts for Number Problems

- Shortcuts for Variable Problems

- Working with Diagrams

Disguised Problem Solving

To drive home the point that comparison is the *raison d'être* of this question type, some books and courses suggest that you'll never need to perform calculations on QCs. We believe that's taking things too far. The truth is, sometimes calculating the values to compare them is the fastest, easiest, and surest way to go, especially on questions in the beginning of the section where the CAT program is simply getting a feel for whether you know how the QC question format works. Despite the relatively odd format, some QC questions are little more than Problem Solving questions in disguise and benefit from the kinds of standard applications of math concepts we discussed in the previous chapter. The only difference is that once you get your answer, you won't search for it among the choices but will instead compare your answer to the quantity or expression presented in the other column. Let's turn the page and look at a few examples.

Single-Column Calculations

A very common QC format consists of a typical Problem Solving type of question in Column A and a number to compare your answer to in Column B. Here's an example (the same one you saw earlier in the X-ray):

A certain bread recipe calls for water, flour, and yeast to be mixed in a ratio of 4:5:2 ounces, respectively.

Column A	Column B
The amount of flour needed to make 220 ounces of bread according to the recipe	100 ounces

○ The quantity in Column A is greater.
○ The quantity in Column B is greater.
○ The two quantities are equal.
○ The relationship cannot be determined from the information given.

There's simply nothing to do here but use one of the Math 101 concepts, in this case, the **mixture ratio formula: Set x equal to the factor by which each element is multiplied in the final mixture.*** In this case, that produces the equation $4x + 5x + 2x = 220$. Adding the x terms gives $11x = 220$, and dividing both sides by 11 gives $x = 20$. Flour corresponds to the 5 term in the ratio, so there are $(5)(20) = 100$ ounces of flour in the bread. Simply comparing that with the number in Column B tells us that the columns are equal, and **C** is correct.

Double-Column Calculations

Other QCs may require you to use your Problem Solving skills to figure out the values in *both* columns. Here's a fairly simple example that you might see near the beginning of the Math section:

$$x + 3y = 15$$

$$y + 12 = 16$$

Column A	Column B
x	y

○ The quantity in Column A is greater.
○ The quantity in Column B is greater.
○ The two quantities are equal.
○ The relationship cannot be determined from the information given.

---

* Note that in keeping with the convention established in the previous chapter, we'll continue to bold the concepts from Math 101 as they come up in the solutions to problems. See pages 27–143 if you need to brush up on any of these basic principles.

Now, we could knock ourselves out looking for clever, elegant shortcuts to solve this, but the truth is, it's just not necessary. (Later, you'll see examples for which such shortcuts are appropriate.) The math is far from difficult, so as the sneaker commercial implores, we should *just do it*. Subtracting 12 from both sides of the second equation allows us to determine that $y = 4$. Substituting 4 for y in the first equation gives us $x + (3)(4) = 15$, which simplifies to $x + 12 = 15$ and $x = 3$. Four is bigger than 3, so Column B is bigger than Column A, meaning choice **B** is correct.

This may seem fairly simple, but at least one QC question will most likely contain relatively basic math while really testing whether you understand the question format. Here's another example of a QC that's nothing more than a Problem Solving challenge without the standard choices:

$$20 < n < 22$$

Column A	Column B
$\dfrac{14}{n}$	$\dfrac{1}{2} + \dfrac{1}{6}$

○ The quantity in Column A is greater.
○ The quantity in Column B is greater.
○ The two quantities are equal.
○ The relationship cannot be determined from the information given.

Column B contains a straightforward fraction addition, and we can use the **Magic X** to determine that the sum equals 6×1, or 6, $+ 2 \times 1$, or 2, divided by the product of the denominators, 12. That comes out to $\dfrac{8}{12}$, or $\dfrac{2}{3}$. (If you're still not up on the Magic X, review it in Math 101. If you prefer adding simple fractions the standard way, that's fine too.) As for Column A, 21 is as good as any value to substitute for n, since n is limited to values between 20 and 22. It works out nicely too: $\dfrac{14}{21}$ simplifies to $\dfrac{2}{3}$, so the quantities are equal, right?

Wrong. The quantities *could* be equal, but there are more numbers between 20 and 22 than just 21. Remember, **fractions and decimals exist between any two integers.** If the question doesn't specify integers only, then fractions and decimals are in play as well. If we set n equal to 20.5, then the value of Column A would be larger than $\dfrac{2}{3}$. Similarly, if we make n equal to 21.5, then Column A would be smaller than $\dfrac{2}{3}$. So the correct answer is **D**—there's not enough information to make a surefire determination. Note that if the test makers included the additional requirement that "n is an integer," then the quantities would be equal and the answer would be **C**, since 21 is the only integer between 20 and 22.

The bottom line is that some QCs merely require you to apply your Math 101 concepts in standard ways to come up with values to use in your comparisons.

When you have to "power through," Problem Solving–style, do it. Some questions will naturally be more difficult than others, but the way you go about it should be familiar enough.

Many other QCs, however, call for a different approach. There are, in fact, numerous ways to cut QCs down to size so that you don't have to power through full-fledged calculations. The first involves using a bit of cleverness to save you time and effort.

Math Logic

The GRE test makers point out that the Math section tests more than just your knowledge of math concepts; it also tests something they call *quantitative reasoning*. There are enough big words floating around in GRE lingo, so we'll just call this *math logic*. It refers to the ability to reason logically using math concepts, rather than simply crunching the numbers. Let's look at a couple of forms of math logic at work.

Basic Deductive Reasoning

Some questions hinge on a basic deduction. It's not that such deductions are necessarily difficult or obscure—many test takers simply don't know they're supposed to look for them. That's part of that old-school mindset that we discussed in chapter 1, the mindset that you need to change if you want to succeed on this section. While it's true that to a certain extent deductive reasoning, or cleverness, can't be taught, we can teach you to recognize situations in which these things may be required. Our practice questions will also help you hone the math logic skills you already possess. Consider, for example, the following QC:

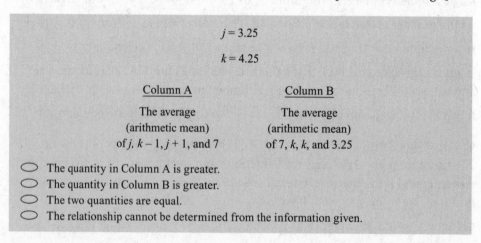

$j = 3.25$

$k = 4.25$

Column A	Column B
The average (arithmetic mean) of j, $k-1$, $j+1$, and 7	The average (arithmetic mean) of 7, k, k, and 3.25

○ The quantity in Column A is greater.
○ The quantity in Column B is greater.
○ The two quantities are equal.
○ The relationship cannot be determined from the information given.

A few bits of math logic can greatly simplify your task here. First, the numbers given for j and k are unwieldy, so the clever test taker will realize right off the bat that she's probably not expected to just plug them into the arithmetic mean formula to solve for the quantities in both columns. Sure, you could try that, but it might be a long slog, fraught with the risk of careless mistakes. Having realized that there's probably a shortcut, the clever test taker might then realize that 3.25 is exactly one less than 4.25; in other words, that $j = k - 1$. This is a particularly helpful deduction since $k - 1$ happens to be a term in Column A. Hey, that also means that $k = j + 1$, another term that shows up in Column A. 3.25 in Column B is merely the same as j, so recognizing that might help our cause too.

If you think the cleverness ends there, think again: The **average formula states that average is equal to the sum of the terms divided by the number of the terms.** It follows that adding the same number to two averages containing the same number of terms would be a wash, which means we can ignore the 7 altogether. If we were looking for the actual averages here, we'd have to use the 7, but since we're only interested in *comparing* the two averages, we can ditch it. All of these realizations fall into the category of *math logic*; using reason in the context of Math 101 concepts to simplify the QC.

Now that we've taken it this far, we may as well solve it. Through the deductions above, we've essentially translated the columns into this:

$$j = 3.25$$

$$k = 4.25$$

$$j = k - 1$$

$$k = j + 1$$

Column A	Column B
The average (arithmetic mean) of j, j, and k	The average (arithmetic mean) of k, k, and j

We went ahead and changed the 3.25 in Column B into j to resemble the j's in Column A—another example of "mirroring," a concept we've already seen and will discuss more later. Since k is larger than j, the average of two ks and a j must be larger than the average of two js and a k, so **B** is correct. Notice again how math reasoning entered the picture based on an understanding of how averages work, even here in the final step.

Overall, a deduction, a couple of clever substitutions, and the strategic deletion of the 7s allowed us to compare the quantities without actually doing any math. Try to use reason in place of brute force whenever the quantities in the question seem unmanageable. But if the quantities look easy enough, go ahead and power through.

Missing Info

Another way to use math logic is to home in on the essentials of the concept under consideration to help you recognize right off the bat that you don't have enough information to answer the question. It may be possible to select choice **D** without crunching any numbers if you notice that a piece is missing from a required formula. For example, see if you can spot what's missing here:

Train x traveled 175 miles to Daling Farm at an average rate of 70 miles per hour. Train y traveled to Daling Farm at an average rate of 85 miles per hour.

Column A	Column B
The time it took train x to travel to Daling Farm	The time it took train y to travel to Daling Farm

- ○ The quantity in Column A is greater.
- ○ The quantity in Column B is greater.
- ○ The two quantities are equal.
- ○ The relationship cannot be determined from the information given.

The handy distance formula should pop into your head immediately: **rate × time = distance.** Now, we have two of those variables for train x but only one variable for train y. So while we can figure out the time it took train x to get to Daling Farm, we're missing a key piece of information regarding train y's journey: namely, how far it traveled. The fact that y traveled faster than x might lead some to conclude that y got there sooner. However, y may have come from much farther away, so **D** is correct.

The moral is this: As soon as you call up a formula to use in a QC question, first check to see if you have all the relevant facts you need to solve it. If not, don't waste another second—choose **D** and move on.

Shortcuts for Number Problems

QCs come in two main varieties: problems that contain variables and problems that don't. In this section, we provide you with strategies to simplify and shorten your work on QCs containing only numbers. Some of these strategies may overlap with math logic, but we think they're important enough to present in their own category.

Chopping Choice D

We ended the previous section with a discussion of one good reason to select choice **D**: not enough information. Now we're going to tell you a reason *not* to choose it: when the quantities in the two columns contain no variables.

Why can't **D** be the answer if the columns contain only numbers? Because values are values. It doesn't matter if you can't figure out the size of one or both; the fact remains that one must be bigger than the other, or they must be equal. There are no other alternatives. If the columns contain only numbers, never choose **D**. Even if you find yourself totally baffled, if there are no variables involved, guess among **A**, **B**, and **C**. If nothing else, you'll increase your odds to one out of three.

Approximating

We discussed the value of approximating in chapter 1's General Math Strategies. Approximating comes in particularly handy in some QCs since, as you've already seen, you don't always need to calculate precise answers to effectively compare the quantities. As a quick refresher, here's the approximation example we presented in that earlier chapter, already in QC form:

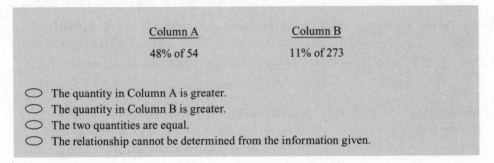

Column A

48% of 54

Column B

11% of 273

○ The quantity in Column A is greater.
○ The quantity in Column B is greater.
○ The two quantities are equal.
○ The relationship cannot be determined from the information given.

We demonstrated how one could quickly eyeball these quantities to approximate their values: Less than half of 54 is less than 27, and more than 10% of 273 is more than 27. A quick dose of solid math logic helps us to choose **B** without having to perform any tedious calculations. You'll get lots of practice with approximating when we get to Data Interpretation in the following chapter.

Positive vs. Negative Numbers

The test makers get a lot of mileage out of positive and negative numbers. Sometimes they'll test your understanding in a straightforward Problem Solving question. You know the kind: "If such and such is true, which of the following must be positive," or something along those lines. But a solid understanding of what makes numbers positive or negative can really come in handy in QCs. You won't need to perform difficult or time-consuming calculations if you can instead compare the two quantities on the basis of where they fall in relation to the zero point. As always, the concept makes the most sense in the context of an example, so let's do one. See how this QC strikes you:

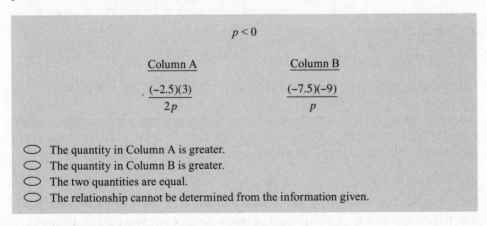

$p < 0$

Column A

$$\frac{(-2.5)(3)}{2p}$$

Column B

$$\frac{(-7.5)(-9)}{p}$$

○ The quantity in Column A is greater.
○ The quantity in Column B is greater.
○ The two quantities are equal.
○ The relationship cannot be determined from the information given.

Many test takers would assume that because we don't know the exact value of p here, the answer must be "not enough information," choice **D**. Those test takers would be wrong. The additional information tells us that p is less than 0, which means p is a negative number (which is why we include this one in this section on number problems). The numerator and denominator of the fraction in Column A must both be negative since **the product of a negative and a positive number is negative.** Since the numerator and denominator in Column A are both negative, the fraction itself must be positive. The fraction in Column B, however, is negative, since **two negatives in the numerator multiply out to a positive,** which is then divided by a negative denominator. So without even knowing the value of p, we can use our knowledge of number properties to determine that Column A is positive and Column B is negative, which means choice **A** is correct.

Also keep in mind that **anything multiplied by 0 is 0,** and that **0 divided by any number is also 0.** If 0 turns up as one of the quantities, determining whether the quantity in the other column is positive or negative (or also 0) will give you the answer without having to figure out its exact value.

Greater than 1 vs. Less than 1

They say 1 is the loneliest number. We don't know about that, but we do know that for the sake of GRE QCs, 1 is one of the most helpful numbers around. Some QCs that appear to contain complex calculations can be solved by noting whether each quantity is greater or less than 1. Consider the following:

Column A	Column B
$\frac{11}{21} + \frac{15}{29}$	$\left(\frac{11}{21}\right)^2 \times \left(\frac{15}{29}\right)^3$

○ The quantity in Column A is greater.
○ The quantity in Column B is greater.
○ The two quantities are equal.
○ The relationship cannot be determined from the information given.

Who wants to add the unwieldy numbers in Column A, or face the nightmare in Column B? Not you, that's who. Luckily there's a quick way around this. Did you notice anything interesting about the fractions in Column A? $\frac{11}{22}$ would be exactly equal to $\frac{1}{2}$, so $\frac{11}{21}$ must be more than $\frac{1}{2}$. Same for the second fraction: $\frac{15}{30}$ is equal to $\frac{1}{2}$, so $\frac{15}{29}$ must be more than $\frac{1}{2}$. We now have two numbers, each greater than $\frac{1}{2}$, added together, which means Column A is more than 1.

The quantity in Column B, on the other hand, must be less than 1. That's because **a fraction between 0 and 1 raised to a power results in a smaller fraction between 0 and 1,** and **multiplying two fractions between 0 and 1 results in another fraction between 0 and 1.** Without having to crunch through the difficult math, we can still determine that Column A must be greater than Column B by checking each quantity's relationship to the number 1.

Mirroring

Mirroring is a technique whereby you make the values given in one column look like the values in the other column. Notice we're not saying you should solve for either quantity—just get them into the same basic form so you'll be able to figure out which, if either, is bigger. We've seen this technique in action twice already: in the introduction to the chapter, where we expressed 144^6 as 12^{12} to compare it to 11^{12} more easily, and in the averages questions, where we used some cleverness to delete an identical number and express both columns in simple terms of j and k. Here we'll tackle a mirroring example with numbers; later we'll see more examples of mirroring in problems containing variables. (You may note that the question below does contain a variable, but it's defined numerically in the additional information, so we'll consider this a numbers problem.) Try to work some mirroring magic on the following:

$$n > 2$$

Column A	Column B
$\dfrac{1}{2} + \dfrac{1}{27} + \dfrac{1}{277}$	$\dfrac{1}{27} + \dfrac{1}{277} + \dfrac{1}{n}$

○ The quantity in Column A is greater.
○ The quantity in Column B is greater.
○ The two quantities are equal.
○ The relationship cannot be determined from the information given.

The key is to recognize the repeated terms and cancel them out. Since the terms $\dfrac{1}{27} + \dfrac{1}{277}$ appear in both quantities, we can disregard them since they add the same amount to both and are thus a wash. That reduces the problem to a comparison between $\dfrac{1}{2}$ and $\dfrac{1}{n}$, with the condition that n is greater than 2. **As n gets larger and larger, the fraction $\dfrac{1}{n}$ gets smaller and smaller.** $\dfrac{1}{3}$ is less than $\dfrac{1}{2}$, and even substituting fractions between 2 and 3 for n doesn't change the relationship; Column B will still be less than $\dfrac{1}{2}$ if n is greater than 2, so **A** is correct.

Notice that if instead of the condition $n > 2$ the test makers specified $n > 1$, then **D** would be correct, since then the quantities could be equal (if n is exactly 2) or Column B could even be greater (if n is between 1 and 2). So you have to pay very careful attention to all aspects of QC questions, since the slightest change in the quantities, or the additional information provided, could make a big difference.

This is a fairly simple example of mirroring. You saw some more difficult examples earlier, and you'll see a particularly tough mirroring example involving exponents in the practice set at the end of the chapter. But right now, more mirroring is on hand as we move to our discussion of how to handle QCs containing variables.

Shortcuts for Variable Problems

The strategies discussed in the previous section should give you a great sense of the options you have when dealing with QCs made up only of numbers. However, many QCs contain variables as well, so let's take a look at a couple of powerful approaches to handling these, beginning with a continuation of the mirroring technique.

Mirroring

The same mirroring technique that applies to pure numbers applies to quantities containing variables: If you can manipulate the expressions in Columns A and B to resemble each other, you may not need to actually solve anything to get the answer. One way to mirror quantities with variables is to reduce or multiply them out, and again we saw an example of this back in chapter 1. We'll repeat it here for your convenience to remind you of the technique, but this time in QC form:

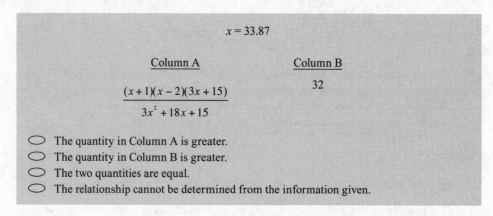

$$x = 33.87$$

Column A	Column B
$\dfrac{(x+1)(x-2)(3x+15)}{3x^2 + 18x + 15}$	32

○ The quantity in Column A is greater.
○ The quantity in Column B is greater.
○ The two quantities are equal.
○ The relationship cannot be determined from the information given.

While we might consider this one basically a Problem Solving question in disguise, the mess in Column A needs some serious work since we really don't want to plug 33.87 into it. A root canal may be more fun. But we can get around that by mirroring the numerator and denominator, in this case by **multiplying terms** in the numerator, or by **factoring** the denominator. As we saw back in chapter 1, the denominator factors into $(3x + 15)(x + 1)$, and we can cancel these terms out of both the numerator and denominator, leaving the whole expression as $(x - 2)$. If we then simply substitute 33.87 for x, the value in Column A becomes 31.87, which is less than 32. So Column B is bigger, and choice **B** is correct.

See how you do with this one:

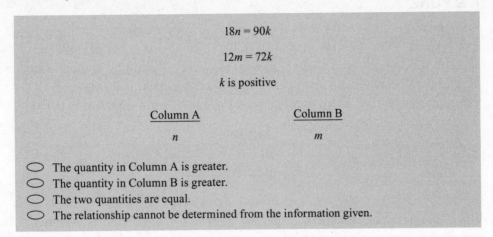

$$18n = 90k$$

$$12m = 72k$$

k is positive

Column A	Column B
n	m

○ The quantity in Column A is greater.
○ The quantity in Column B is greater.
○ The two quantities are equal.
○ The relationship cannot be determined from the information given.

Note first that your task is to compare n and m, and we can mirror them by manipulating the equations in the additional information to express both of these variables in terms of k. Dividing both sides of the first equation by 18 yields $n = 5k$, and dividing both sides of the second equation by 12 gives us $m = 6k$. Now we have quantities that are much easier to compare since they look a lot alike:

$$n = 5k$$
$$m = 6k$$

Given that k is positive, m must be bigger than n since 6 times a positive number is bigger than 5 times that same positive number. **B** is therefore correct.

Note, however, that if they said that k was *negative*, then the answer would switch to **A**, since 6 times a negative number is more negative (i.e., smaller) than 5 times the same negative number. And we hope you anticipated the final possibility: They might leave out the additional information entirely, in which case we *wouldn't know* which was bigger, since it changes depending on whether k is positive or negative. For that matter, the quantities could even be equal if we make k zero. With no information on k, we couldn't tell for sure which is bigger, and **D** would be correct.

The mirroring technique puts us in the ballpark, but we still have to be mighty careful when considering just what values our QC variables might take. If only there was a strategy to help us test out various numbers in such a situation . . .

Wait—there is! And we call it . . .

The FONZ

Sure, the rest of the world knows the Fonz as the leather-jacketed epitome of cool from the 1970s TV show *Happy Days*. Let them have their sitcom silliness—to you, it's an acronym for values to test when substituting numbers into QC questions. In fact, it's a specialized version of the "making up numbers" technique you learned about in the previous chapter. Here's what it stands for:

$$F = \text{fractions}$$
$$O = \text{one}$$
$$N = \text{negative numbers}$$
$$Z = \text{zero}$$

When the quantities provided include variables, you can plug in these values and see what you get. These are particularly good values to try, since they each have special properties that often reveal if more than one relationship between the quantities is possible. As you know, if the relationship between the quantities changes as you try different values, then **D** is correct. If not, the correct answer will be **A**, **B**, or **C**, depending on the exact relationship that has emerged. Let's consider a simple example to see how this works:

Column A	Column B
x^2	x^3

○ The quantity in Column A is greater.
○ The quantity in Column B is greater.
○ The two quantities are equal.
○ The relationship cannot be determined from the information given.

Your first reaction might be that the quantity in Column B is greater; a totally understandable reaction, since x^3 is greater than x^2 for most whole numbers: 4^3 is greater than 4^2, 10^3 is greater than 10^2, and so on. So it's looking like **B** may be correct.

The FONZ, however, begs to differ. The number 1, the O in FONZ, is the simplest test. If we substitute 1 for x, the quantities are equal, and we can stop right there: The answer must be **D** since we've now seen that the quantity in Column B might be bigger, but the two quantities might also be the same. Perhaps you tried a fraction instead—the F in FONZ. If $x = \dfrac{1}{2}$, then $x^2 = \dfrac{1}{2} \times \dfrac{1}{2} = \dfrac{1}{4}$, and $x^3 = \dfrac{1}{2} \times \dfrac{1}{2} \times \dfrac{1}{2} = \dfrac{1}{8}$. Under these circumstances, Column A is bigger. Whenever the relationship changes depending on the value of the variables, the fourth oval, what we call choice **D**, is correct.

Let's try one more before we move on:

	Column A	Column B
	$-5z$	$\dfrac{z}{2}+2$

○ The quantity in Column A is greater.
○ The quantity in Column B is greater.
○ The two quantities are equal.
○ The relationship cannot be determined from the information given.

The easiest FONZ number types to try are usually 0 and 1, so it makes sense to try these first. If z is 0, then Column A = 0 and Column B = 0 + 2, or 2. If z is 1, then Column A = –5 and Column B = 2.5. Column B contains the larger quantity in both cases, but let's not jump the gun; we've only done a half FONZ maneuver so far. (If that sounds like a wrestling move, that's not inappropriate considering how we're wrestling with GRE math.) Let's try a negative number next, and an easy one at that: say, –1. If $z = -1$, then Column A = 5 (remember that **multiplying two negatives yields a positive**), and Column B $= -\dfrac{1}{2}+2=1\dfrac{1}{2}$.

Ah, so the tables have turned, and now A is larger than B. No need to even try a fraction, as we know by now that the answer must be **D**.

As mentioned earlier, the FONZ technique is part of the general "making up numbers" strategy. If there are no restrictions on the variables provided by the additional information above the columns, then by all means FONZ away, beginning with 0 and 1 and moving on to fractions and negatives if necessary. However, if there are restrictions provided, such as "$x < 0$" or "x is a positive even integer," then be sure to test out only permitted values when attempting to pinpoint the relationship between the columns.

You'll get more FONZing practice in the practice set at the end of the chapter. Before we finish up this section on QC fundamentals and move on to the step method, let's first consider one important point about QCs containing diagrams.

Working with Diagrams

When you see a diagram in a Problem Solving question, you can generally assume that it's drawn to scale. However, the opposite is true for QCs: If the test makers intend the diagram to be to scale, they'll tell you. If they don't say a word about the picture, then there may be a trap afoot, since the actual values of angles or areas or other aspects of the figure may be different from how they appear. For example, an angle that looks like a right angle may in fact have a value of 60° when you work out the math. Answering QCs based on how the pictures attached to them look can be risky business. Take the following, for example:

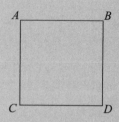

The perimeter of rectangle *ABCD* is 12.

Column A	Column B
The area of rectangle *ABCD*	7

◯ The quantity in Column A is greater.
◯ The quantity in Column B is greater.
◯ The two quantities are equal.
◯ The relationship cannot be determined from the information given.

The figure is described as a rectangle but actually looks like a square. That's certainly permissible, as **a square is a special form of rectangle with all its sides equal.** But just because *ABCD* looks like a square doesn't mean it actually is, since there's no indication that the figure is drawn to scale. No doubt, the test makers would be checking to see whether you simply assumed the figure is a square just because it looks like the sides are equal. If you did, then you'd simply divide the perimeter, 12, by 4 to come up with four equal sides of length 3, since **the length of each side of a square is the perimeter divided by 4:**

In this case, the area would be $3 \times 3 = 9$, and you'd choose **A** because 9 is larger than 7. However, with no indication that the sides must in fact be equal, there's no reason that our rectangle couldn't look like this:

This rectangle also has a perimeter of 12, so we haven't broken any rules. But note that its area has dwindled to $5 \times 1 = 5$, less than the 7 in Column B. If we go simply by the original picture provided, Column A seems bigger. If we remember that the picture is not necessarily drawn to scale, we find that another relationship is possible. **D** is therefore the choice to select.

QC STEP METHOD

We've provided many fundamentals to get you thinking the right way about QCs. Now we'll give you a method to employ your newfound knowledge. Here's a preview:

Step 1: Get the Specs.

Step 2: Plan the Attack.

Step 3: Mine the Math.

Step 4: Make the Comparison.

As you can see, the first three steps are identical to those of the Problem Solving method: You'll see what the problem presents (Get the Specs), settle on an approach (Plan the Attack), and extract Math 101 concepts as necessary from the extensive list in chapter 2 (Mine the Math). However, since QCs differ in format from PS questions, Step 4 (Power Through, in the PS method) must be changed accordingly. While in some cases you *will* "power through" to arrive at quantities to compare, other questions are best handled with alternative approaches, as you've seen. Step 4 will consist of making the final comparison, no matter how you arrive at your determination.

Let's take a closer look at how the steps play out before trying out the method on QC practice problems.

Step 1: Get the Specs. Step 1 helps you to adopt the proper mindset to attack the question. Here are the kinds of things you should notice about each new QC that appears:

- Is the question a Problem Solving challenge in disguise?

- Is there additional information to take into account, or are you to focus entirely on the quantities in Columns A and B?

- If there is additional information, does it place restrictions on any variables appearing in the problem? If you're planning on testing out choices, check to see whether you're free to try all four kinds of FONZ numbers or whether the additional information limits the numbers you can test.

- Does the question contain only numbers, allowing you to chop choice **D** right off the bat?

- What specific math concept or concepts does the question concern? Recognizing the relevant concepts will help you mine the math in Step 3 and make the comparison in Step 4.

- If a diagram is provided, do the test makers indicate that it's drawn to scale? If not, realize that elements of the figure may not be as they appear.

Step 2: Plan the Attack. Here your main decision will be to decide whether to treat the problem as a basic Problem Solving question, working through the math as appropriate, or whether you may be able to use one of the shortcuts discussed in the previous section. It takes practice to make this determination, and we'll give you that practice in the rest of this chapter and in the practice test at the end of the book.

Step 3: Mine the Math. No matter which approach you settle on, there are bound to be Math 101 concepts required to solve the problem. We'll continue to help you figure out which math concepts are required for each question and will continue to put them in bold for easy reference.

Step 4: Make the Comparison. In the end, every QC comes down to the same three questions:

- Is one column bigger?

- Are the two columns equal?

- Is it impossible to tell?

Everything you do in Steps 1–3 is geared to helping you close the deal and make the proper determination in Step 4.

Guided Practice

We've seen lots of QC questions already, but let's do another one to illustrate the step method. This will put you in the right frame of mind to try a bunch of these on your own. Give this one a shot and then follow along with the steps in the explanation that follows.

> Film contains 24 frames per second.
> Video contains 30 frames per second.
>
> | Column A | Column B |
> | --- | --- |
> | The number of frames in 595 seconds of film | The number of frames in .2 hours of video |
>
> ○ The quantity in Column A is greater.
> ○ The quantity in Column B is greater.
> ○ The two quantities are equal.
> ○ The relationship cannot be determined from the information given.

Step 1: Get the Specs. There's additional information concerning the precise number of frames per second for two different kinds of movie, and we're given precise times in columns A and B to work with. So, there are no variables, and we do have enough information to figure out the number of frames in each scenario. Therefore, we can eliminate **D** from contention immediately. The other thing to notice is that the times in the columns are in different units (seconds and hours) and the numbers are not particularly simple ones to multiply, especially the 595 seconds of film.

Step 2: Plan the Attack. Since 595 × 24 isn't the easiest calculation without a calculator, we can assume there may be a cleverer way to go about this, perhaps involving approximating. Because the units in Columns A and B are different, some mirroring may also be in order, since they'd be easier to compare if they better resembled one another.

Step 3: Mine the Math. The formula in play here is an offshoot of our typical work formula: **total = rate × time**. In this case, total frames = # of frames per second × # of seconds. But since our plan of attack is to use some math *logic* to get us through, don't assume you'll need to perform the actual calculations; understanding the gist of *how* to calculate the number of frames in each column may be enough.

Step 4: Make the Comparison. Column B is a bit easier to work with, and there's no reason why we can't start there. The length of the video is .2 hours, which multiplied by 60 minutes in an hour gives us 12 minutes. Not too tough. Now, you could convert that to seconds and then multiply by 30 to arrive at the precise value of Column B, but we're trying to avoid lengthy calculations, so let's leave it at 12 minutes for the video and move on to Column A. But 595 seconds isn't so easy to work with, while 600 seconds is: Dividing by 60 seconds per minute gives us 10 minutes, so 595 seconds is just under 10 minutes of film. Aha! The video is longer and contains more frames per second as well, so without even figuring out the exact number of frames in each, we can conclude with certainty that there are more frames in Column B. Choice **B** is correct.

Sure, you could have multiplied it all out, but with a little mirroring (expressing both movie times in minutes), a little approximating, and a little general cleverness, we arrive at the same point—hopefully faster, and with less risk.

PRACTICE PROBLEMS

Ready for some on your own? Good—have a crack at the five questions in this set, and then thoroughly review the explanations to see how you did.

Directions: Each of the following questions consists of two quantities, one in Column A and one in Column B. There may be additional information, centered above the two columns, that concerns one or both of the quantities. A symbol that appears in both columns represents the same thing in Column A as it does in Column B.

You are to compare the quantity in Column A with the quantity in Column B and decide whether:

(A) The quantity in Column A is greater.
(B) The quantity in Column B is greater.
(C) The two quantities are equal.
(D) The relationship cannot be determined from the information given.

In a question, there may be additional information, centered above the two columns, that concerns one or both of the quantities to be compared. A symbol that appears in both columns represents the same thing in Column A as it does in Column B.

1. $p < q < r < s < 0$

Column A	Column B
$\dfrac{pq}{rs}$	1

◯ The quantity in Column A is greater.
◯ The quantity in Column B is greater.
◯ The two quantities are equal.
◯ The relationship cannot be determined from the information given.

2.   Let $a* = a^a$ and $a\# = \dfrac{1}{a}$

Column A	Column B
$(((3*)\#)\#)\#$	27

◯ The quantity in Column A is greater.
◯ The quantity in Column B is greater.
◯ The two quantities are equal.
◯ The relationship cannot be determined from the information given.

3.

Column A	Column B
The number of prime numbers between 1 and 7, inclusive	The number of prime numbers between 12 and 29, exclusive

- ○ The quantity in Column A is greater.
- ○ The quantity in Column B is greater.
- ○ The two quantities are equal.
- ○ The relationship cannot be determined from the information given.

4.

Column A	Column B
$500^{100} - 500^{99}$	499×500^{99}

- ○ The quantity in Column A is greater.
- ○ The quantity in Column B is greater.
- ○ The two quantities are equal.
- ○ The relationship cannot be determined from the information given.

5. On tests graded out of 100, Nancy received an 85 on each of her first three tests and an average of 80 on her last two tests. Alfonso received a 90 on each of his first three tests and a 100 on each of his last two tests.

Column A	Column B
The standard deviation of Nancy's five test scores	The standard deviation of Alfonso's five test scores

- ○ The quantity in Column A is greater.
- ○ The quantity in Column B is greater.
- ○ The two quantities are equal.
- ○ The relationship cannot be determined from the information given.

Guided Explanations

---

1.   **A**

Step 1: Get the Specs. We've got variables in Column A, which means choice **D** remains on the table. It's also worth noticing the restrictions on the variables set out in the additional information: All four variables must be negative and decrease in size from s to p.

Step 2: Plan the Attack. FONZing seems to be a promising route, since making up numbers for the variables might help us to compare the expression in Column A to the number 1 in Column B. Just make sure to obey the restrictions in the additional information.

Step 3: Mine the Math. The **rules of negative numbers** come into play here: **A negative × a negative = a positive,** and **a negative ÷ a negative equals a positive** too. Those are really the only math concepts we'll need, other than some simple arithmetic, to test out some numbers.

Step 4: Make the Comparison. Ready . . . set . . . FONZ! Since the variables must be negative, 0 and 1 are out, so let's make s our simplest negative number, –1, and decrease from there: $r = -2$, $q = -3$, and $p = -4$. This gives $\frac{pq}{rs} = \frac{-4 \times -3}{-2 \times -1} = \frac{12}{2} = 6$. This is greater than 1 in Column B, so the answer could be **A**. If we pick other negative integers, such as –2, –3, –4, and –5, the result is the same: a positive number greater than 1. Just to be sure, though, we'd better try some fractions, because they sometimes cause funny things to happen. Let's go with these: $s = \frac{-1}{5}$, $r = \frac{-1}{4}$, $q = \frac{-1}{3}$, and $p = \frac{-1}{2}$. This maintains the relationship in the additional information since $\frac{-1}{5}$ is closer to 0 than $\frac{-1}{4}$, and hence bigger, and so on down the line. Filling in these for the variables yields the numerator $pq = \frac{-1}{2} \times \frac{-1}{3} = \frac{1}{6}$, and the denominator $rs = \frac{-1}{4} \times \frac{-1}{5} = \frac{1}{20}$. The entire fraction is then $\frac{pq}{rs} = \frac{\frac{1}{6}}{\frac{1}{20}} = \frac{1}{6} \times \frac{20}{1} = \frac{20}{6} = 3\frac{1}{3}$. Again, we get a positive number greater than 1 and can conclude that **A** is indeed correct.

---

2.   **B**

Step 1: Get the Specs. Even though this may look intimidating, it's nothing more than a made-up symbol problem. The expression in Column A and the whole number in Column B suggest that we can treat this as a disguised Problem Solving question testing whether we understand how made-up symbol problems work.

Step 2: Plan the Attack. There are no real shortcuts to made-up-symbol problems; we simply need to follow the rule to calculate the quantity in Column A and then compare what we get to the number in Column B.

Step 3: Mine the Math. Exponents and **fractions** seem to be the relevant math concepts, and $\frac{1}{a}$ is a special kind of fraction, called a **reciprocal. We form the reciprocal of a number by flipping its numerator and denominator.** If you're up on these arithmetic concepts, you should have little problem following the rules to arrive at an answer.

Step 4: Make the Comparison. Let's crunch through Column A and then compare what we get to 27. The first rule, $a^* = a^a$, means that whenever we see a number followed by an asterisk, we need to take that number to its own power. So 3* means we need to calculate $3^3 = 27$. Anyone who stopped there would have been tempted to choose **C**, but of course we need to continue through the rest of the expression containing the # signs. The second rule, $a\# = \frac{1}{a}$, means that whenever we see a number followed by a #, we need to take the reciprocal of that number. The expression 27# therefore means $\frac{1}{27}$, which takes care of the first #. Performing the same for the second # brings us back to plain old 27, and doing it for the third and final time yields $\frac{1}{27}$ yet again as our final answer. That's a lot of back and forth, but if you kept things straight, and took the reciprocal the right number of times (three), you'd find that 27 in Column B is bigger than $\frac{1}{27}$ in Column A. That means the second oval (what we call choice **B**) is the oval to click.

---

3.   **C**

Step 1: Get the Specs. All of the information is found in the columns themselves, and the problem deals with prime numbers. There's also this "inclusive/exclusive" business, but that's about all we're up against. That means we're basically looking at another Problem Solving question in disguise.

Step 2: Plan the Attack. They're not asking us to come up with dozens of primes, so we may as well just do the work and count 'em up.

Step 3: Mine the Math. Of course, to count them, we have to know what a prime number is, something we covered in the Math 101 chapter. **A prime number is a number that has exactly two positive factors, 1 and itself.** We also need to know that *inclusive* **means we are to include the outer values of the set** (if they apply), while **exclusive means we must exclude the outer values of the set** (even if they apply).

Step 4: Make the Comparison. Let's get counting, beginning with Column A. As we just saw, the word *inclusive* means we have to include the 1 and the 7, if they apply. Seven is prime, so it counts, but **1 *isn't* a prime number because it**

doesn't have two distinct factors. So the numbers in the set defined in Column A are 2, 3, 5, and 7—four numbers total. The set defined in Column B contains these numbers: 13, 17, 19, and 23. The word *exclusive* means we have to exclude prime number 29 from our list, so there are four numbers in this set as well. Four primes in A, four primes in B, so the columns are equal, choice **C**.

---

4. **C**

Step 1: Get the Specs. No computer—let alone person—in its right mind would be happy crunching these numbers, which means there must be a logical way into it. There's no additional information, and the columns contain pure numbers, no variables, so we can chop **D** from the get-go. But we'd better find a shortcut, since there's no way we can possibly calculate these expressions. The shortcut to employ is suggested by the look of the quantities in the two columns. They look kind of similar, don't they, what with all those 500s and a couple of 99th powers floating around? That can only mean one thing . . .

Step 2: Plan the Attack. Mirroring! These expressions look so similar that there simply has to be a way to make them resemble one another even further, making a comparison possible. But that's gonna require some math chops, which is another way to say it's time for Step 3:

Step 3: Mine the Math. Clearly exponents is the name of the game, and here's the main thing you need to know about them to get over the hump: $x^y = (x)(x^{y-1})$. For example, since x^{10} is the same as x multiplied by itself 10 times, it's also the same as $(x) \times (x$ multiplied by itself 9 times). Either way, you get x times itself 10 times. Why does this help us, you ask? Here's why:

Step 4: Make the Comparison. $500^{100} = (500)(500^{99})$. Substituting that for 500^{100} in Column A gives us:

$$(500)(500^{99}) - 500^{99}$$

Factoring out the common 500^{99} term results in:

$$(500^{99})(500 - 1)$$

which equals:

$$(500^{99})(499)$$

That's the same as Column B, even though the terms are reversed. **(The order of terms doesn't matter for multiplication: A × B = B × A.)** The quantities are equal, so **C** is correct.

---

5. **D**

Step 1: Get the Specs. Next up is a standard deviation question. As we discussed in our Math 101 chapter, you'll never be asked to actually calculate standard deviation since the formula is too complex to be tested on the GRE. We have to assume therefore that the question is merely testing our *understanding* of the mechanics—that is, the principle behind it. We'll need to mine our reservoir of math concepts for that principle, but first let's get our plan of attack in place.

Step 2: Plan the Attack. We'll use the numbers given but not expect to calculate the actual standard deviations for the two columns. Instead, we'll rely on math logic to determine the relationship between them. First we have to know what standard deviation is, and that's the purpose of Step 3.

Step 3: Mine the Math. **Standard deviation is a measure of the spread of a group of numbers.** In other words, a group whose numbers are all close to the same value has a smaller standard deviation than a group whose numbers differ widely from one another.

Step 4: Make the Comparison. Based on the definition in Step 3, our task is to figure out which set of numbers is more spread out. Alfonso's performance is better defined: We know that his test scores are 90, 90, 90, 100, and 100. That gives us a good sense of the spread of his scores, but we'll need to compare that to the spread of Nancy's scores to get our answer. Her scores are less defined. While we know she definitely received 85, 85, and 85 on her first three tests, we don't know exactly what she got on the last two; all we know is that they average out to 80.

Now, anyone who assumed that means her last two scores were 80 and 80 would be likely to choose **B** as the answer, since the spread of 85, 85, 85, 80, and 80 is less than the spread of 90, 90, 90, 100, and 100. That's because 80 is closer to 85 than 100 is to 90. The problem is, we don't know that Nancy's final two scores are 80 and 80. They could be, in which case her standard deviation would be smaller than Alfonso's, and **B** would be correct. But we have to use some cleverness and ask ourselves how else her final two scores could possibly average out to 80. The other extreme, given that the tests are out of 100, is that she got 100 on one test and 60 on the other. Those numbers also average out to 80, keeping with the requirement in the additional information, but change her test score distribution to 85, 85, 85, 100, and 60. Now Nancy's last two scores differ from her previous scores by 15 and 25 points, respectively. This is greater than the 10-point spread in Alfonso's scores, so in this scenario Nancy has the greater standard deviation. The answer must be **D**, since we get two different results from two different but equally plausible scenarios.

———————————————————

So there you have it: the wonderful world of Quantitative Comparisons, in a bit more than a nutshell. Sure, we covered a lot of ground in this chapter, but the fundamentals and step method will sink in as you get more practice with this question type. A little extra work on QCs is warranted since QCs make up the majority of GRE math questions: approximately 14 compared to 10 Problem Solving and only 4 Data Interpretation questions. It is to this final math question type, Data Interpretation, that we turn our attention now.

Chapter 5

Data Interpretation

Following that heavy-duty QC workout, you'll be happy to know that Data Interpretation (DI) questions require much less rigorous math than either of the math question types covered in the previous two chapters. No Pythagorean theorem, no exponents, no quadratic equations—these things simply have no place in DI. As the name implies, these questions concern *data*: numbers, figures, percentages, ratios, and so on. The data is contained in one or more diagrams. Your job is to find the relevant data for each question and, in most cases, manipulate it to arrive at an answer. Occasionally, you'll need to determine that not enough information is provided to answer the question asked. There are usually four DI questions in the GRE Math section. This chapter will give you what you need to approach this question type with confidence.

As always, let's begin with an X-ray.

DI X-RAY

You'll see a number of different diagram types soon enough, but turn the page to get us started. Take a quick scan through this one, but don't worry about answering the question just yet; we'll come back to it later on.

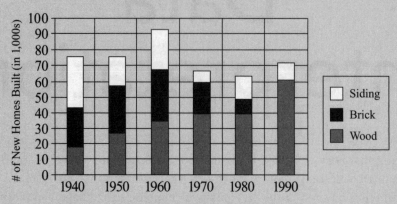

Exterior Surface of New Homes Built from 1940 to 1990

Note: All homes represented in the data were built with single exterior surface material.

In which of the following years was the number of new homes built with a wood exterior less than the number of new homes built with a siding exterior?

○ 1940
○ 1950
○ 1960
○ 1970
○ 1980

You'll probably see two distinct sets of DI questions on your test, each consisting of two questions. That is, if a graph like the one above appears in the first DI set, you'll answer two questions based on it. Then, after some Problem Solving and Quantitative Comparison problems, another DI set will appear with new diagrams and another two questions, which combined makes for four DI questions total.

The DI example above has only one diagram, although a set may contain two or even three diagrams. In this case, the diagram is a bar graph. Other kinds of diagrams include circle graphs, line graphs, and tables. The graph will appear on the left side of the screen while the questions appear on the right (one at a time). If the graph and any accompanying information don't fit on the screen, they will appear in a scroll box, much like the longer Reading Comprehension passages you'll see in the Verbal section. The directions are standard fare for multiple-choice questions: Choose the best answer out of the five provided.

DI FUNDAMENTALS

As mentioned earlier, DI is not primarily about the mastery of esoteric math concepts; instead, it's kind of like math's version of Reading Comprehension. Familiarity with the question type is crucial for DI success. The following fundamentals will acclimate you to the kinds of diagrams and questions you're likely to face and the approaches that will take you through them:

- Eyeballing

- Simple Arithmetic

- Percentage Questions

- Multistep Questions

- Standard Data Analysis

- Not Enough Information

Eyeballing

The most basic DI questions test nothing more than whether you can track down and properly interpret relevant data to answer a question. These don't require any actual calculations; they require you to *eyeball*, or scan the diagrams, for the data you need. There are two main kinds of questions that benefit from eyeballing. Let's look at both.

Single Eyeballing

The most basic question of this type asks you to scan a diagram to locate a single piece of information. Even if the DI set comes with more than one diagram, only one will be in play for this type of question. We return to our X-ray example for a question of this type:

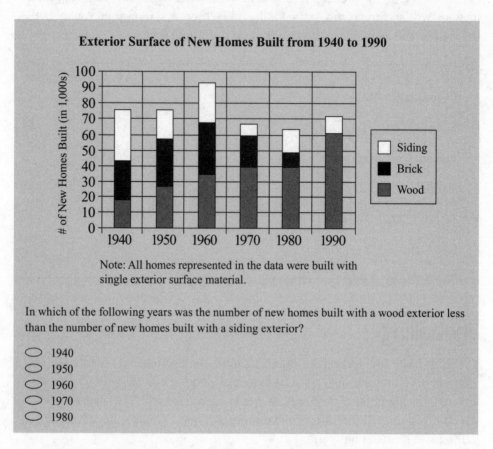

Exterior Surface of New Homes Built from 1940 to 1990

Note: All homes represented in the data were built with single exterior surface material.

In which of the following years was the number of new homes built with a wood exterior less than the number of new homes built with a siding exterior?

- ◯ 1940
- ◯ 1950
- ◯ 1960
- ◯ 1970
- ◯ 1980

As you'll see later in our discussion of the DI step method, the first step is to get a handle on the data presented, so let's take a quick look at the graph before eyeballing the answer.

This graph depicts three types of exterior surface materials used for new houses over the course of six decades. The graph is a "multipart" bar graph in that each bar contains data concerning three different categories—in this case, siding, brick, and wood. When asked to estimate the number of new homes built with siding in 1970, some test takers might say a little less than 70,000, since that's where the top of the siding bar reaches in that year. However, a little less than 70,000 is the *total* number of new homes built with all three surfaces in 1970—not the number of homes built with siding. So for multipart bar graphs, make sure you estimate the *difference between the top and bottom of each segment* to obtain the correct values.

Notice the caveat at the bottom stating that all the homes represented in the data were built with a single material. That's simply to ward off any complications regarding double or triple surfaces. If a house falls into the siding category, for example, it can't also be counted in the brick or wood categories. Finally, notice that the *y*-axis values for the data are all given in 1,000s. This means that eight units on the chart (for example, corresponding to the approximate number of new homes built with siding in 1970) means 8,000 houses, not 8. Once you've become accustomed to multipart bar graphs, analyzing the diagram should take only a few moments.

Now that we have a good handle on the data, we can eyeball it to answer the question. We're asked to compare the number of new homes with wood exteriors to the number of new homes with siding. According to the boxed labels on the side, the graph represents wood in gray and siding in white, which means we need to find the bar in which the white section is bigger than the gray. Eyeballing the graph immediately tells us that 1970, 1980, and 1990 are out, since the gray portions of these bars dwarf the white portions. The year 1990 isn't even a choice, but we can at least chop **D** and **E**.

Of the others, it's probably easier to see that the siding bar is bigger than the wood bar in 1940 than it is to compare the two surface materials in 1950 and 1960, so you may have been comfortable at this point choosing **A** and moving on. If you wanted to make sure, you'd have to take a closer look at those other two years, and let's do just that to get some more practice eyeballing this kind of graph. The wood bar in 1950 reaches through two full boxes and almost to a third, while the siding bar in that year covers a little more than one box. So wood trumps siding in 1950, showing **B** to be incorrect. Similarly, eyeballing the 1960 bar shows that wood clocks in at over 30,000, while siding comes in under 30,000, so **C** is out, confirming **A** as the correct choice.

Double Eyeballing

The test makers may ratchet up the difficulty level by asking you to eyeball multiple scenarios, as in the following question:

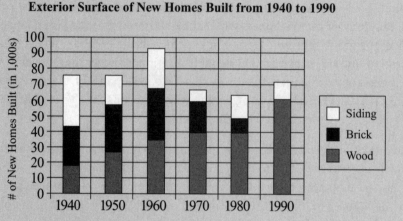

Exterior Surface of New Homes Built from 1940 to 1990

Note: All homes represented in the data were built with single exterior surface material.

Price per Square Foot of Exterior Surface Materials from 1940 to 1990

	1940	1950	1960	1970	1980	1990
Siding	$4.59	$4.79	$5.79	$6.29	$8.99	$8.99
Brick	$12.00	$12.00	$15.00	$16.50	$22.50	$34.00
Wood	$9.00	$11.50	$11.00	$13.00	$15.00	$18.00

Which of the following is true of the year in which the price per square foot of one of the exterior building materials decreased from that of the previous decade?

○ No new brick homes were built.
○ The number of new siding homes built outnumbered the number of new wood homes built.
○ The number of new wood homes built was approximately double the number of new brick homes built.
○ The number of new brick homes built outnumbered the number of new siding homes built.
○ More than 90,000 new homes were built with siding.

Notice now that another diagram—a table—has been added to the mix. (We're introducing it here for the sake of instruction. On the actual test, all diagrams included in a DI question set will appear on the screen from the get-go.) The question concerns prices, but the choices concern number of homes built, which means we'll need to look in two places to get our answer. First we should eyeball the table, looking for a price decrease from one decade to the next. Indeed, this happens only in one place: The price per square foot of wood decreased in 1960 from its 1950 level. So our first eyeballing venture yields 1960 as the target year. Now we need to eyeball the 1960 bar of the new homes graph to see which choice accords with that bar. Let's test the choices in order, with our eyeballing skills at the ready:

A: No, there were brick homes built in 1960. This choice seems to refer to 1990.

B: As we saw in the previous question, wood homes outnumbered siding homes in 1960, so **B** is out.

C: At a glance, the wood and brick segments look nearly equal in 1960, so this "approximately double" business is off the mark.

D has it right: The 1960 black brick bar (try that ten times fast) spans two full boxes plus most of two other boxes, while the white bar in that year covers just a little more than two full boxes. Eyeballing shows that the brick section of the 1960 bar is bigger than the siding section of that bar, so **D** is correct for this double eyeballing challenge.

E: Nuh-uh! This one's written as a trap to tempt people who confuse the total number of homes with the individual segment numbers. *Total* homes built top 90,000 in 1960, but *siding* homes account for only a little more than 20,000 of those.

Simple Arithmetic

Eyeballing questions involve reading the answers right off the diagrams. The next step up in difficulty is questions requiring you to *do something* with the values you eyeball. In simple arithmetic questions, you need to find the relevant data and then perform some basic calculations. Sometimes you'll be looking for a precise answer; other times, an approximation. Let's look at an example of each.

Precise Calculations

If a question looking for a numerical answer doesn't include the word *approximate* or *approximately*, then that answer must be exact. That means that you'll need to read precise figures off of a graph or table provided and perform some simple math based on those figures. Consider the following, based on the materials pricing table from the previous question:

Price per Square Foot of Exterior Surface Materials from 1940 to 1990

	1940	1950	1960	1970	1980	1990
Siding	$4.59	$4.79	$5.79	$6.29	$8.99	$8.99
Brick	$12.00	$12.00	$15.00	$16.50	$22.50	$34.00
Wood	$9.00	$11.50	$11.00	$13.00	$15.00	$18.00

The difference between the lowest price per square foot of brick and the highest price per square foot of brick for the years cited is

  I. greater than the combined price per square foot of all three building materials in 1950
 II. one dollar more than the combined price per square foot of brick and wood in 1940
III. two dollars less than the combined 1960 and 1970 prices per square foot of wood

- I only
- II only
- III only
- I and II
- II and III

The question and choices may sound confusing, and the Roman numeral format may seem a bit odd as well, but all the question requires is that you track down the right information and then do a bit of adding and subtracting. First let's work with the information in the question. The lowest price per square foot of brick is $12, both in 1940 and 1950. The highest price per square foot of brick is $34 in 1990. The difference is therefore 34 – 12 = 22. Now all we have to do is check the three Roman numeral statements to see which ones accord with this value of 22.

Even leaving out the cents, the combined price per square foot of all three building materials in 1950 is 4 + 12 + 11 = 27, which is greater than 22, so statement I is incorrect. The combined price per square foot of brick and wood in 1940 is 12 + 9 = 21, and the 22 figure we calculated is in fact one dollar more than this amount, so II provides an accurate completion of the question. The combined 1960 and 1970 prices per square foot of wood is 11 + 13 = 24. Our 22 figure is certainly two dollars less than this amount, so III works also. Therefore **E** is correct.

It may seem involved at the outset, but all we really did was get the numbers and do some very simple math.

Approximating Values

If a question *does* include the word *approximate* or *approximately*, then estimate the relevant values via eyeballing, and then work through the math with the values you get. Here's an example:

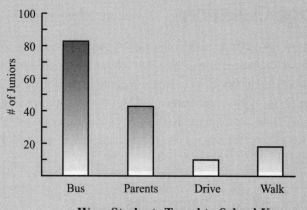

Ways Students Travel to School X

Approximately how many times greater is the number of juniors who take the bus to school X than the combined number of juniors who drive and walk to school X?

- $1\frac{1}{2}$
- $2\frac{2}{3}$
- $5\frac{1}{3}$
- 24
- 50

First, approximate the figures: The bus bar clocks in at a tad over 80, so go with 80 for now. The drive bar looks roughly equal to 10, while the walk bar is a shade under 20. The amount that the bus bar is over 80 roughly cancels out the amount the walk bar is below 20, so we can simply go with these values as our approximations.

Now let's do the math: If there are 80 bussers and 10 + 20 = 30 combined drivers and walkers, then we must need to calculate how much bigger 80 is than 30. **To calculate how much bigger x is than y, divide x by y.***

$80 \div 30 = 8 \div 3 = 2\frac{2}{3}$, choice **B**.

Notice that **D** and **E** are "left field" choices that are far too big to fit the scenario here. The bus figure is only roughly ten times the drive figure, so the bus figure can't be more than ten times the drive and walk figures combined. Moreover, they're traps to boot: You'd get 24 if you multiplied 8 by 3, and 50 is the *difference* between 80 and 30, not the *number of times greater* 80 is than 30.

---

* Note that in keeping with the convention established in the previous two chapters, we'll continue to bold the concepts from Math 101 as they come up in the solutions to problems. See pages 27–143 if you need to brush up on any of these basic principles.

THE
GRE

Percentage Questions

There are many ways that DI questions might test your understanding of percentages, so if you're shaky in this area, we advise you to go back to chapter 2 to review the Math 101 percentages concepts before going any further. As with simple arithmetic questions, sometimes the test makers are looking for a precise answer and other times an approximation. A third kind of common percentage problem involves percent increases and decreases, based on the formulas you learned in Math 101. Let's look at all three kinds.

Precise Calculations Using Percentages

Try the following:

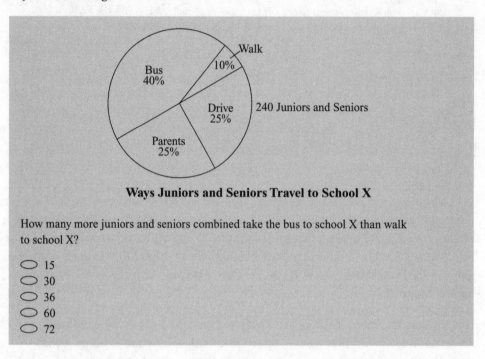

Ways Juniors and Seniors Travel to School X

How many more juniors and seniors combined take the bus to school X than walk to school X?

- ⬭ 15
- ⬭ 30
- ⬭ 36
- ⬭ 60
- ⬭ 72

The first thing to notice is that the data is presented in terms of percentages, not raw numbers. Overlooking this fact would lead one to simply calculate 40 – 10 = 30. Not surprisingly, the test makers have included 30 as an enticement for those who make this mistake. We need to calculate both figures, and then subtract.

If 40% of 240 juniors and seniors take the bus to school, then we need to multiply 240 × .4 to get 96 juniors and seniors who bus it to school. You may have had to use your scratch paper for this calculation, but hey, that's what it's for. The walking figure could be done in your head, since **taking 10% of any number means moving the decimal one place to the left.** The number of walkers therefore equals 10% of 240, or 24. 96 – 24 = 72, choice **E**.

Approximating Percentages

Again, if the word *approximate* or *approximately* shows up in a question, then you shouldn't expect the figures to be particularly tidy or the calculations to be simple. In such cases, use your powers of approximation to get into the ballpark, as we advised in our introduction to GRE math in chapter 1. Try it out in the following question. Hint: You'll need to do a precise percentage calculation before approximating for the final answer.

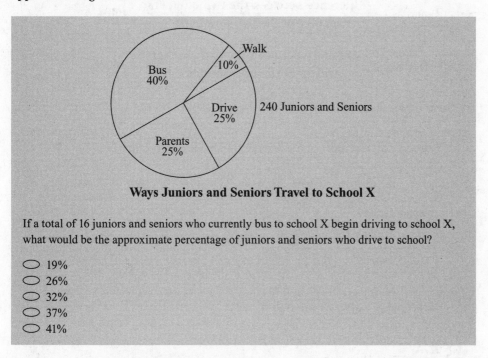

Ways Juniors and Seniors Travel to School X

If a total of 16 juniors and seniors who currently bus to school X begin driving to school X, what would be the approximate percentage of juniors and seniors who drive to school?

- ⬯ 19%
- ⬯ 26%
- ⬯ 32%
- ⬯ 37%
- ⬯ 41%

We know the number of additional drivers (16), but we need to add that to the number of current drivers before we can approximate the new percentage of drivers overall. Here's where a precise calculation comes in: The number of current drivers equals 25% of 240, or 60. Combining this with the 16 new drivers, we now have 76 junior and senior drivers out of 240 total juniors and seniors. The new percentage of drivers is therefore (76 ÷ 240) × 100%. The number 76 is fairly awkward, but 80, which is not too far from 76, works better. $\frac{80}{240}$ reduces to $\frac{1}{3}$, which is roughly equal to 33%. Since we rounded up from 76, 76 out of 240 is a little less than 33%, so **C** is the closest approximation. **A** is a left-field choice, since the percentage of drivers can't decrease if more drivers are added and the total number stays the same, and **E** is a trap that you'd get if you simply added 16 to 25.

Percent Increase and Decrease

When a value changes, it's possible to calculate the percentage that that value goes up or down, whichever the case may be. You may be tested on this concept in any of the three math question types, but the GRE test makers particularly enjoy utilizing this concept in Data Interpretation. In all cases, the formulas remain the same, and we'll repeat them here for your convenience:

$$\text{percent increase} = \frac{\text{difference between the two numbers}}{\text{smaller of the two numbers}} \times 100\%$$

$$\text{percent decrease} = \frac{\text{difference between the two numbers}}{\text{greater of the two numbers}} \times 100\%$$

Try the following question to see how this concept plays out in the context of DI.

Price per Square Foot of Exterior Surface Materials from 1940 to 1990

	1940	1950	1960	1970	1980	1990
Siding	$4.59	$4.79	$5.79	$6.29	$8.99	$8.99
Brick	$12.00	$12.00	$15.00	$16.50	$22.50	$34.00
Wood	$9.00	$11.50	$11.00	$13.00	$15.00	$18.00

The price per square foot of wood in 1990 represents what percentage increase compared to the price per square foot of wood in 1980?

- ⬭ 3%
- ⬭ 17%
- ⬭ 18%
- ⬭ 20%
- ⬭ 33%

The question isolates wood as the featured surface material, and tracking down the relevant figures we see that the price of wood increased from $15 in 1980 to $18 in 1990. Plugging these values into our handy percent increase formula yields: $\frac{18-15}{15} \times 100\% = \frac{3}{15} \times 100\% = \frac{1}{5} \times 100\% = 20\%$.

So the answer is a 20% increase, choice **D**. Notice the distractors included among the choices:

A is the total difference per square foot between the dollar amounts, 3, not the *percent increase* in price per square foot from 1980 to 1990.

B, 17%, is approximately what you'd get if you mixed up the formula and divided the difference by the greater amount (18) instead of the smaller amount (15).

C repeats a number from the problem (18).

E (33) is what you'd get if for some reason you added the 15 and 18 figures together. As an extra enticement, 33% is a fairly common percentage (roughly $\frac{1}{3}$), which may have caught your eye for that reason as well.

But if you isolated the correct information from the table, plugged it into the correct formula, and did the math correctly, no distractor would deter you from **D**.

Multistep Questions

So far the questions you've seen aren't overly complex, but if you're doing well on the section, the CAT software program may see fit to throw more difficult DI questions your way. One way to toughen these up is to require you to perform multiple steps to get the answer. You've already seen some basic examples. For instance, a double eyeballing question requires you to bounce from one part of a diagram to another or from one diagram to a different one altogether. Still, your main task in those is to just find the relevant information. Harder questions may involve bouncing between the diagrams, multiple calculations, and occasionally even some math reasoning. Let's look at a difficult example of this type. See what you can make of this one:

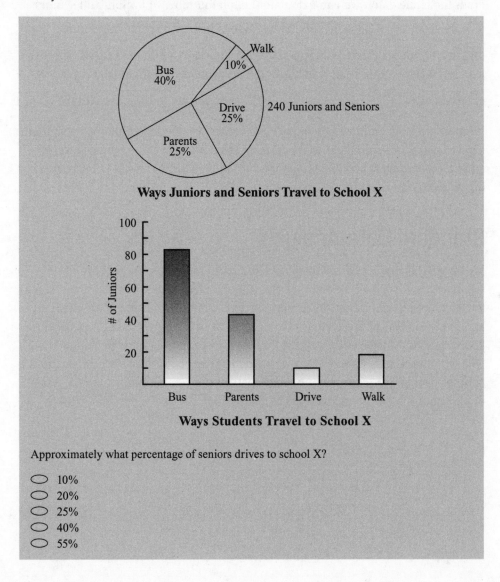

Ways Juniors and Seniors Travel to School X

Ways Students Travel to School X

Approximately what percentage of seniors drives to school X?

- 10%
- 20%
- 25%
- 40%
- 55%

Doesn't seem so tough, but the problem is that the circle graph doesn't differentiate between juniors and seniors. Fortunately we have the bar chart depicting the travel arrangements of the juniors, which makes it possible to bounce between the diagrams to arrive at a solution.

Our general percentage formula is **percent of a specific occurrence =** $\dfrac{\textbf{the number of specific occurences}}{\textbf{the total number}} \times$ **100%**. The percent of seniors that drives to school is therefore equal to $\dfrac{\textbf{the number of seniors who drive to school}}{\textbf{the total number of seniors}} \times$ **100%**.

We don't have either of these numbers yet, but we can get them. By adding together the bars on the bar graph, we can calculate the number of juniors as approximately 80 + 40 + 20 + 10 = 150. The circle graph tells us that there are 240 total juniors and seniors, so if we subtract the 150 juniors, we're left with 240 – 150 = 90 seniors total (approximately). That gives us our denominator. From the circle graph we can calculate the total number of juniors and seniors who drive as $\dfrac{25}{100} \times 240 = 60$. Bouncing back to our bar graph, we see that roughly 10 juniors drive, which means that 60 – 10 = 50 seniors drive (approximately). Now we can finally calculate the percentage of seniors who drive as approximately $\dfrac{50}{90}$. That's more than half, leaving only **E** as a possibility.

What makes this multistep question hard is that we need to employ a bit of math logic to extract the numbers we need from the data, as well as bounce around quite a bit on our way to our final approximation. This is the kind of maneuvering you should expect to see on the more difficult DI questions.

Standard Data Analysis

We began the chapter by mentioning some math topics you'll probably never see in a DI set, such as the Pythagorean theorem. Now we'll tell you about some topics you very well might see. Since concepts such as average, mean, median, and mode all deal with various ways to analyze data, they're all fair game in DI. You've gotten practice with some of these concepts in the previous chapters, and will see others in the practice test at the end of the book. But let's now see how another data analysis topic—frequency distribution—might appear as the basis of a DI question. Try your hand at the following:

Size of Litter *(numbers of kittens)*	Number of Litters
3	9
4	5
5	16
6	11
7	26

The table shows the frequency distribution of litter size for feline litters in a certain study.

What is the average (arithmetic mean) of the number of kittens in all litters in the study containing fewer than five kittens but more than six kittens?

○ 3.275
○ 4.125
○ 5.725
○ 6.125
○ It cannot be determined from the information given.

First off, we'll need to pull the frequency distribution concept from our reservoir of Math 101 knowledge. **A frequency distribution lists a set of values and the frequency of occurrence for each value.** In this example, the first row tells us that nine litters contained three kittens each. The second row tells us that five litters contained four kittens each, and so on. We're asked for the average of specific litters, so be careful: This "fewer than five, more than six" business is simply another obstacle set in your path to deter you from finding the data you need. If you read carefully, however, you'll see that you need to average the litters of three and fours kittens ("fewer than five") with the litter of seven kittens ("more than six"). That means we need to work with the first, second, and last rows of the table.

So how do we average these? We need to use the standard average formula: **Average equals the sum of the terms divided by the number of terms.** In this case, the *sum of the terms* means the total number of kittens in the three litter size categories we singled out. The *number of terms* is the number of litters contributing to this total number of kittens. First let's figure out the number of kittens: Nine litters of three kittens is simply $9 \times 3 = 27$ kittens. Doing the same for the four- and seven-kitten litters gives us $5 \times 4 = 20$ kittens and $26 \times 7 = 182$ kittens. The total number of kittens is therefore $27 + 20 + 182 = 229$. That's a lot of kitties!

Now we have to divide this total number of kittens by the number of litters producing these kittens to get our average. There are $9 + 5 + 26 = 40$ litters in the sample we're considering, so the final average litter size comes to $\frac{229}{40} = 5.725$, choice **C**. Now surely no one would want .725 of a kitten, but averages are often expressed this specifically and do provide useful information (think of the common average of 2.3 children per American household). Here we know the litter average is between five and six kittens, closer to six.

So, what's the deal with funky choice **E**? Glad you asked. That's the very topic of the next section.

Not Enough Information

Have you ever heard someone in a group conversation discuss an overly personal situation, and someone else mutter the phrase "too much information . . ."? Our next form of DI question has the opposite problem: not enough information. In some DI questions, the data presented is insufficient to allow you to calculate an answer. When that's the case, choice **E** will state that there's not enough information to answer the question. That doesn't mean that every time you see a choice like this, it will be correct—the previous question is a case in point. But it does mean that when a question contains a "cannot be determined" choice, you should be alert to the possibility that you may not be able to solve the problem. Some test takers, ignoring the choices, spend many minutes agonizing over a question, only to find to their dismay that there's no way to solve it and all along a choice said just that. So if you can't see a way into a problem and don't think you have the data you need, check the choices to see if "not enough information" is an option.

Let's look at an example. If you've been paying attention, you'll know the answer to the following question is **E**. But for practice, think about why you don't have enough information to solve it.

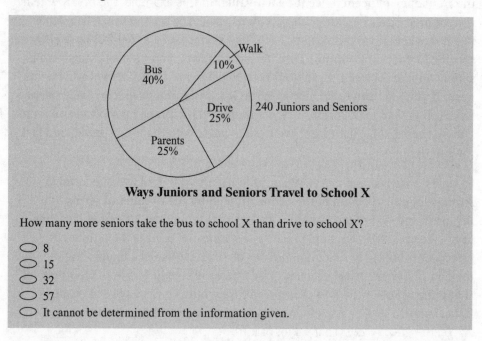

Ways Juniors and Seniors Travel to School X

How many more seniors take the bus to school X than drive to school X?

- ⬭ 8
- ⬭ 15
- ⬭ 32
- ⬭ 57
- ⬭ It cannot be determined from the information given.

Okay, so the answer is **E**—not a real shocker, since we told you that above. But did you figure out *why*? The percentages in the graph represent the combined junior and senior populations; there's no way to figure out from this circle graph alone the breakdown of juniors and seniors within each category. We therefore can't answer the question since we don't know the actual number of seniors that take the bus or drive to school. If we had the bar chart from earlier listing the number of juniors in each category, that would be a different story. But given only the circle chart to work with, no-go. Be aware of the fact that some DI questions test not whether you can find the right information to answer a question but whether you recognize that it doesn't exist.

DI STEP METHOD

You've now seen numerous DI scenarios and worked your way to many DI answers (and even one nonanswer). It's time to put your knowledge to work in the context of our DI step method. Here's a rundown of the steps:

Step 1: Get the Specs.

Step 2: Grill the Interrogator.

Step 3: Gather the Data.

Step 4 (if necessary): Power Through.

Why is Step 4 labeled "if necessary"? What does "Grill the Interrogator" mean? How does the little refrigerator light turn off when you close the door? All excellent questions! All (except that last one) will be answered right now as we take a closer look at each step.

Step 1: Get the Specs. You're familiar with this step from both the Problem Solving and Quantitative Comparison step methods. The difference here in DI is that you have to scope out and get a firm handle on the elements of the diagram(s) before you have any chance of answering the questions. So, the "specs" in this question type are the parameters of the graphs or tables presented. You need to perform this step only before the first question, since the diagrams don't change from question to question. Issues you need to notice up front include the following:

- What does the data represent?

- What is the scale of the data presented? Make sure you know how the things represented in the diagrams are measured. Take note of the units (thousands, millions, feet, seconds, hours, etc.). If a diagram contains multiple scales, notice whether they're the same or different. In tricky DI sets, multiple scales may be indicated in different units, which makes eyeballing much more risky.

- If there is more than one diagram, what's the relationship between them? Does any obvious correlation emerge? Does one diagram contain information that represents a subset of the data contained in the other diagram?

- Are any trends evident from eyeballing the data? Take a quick look at the big picture to help you get the gist of the information before moving on to the first question.

Step 2: Grill the Interrogator. Once you know what the diagrams are about, it's time to tackle the first question. Each question provides a wealth of information that should alert you to the math concepts (if any) in play and direct you to the data you'll need to answer it. Grill the question itself to unearth clues that will lead you in the right direction. When you know what they're asking, you'll recognize what you need to know, which will further help you determine where you need to look.

Step 3: Gather the Data. By this point, you've gotten the diagrams under your belt and have determined what the question is asking, which should allow you to venture forth to find the data you need to answer the question. In some cases you may also need a Math 101 concept to set you on the right track, but you can get by on many DI questions without "mining the math" (Step 3 of the PS and QC step methods). You certainly should know how to work with percentages and be familiar with common data analysis concepts, but overall you shouldn't have to dive too deep into your Math 101 knowledge base. If the question set contains only one diagram, use your information from steps 1 and 2 to direct you to the part of that diagram containing the data relevant to the question at hand. If the set contains multiple diagrams, then use the information in the question to tell you where to head, in what order, to get the numbers you need.

Now, it's possible you won't need to "Power Through" in Step 4, which is why we label this final step *if necessary*. That's because the simpler DI questions test only whether you understand the question asked and can read the answer right off a graph or table. In those cases, you'll be done by Step 3. Questions answered by eyeballing generally fall into this category. More complex questions, however, require not only that you find the relevant information but also that you manipulate it after you have it. That's where Step 4 comes into play.

Step 4 (if necessary): Power Through. If you can't simply read the answer off a graph or table, you'll have to crunch the numbers you extracted from the diagram(s) in Step 3. You may need to calculate precisely, or you may get away with approximating. In any case, expect many DI questions to require at least a bit of work after you've gathered your information.

Guided Practice

Don't worry if you're not totally on top of DI just yet. It's going to take practice, more of which awaits you in the practice set at the end of this chapter and the practice test at the end of the book. But first we'll walk you through our step method in the context of another question, resurrecting one last time our good old home-building scenario.

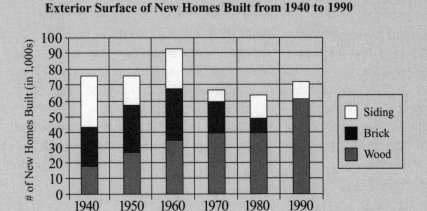

Exterior Surface of New Homes Built from 1940 to 1990

Note: All homes represented in the data were built with single exterior surface material.

Price per Square Foot of Exterior Surface Materials from 1940 to 1990

	1940	1950	1960	1970	1980	1990
Siding	$4.59	$4.79	$5.79	$6.29	$8.99	$8.99
Brick	$12.00	$12.00	$15.00	$16.50	$22.50	$34.00
Wood	$9.00	$11.50	$11.00	$13.00	$15.00	$18.00

If new homes built with siding in 1970 averaged 915 square feet of exterior surface material, approximately how much money was spent on siding for new homes in that year?

- ○ $700,000
- ○ $3,600,000
- ○ $29,000,000
- ○ $46,000,000
- ○ $140,000,000

Step 1: Get the Specs. We've seen these diagrams already, but let's reiterate the specs for good measure. There are two diagrams, one graph and one table, each containing siding, brick, and wood information for six different years. The multipart graph depicts the number of homes built with each surface material, and the scale is in thousands. We need to be careful to consider the correct beginning and end points for each segment of the graph. The note at the bottom eliminates the possibility of multiple-surface houses, averting possible confusion on that front. The table contains the prices per square foot of the material in the various years. Prices generally seem to rise across the years, with one exception in the wood row.

Step 2: Grill the Interrogator. The question limits its inquiry to 1970 siding homes, which narrows things down considerably. It provides the average number of square feet per siding homes built that year and asks for the approximate amount of money spent on that surface in 1970. The word *approximately* and the large difference between the dollar figures in the choices tell us we can estimate the values to make our lives easier. That's a great jump on the question, so let's move on to Step 3.

Step 3: Gather the Data. We know that money is involved, so the table will come into play, but what else do we need to know to calculate the total amount of money spent on siding in 1970? The basic formula **total cost = cost per unit × number of units** comes into play. In this case, *number of units* is itself broken down into average number of square feet per house (915, given) and the number of houses built in that year. So the total siding cost in 1970 = number of siding houses built in 1970 × 915 square feet per house × cost per square foot of siding in 1970. The cost per square foot of siding in 1970 is $6.29, and the number of siding homes built in 1970 was around 8,000. (The siding segment in that year starts just around 60,000 and ends before the 70,000 line.)

Step 4: Power Through. We've got our figures, so let's bring it on home: Since we're looking for an approximate value, we can round 915 square feet per house up to 1,000 to make matters simpler. Multiplying that by 8,000 houses gives us 8,000,000 square feet of siding used for new homes in 1970. While we're at it, let's approximate $6.29 as plain old $6.00, which gives us 8,000,000 square feet × $6.00 per square foot = $48,000,000. Is there anything close among the choices? Yup—$46,000,000, choice **D**. That number makes sense too, since we rounded 915 up to 1,000, so we should expect that our answer might skew a bit high, despite the fact that we also rounded the price down a bit.

PRACTICE PROBLEMS

The best way to reinforce all we've taught you in this chapter is to try some DI problems on your own. Keep the fundamentals and step method in mind as you try the questions in the following set. Note that each DI question set will contain two questions. We've provided *five* in this set for additional practice. See how you make out and then check out the explanations that follow.

Directions: Questions 1–5 refer to the following graphs. For each question, select the best of the answer choices given.

Food Budget for School District X

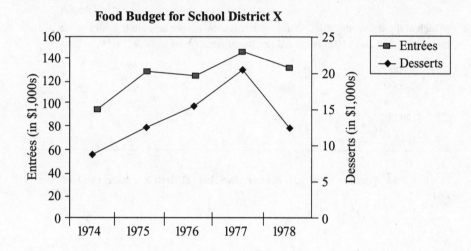

Breakdown of Entrée Budget for 1975

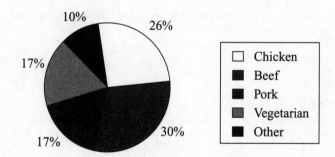

Note: "Other" represents turkey, lamb, and duck.

1. In which of the following years was the difference between School District X's budget for entrées and its budget for desserts the lowest?

    ◯ 1974
    ◯ 1975
    ◯ 1976
    ◯ 1977
    ◯ 1978

2. Which of the following statements can be inferred from the data?

    I. School District X's entrée budget increased from the previous year in every year its dessert budget increased from the previous year.

    II. School District X's dessert budget in 1975 was within $2,000 of its 1975 combined budget for turkey, lamb, and duck.

    III. School District X budgeted a greater amount for pork in 1975 than it budgeted for pork in 1974.

    ◯ I only
    ◯ II only
    ◯ III only
    ◯ I and II
    ◯ II and III

3. Which of the following is the closest approximation for the amount School District X's budget for chicken in 1975 exceeded its budget for desserts in 1974?

    ◯ $4,000
    ◯ $24,000
    ◯ $32,000
    ◯ $120,000
    ◯ $125,000

4. What was the approximate percent decrease in School District X's dessert budget from 1977 to 1978?

    ◯ 8%
    ◯ 12%
    ◯ 20%
    ◯ 40%
    ◯ 75%

5. What was School District X's approximate budget for vegetarian entrées in 1975?

    ◯ $7,500
    ◯ $13,000
    ◯ $21,500
    ◯ $37,500
    ◯ $58,250

Guided Explanations

1.   **A**

Step 1: Get the Specs. The two graphs concern a food budget for School District X. Evidently GRE–land has only one name for schools: X (see the traveling to school questions earlier in the chapter). Be that as it may . . .

The first line graph depicts the budgets for both entrées and desserts over the course of five years. The key to the right tells us which line is which. The left label on the *y*-axis indicates that the figures for entrées are in thousands of dollars, and the right label tells us that the figures for desserts are also in thousands of dollars. Note, however, that the two *y*-axes contain radically different numerical scales. (Those who missed this were in for a big surprise here in question 1.) The two budgets appear to follow a similar pattern, but we'll have to be careful about the different scales.

The circle graph shows the percentage breakdown of different types of entrées served in 1975, so it represents a subset of data from the first graph. We should expect at some point to have to bounce these percentages from the circle graph off the 1975 entrée number from the line graph. The box to the right provides the legend for the circle graph, which enables us to figure out which slice represents which type of entrée. There were five main types: chicken, beef, pork, vegetarian, and "other," which the note informs us consists of turkey, lamb, and duck. So in actuality, there were seven types of entrées served; only three of them are grouped together in a single slice of the pie.

Step 2: Grill the Interrogator. The first question concerns the difference between the entrée and dessert budgets across the board, so it appears that only the line graph will be in play here.

Step 3: Gather the Data. Normally a quick bit of eyeballing would work fine for a question like this, except for the fact that, as we mentioned, the two *y*-axis scales are radically different. Anyone going with a quick general scan of the line graph would no doubt choose 1977, choice **D**, as the year with the smallest difference in budgets. However, since the scales are different for the two budgets, we'll have to approximate the actual numbers to calculate the differences. You can approximate the values of each year if you remember to read the entrée number off the left vertical axis and the dessert number off the right.

Step 4: Power Through. Since the entrée budget increases far faster than the dessert budget, the smallest difference between them is likely to occur when the entrée budget is the smallest. This happens in 1974. Here the entrée budget is roughly $95,000 and the dessert budget is roughly $8,000. The difference between these two budgets, roughly $87,000, turns out to be less than that for any of the other years, each of which exhibits a difference of more than $100,000. **A** is therefore correct.

2. **B**

Step 1: Get the Specs. We performed this step for question 1, so we don't need to repeat it here.

Step 2: Grill the Interrogator. The next question is in Roman numeral format, which means we'll simply have to test each statement individually to see which can be inferred.

Steps 3 and 4: Gather the Data/Power Through. Since we have to essentially work out three separate problems, we'll combine these steps as we first gather the data and power through statement I and then repeat the same process for statements II and III.

Statement I isn't true because eyeballing alone shows that the school district's dessert budget rose from 1975 to 1976, while its entrée budget fell during the same period. That eliminates choices **A** and **D**.

Statement II is inferable: The 1975 dessert budget looks to be just about in the middle of $10,000 and $15,000, so it's approximately $12,500. Turkey, lamb, and duck compose the "other" category in the circle graph, and we can see from that figure that these made up 10% of the entrée budget in 1975, which we can approximate as 10% of 125,000, or $12,500 as well. So the budgets in question in statement II are nearly equal, and certainly within $2,000 of each other.

Statement III, however, isn't inferable since we know nothing of the percentage of the 1974 entrée budget comprising pork; remember, the entrée breakdown represented in the circle graph deals only with the year 1975. For all we know, pork wasn't on the menu in 1974—or it made up the entire menu. Notice how this Roman numeral format provides the test makers with another way to test your understanding of "not enough information." Since we don't know the pork situation in 1974, we can't infer statement III, and choice **B**, II only, is correct.

---

3. **B**

Step 1: Get the Specs. Been there, done that. Onward!

Step 2: Grill the Interrogator. In this one we're asked to *approximate* the difference between the 1975 chicken budget and the 1974 dessert budget, so it appears we'll need to approximate two values and then do some simple subtraction. It's therefore looking like we'll need to use both diagrams for this multistep question. We also know from the question's wording that the chicken number will be higher, for whatever that's worth.

Step 3: Gather the Data. Hunting we go: The dessert budget is easier to find since we only need eyeballing for that. Remembering to read the value from the *y*-axis on the right, we see that the budget for desserts in 1974 clocked in at just under $10,000, so we'll say approximately $8,000. The chicken budget, however, requires a few steps. In 1975 the total entrée budget was a little more than $120,000, but let's go ahead and round it down to that nice round number to make things easier. (Remember, we can do that when the question asks for an *approximate* value.) Moving to the circle graph, we see that chicken represents 26% of the 1975 budget, which we'll again round off to the more user-friendly figure of 25%.

Step 4: Power Through. We have all the numbers we need from the graphs, so let's do the math. The 1975 chicken budget is equal to the total entrée budget that year multiplied by the percentage of it devoted to chicken. Since we rounded down a bit, that comes to a little more than $0.25 \times \$120,000$. In this case it helps to convert .25 to $\frac{1}{4}$, allowing us to calculate the 1975 chicken budget as $\frac{1}{4} \times 120,000 = \frac{120,000}{4} = 30,000$. We estimated the budget for desserts in 1974 at approximately $8,000, so the difference is roughly $30,000 - \$8,000 = \$22,000$. Scanning the answer choices shows that **B**, $24,000, is closest to our estimation. Since $30,000 was an underestimate of the true value, it makes sense that the actual answer is slightly larger than our calculation.

---

4.   **D**

Step 1: Get the Specs. We took care of this in question 1, so on to Step 2.

Step 2: Grill the Interrogator. We're looking for a rough estimate of the percent decrease in the dessert budget from 1977 to 1978, which means we need to find those approximate figures on the graph and plug them into our handy percent decrease formula. So let's move on to Step 3 with this plan in mind.

Step 3: Gather the Data.

$$\textbf{Percent decrease} = \frac{\textbf{difference between the two numbers}}{\textbf{greater of the two numbers}} \times \textbf{100\%}$$

The question tells us exactly what numbers to plug into the formula: Dessert budget numbers from 1977 and 1978. The 1977 dessert budget clocks in just around $20,000 (remember to use the scale on the right side of the graph for dessert budget figures), and the 1978 dessert budget looks to be somewhere close to $12,000.

Step 4: Power Through. With our numbers in place, we simply plug them into the formula: $\frac{20,000 - 12,000}{20,000} = \frac{8,000}{20,000} = \frac{8}{20} = \frac{2}{5} = .4$. Multiplying by 100% gives 40%, choice **D**.

---

5.   **C**

Step 1: Get the Specs. Already got 'em, so let's see what the final question has to offer.

Step 2: Grill the Interrogator. The reference to 1975 and the word *vegetarian* combine to tell us that we're again up against another multistep question requiring both graphs to solve. Let's gather our data.

Step 3: Gather the Data. The first graph tells us that the total entrée budget was approximately $125,000 in 1975. According to the second graph, 17% of this was for vegetarian entrées. We'll take these figures with us into Step 4.

Step 4: Power Through. We can round up the 17% to 20% to make our lives easier, and then take $\frac{1}{5}$ of $125,000 to get an approximate answer of $25,000. The closest we get to this among the choices is $21,500 in choice **C**. This makes sense since we overestimated the percentage, and we'd therefore expect the real answer to be a little less than the $25,000 figure we came up with. **C**'s our pick, and we're sticking with it.

That finishes off Data Interpretation, our third and final GRE math question type. We hope that by the end of this portion of the book the Math section seems more manageable to you. Sure, there's a lot to know, but the concepts are tested in systematic and predictable ways in the three question formats we've discussed. We've provided you with strategies and step methods to handle each one. If you apply what you've learned to the questions in the practice test at the end of the book, and to all other practice questions you face, you should be in fine form to handle the math section on test day.

By the way, in case you were wondering, here's the reason the light goes off when you close the refrigerator door: A little man lives in your refrigerator, and he turns it off every time. At SparkNotes, we draw on many different resources to make sure you get the most accurate and up-to-date information. And now, we imagine many of you will be delighted to leave math and head straight into a totally different world: the GRE Verbal section.

Part II

THE VERBAL SECTION

Gameplan

Here's how we organized this section so that your test preparation is in fact useful:

- **Meet GRE Verbal.** First we'll learn the basics: how this section is scored and what the question types look like. We'll also introduce you to essential verbal strategies for approaching all the questions you'll encounter in this section.

- **Sentence Completions.** Here we focus on the question type, which has three variations. We also provide a step method to ensure that you know how to pick the correct answer choice for each one.

- **Reading Comprehension.** We show you how to "read" passages when you are taking the GRE test, and we also provide a step method that will help you avoid GRE traps and pick the right answers for each kind of passage.

- **Antonyms.** This question type tests your vocabulary and your ability to use logic to determine a word's opposite meaning. Our specific strategies and step method will improve your odds for choosing the correct answer even when you're unsure of the meaning of a word.

- **Analogies.** These questions test your ability to understand the relationship between words and to recognize pairs of words with parallel structures. Here we'll teach you the most common relationships tested and provide strategies for eliminating wrong answers, as well as spotting the pair of words that best matches the original.

Chapter 6

Meet GRE Verbal

On test day, you'll answer 30 Verbal questions in 30 minutes. The Verbal section has a mix of Sentence Completions, Reading Comprehension, Antonyms, and Analogies. Vocabulary and what the GRE calls "critical reading" play a key role on the test. We will not only teach you how to "read critically," but we'll also provide strategies and step methods that will improve your score on this section. We've also provided a list of the tough vocabulary words found on the test on a tear-out chart in this book.

SCORING

You'll receive a Verbal score between 200 and 800. The computer will calculate your score as you proceed throughout the section, taking into account not only right and wrong answers but also the level of difficulty of each question you answer.

Since you cannot proceed to the next question until you answer the current one, you should always guess when you don't know the answer. We'll tell you how to guess smartly and avoid being caught by traps in the Verbal strategies section of this chapter.

VERBAL QUESTION TYPES

The GRE Verbal section has four types of questions. On the next page you can look at our chart, which also provides the approximate percentage of the section devoted to each type:

Question Type	Number of Questions per Section (approximately)	Percent of Verbal Section
1. Sentence Completions (SCs)	6	20%
2. Reading Comprehension (RC)	8	27%
3. Antonyms	9	30%
4. Analogies	7	23%
Total	30	100%

Within the Verbal section, the question types will be interspersed—that is, you might see an Antonym question, a couple of Analogies, a Reading Comp passage, some Sentence Completions, and so on. The Reading Comp questions will naturally be grouped together since they all relate to the same passage, but the others function as stand–alone questions and thus will appear randomly. We'll give you a brief introduction to these question types below, saving the strategies and directions for the individual chapters devoted to each.

1. Sentence Completions

Sentence Completions, or SCs, test your knowledge of words and their proper contexts. These questions emphasize logic: You'll be asked to determine which words make *logical* sense in the sentence. Some sentences will require one word or phrase to complete them; others will contain two blanks to be filled in.

2. Reading Comprehension

Reading Comprehension consists of a prose passage followed by questions. The test makers take the passages from all academic disciplines, including English, history, philosophy, natural science, and psychology. Some passages are fairly long and come with four or five questions; others are shorter and may be accompanied by only two questions.

3. Antonyms

Antonym questions are fairly straightforward in structure, although that doesn't necessarily mean they're easy. You're given a word followed by five choices and will have to select the choice that most closely expresses the opposite of the word provided. These questions are certainly easier if you know the meaning of the word at hand. However, since this question type tests *reasoning* as well as vocabulary, there are ways to narrow down the choices and improve your odds even on questions containing difficult words. We'll review those strategies in the Antonyms chapter in this book.

4. Analogies

Analogy questions test your ability to recognize the relationship between two words and to locate pairs of words containing similar relationships. You'll be given one pair of words in the question and five pairs of words in the answer choices to choose from. The correct choice will be the one with the pair of words exhibiting the same logical connection as the original pair. Word order matters: A pair that contains the same basic relationship but in reverse won't be correct. In the Analogies chapter, we'll show you how to recognize the common types of relationships tested and how to reason out the relationships so that you can spot the parallel pairs and eliminate the imposters.

GENERAL VERBAL STRATEGIES

First, let's take a quick look:

- Read Widely and Deeply

- Ken Thy Lexicon (Know Your Vocabulary)

- Avert Distractors (and Guess!)

Now let's see how they work.

Read Widely and Deeply

If you're not a reader, become one. Reading high-quality prose and learning by example are two of the most important (and pleasant!) ways to gain a better vocabulary, as well as develop the ability to read at a faster rate.

Make reading a part of your daily routine, even if only for fifteen or twenty minutes. If you're not a natural reader, read stuff you're interested in just to get in the habit. Read the sports pages, the fashion blogs, *People* magazine, cereal boxes, *Ulysses*. In other words, read widely and deeply.

Practice makes perfect, as the saying goes. The more you read, the better a reader you'll become. You'll learn how to quickly absorb information, how to make inferences and identify the author's main point, and how to understand words in context—all of which are skills tested by the GRE.

What to Read

Eventually, you'll want to start reading material similar to that found on the test. Don't worry—you don't have to pore through dusty old anthologies. The test makers cull the reading passages from all kinds of sources that appeal to a smart, general audience. Keep this in mind as you prepare for the test: You don't

THE
GRE

have to be an expert to understand GRE passages. You just have to be able to quickly grasp the main ideas and answer the questions.

Reading any of the following on a regular basis will help you improve your literacy skills:

- The *Wall Street Journal* (www.wsj.com)

- The *New York Times* (www.nytimes.com)

- The *New Yorker* (www.newyorker.com)

- *Harper's* (www.harpers.org)

- The *New York Review of Books* (www.nybooks.com)

- The *Economist* (www.economist.com)

- *Scientific American* (www.sciam.com)

- *Arts and Letters Daily* (basically an electronic broadsheet, this site has links to articles from all kinds of scholarly publications. Check it out at www.aldaily.com.)

- The *Onion* (that's right, the *Onion*. Who says funny writing can't be smart writing? The articles are surprisingly advanced. See for yourself at www.theonion.com.)

Ken Thy Lexicon (Know Your Vocabulary)

The GRE wants to make sure that you know how to use words correctly, and vocabulary remains a critical component of getting a good score. People with better vocabularies will recognize words faster and more easily avoid traps than people with limited vocabularies. Vocabulary is tested directly in Antonym and Analogy questions and in context in Sentence Completions. Of course, vocabulary also comes into play in understanding Reading Comp passages, a key factor in answering those questions correctly. The bottom line is that having a solid vocabulary is a crucial requirement of achieving a great Verbal score.

Begin by reading with a dictionary by your side. Look up any unfamiliar words you come across as you peruse the *Economist* or the *New York Times*. You might consider keeping a list of words you don't know or don't know well.

We also provide you with the 400 most commonly tested GRE words in a tear-out chart in this book. You should have these babies down cold by test day.

Avert Distractors (and Guess!)

As the GRE is a CAT, you have no choice but to answer every question you see before moving on to the next question. So if you're in a position where you have to guess, you may as well guess intelligently. By guessing intelligently on questions you don't know, you'll increase your score. Guessing intelligently is *not* cheating: It's using what you know to eliminate wrong answers and find the correct answer.

But the test makers don't want you to stumble across the right answer, so they've designed two types of traps, or what we call "distractors":

- **Sentimental Counterfeits.** These distractors will frequently seem to fit into the question by associating themselves with a feeling or idea in the question. But they're really fakes, designed to distract you from the correct answer.

- **Look-alikes.** These are words with similar, but not identical, meanings to either other answer choices or to words in the question.

Sentimental Counterfeits

Let's take a look at this sample sentimental counterfeit:

> Medieval kingdoms did not become constitutional republics overnight; on the contrary, the change was _____.
>
> ⬭ ostracizing
> ⬭ unexpected
> ⬭ advantageous
> ⬭ sufficient
> ⬭ gradual

If you zipped through this one, you might have instinctively gone for **C**, figuring that, within the context of the sentence, *constitutional republics* are preferable to *medieval kingdoms*. And the word *advantageous* has positive associations that fit with the sentence's sense of historical progression. You would have been wrong, though: **C** is a "sentimental counterfeit."

Take another look at this question. The phrase *on the contrary* should tip you off that the correct answer must somehow contradict, or be in contrast to, the first clause. *Advantageous* doesn't work, because it doesn't contradict anything in the first clause.

Likewise, you might also have been tempted by **B**, *unexpected*, or **D**, *sufficient*, since both words also seem to fit with the gist of the sentence. Or you might have gone for **A**, *ostracizing*, because that seems just weird enough to fit the GRE. And, as you'll see in the list of the top 400 GRE words, the test makers do like esoteric, polysyllabic words.

The correct answer, **E**, is the only word that makes logical sense: *Gradual* contrasts with *overnight*. You can eliminate distractors by always double-checking that your answer makes logical sense and coherently fills in the blank.

Look-alikes

Although memorizing roots, suffixes, and prefixes can help increase your vocabulary, be careful about assuming that *all* words that look alike have similar meanings. For instance, *ingenue*, a noun, means "a naïve young woman," but *disingenuous*, an adjective, means "insincere." Likewise, be careful about confusing words that sound the same but mean something totally different, like *discrete* ("separate") and *discreet* ("exhibiting good judgment or modest").

Chapter 7

Sentence Completions

Sentence Completions (SCs) are exactly what they sound like: You're given a sentence with one or two blanks and asked to pick the word or words that best complete the sentence. The test makers use SCs to assess your level of literacy and your ability to use reason to figure out how words relate to one another within the sentence. In short, SCs test your understanding of *vocabulary in context*.

SC X-RAY

Before we get into the nitty-gritty, we want to emphasize three important facts about SCs:

1. SCs contain everything you need to define the word or words correctly. You can use the context of the sentence to figure out what the missing words mean. You don't need to look at the answer choices first.

2. All of the answer choices will work grammatically in the sentence, so you can't use grammar to rule out any choices. Only the meanings of words matter.

3. Regardless of the number of blanks or answer choices, you'll always want to choose the answer that best fits and makes the most logical sense.

Turn the page to see what a typical Sentence Completions question looks like.

<u>Directions</u>: The sentence below has one blank indicating that something has been omitted. Beneath the sentence are five words or sets of words. Choose the word or set of words for the blank that <u>best</u> fits the meaning of the sentence as a whole.

Most corporations are not in the business of philanthropy; instead, their primary concern is to maximize _____ .

○ goodwill
○ profits
○ open trade
○ employee loyalty
○ customer satisfaction

Your job is to choose the one correct answer from among the five choices. Here we need to choose the word or phrase that makes logical sense in the context of the sentence. In other cases, you'll need to find appropriate words to fill in two blanks. In the example above, it would help to know the meaning of *philanthropy* ("effort to help others"). In case you're wondering, the correct answer, **B**, makes sense in the given context. If you don't know the meaning of a word in the question, don't worry; we provide strategies to help you take a good, solid guess.

SC FUNDAMENTALS

Before we introduce our SC Step Method, we want to highlight two SC fundamentals that are integral to mastering Sentence Completions on the GRE:

• Sentence Types

• The Easier Blank

Sentence Types

SC sentences follow predictable patterns, and if you recognize the type of sentence you're up against, you'll have an easier time with it. Here are three common sentence types that you'll find on the GRE:

1. Definition

2. Contrast

3. Amplification

Later, in our step method discussion, you'll learn about "road signs" that will help you to identify these types of sentences. For now, let's take a look at the specifics of each.

Definition

Consider the following sentence:

> The drummer's playing was so _____ that the other instruments couldn't be heard above the din.

What kind of drum playing would cause other instruments not to be heard? It's clear from the context of the sentence that the missing word or phrase must mean something along the lines of "loud." This word defines that which drowns out other things. Some blanks will be filled by words that simply provide the appropriate definition for something defined in another part of the sentence.

Contrast

But what if we changed the sentence to this?

> Although the drummer played loudly, the other instruments were still clearly _____.

This sentence has a twist, as something exceptional is implied: The drummer plays loudly, but the other instruments were still clearly *something*. The word *Although* signals a contrast contained in the structure of the sentence. The drummer is loud, but we can still *hear* the other instruments. The GRE would most likely use a slightly more sophisticated word to fill in the blank, such as *audible*.

COMMON CONTRAST WORDS
Familiarize yourself with these contrast words.

Contrast Words		
actually	all the same	although
anyway	at any rate	at length
but	by contrast	however
in any case	in contrast	in reality
in spite of this	instead	nevertheless
on the contrary	on the other hand	otherwise
though	while	yet

Amplification

Finally, those crafty test makers might concoct something of this form:

> At first merely loud, the drummer's playing ascended to _____ levels as the concert progressed, drowning out the other instruments.

In this case, one element of the sentence is intensified: Something that was *merely loud* has become even more so, so we'd expect a word like *deafening* to fit the bill. The sentence, as well as the drumming it describes, has been amplified.

Definition, contrast, and amplification represent three common SC sentence types, but there are others. The key is to recognize that the *form* of the sentence may tip you off as to the words that logically fill in the blanks.

The Easier Blank

In SCs with two blanks, start with whichever blank seems easier to you. Don't start with the first blank simply because the test makers put that blank first. Instead, skim the sentence and predict the answer of the easier blank. Then narrow the choices down to the ones that work with that easier blank, and only engage the harder blank to help you pick the final winner. The advantage of this approach is that you can avoid testing all five choices on the tough part of the sentence, using the easier part to narrow the field. Let's go through an example to show you how this works.

> Siberian tigers are considered among the most _____ of animals; their striking coloration, powerful musculature, and regal bearing leave many people _____ .
>
> ○ obsequious . . defiant
> ○ anomalous . . fearful
> ○ desultory . . captivated
> ○ splendid . . indifferent
> ○ stately . . awestruck

The second blank is easier because there are clues that hint at its function in the sentence, whereas we aren't given much to work with in the first blank. How would something *striking, powerful*, and *regal* most likely make people feel? Scanning the second word of each choice, *captivated* and *awestruck* jump out as possibilities. *Fearful* is a common trap, playing off a common perception of tigers instead of the positively tinged clues provided in the second part of the sentence. *Indifferent* seems to be the opposite of how one would feel toward something *striking, powerful*, and *regal*, and *defiant* doesn't flow with the logic of the sentence either.

So we can quickly narrow the choices down to **C** and **E**, which means we don't have to even bother with difficult words like *obsequious* and *anomalous*. Nor are we likely to be tempted by **D**, which contains a first word, *splendid*, which could theoretically work. Checking the first words of **C** and **E**, we find that **E** creates a logical and complete sentence (*stately* means "majestic" or "grand") while **C** does not. Focusing on the easier blank first—in this case, the second, although sometimes it will be the first—will help you cut through complicated double-blank SCs.

SC STEP METHOD

Here's a preview of our five-step method to help you find the answer choices that best fill in the blank(s).

Step 1: Find the Keywords.

Step 2: Look for Road Signs.

Step 3: Make a Prediction.

Step 4: Compare Your Answer(s) to the Answer Choices.

Step 5: Plug It In.

Now let's go through the step method in slow motion to see what this all means.

Step 1: Find the Keywords. Quick, what's the correct answer for the following SC?

> Mrs. Patel was very _____ .
>
> ○ nice
> ○ rich
> ○ pretty
> ○ smart
> ○ curious

Unless you know something about Mrs. Patel that we don't, *any* of the five answer choices (and, for that matter, just about any reasonable adjective) would work in this sentence. But since any answer could work, any answer could also *not* work.

This question would never appear on the GRE, because it's missing *keywords*, or the information that lets you know how to fill in the blank. Keywords are essential to the meaning of the sentence, so every SC on the GRE will have them.

Here's our example again, this time with keywords:

> A two-time beauty pageant winner, Mrs. Patel was very _____ .
>
> ○ nice
> ○ rich
> ○ pretty
> ○ smart
> ○ curious

The keywords are *beauty pageant winner,* because these words tell us important information about Mrs. Patel, information that lets us correctly fill in the blank.

Of the five answer choices, *pretty* is the only one that fits with the context provided by the keywords. *Smart, curious, rich,* and *nice* might all work grammatically, but they don't logically fit in with the rest of the sentence.

Let's look at an example that more closely resembles the SCs you'll find on the GRE. This time, we'll try to identify the keywords.

> As more Americans move up the economic ladder, one fixture of the upper-middle-class income bracket often _____ them; searching for a nanny can be an exasperating, humiliating experience.
>
> ○ entertains
> ○ excites
> ○ eludes
> ○ escapes
> ○ disappoints

Although the blank is in the first clause, the first clause doesn't tell us much about the missing words. So let's take a look at the second clause: *searching for a nanny can be an exasperating, humiliating experience.* This clause explains the first clause by implying that *a nanny is one fixture of the upper-middle-class income bracket.* The second clause also makes it clear that finding a nanny isn't much fun.

Now let's take a look at the answers: *Entertains* and *excites* are out, since finding a nanny is exasperating and humiliating. *Eludes* and *escapes* seem like reasonable choices, but *disappoints* doesn't work well grammatically: *One fixture disappoints them* is technically correct, but it sounds bad. SC sentences always flow smoothly when the correct words are inserted.

Escapes works in the sentence, but *eludes* works better, since this word indicates that finding a nanny is easier for some people than for others, as implied by the word *can* in the second clause.

Step 2: Look for Road Signs. *Road signs* are words that indicate whether a sentence has changed direction. They will also key you in to the sentence type, as we described above. Some sentences are straightforward, like our example with Mrs. Patel:

> A two-time beauty pageant winner, Mrs. Patel was very _____ .

This fits into the "definition" sentence type discussed in the previous section, since the word *pretty* essentially defines *beauty pageant winner.*

But as we saw in the "contrast" sentence type, some SCs will contain twists and turns; for example, they start positively but end negatively, start neutrally but end positively, and so on. Road signs let us know when an SC sentence will wind up in a place very different from where it started. Take a look at this example:

Scenes of extreme poverty stand in contrast here with the construction of _____ headquarters of corporations from North America.

○ unprepossessing
○ simpatico
○ bankrupt
○ opulent
○ intemperate

This SC has switched directions. It starts with *scenes of extreme poverty* but winds up talking about corporate *headquarters*. These *headquarters* stand *in contrast* to the *scenes of extreme poverty*, so we can predict that the blank might be filled with a word that means the opposite of *scenes of poverty*, a word such as *expensive*. *In contrast* is our road sign, and the answer is **D**.

The bottom line is that you should always pay attention to the context given in an SC—and let the context, including its keywords and road signs, lead you to the correct answer.

Let's take a look at another SC:

Far and above the typical rowdiness and harmless pranks of his fraternity brothers, Matthew's behavior bordered on unadulterated _____ .

○ disorderliness
○ etiquette
○ debauchery
○ morality
○ cleverness

The phrase "Far and above" is a road sign that suggests that the missing word must be characterized by a more extreme form of "typical rowdiness" and "harmless pranks." That means that we have an amplification sentence structure on our hands, and our job will be to bump up from *typical* and *harmless* behavior to something more intense. It helps to know that *unadulterated* means "utter," "absolute," or "complete," but even if you didn't know this, recognizing the amplification sentence structure can help you sniff out the right answer anyway. *Etiquette* and *morality* suggest good behavior, things we might be looking for if this were a contrast sentence. However, these words defy the logic here, so we can cut **B** and **D** from the get-go. *Cleverness* is out of place in a sentence concerning rowdy behavior, so we can eliminate **E** as well.

That leaves **A** and **C** as potential candidates, and it's a close call between them since both *disorderliness* and *debauchery* indicate forms of negative behavior. However, only *debauchery* ("depravity," "decadence," "wickedness") ups the ante by amplifying the behavior described in the beginning of the sentence, whereas *disorderliness* could theoretically have the same intensity as *typical rowdiness* and *harmless pranks*. **C** therefore best completes the sentence. Recognizing that the sentence calls for an amplification helps us to eliminate some choices right off the bat and then to choose successfully between the two closest candidates.

Step 3: Make a Prediction. Anticipating the correct answers before looking at the choices makes it much less likely that you'll be tempted by traps and much more likely that you'll choose the correct answer. In steps 1 and 2, you looked for keywords and road signs, both of which will lead you to accurately predict the answer or answers *before* you look at the actual choices.

Step 4: Compare Your Answer(s) to the Answer Choices. After you've made your prediction, take a look at the answer choices and match your prediction to the answers. Rarely will your predictions be a perfect fit with the answers. Don't worry. Remember to choose the answers that are closest in meaning to your predictions.

Step 5: Plug It In. When you've got a new electrical device like a microwave or TV, there's only one way to make sure it works: Plug it in! Same goes for testing out answer choices.

Now that you've seen all the steps, let's give this method a whirl.

Guided Practice

Here's a double-blank example similar to an SC you'll see on test day. We haven't included the answer choices in order to emphasize the importance of following Step 3 and coming up with your own answer first.

> Despite its repeated claims of _____ , the heavy metal group actually had an exceptionally _____ history.

Step 1: Find the Keywords. For keywords, we've got *actually* and *exceptionally*. We've also got *heavy metal group*, because that's what the blanks and sentences are talking about.

Step 2: Look for Road Signs. For road signs, we've got the word *despite*. The *despite* here tips us off that the second blank should contrast with the first. This sentence is really saying something along the lines of *despite* saying one thing, *the heavy metal group* was really something else. So, the correct words for the two blanks should contrast with each other.

Step 3: Make a Prediction. The music group is claiming to be something it isn't, and its present claims contrast with its *history*. Maybe the band is claiming it's *tough* or has *a lot of street cred*. Being tough seems to go along with being in a heavy metal band.

The first blank contrasts with the second, so we need a prediction for the second blank along the lines of *wimpy* or *harmless*. Now that we've got a prediction, let's go to Step 4.

Step 4: Compare Your Answer(s) to the Answer Choices. We predicted *toughness* or *a lot of street cred* for the first blank and *wimpy* or *harmless* for the second blank. Now we'll compare our predictions with the answer choices:

◯   musical excellence . . notable
◯   having a traditional style . . felonious
◯   being made up of hardened criminals . . innocent
◯   aesthetic purity . . unrenowned
◯   fiscal propriety . . affluent

Being made up of hardened criminals definitely fits with our prediction of *tough* for the first blank, and *innocent* fits with our prediction of *wimpy* or *harmless* for the second. Don't worry if your predictions don't match the answers exactly; choose the closest approximation to your prediction, and move on to Step 5.

Step 5: Plug It In. It's tempting to skip this step. Don't. You *must* plug your answer choices back into the sentence to make sure they work.

> Despite its repeated claims *of being made up of hardened criminals*, the heavy metal group actually had an exceptionally *innocent* history.

So **C** is correct. Remember: After you've made your predictions and checked out the choices, eliminate the answers that don't match, and plug in the ones that do. You're looking for the best, most logical answer for every blank.

Let's do one more SC together. After that, you'll be ready to try your hand at the practice problems at the end of this chapter.

Born _____ , baby howler monkeys will explore every inch of their surroundings without any sense of fear, since they are not _____ of the possibility of danger at such a young age.

◯   inquisitive . . cognizant
◯   pugnacious . . impudent
◯   timorous . . apprehensive
◯   listless . . mindful
◯   questioning . . unwary

Step 1: Find the Keywords. Let's find the keywords by looking at the sentence in parts. The first part describes how *baby howler monkeys* are when they are *born*: They *will explore every inch of their surroundings without any sense of fear*. There's our first group of keywords. The first blank describes the monkeys at birth: They like to explore.

The second blank further describes the monkeys: They are *without any sense of fear*. But note the phrase that precedes this blank: *They are not*. So we're looking for a word that contrasts with the phrase *without any sense of fear*. That makes this blank a little trickier.

Step 2: Look for Road Signs. This sentence has just one road sign: *since*. This road sign means "because," and thus it clues us in to the relationship among the parts of the sentence: The second part of the sentence provides the reason for or explains something about the first part. Now we know that the two are related, and not in contrast to one another.

Step 3: Make a Prediction. Uncovering the keywords in Step 1 lets us know that the first blank describes how baby howler monkeys are at birth: They like to explore. A good word for the first blank, then, would be something like *curious*.

The second blank describes how the monkeys are in relation to danger. Since the baby howler monkeys are basically fearless, it makes sense that they either *don't care* about the possibility of danger or they are *unaware* of the possibility of danger. But note that *not* before the second blank: We need to then look for a word that means either "care" or "aware."

Step 4: Compare Your Answer(s) to the Answer Choices. To recap, we're looking for the first blank to mean something like "curious" and the second blank to mean something like "care" or "aware." *Inquisitive* and *questioning* are good matches for *curious*; *pugnacious*, which means "aggressive," and *timorous*, which means "nervous," are not. *Listless*, meaning "lacking energy," also goes against the idea of enthusiastic, exploring monkeys, so we can chop **B**, **C**, and **D** after working with the easier of the two blanks.

For the second blank, choice **A** contains *cognizant*, which matches "aware." Bingo! Let's double-check remaining choice **E** just to make sure it's not a better match: *Unwary* means "unsuspecting," so to say that the monkeys are *not unwary* would mean that they are cautious and careful, which is close to the opposite of what the logic here requires.

Step 5: Plug It In. Before we can click the answer and move on, we need to double-check that the two words in **A** work in the sentence by plugging them in:

> Born *inquisitive*, baby howler monkeys will explore every inch of their surroundings without any sense of fear, since they are not *cognizant* of the possibility of danger at such a young age.

Perfect. We're done.

PRACTICE PROBLEMS

Figure out where you stand by trying these SCs.

1. Although critics are quick to point out that the media is biased and subjective, its supporters maintain that one would have difficulty finding a convenient source that is more _____ .

   ○ credible
   ○ lucid
   ○ convoluted
   ○ entertaining
   ○ underrated

2. Previous theories explained the phenomenon through logical, scientific reasoning; today, perhaps surprisingly, _____ theories are in favor.

   ○ pragmatic
   ○ impecunious
   ○ irresolute
   ○ shocking
   ○ paranormal

3. No one but the most astute collector would have appraised the recent piece so highly; all previous work by the artist was considered _____ , and it would have been natural to assume this latest entry was no exception.

   ○ Machiavellian
   ○ insipid
   ○ praiseworthy
   ○ beautiful
   ○ urbane

4. Ashley's work ethic was never in doubt, and she performed even _____ tasks with _____ .

   ○ indubitable . . alarm
   ○ reckless . . zeal
   ○ officious . . hesitation
   ○ formidable . . alacrity
   ○ multifaceted . . perfidy

5. Supporters of physiognomy claim that experts can predict people's _____ characteristics, such as a predisposition to violence or tendency toward self-deprecation, by _____ facial features or body structure.

○ inherent . . dismissing
○ cogent . . recognizing
○ psychological . . scrutinizing
○ sensory . . mimicking
○ extant . . insinuating

Guided Explanations

1. **A**

Step 1: Find the Keywords. The keywords here are *biased* and *subjective*.

Step 2: Look for Road Signs. The road sign is *although*, which indicates that the blank slightly contrasts with the first part of the sentence.

Step 3: Make a Prediction. The road sign combined with the keywords indicate that the correct answers will mean something along the lines of *unbiased* and *objective*.

Step 4: Compare Your Answer(s) to the Answer Choices. Of the answers given, *credible* is the only reasonable choice.

Step 5: Plug It In. Plugging this word back into the original sentence confirms that **A** is correct.

2. **E**

Step 1: Find the Keywords. The keywords here are *stark* and *scientific*.

Step 2: Look for Road Signs. Here, the road signs are *previous* and *today*. There's been a change between the way things used to be and the way things are now.

Step 3: Make a Prediction. The road signs combined with the keywords indicate that the correct answers will mean something along the lines of *illogical* and *unscientific*.

Step 4: Compare Your Answer(s) to the Answer Choices. The closest answer choice is *paranormal*.

Step 5: Plug It In. Plugging *paranormal* back into the sentence confirms that the logic of the sentence holds up with this word inserted. Thus, **E** is correct.

3.   **B**

Step 1: Find the Keywords. This SC is a little trickier than the previous two. What words are crucial to this sentence's meaning? *No one but the most astute collector would have appraised the recent piece so highly* certainly gives us a clue about the rest of the sentence.

Step 2: Look for Road Signs. The sentence has one road sign, *previous*, but you might find it difficult to determine just how this word is used. Not to worry—a careful reading of the sentence will still allow you to make a prediction for the correct answer.

Step 3: Make a Prediction. Now we have to consider what the previous pieces must have been like for it to take a rare person (*astute collector*) to *appraise the recent piece so highly*. If all the previous work had been excellent, many people—not just a few smart collectors—would probably appraise a recent piece highly. For it to take a *rare* person to see the value of the current work, the previous pieces were probably *not* excellent.

Step 4: Compare Your Answer(s) to the Answer Choices. Of the answers given, *insipid*, which means "dull," is the best choice.

Step 5: Plug It In. Inserting *insipid* into the original sentence confirms that **B** is the correct answer.

---

4.   **D**

Step 1: Find the Keywords. The keywords here are *never in doubt*. What was *never in doubt*? Her *work ethic*.

Step 2: Look for Road Signs. Since there are no road signs, the sentence is going to go in one direction, from start to finish.

Step 3: Make a Prediction. We'll start with the easier blank. This is a matter of personal choice, obviously, but most people would probably find the second blank to be easier. In what manner does a person with a great work ethic perform tasks? *With enthusiasm* or *willingly* are reasonable guesses.

Now for the first blank. What kinds of tasks would this person perform *with enthusiasm* (our prediction for the second blank)? Well, technically speaking, she'd perform just about any task in such a manner. But the sentence has to reinforce this person's great work ethic. Having her perform *difficult* tasks would accomplish this.

Step 4: Compare Your Answer(s) to the Answer Choices. For the second blank, we predicted *with enthusiasm* or *willingly*. *Alacrity* ("eagerness") works. Among the choices for the first blank, *formidable* has a meaning most similar to *difficult*, our prediction.

Step 5: Plug It In. Plugging *formidable* and *alacrity* back into the original sentence produces a perfectly logical, clear result, and so **D** is correct.

___

5.   **C**

Step 1: Find the Keywords. The keywords are *predict characteristics*, which tell us a bit about what the supporters claim. What kind of characteristics? That's the essence of the first blank, and a clue is provided by a handy road sign, so let's head to Step 2.

Step 2: Look for Road Signs. The road sign *such as* indicates that examples of the characteristic in question are about to emerge: *a predisposition to violence or tendency toward self-deprecation*.

Step 3: Make a Prediction. The examples given don't sound like physical characteristics; they sound like things that go on inside our heads, like *mental* or *emotional* states. That's a good prediction for the first blank. As for the second blank, what can one do to facial features to make such a prediction? Probably *study* them, or something along those lines.

Step 4: Compare Your Answer(s) to the Answer Choices. Given our predictions, *psychological* seems like a good bet for the kinds of characteristics the author is talking about, and *scrutinizing*, meaning "analyzing" or "studying," seems to work for the second blank.

Step 5: Plug It In. Inserting the words in choice **C** into the sentence as written produces a clear, logical thought.

Chapter 8

Reading Comprehension

Reading Comprehension (RC) tests your ability to read and process written information. But GRE reading isn't like normal, everyday reading. This chapter will show you how to read GRE passages effectively, what to look for when you read, and most important, how to pick the right answers.

RC passages are generally taken from the fields of natural science, social science, and the humanities. The test makers draw the passages from various sources, including scholarly journals, magazines, biographies, works of literature, and textbooks. The passages mimic the material you'll be reading in grad school, with advanced vocabulary, complex sentence structure, and complicated ideas.

RC X-RAY

On test day, you'll see about eight questions spread out among roughly three passages. A common breakdown consists of two questions accompanying a short passage (roughly 150 words), two questions on another short passage, and four questions on a longer passage (roughly 450 words). The passages will be interspersed among the other Verbal question types—Analogies, Antonyms, and Sentence Completions. Once a Reading Comp passage appears, you'll have to answer all of its accompanying questions before moving on to the other question types.

On the actual test, the passages will always appear alongside the questions. Most passages don't fit on the screen, so you'll usually have to scroll to see the entire thing. You'll see only one question at a time, but a heading at the top of the passage will let you know how many questions accompany each passage.

Here is what a typical RC passage and question look like:

On two tragic occasions, at a century's distance, the fate of the United States has trembled in the balance: Would it be a free nation? Would the states continue to be one nation? A leader was wanted on both occasions, a very different one in each case. Twice America got the leader that the country needed: The American
5people had a Washington when a Washington was needed and a Lincoln when a Lincoln could save them. Neither would have adequately performed the other's task. A century of gradually increasing prosperity had elapsed when came the hour of the nation's second trial. Though it may seem to us small, compared with what we have seen in our days, the development had been considerable,
10the scattered colonies of yore had become one of the great powers of the world, with domains reaching from one ocean to the other; the immense continent had been explored; new cities were dotting the wilderness of former days. In 1803 France had, of her own will, ceded the Louisiana territories, which have been divided since into fourteen states. Many in the Senate had shown themselves
15averse to the ratification of the treaty, thinking that it might prove rather a curse than a boon. "As to Louisiana, this new, immense, unbounded world," Senator White, of Delaware, had said, "if it should ever be incorporated into this Union . . . I believe it will be the greatest curse that could at present befall us; it may be productive of innumerable evils, and especially of one that I fear even to
20look upon."

1. According to the passage, Senator White was opposed to what event?

   ○ Delaware's inclusion in the United States
   ○ The Civil War
   ○ The French Revolution
   ○ The Louisiana Purchase
   ○ The ratification of the Constitution

You'll be given a standard multiple-choice question, followed by five answer choices, and asked to choose the single correct answer by clicking on the oval that precedes your choice. Your job here is to click the correct answer's oval and continue onto the next question. In this case, the correct answer is **D**.

RC FUNDAMENTALS

Before we get to our step method for this section of the test, we'd like to introduce two essential skills that will be key to your success when tackling RC:

- Skimming

- Outlining

Let's see how they work.

Skimming

The only reason you are "reading" a GRE passage is to gain points. That is why skimming is an essential skill you'll need to maximize your score. Normal, everyday *reading* means reading every single word of a passage at least once. *Skimming* means reading only some of the words in a passage and letting your eyes dart across the rest. This will allow you to save significant time and search for the passage's most salient features.

Read only the first and last sentences in paragraphs. Use a pencil or pen to help you break the habit of reading every word. Practice dragging your pencil or pen along passages in a book or magazine quickly enough to make it impossible for you to read every word. This will train your eye to skip over some words and phrases, which means you are actually skimming.

As you skim, note the passage's major features:

- Topic, argument, main idea

- Evidence (facts, statistics, examples, quotations, etc.)

- Author's tone and attitude

Trying to understand every detail your first time through a passage is a waste of time. Given the relatively small number of questions, there's no guarantee you'll even be asked about a particular detail. In the event that you're asked about something you didn't quite get, the split-screen format lets you easily refer back to the passage.

We don't recommend that you skip any part of the passage—only that you read it as quickly as you can to get the gist.

Outlining

Staying focused on RC is difficult. You'll be reading long, difficult passages on a computer screen, which makes the Verbal section somewhat challenging. You can maintain your focus by taking brief outline-style notes as you skim the passage.

Jot down the passage's most salient features, and make a brief note about each one. As noted above, you want to concentrate on identifying the topic or main idea, the evidence used, and the author's tone or attitude. Use abbreviations and symbols to help you jot down your notes faster, and don't worry about poor grammar or spelling errors. Remember: You won't be handing your notes in at the end of the test, and you're the only one who will be using them. When it comes time to answer the questions, your notes will provide a road map to the passage.

Don't try to provide a complete reference guide to the passage. Your outline is meant to keep you focused as you read and avoid getting distracted.

Let's skim the sample RC passage below, taking brief notes as we go, to show you how it's done.

> On two tragic occasions, at a century's distance, the fate of the United States has trembled in the balance: Would it be a free nation? Would the states continue to be one nation? A leader was wanted on both occasions, a very different one in each case. Twice America got the leader that the country needed: The American people had a Washington when a Washington was needed and a Lincoln when a Lincoln could save them. Neither would have adequately performed the other's task. A century of gradually increasing prosperity had elapsed when came the hour of the nation's second trial. Though it may seem to us small, compared with what we have seen in our days, the development had been considerable, the scattered colonies of yore had become one of the great Powers of the world, with domains reaching from one ocean to the other; the immense continent had been explored; new cities were dotting the wilderness of former days. In 1803 France had, of her own will, ceded the Louisiana territories, which have been divided since into fourteen states. Many in the Senate had shown themselves averse to the ratification of the treaty, thinking that it might prove rather a curse than a boon. "As to Louisiana, this new, immense, unbounded world," Senator White, of Delaware, had said, "if it should ever be incorporated into this Union . . . I believe it will be the greatest curse that could at present befall us; it may be productive of innumerable evils, and especially of one that I fear even to look upon."

Again, here are the things to look for as we skim:

- Topic, argument, main idea

- Evidence (facts, statistics, examples, quotations, etc.)

- Author's tone and attitude

Although there is no single right or wrong way to take notes, your notes should be comparable to ours in terms of length, style, and scope:

Pass. about: U.S. free? One nation? Two times of change

Washington & Lincoln = good

Evidence: Quotation from senator, lots of description

French gave L. territories—could be bad

Author: Informed, neutral

These notes will not only keep your mind on task but also will allow you to answer the questions a whole lot faster. Now let's get to our step method and see how it all ties together.

RC STEP METHOD

Here are the steps you should follow on RC passages and their questions:

Step 1: **Skim and Outline.**

Step 2: **Read the Question and Search for Triggers.**

Step 3: **Locate Relevant Information in the Passage and Make a Prediction.**

Step 4: **Match Your Prediction to the Answer Choices.**

Step 1: Skim and Outline. Read the passage first, paying no attention to the first question on the screen if you think it may distract you. However, you may find that previewing that first question will help you locate the answer to it as you perform your initial skim of the passage. Decide what works best for you.

You should never spend more than *three minutes* with a long 450-word passage, and give yourself about a minute or so to read the shorter 150-word passages. While you skim, focus on the most important parts of every passage: the introduction, the conclusion, and the first and last sentences of each paragraph. This will ensure that you are not just skimming but *actively* absorbing information. Jot down and outline the key features on your scrap paper.

Step 2: Read the Question and Search for Triggers. The questions will appear individually on the right side of the screen. You won't see a new question until you answer the current one. Read the question, but not the answer choices. Specific questions refer directly to words or lines in the passage. Look for these "trigger words" and line numbers that indicate what the question is looking for. Before going back to the passage, articulate to yourself exactly what the question is asking. Don't look at the answers (this will help you avoid being caught by traps).

Step 3: Locate Relevant Information in the Passage and Make a Prediction. Go back to the specified area in the passage dealing with the topic of the question at hand and read the few lines before and after it to get a sense of the context. This will enable you to come up with your own answer to the question so you can go on to the next step.

Step 4: Match Your Prediction to the Answer Choices. Go back and find the answer that best matches your prediction. If no prediction is possible, let the choices guide your work.

Be Flexible

You may also find you're able to answer some general questions without looking back at the passage at all. General questions do not refer to specific locations in the passage. Instead, they ask about broad aspects of the passage such as its main idea, primary purpose, and tone. Sometimes the best way to answer general questions like these is to refer to the notes on the passage you made in Step 1. If you've already jotted down notes on the purpose of each paragraph, the tone, and the overall argument of the passage, you may be able to answer some of the questions without even looking back at the passage.

Now let's see how the step method works on a practice passage.

Guided Practice

The word *hurricane* comes from the word Hunraken, the Mayan god of winds. Today we use the term to refer to tropic cyclones, storms with winds of more than 75 miles per hour. They begin as thunderstorms that form over areas of the ocean where the water temperature exceeds 81 degrees Fahrenheit. The warmth and moisture in these regions provide the hurricane with its tremendous power, which explains why hurricanes quickly weaken when they pass over cool water and dissipate soon after they hit land.

Meteorologists measure hurricanes using the Beaufort Wind Force Scale. The scale has thirteen "Beaufort numbers," a shorthand method of describing a hurricane's type of wind and speed of wind, as well as the conditions of the ocean and on nearby land. On this scale, a Beaufort number of 0 means calm, peaceful conditions, whereas a 12 describes a violent, powerful hurricane.

Although hurricanes themselves are only a real concern to coastal areas, they often give birth to tornadoes. These funnel clouds turn inland, leaving swaths of destruction in their wakes. Tornadoes destroy power lines, damage homes and other property, and are responsible for dozens of deaths every year. These tragedies are becoming less common, however, as new weather technology makes it easier to predict the formation of tornadoes and provide early warning to the areas that may be affected.

1. According to the passage, the source of a hurricane's power is directly related to the

   ◯ likelihood that a hurricane will give birth to a tornado
   ◯ type of wind that characterizes that hurricane
   ◯ climatic conditions of its point of origin
   ◯ cool water it encounters upon approaching land
   ◯ number of deaths it causes in and around coastal areas

Step 1: Skim and Outline. After skimming the passage quickly, you probably noticed that it's primarily about hurricanes. Your notes might say something like the following:

Main idea: Hurricanes, tornadoes

Scary weather = bad

Bea. Wind Scale — measure weather

Evidence: Facts, numbers, 81F

Author: Objective, pure description, no opinion?

Step 2: Read the Question and Search for Triggers. The trigger words in question 1 are *power of a hurricane*, and the question wants to know what causes it.

Step 3: Locate Relevant Information in the Passage and Make a Prediction. Scanning for our trigger words leads us to the last sentence of paragraph 1, and we want to read that sentence, and even the one before it, carefully. The sentences we targeted indicate that hurricanes form over hot ocean areas and that the warmth and moisture in these areas "provide the hurricane with its tremendous power." Therefore we can predict that the answer will have something to do with a hot and wet climate.

Step 4: Match Your Prediction to the Answer Choices. Warmth and moisture are certainly climatic conditions, so **C** provides a perfect match to the relevant information in the passage relating to the source of a hurricane's power.

Tornadoes are discussed in paragraph 3, far from the discussion of the source of a hurricane's power, so **A** is incorrect. As for **B**, nothing in the passage indicates that the type of wind and speed of wind are related. **D** goes in the wrong direction, because the cooler water of coastal areas tends to sap a hurricane's power. **E** is wrong because deaths are discussed in the context of tornadoes, not hurricanes. In any case, it seems illogical that deaths would be a *source* of a hurricane's power; if anything, it would be the other way around.

As soon as you answer and confirm your selection, question 1 would disappear from the screen and be replaced by question 2. The passage would remain on the left of the screen for you to consult. Give question 2 a shot now.

> 2. What is the main purpose of the final paragraph?
>
> ○ To convince the reader that hurricanes pose no threat to inland areas
> ○ To explain in more detail the ideas introduced in the first paragraph
> ○ To explain the most dangerous aspect of hurricanes
> ○ To inform the reader why even people who live far from the ocean should be aware of hurricanes
> ○ To assure the reader that the development of new early-warning systems will render hurricanes harmless

Step 1: Skim and Outline. We've performed this step before answering question 1, so we can now proceed right to Step 2.

Step 2: Read the Question and Search for Triggers. The trigger words in this one are *final paragraph*, which tells us where in the passage to look for the answer. Specifically, we're asked for what purpose this paragraph serves in the context of the passage.

Step 3: Locate Relevant Information in the Passage and Make a Prediction. We've determined that the relevant information is the whole third paragraph, so a quick scan through it is in order. The third paragraph states that "hurricanes themselves are only a real concern to coastal areas" but goes on to say that they give birth to tornadoes that "turn inland." The paragraph clearly provides a reason why even people who live far from the ocean should be aware of hurricanes.

Step 4: Match Your Prediction to the Answer Choices. D is a perfect match and is correct.

A is incorrect because the paragraph only states that hurricanes pose no *direct* threat to inland areas, not that they pose no threat to inland areas at all. **B** is simply inaccurate. **C** is incorrect because the passage does not state or imply that tornadoes are the *most dangerous* aspect of hurricanes, only that they are dangerous to inland areas. **E** is incorrect because the passage does not suggest that early-warning systems will render hurricanes harmless, only that they will give people more time to prepare for tornadoes.

Now that your RC method is in place, you'll also need to know the types of questions you'll see on test day, which is the focus of the next section.

RC QUESTION TYPES

The questions that follow RC passages will fall into six main categories:

1. Implied Information

2. Detail

3. Detail Purpose

4. Primary Purpose

5. Organization

6. Tone, Style, or Attitude

We'll work through each type of question using the sample passage on the following page. Following Step 1 of our method, you should take a couple of minutes to skim and outline.

Common to most interpretations of the role of art is the notion that art correlates directly with the environmental characteristics of its period of origin. If we understand technology not only as a practical set of techniques and machines but also as an evolving dominant ideology of the modern age, it follows that we should
5 witness an infiltration of technology into art, not just in terms of the tools and processes at artists' disposal but also in terms of technology's influence on art's place within society. The latter supposition is explored by American writer and critic Lewis Mumford during various stages of his prolific career.

Mumford posited an integrative role of medieval art corresponding to the unity of
10 life characteristic of this pre-technological period. Medieval citizens, he argued, did not attend the theater, concert hall, and museum as activities unto themselves as we do, but rather witnessed a fusion of music, painting, sculpture, architecture, and drama in unified religious ceremonies that incorporated people into the shared social and spiritual life of the community. Integral to this phenomenon was the non-
15 repeatability of the experience—live musicians, specially commissioned scores, unique paintings and sculptures, and inimitable speakers filling incomparable cathedrals with exhortation and prayer. Everything in the artist's repertoire was brought to bear to ensure maximum receptivity to the political, social, and religious teachings at the heart of this medieval spectacle.

20 Mumford further speculated that the mass production of text and images from the sixteenth century forward ultimately disrupted the unity exemplified by the medieval experience, and with it, the role of art as a testament to and reinforcement of that unity. He believed that modern communication technologies encourage the fragmentation of time, the dissociation of event and space, and the degradation of the
25 symbolic environment via an endless repetition of cultural elements. The result is the oft-commented-upon "alienating" experience of modern life.

A new aesthetic orientation emerged to express this new reality. Art turned inward to focus on man's struggle against a bureaucratized, impersonal, technological civilization. Mumford readily admits that the dissociation of the artist from
30 communal obligations greatly expanded the realm of artistic possibilities; freed from its integrative purpose, art was set loose to traverse previously inappropriate realms of psychology and individualism in startling new ways. However, the magnificent innovation born of this freedom has been somewhat hindered by art's apprenticeship to the dominant force of the technological milieu: the market. Out of necessity,
35 money has replaced muse as motivation for many artists, resulting in the art world of today: a collection of "industries," each concerned with nothing loftier than its own perpetuation. Mumford testified admirably to a unity of art greater than the sum of its parts. Despite modern art's potential, it is reasonable to infer the converse: that the individual arts of our technological landscape are diminished in isolation.

1. Implied Information

By definition, information that a passage implies, or that you infer, is not stated anywhere in the passage. To answer these questions, look for a statement that, although not stated directly, must almost certainly be true, given the information in the passage.

Remember that RC questions are open book, meaning that the answers are right in front of you. As you answer these questions, refer back to the passage to see which answer is definitely supported. Be careful to use *only* information from the passage. Don't make large leaps in logic or use outside information to draw inferences.

Which of the following can most reasonably be inferred from the passage?

○ Modern religious ceremonies never make use of specially commissioned scores.
○ Most artists are grateful to be relieved of their communal obligations.
○ Only art that turns inward is suitable to express dissatisfaction with one's social and cultural environment.
○ Medieval life was generally not alienating and impersonal.
○ Mumford did not investigate the tools and processes at the disposal of modern artists.

There are no helpful trigger words, so we have no clue as to where the answer will be found. Moreover, in a general Implied Information question, it is impossible to predict the answer. Here we'll simply have to attack the choices one by one.

A: *Modern* religious ceremonies are irrelevant—we're told nothing about those, so we can't determine where the music for those ceremonies comes from.

B is also irrelevant. We don't know whether modern artists are even aware of the paradigm shift that Mumford outlines, or if they are, that they care.

C centers around the idea of necessity. While the passage does suggest that inward-turning art is effective at expressing dissatisfaction with one's environment, nothing suggests that it is necessary for this purpose; that is, that it's the only way to express this angst.

D is inferable. The author contrasts the unity and communal spirit of medieval life (both aided and expressed by the arts) with the impersonal alienation of modern times. It is thus inferable that medieval life was not generally alienating and impersonal, even if the author never quite states that directly.

E: We know what Mumford *did* investigate; as for what he *didn't*, there's no way to tell.

2. Detail

These questions require you to find specific details in the passage. You'll be using the trigger words you discover in Step 2 to help you go back to the passage to search for specific words or phrases to answer these questions.

Let's look at an example:

The author indicates that Mumford believed which of the following regarding modern communication technologies?

○ Modern communication technologies play a part in engendering alienation.
○ Modern communication technologies represent a unifying force in society.
○ Modern communication technologies are the only factors degrading the symbolic environment.
○ Modern communication technologies were invented to express the new aesthetic orientation that has arisen in the modern period.
○ No culture experienced the fragmentation of time before the advent of modern communication technologies.

"The author indicates" tells us the answer is in the passage. It's not implied. Therefore, we're dealing with a Detail question: The answer is stated right in the passage itself. Mumford's view on modern communication technologies appears in paragraph 3. The author tells us that Mumford believed that modern communication technologies fragment time, dissociate events and space, and degrade the symbolic environment, resulting in the alienating experience of modern life. **A** captures this notion best.

B goes against the grain of the passage. Mumford thought that modern communication technologies have diminished the kind of societal unity exhibited in the Middle Ages.

C goes too far. While Mumford believes that these technologies degrade the symbolic environment, nothing suggests that he thinks they're the only things to do so.

D reverses cause and effect, at least as far as the author sees things. The author states that a new aesthetic orientation emerged to express the new reality created by the disintegrating effects of modern communication technologies. **D** gets it backward.

E: Just because Mumford believed that modern communication technologies have this fragmentation effect doesn't mean he necessarily thinks this is the first time in history a society has experienced this.

3. Detail Purpose

Some RC questions ask for the purpose of some specific detail in the passage; not what the detail *says* (which would make it a Detail question proper), but why the author chose to include it. You'll be given a specific issue to focus on, so you'll enact Step 2 of the RC method to find the relevant passage material. When you've located the detail in question, analyze it in terms of its function. Think in terms of *context*—that is, how the detail relates to everything around it. That means going beyond the simple question of what is said to the more complicated issue of *why* it's said. Let's look at an example.

> The author discusses the non-repeatability inherent in medieval citizens' experience of art in lines 14–15 primarily in order to
>
> ○ support Mumford's contention that medieval citizens attended art events in isolation
> ○ support the assertion that medieval life was characterized by alienation
> ○ suggest the medieval disdain for the fragmentation of time and the dissociation of event and space
> ○ demonstrate Mumford's belief that the artist's repertoire was brought to bear to ensure maximum receptivity to the political, social, and religious teachings at the heart of this medieval spectacle
> ○ describe an orientation toward art that Mumford believes will be compromised by modern technology

"Non-repeatable" is the way Mumford characterized the artistic elements of the medieval religious experience. The terms *live, specially commissioned, unique,* and *inimitable* all reinforce the idea that the music, paintings, sculpture, architecture, and drama of religious ceremonies were all one-of-a-kind experiences not to be exactly repeated in the future. But why does the author make this point? To present a contrast to modern civilization, which, we're told in paragraph 3, is characterized by the exact opposite: "an endless repetition of cultural elements." The "non-repeatability" claim therefore serves to present a kind of art—unique, nonstandardized, nonrepetitive—that Mumford goes on to argue is compromised by modern communication technologies. **E** is correct.

A and **B** have it backward. Mumford argues that the medieval arts were not isolated but integrated into the life of the community, and that medieval life was characterized by unity, as opposed to the alienation of modern times discussed later in the passage. So these two choices go beyond distorting the author's intention—they assert the exact opposite of it.

C: The fragmentation and dissociation discussed apply to the modern era. For all we know, medieval citizens couldn't even conceptualize such things, living hundreds of years before even the invention of the telegraph.

D: The assertion that the artistic elements of medieval ceremonies were what the author calls "non-repeatable" speaks to the way that medieval audiences experienced the arts as a unique totality, not one by one in isolation. Nothing about this demonstrates Mumford's claim regarding the way artists' works were specifically used to support the societal framework and ideologies of the Middle Ages.

4. Primary Purpose

Some questions ask you about the passage as a whole. For example, you may be asked for the passage's main idea, or for an appropriate title, which is essentially the main idea in sound-bite form. A very common question dealing with the passage in a global sense is the Primary Purpose question, which asks for the main reason why the author wrote the passage. Since the correct answer must reflect the author's overall intention in the entire passage, beware of choices that deal with only part of the story. The correct choice will not be too broad or too narrow; it must be just right. Let's look at a typical Primary Purpose question:

> The author's primary purpose in the passage is to
>
> ◯ outline an effect of a feature of modern society
> ◯ recommend a solution to a cultural problem
> ◯ bolster a critic's speculations with supporting evidence
> ◯ describe a difference between two historical periods
> ◯ advocate for a change in society's modes of communication

A presents a perfect match. Technology is the feature of modern society under consideration, and its influence on art, the main focus of the passage, is the "effect" to which the choice refers. So **A** is correct. As for the others:

B: The author laments what she perceives to be the degradation of modern art but proposes no solutions to this or any other cultural problem.

C: "Here's what Mumford says, and here's evidence to show that he's correct" would have to be the main thing we get in this passage in order for **C** to be correct. "Here's what Mumford says, and here's how it supports my take on art and technology" is more like it.

D: The difference between the historical periods described by the author is intended to support a larger point about technology's influence on art. The author did not write this passage *primarily* to compare the medieval world to the modern, despite the fact that that comparison does play a part in the passage.

E: The author spends most of her time describing things and only in the end ventures the opinion that modern art has suffered somewhat from changes in technology. Nowhere does she come close to *advocating* anything, let alone a change in communication techniques.

5. Organization

Like Primary Purpose questions, Organization questions deal with the passage as a whole, specifically how the passage unfolds. In addition to capturing the passage as a whole, the correct answers to these questions will always provide an accurate summary of the *order* in which the author presented ideas.

Here's an example of an Organization question:

Which of the following most accurately describes the structure of the material presented in the passage?

◯ A theory is put forward, a specific means of testing the theory is outlined, and obstacles to carrying out the test are detailed.

◯ A consequence of accepting a particular definition is proposed, the validity of that proposal is affirmed, and a judgment based on that affirmation is stated.

◯ A supposition is introduced, a speculation regarding that supposition is described, and further speculations are detailed that counter the original supposition.

◯ An interpretation is offered, expert testimony opposing that interpretation is provided, and a consequence of that testimony is explored.

◯ A question is raised, and evidence from one time period and then another time period is presented to deem the question unanswerable.

The wording of the question itself identifies this as an Organization question. The best way to handle an Organization question is to meticulously compare the parts of each choice against your understanding of the passage. As soon as you find a single part of a choice that doesn't work, eliminate that choice. Note that here you are working backward from the choices as it is much easier than making your own prediction. Remember, be flexible. The answers are right on the page. Let's practice on the five choices of this question.

A: Is a theory put forward? Sure—the author's notion that "we should witness an infiltration of technology into art" in numerous ways. But the author never veers off into any kind of discussion of how to test the theory or, even further afield, obstacles to such a test.

B: Is a particular definition presented? Yes; the author defines technology as both a practical set of techniques and an evolving dominant ideology. Is a consequence of accepting this definition proposed? Yes again: The author says that if we view technology in this particular light, something should follow; namely a particular relationship between technology and art. Is that proposed consequence affirmed? Yup; the next few paragraphs describe, with Mumford's help, this very issue of technology's influence over art. We've come this far—it would be a damn shame for it to fall to pieces now, and it doesn't. A judgment (art has been diminished through this process) is rendered in the end.

C: The words *supposition* and *speculation* aren't so egregious to raise red flags right off the bat, as there certainly is a lot of supposing and speculating going on in the beginning. We'll even let "further speculations are detailed" slide, since Mumford does offer speculations in bulk. But we can't be as forgiving of the phrase *"counter* the original supposition," since no big turnaround occurs. The original supposition that technology should influence art in a particular way is affirmed, not countered.

D: No opposition to an interpretation appears in the passage. The closest we get to "expert testimony" are Mumford's theories, which serve to support the author's overall point.

E: It's fair to deem the initial inquiry a "question," as the author basically sets up the question of whether technology's infiltration into art pans out as she supposes it should based on her conception of technology. Moreover, evidence from both the medieval and modern periods *is* provided in the course of the passage in the hopes of investigating this issue. This one breaks down over the phrase "deeming the question unanswerable." The question is answered (technology does indeed affect art), and a value judgment based on this answer (art is diminished) is asserted.

6. Tone, Style, or Attitude

Questions about a passage's tone, style, or attitude refer to *how* the passage is presented as opposed to *what* is presented in the passage.

Here's a sample Attitude question:

> Which of the following most accurately describes the author's attitude toward modern art as expressed in the passage?
>
> ○ Unqualified derision
> ○ Bemused indifference
> ○ Reserved disappointment
> ○ Boundless optimism
> ○ Mild puzzlement

In your initial skim of the passage, you should have noted that no authorial attitude emerges in this passage until the fourth paragraph, where *hindered* and *diminished* in isolation were our first hints as to the author's feelings about modern art. That rules out "totally positive" as the author's attitude, which kills **D**, and shows that she's more than "neutral" too, which allows us to toss **B** as well. Having discarded these choices quickly for failing to even get in the ballpark, we can now turn our attention to the negatively tinged choices.

E fails on account of *puzzlement*. The author's stance is too assured to qualify as puzzled, considering that she's just spent an entire passage explaining to us the mechanism that has led to modern art's diminishment.

That leaves **A** and **C**, which differ mainly in the author's degree of negativity. You might ask yourself: What does "unqualified derision" sound like? Well, kind of like this: "THIS SUCKS! IT REALLY, REALLY, SUCKS!! No two ways about it . . . IT SUCKS!!" In fact, our mild-mannered author actually has some *positive* things to say about the change that has taken place, despite its overall negative impact: It "greatly expanded the realm of artistic possibilities," "art was set loose" to cover new ground in "startling new ways," and even the thing that has been "somewhat hindered" (notice the qualifier *somewhat*, which by itself works against **A**'s "unqualified derision") is referred to as "magnificent innovation." So putting it all together, she thinks modern art is worse off, despite great promise. "Reserved disappointment" best matches this attitude toward modern art, so **C** is the answer we seek.

COMMON RC TRAPS

Simply put, your job on RC sets is to answer the questions correctly. This means, of course, choosing the correct answer, but it also means that you need to know how to avoid the three RC traps:

1. Extreme Answers

2. True, Eloquent, but Irrelevant Answers

3. Answers That Repeat Wording from the Passage

Extreme Answers

Extreme Answers are too broad, are too narrow, or use polarizing language. An answer choice that indicates something is *always* true or *never* true will be very hard for the test makers to defend as correct. Extreme words include *all*, *always*, *never*, *none*, and *will*.

That last word, *will*, may surprise you. Think about what *will* means. It indicates that something *is definitely going to happen in the future*. This is just as extreme as using a word like *always* or *never*. Also, rarely do passages on the GRE try to predict something. They're usually about the past and the present. Unless a passage specifically says so, don't assume that what's true today, or was true yesterday, will also be true tomorrow.

Take another look at this question, but now, instead of picking out the correct answer, try to recognize the Extreme Answers:

The author's primary purpose in the passage is to

○ outline an effect of a feature of modern society
○ recommend a solution to a cultural problem
○ bolster a critic's speculations with supporting evidence
○ describe a difference between two historical periods
○ advocate for a change in society's modes of communication

We saw earlier that **A** is correct, but notice how **B** and **E** go to extremes since the author never goes so far as to recommend a solution or advocate for a change. These are typical examples of Extreme choices—choices that take the information in the passage too far.

True, Eloquent, but Irrelevant Answers

This trap has a lot going for it: It makes a statement that's true according to the information in the passage but does not answer the question at hand. Just because a choice contains something that's "in there somewhere" doesn't mean it's right, even if it's impressively written and official-sounding. The question discussed just above contains one of these traps:

(D) describe a difference between two historical periods

In fact, the author absolutely *does* describe a difference between the medieval and modern periods, but that doesn't mean this is the primary purpose of the passage. Remember, your job is to answer the question asked, not to find statements that are merely true. Sometimes, true will not equal correct. You're not searching for truth or beauty on the GRE. You're searching for answers that get you points.

Answers That Repeat Wording from the Passage

Be wary of answers that use exactly the same wording as the passage. Instead of thinking, "Ahh . . . I remember seeing something like that in the passage—this answer must be right . . . ," think, "Ahh . . . I remember seeing something like that in the passage. The GRE can be tricky, so this answer is probably wrong." Pay attention to what the question asks you, and make sure that you choose the answer that best answers the question—not the answer that simply repeats information found in the passage.

Identify the Repeated Wording trap in the following question:

The author discusses the non-repeatability inherent in medieval citizens' experience of art in lines 14–15 primarily in order to

◯ support Mumford's contention that medieval citizens attended art events in isolation

◯ support the assertion that medieval life was characterized by alienation

◯ suggest the medieval disdain for the fragmentation of time and the dissociation of event and space

◯ demonstrate Mumford's belief that the artist's repertoire was brought to bear to ensure maximum receptivity to the political, social, and religious teachings at the heart of the medieval spectacle

◯ describe an orientation toward art that Mumford believes will be compromised by modern technology

We saw this question earlier, so we know that **E** is correct. Why is **D** wrong? It restates part of the passage nearly verbatim. This wording should immediately make you wary of the answer. While **D** sounds impressive because it comes right out of the passage, it doesn't represent the reason the author discusses the non-repeatability aspect of medieval art. Notice also that choices **A**, **B**, and **C** contain significant chunks of passage text, perhaps tempting some test takers, but they all go astray for the reasons discussed earlier.

We've covered a lot of ground in this chapter. Go back and review anything that's still unclear, take a deep breath, and then dive into the following practice problems.

PRACTICE PROBLEMS

On test day, you're likely to see one long RC passage and a couple of short ones. This practice set includes an example of each. Don't forget to go over the answers and explanations that follow.

Directions: After reading each passage, choose the best answer to each question. Answer all questions following a passage on the basis of what is stated or implied in that passage.

Pure science is a science of discovery, a science of figuring out the physical, chemical, and biological laws governing the universe. A scientist engaged in pure science gains knowledge of a limited sort. He or she may gain an understanding of the actions of particles under certain circumstances, or of the processes which make up the
5   nitrogen cycle, but a researcher who discovers the whys and hows of scientific laws does not attempt to change those laws. Pure scientific research thus does not impinge on the rights or privacy of particular individuals or communities.

Applied science, in contrast, involves an effort to harness the knowledge gained by pure science for the purpose of achieving specific ends. As a result, applied science
10   holds the potential to greatly benefit humanity, but it also holds the potential to cause great harm, such as the construction of the atomic bomb built specifically to destroy. It is only when science has become manifest in society through application that it can impinge on human rights.

1. According to the passage, applied science differs from pure science in

    I. its ability to impact upon the rights of individuals
    II. the complexity of its effects
    III. the scope of its intentions

    ◯ I only
    ◯ I and II only
    ◯ I and III only
    ◯ II and III only
    ◯ I, II, and III

2. Which of the following would the author consider an example of pure science?

    ◯ Researching ways to combat air pollution
    ◯ Using biochemical data to clean up hazardous waste
    ◯ Discovering which rock formations are likely to contain gold
    ◯ Using mathematical formulas to estimate the mass of the earth
    ◯ Developing a technique to extract oil from small deposits

Literary audiences have traditionally favored writers whose works appear to spring from the richness of lived experience. Ernest Hemingway and Jack London come to mind as semi-mythic action figures who documented their experiences in art. Next to the travails of nineteenth-century Russian novelist Fyodor Dostoyevsky, the
5   adventures of even these lively American writers pale in comparison. Dostoyevsky was arrested for treason against the state, kept in solitary confinement for ten months, tried and condemned to death, and brought to the scaffold only to have his execution stayed at the last moment by an order of the Czar delivered dramatically on horseback. To say that his life was as dark and dramatic as the books he wrote
10   is no mere marketing gimmick, no ritual of hyperbole characterizing the incessant and obligatory hype announcing the release of every modern novel and Hollywood spectacular.

Considering such a biography, it is commonplace to emphasize the direct link between Dostoyevsky's life and his novels. This view is not without merit:
15   Dostoyevsky suffered greatly, and he wrote with great power and passion about the prospect of attaining redemption through suffering. Years of communing with hardened criminals in a Siberian prison yielded passages of penetrating insights into the criminal mind. Dostoyevsky suffered from a destructive gambling addiction and debilitating epileptic seizures, maladies he imparted to some of his characters. He
20   faithfully and poignantly reproduced in his writing his most harrowing personal experience: the excruciating moments awaiting execution and the confused euphoria following its sudden, seemingly miraculous annulment.

However, the popular view of Dostoyevsky as a preeminent example of the synergistic relation between the artist and his work tends to obscure the contradictions that
25   inevitably infuse even the most coherent artist's life. As Dostoyevsky himself taught via brilliantly realistic character portrayals, each human being consists of a labyrinth of internal inconsistencies, competing desires, and mysterious motivations that belie the notion of a completely unified personality. One of Dostoyevsky's most vital insights concerns the individual's struggle to bring his contradictory being into
30   harmony with the world. The fact that Dostoyevsky himself fused his being with his art to a near miraculous extent does not suggest the absence of contradiction between the two. He was, by fellow Russian writer Ivan Turgenev's account, an odious and obstinate individual who nonetheless managed to portray the highest

human types in characters such as Prince Myshkin in *The Idiot* and Alyosha in
35   *The Brothers Karamazov*. In his writings Dostoyevsky vehemently challenged
rationality as the supreme guide to human affairs, yet in his life he strove to
perfect an ultra-rational gambling methodology to alleviate his crushing financial
difficulties. Far from masking his brilliance, such contradictions reveal the fallible
human behind it, making Dostoyevsky's accomplishments all the more remarkable.

3. The author is primarily concerned with demonstrating that

⭕ both synergy and conflict characterize the relationship between the life Dostoyevsky
lived and the novels he wrote

⭕ Dostoyevsky expressed the need for individuals to resolve inner conflicts and attempt
to achieve harmony with the world

⭕ people who emphasize a direct link between Dostoyevsky's life and his novels fail to
recognize that contradictions in his life made his achievements possible

⭕ Dostoyevsky deserves the distinction of semi-mythic action figure more than American
adventurers such as Jack London and Ernest Hemingway

⭕ the numerous contradictions between Dostoyevsky's life and works overshadow the
near miraculous degree to which he managed to fuse his being with his art

4. The passage cites each of the following as an element of Dostoyevsky's novels that was
drawn from the writer's personal experience EXCEPT:

⭕ characters suffering from epilepsy or an addiction to gambling
⭕ perceptive observations on criminal psychology
⭕ the possibility of achieving redemption through suffering
⭕ the sudden and dramatic reversal of a death sentence
⭕ the experience of isolation brought on by solitary confinement

5. Which one of the following most accurately describes the author's purpose in referring to
Turgenev's view of Dostoyevsky?

⭕ To demonstrate the incongruity between Dostoyevsky's actual personality and the
perception of him among the reading public

⭕ To show that even an odious and obstinate person is incapable of creating characters
other than those of the highest human type

⭕ To lend credence to the idea that emphasizing the synergy between Dostoyevsky's life
and works is not without merit

⭕ To support the claim that the relationship between Dostoyevsky's life and art was not
free from contradiction

⭕ To provide evidence for the assertion that Dostoyevsky created characters noted for
internal inconsistencies, competing desires, and mysterious motivations

Guided Explanations

1.   **E**

Step 1: Skim and Outline. We trust that you made your way through the passage
and jotted down its main features in a way that makes sense to you.

Step 2: Read the Question and Search for Triggers. The triggers are *According to the passage*, which tells us we're dealing with a Detail question, and *differs*, which tells us we're looking for differences between pure and applied science.

Step 3: Locate Relevant Information and Make a Prediction. The phrase *in contrast* in the first line of paragraph 2 is a great clue as to where the difference between pure and applied science will be found. Reread that part carefully if you feel you need to enhance your quick skim of that section.

The contrast cited is that applied science tries to harness scientific knowledge to have an effect on the world, so it does differ from pure science in the scope of its intentions, statement III. The last line of both paragraphs also indicate that statement I is correct: Applied science can impact negatively upon people's lives in a way that pure science cannot. Statement II is cited as well in the author's discussion of the idea that applied science has the potential to produce both benefits and harm, a more complex scenario than the neutral fact-seeking of pure scientific endeavors.

Step 4: Match Your Prediction to the Answer Choices. E is correct because as we have seen, statements I, II, and III all represent differences between pure and applied science.

---

2.   **D**

Step 1: Skim and Outline. You've already done this before tackling the first question, so move on to Step 2.

Step 2: Read the Question and Search for Triggers. The trigger phrase is *author consider an example of pure science*, which tells us we'll need to reason from the information presented to deduce something about the author's beliefs. That means this is an Implied Information question.

Step 3: Locate Relevant Information and Make a Prediction. Our trigger words tell us that pure science is the subject of this one, and we know from our skim of the passage and our brief notes that that subject is treated mainly in paragraph 1. So that's the paragraph to head for if you need to quickly review what pure science is all about. To this author, pure science is research that has no relation to human industry or other activities.

Step 4: Match Your Prediction to the Answer Choices. Only **D** fits this description, since merely estimating how much the earth weighs doesn't in and of itself accomplish anything other than adding to our knowledge of the universe. The other four choices describe things that fit quite well into the author's definition of applied science: undertakings meant "for the purpose of achieving specific ends."

---

3.   **A**

Step 1: Skim and Outline. As always, perform a quick skim of the passage and take note on your scrap paper of what you consider the most relevant points.

Step 2: Read the Question and Search for Triggers. Since this is a Primary Purpose question, there are no trigger words to speak of, and the correct answer will reflect a general understanding of what the author set out to accomplish.

Step 3: Locate Relevant Information and Make a Prediction. There is no specific information to look for as we're looking for the overall purpose of the entire passage. Rather than make a prediction, the best thing to do is work from the answer choices, so we'll test the answers one by one. Remember, we encourage you to "be flexible" as to how to apply the step method.

A: Choice **A** comes closest to capturing the author's main purpose in the passage. The author doesn't discount the popular view regarding the link between Dostoyevsky's life and works—indeed, he says that Dostoyevsky "fused his being with his art to a near miraculous extent." And if he wanted to disavow the popular view entirely, he wouldn't have gone out of his way to support the general merit of this view with numerous examples in paragraph 2. Instead, he's trying to take it down a notch; trying to show that while there *was* a remarkable amount of synergy between Dostoyevsky's life and works, it didn't reach the epic proportions that some would have us believe. The author tries to complete the story by suggesting that there were also contradictions.

B: Achieving harmony with the world is merely an idea from paragraph 3 that doesn't encompass the author's main intention of discussing synergy and contradiction in Dostoyevsky's life and works.

C: The author states that the contradictions between Dostoyevsky's life and art don't detract from his accomplishments and even make them more remarkable. That's not to say that the author is arguing that these contradictions *enabled* his achievements.

D harks back to role players Jack London and Ernest Hemingway, who aren't important enough figures to be included as part of the author's primary concern. The author didn't write all of this to merely compare Dostoyevsky to his American counterparts.

E gets it backward. The author believes that the popular view of the synergy between Dostoyevsky's life and art overshadows the contradictions between those things, not that the contradictions overshadow the popular view.

---

4.   **E**

Step 1: Skim and Outline. You've already done this, so move right on to Step 2.

Step 2: Read the Question and Search for Triggers. *The passage cites* indicates that this is a Detail question testing your understanding of some fact presented in the passage. *Elements of novels drawn from personal experience* tells us which fact is being tested, so that is your trigger. Moreover, the word EXCEPT tells us that this is a special kind of question looking for the one choice that doesn't represent something from Dostoyevsky's experience that wound up in one of his books.

Step 3: Locate Relevant Information and Make a Prediction. Elements of Dostoyevsky's life encapsulated in his novels are found in paragraph 2, so it makes sense to refresh your memory of those before trying to answer the question. As we are looking for the *exception*, it makes more sense to work from the answer choices and cross off the ones that appear in paragraph 2.

A, B, C, and **D** are explicitly mentioned in the second paragraph as elements of Dostoyevsky's life that he wrote about in his books.

E, however, is the odd man out: While the author states in paragraph 1 that Dostoyevsky was kept in solitary confinement following his arrest, this event is not mentioned in paragraph 2 as something from Dostoyevsky's life that he depicted in his novels.

---

5.   **D**

Step 1: Skim and Outline. One final question to handle, so get right to Step 2 to see what it's after.

Step 2: Read the Question and Search for Triggers. This one's a Detail Purpose question that's interested in why the author mentions Turgenev's view of Dostoyevsky. *Turgenev* is our trigger word.

Step 3: Locate Relevant Information and Make a Prediction. Turgenev is only mentioned once near the middle of paragraph 3. So it pays to reacquaint yourself with this detail by reading a few lines above and a few lines below the Turgenev bit to put that reference in context. Dostoyevsky, according to Turgenev, was a revolting and stubborn person, yet Dostoyevsky portrayed in his works characters embodying the highest human ideals. This information appears in the passage immediately following the assertion that there was contradiction between Dostoyevsky's being and his art.

Therefore, it is likely that Turgenev's opinion of Dostoyevsky is provided as part of an example supporting the author's contention that contradiction existed between Dostoyevsky's life and works.

Step 4: Match Your Prediction to the Answer Choices. Choice **D** is the closest paraphrase to our prediction above.

As for the other choices:

A: The author supplies no evidence that Dostoyevsky *wasn't* odious and obstinate, as Turgenev maintained. Turgenev's depiction therefore isn't provided to contrast the perception of Dostoyevsky's personality with the reality of what he was really like.

B is difficult to decipher, but it appears to be saying that even an odious and obstinate person can only create characters of the highest human type. Not only does this make little sense, but the author's purpose seems to be the opposite: to illustrate the contradiction inherent in the fact that such a revolting person can create such characters *at all*.

C: The detail in question supports the notion of contradiction, not synergy. The evidence referred to in **C** is found in paragraph 2, not where Turgenev appears in paragraph 3.

E refers to Dostoyevsky's insight regarding human contradiction mentioned earlier in paragraph 3. Turgenev's view of Dostoyevsky, expressed later in the paragraph, relates to the *author's theory* regarding *Dostoyevsky's* contradictions.

Chapter 9

Antonyms

One of the milestones of language acquisition is the discovery that things in the world actually have opposites—not just nouns like *day* and *night* but also verbs like *push* and *pull* and adjectives like *rich* and *poor*. Soon after making this discovery, kids find themselves paraded as geniuses by proud parents showing them off to anyone who will listen. "Up," the parents would say, to which the child would dutifully respond "down." This jaw-dropping linguistic display would inevitably be followed by classics like *in* and *out* and *high* and *low,* much to the amazement of the audience. What would really be a neat trick would be if the parents said "obdurate" and the kid responded "compliant." Flashing forward twenty odd years, GRE Antonym questions give you the opportunity to reprise your role as Master of Opposites—except this time no one's applauding. Knocking back these nine or so questions interspersed throughout the Verbal section will, however, help you get into grad school, which should be reward enough.

Antonym questions test not only your vocabulary but also your ability to reason from a concept to its opposite. So while a solid vocabulary is the most important factor in success, a bit of logic comes into play as well. As always, we'll get things started with an X-ray.

ANTONYM X-RAY

Here's what a typical GRE Antonym question looks like:

Directions: The question below consists of a word printed in capital letters, followed by five words or phrases. Choose the word or phrase that is most nearly opposite in meaning to the word in capital letters.

Since some of the questions require you to distinguish fine shades of meaning, be sure to consider all of the choices before deciding which one is best.

BRAZEN:

- ⬭ profound
- ⬭ devilish
- ⬭ reticent
- ⬭ courteous
- ⬭ distressed

The word in capital letters is the one you need to find an antonym for, and it will most likely be a noun, verb, or adjective. The choices may be single words, or they may be phrases. We'll return to the example above in the practice set at the end of the chapter.

There is one small qualification to note: The test makers go out of their way to warn you that these questions deal with "fine shades of meaning," which means you need to consider the words very carefully before settling on a choice. In a booklet of sample questions published by ETS, they go even further by saying that some words used in the questions do not have precise opposites, reiterating that you'll have to look for "the answer choice that expresses a concept most nearly opposite to that of the given word." This means that you have to stay on your toes. A choice that may not seem like the exact opposite of the given word may still be the best of the bunch. Not to worry. This chapter will ensure you know how to successfully tackle GRE Antonyms, regardless of the subtleties.

ANTONYM FUNDAMENTALS

There are three factors that are fundamental to your success on this question type. Let's take a look:

* Vocabulary

* Clues

* Traps

Vocabulary

We know we're stating the obvious, but there's simply no way around it: The better your vocabulary, the better you'll do on Antonym questions. When you know the meaning of the original word and the words in the choices, Antonym questions are perhaps the most straightforward on the GRE. Much like in the childhood opposites act described earlier, the GRE may spit out word X, prompting you to immediately spit back opposite word Y. For example, say the word is *sullen*. You immediately think *gloomy* or *brooding*, which causes something along the lines of *happy* or *joyful* to pop into your head as its opposite. Scanning the choices you come across *gleeful*, and you're done. Boom. Next question. This is the best-case scenario that will play out whenever you know the words, whether those words are easy or difficult.

The best way to improve your performance on GRE Antonyms is therefore to add high-level words to your vocabulary. We encouraged you in the "Meet GRE Verbal" chapter to read widely and deeply, and we suggest that you do so with a dictionary by your side. Look up any unfamiliar words you come across as you peruse the *Economist* or the *New York Times*. You might consider keeping a list of words you don't know or don't know well and adding those to the list of 400 GRE-level vocabulary words we provide in the tear-out chart in this book.

Memorization

Use whatever methods work for you to memorize words. We won't make fun of your silly songs or poems, and no one will hear you chanting strings of polysyllabic nouns in your car. What matters is that your methods work—and that you learn the words.

You could make a CD with words and definitions and listen to it while you drive or while you sleep, which, hopefully, are not simultaneous activities. You could read the dictionary. You could hang out with some really smart people who use big words whenever they can (an annoying behavior practiced by *sesquipedalian* individuals, people who use a big word when a small one would do). Here are some more suggestions.

Use Flash Cards. Flash cards are simple and portable. Write a word on one side and its definition on the other. Take these cards with you wherever you go and use them when you have a free minute or two. Think of a stack of flash cards as a mini-quiz: You look at each word, think of the definition, and then flip the card over to check yourself. If you get it right, set the card aside. If you get it wrong, keep the card in the stack. Repeatedly go through the stack until all the words are in your "got it right" pile. Going through your flash cards in this way gives you a clear-cut method for knowing when you know your words and when you don't.

Create Mnemonic Devices. Some words are hard to remember, plain and simple. These are the words that never seem to make it to your "got it right" pile, no matter how many times you go through them. For these troublesome words, mnemonic devices may be just what you need.

A mnemonic device is a memory aid, usually in the form of a word association. The more off the wall a mnemonic device, the more effective it tends to be. For example, if you have trouble remembering that *craven* means "cowardly or weak-willed," you could think of Cliff Claven, the character from *Cheers*. Among other things, Mr. Claven was pretty cowardly and weak-willed, so *craven* could mean "like Cliff Claven." Be creative—you'll find many tough words can be remembered through suitable mnemonic devices.

Make Up Sentences. Making up sentences is a great way to help you remember difficult words. For each word, make up a sentence that gives a clue to the word's meaning. To be effective, your sentence must be specific. For example, "Edgar is very *philanthropic*" wouldn't be very helpful, but "Since he always gives to charities, Edgar is very *philanthropic*" provides a strong clue that *philanthropic* means "of, relating to, or marked by charity."

Expanding your vocabulary will help you craft a number of "blue sky" antonym scenarios—simply knowing the words and scanning to the correct choice. But it's still likely you'll comes across at least some cases in which you don't know some of the vocab or have only a partial understanding of the words in question.

The rest of the fundamentals in this section are intended to help you at least narrow down the choices in such cases and at best eliminate all but the correct answer.

Clues

There are numerous clues that can shed light on words you don't know. Will these clues help you to define unfamiliar words precisely? Probably not, but they may often help you distinguish possible choices from unlikely ones. Our first clue concerns how words are formed.

Roots, Prefixes, and Suffixes

New words aren't created by people simply sitting around making them up on the spot. If they were, there would probably be more fun words like *blissenfrazzle* and fewer nasty words like *deleterious*. Words are comprised of pieces that reflect their origins and contribute to their definitions. Especially important are roots, prefixes, and suffixes. By learning some of these common building blocks, you'll be able to make intelligent guesses on words whose meanings you may not have memorized. Consider the following fairly difficult Antonym question:

CIRCUMLOCUTION:

- revelation
- brevity
- responsibility
- understanding
- relentlessness

Circum is a prefix that means "around," as in the words *circumference* ("distance around a circle") and *circumvent* ("to go around or bypass"). *Loc* and *loq* are common roots meaning "to speak," as in *eloquent* ("well spoken") and *ventriloquist* ("one who speaks through a wooden dummy"). Putting these two pieces together, *circumlocution* means "a roundabout way of speaking." The opposite of this is *direct speaking* or *concision*, another word for which is *brevity*, choice **B**.

Root, suffix, and prefix clues may not always lead you all the way to the correct choice, as in the example above, but they can help you get in the ballpark. It therefore pays to have a solid command of these common word components. Here are some of the major building blocks of English words, along with the related GRE words you might see on test day. You'll see some of these GRE words again in our vocabulary list in the tear-out chart in this book. If you see a word that you don't know, look it up and learn it.

Helpful Roots

Root	What It Means	Example
aco(u)	to hear, hearing	acoustic
act, ag	to act, to do, to drive	active, agent
agog(ue), agogy	to lead, leader, guiding, inducing	demagogue
agon, agonist	struggle, content	agony, antagonist
alg, algesia, algia	pain	analgesic
am, amat	to love	amiable, amorous
ambul	to walk	circumambulate, amble
andro, andry	male	android, androgynous
anim	mind, feeling, life	animate
anthrop	man, human being	philanthropy, anthropology
aqu	water	aquatic, aquarium
arch	first, ancient, rule	archaic, archive
aud	to hear, hearing, aloud	audible, audience
aug, auct, auth, aux	to increase, to create	augment, author, auxiliary
auto	of, by, for, or in oneself	autobiography, autocrat, autodidact
bene, bon	good	bonus, benefit
brac, brachi	the arm	brachiate, bracelet
cant, cent	to sing	canticle, chant, recant, incantation
cap, capt, cep, cept	box, to take, contain, seize	capture, receipt, capacious
capit, capt, cipit	head, chief	capital, precipitate, chapter, capitulate
carn	flesh	carnal, incarnate, carnivore
caus, cuse	to cause	causal, excuse, accuse
ced, cede, ceed, cess	to yield, to go	cede, accessible, necessary
cern, cert, cret, crim	to separate, to distinguish	discern, uncertain
chrom, chromat	color	chromatic, polychromatic
chron	time	synchronous, chronicle
cid, cide	to kill	regicide, suicide, genocide
cis, cise	to cut	excise, scissors
cog, cogit	to think	cognitive, cogent

Root	What It Means	Example
coll	glue, to stick together	colloquy, collage
corp, cors	body	corporeal, corpulent
cosm	universe, order	cosmic, cosmopolitan
creant, cred, creed	to believe, to trust	credence, credit, incredible
cruc, crus	cross, significant	crux, crusade, crucial
de, div	concerning God or deities	divine, deity
dic, dict, diction	to say, speech, word	dictate, indicate, edict, benediction
doc, doct, dog, dox	to teach, learning	doctrine, dogma, orthodox
dom	house, master	domestic, dominate
equ, qui	equal, even	equate, adequate, equinox
esthe, esthesia	to feel, sensation	anesthesia, esthetics
fid, fidel	faith, trust	fidelity, confidence, infidel
fin, finite	end, purpose	infinite, definite
flu, fluor, flux, fluv	to flow	affluence, fluid, superfluous
for, fort	strong	fortress, enforce, comfort
fract, frag, frang, fring	to shatter	fracture, fragment, fragile, refract
gen, gon	birth, race, kind	genetic, gonad, congenital, gender
ger, gest	to carry, to produce	gestate, gesture, digest
grad, grade, gress	to step, a degree or grade	gradual, degree, progress
gram, graph	a written record, to write	telegram, autograph
grat	pleasing, thankful	gratitude, congratulate, ingratiate
greg	society, group	aggregate, gregarious
gynec, gyn, gynist	female	gynecologist, misogyny
hier, hieratic	holy, sacred	hierarchy, hieroglyphic
hol	whole	holistic, hologram
hydr, hydro	water, liquid	hydraulics, hydrant
ideo	idea, philosophy	ideology, idol, ideal
idi, idio	personal, private	idiosyncratic, idiom
iso	equal, similar	isometric, isotope
ject, jet	to throw	eject, inject, jettison, projectile

Root	What It Means	Example
jud, jur, just	right, law	jury, judgment, judicious, injury, perjury
jug, junct	a link, to join	juncture, conjunction, conjugate
kine, kinesia, kinesis	movement, energy	kinetic, cinema
lat, late, lation	to bear, to carry	collate, correlate, legislate, translate
lect, leg, lig	to choose, to read	legible, intelligent, dialect, collect
lev, lieve, life	to lift, light in weight	alleviate, elevator, relief
lign, line	line	delineate, lineage
locut, loqu, loquy	to speak, speech	locution, circumlocution, eloquent, ventriloquist
log, logue, logy, lexico	speech, word, study of	logic, lecture, analogy
luc, lumin, lux	light, to shine	illuminate, lucent, luminary, elucidate
macro	large	macrocosm
mal	bad	malady, malcontent, malefactor
medi, meso, mid	in the middle of	intermediate, mediocre, medium
micro	small	microscope
mis	hate	misanthrope, misogyny
mor, mort	death	mortal, mortician, mortify
neg	to deny	negate, neglect, renege
neo	new	neologism, neonate
noct, nox	night	nocturnal, equinox
nom, num	law	nomad, economy, astronomy
od, odia	smell	odor, odious
opt, optic	eye, vision	panopticon, optics,
ov, ovul	egg, egg-shaped	oval, ovulate
par, pare	equal	pair, parity, peer, compare
part, patri	father	patriot, patronage, patriarch, paternal
path, pathic, pathy	emotion, suffering	pathological, pathetic, sympathy, empathy
pel, puls	to drive, driven	pulse, compulsion, expel, impulse

Root	What It Means	Example
phil, philia	love, fondness for	philosophy, philanthropy, philander, philology
phob, phobo	fear	phobia
plaud, plaus, plod, plos	to make a loud noise	applaud, explode
plen, plet	to fill, full	plentiful, plethora, replenish
prim, prin	first	primary, primate, premier
pur, purg	to clear of guilt, to get rid of something unwanted	purge, pure, expurgate, purgatory
quest, quir, quisit	to ask	request, inquest, question, acquire, conquer
qui, quil, quit	rest	quiet, quit, acquiesce, acquit
rad, radic	root	radical, eradicate
rati, reas	to think, calculate	rate, ratify, rational, reasonable
rect, reg, rig	to rule or guide, proper, straight	rectify, regal, region, regulate, rigorous
rupt	to break, to sever	rupture, abrupt, disrupt, corrupt, interrupt
salu, salv	safety, health	salubrious, salvage, salutary
scrib, scribe, script	to write, something written	circumscribe, ascribe, describe, inscribe, prescribe
secut, sequ	to follow, to ensue	sequence, consequence, execute, consecutive
sen, senil	old, old age	senior, senator, senescence
ser, sor	a series, attachment	serial, desert, assert
solute, solv	to release, to loosen, to free	dissolve, absolute, insoluble
soph, sophy	wisdom	philosophy, sophisticated
spec, spect, spic	to look, to see	aspect, specific, spectator, spectrum, specimen
spir, spire	to breathe, breath, spirit	aspire, expire, conspire, transpire
stant, stat, stit	to stand, to stay, to state	assistant, consistent, constant, status, stance, destiny
stru, struct	to build, a building or pattern	destructive, instruct, obstruct, structural
tact, tang, teg, ting	to touch	tactile, taste, tangible, contact, contingent
temper, tempor, temp	time, balance	temporize, temporary, contemplate, temperature
ten, tain, tent, tin	to hold	tenable, tenacious, tenet, contain, detain

Root	What It Means	Example
tend, tens	to stretch	extend, distend, tension, tendril
top, tope, topy	place	topic, topology, utopia
tract, treat	to draw, to extend, to attract	extract, treatise, contract, retreat, subtract
trib, tribe, trit	to rub, to wear down	tribulation, trite, attrition
trop, tropic, tropy	to turn, a change or turn	trope, tropic, entropy
troub, turb	confusion, whirling	disturb, perturb, turbine, turbulence
vac, van, vast, void	empty, desolate	vacuum, vacant, vanity, devastate, avoid
vail, val	to be strong, to be worthy	valiant, valor, validate, valence
ver, veri	true	veracious, verdict, verify
vit, viv	life, to live	vital, survive, viable, vivify
voc, vok, vow	voice, to call or summon	vocalize, vociferous, avow, equivocate
vol	will, desire, wish	volition, volunteer, involuntary
vor, vorous, vour	to eat, to swallow	voracious, carnivorous
xene, xeno, xeny	foreign	xenophobe, xenogamy
zoa, zo, zoo, zoon	life, living	zoo, zodiac, metazoan

Helpful Prefixes and Suffixes

Prefix or Suffix	What It Means	Example
a, an	not, without	apathy, analgesic
ab, abs	away, from, separated	abdicate, abort
ac, ad	to, toward	acclaim, accrete, adhere, adjoin
ambi, amphi	both, around	ambiguous, ambidextrous, ambiance
ante, anter	before, prior, in front of	antebellum, antechamber, anterior, antique
ap, apo	away from, detached	apology, apostate, apostle
cata, cat, cath	downwards, against, contrary to	cataclysm, catapult, catharsis

Prefix or Suffix	What It Means	Example
circum	around	circumscribe, circumspect, circumference
co, com, con	with, together	cohabitation, comfort, collude, colloquy
contra	against	contradict, contrast
de	down from, reverse, remove, out of, derived from	decapitate, declare, deface, delegate, delineate
di, dif, dis	separation	disable, dispute, decrease, divert
dys	bad, difficult	dysentery, dysphoria
ec, ecto, ex	outside of, external, away from	eclectic, ecstasy, excursion, excuse, explode
em, en, ent	in, into, within	encourage, endemic, embryo, embargo, enchant
epi	over, above, around	epilogue, epitome, epidemic
eu, ev	well, good	euphoria, eulogy, euphemism
hyper	more, beyond normal, excessive	hyperkinetic, hypersonic
hypo	less, under, below	hypochondria, hypothesis
in, im, em, en	in, on, amongst, within	incarnate, insert, inspire, instruct, immolate, employ, enchant
in, im	not	immeasurable, improper, inadequate
men, ment	result, means of or product of an action	instrument, ailment, compartment, entanglement
meta, meth	after, along with, transfer, changed	metabolism, metaphor, metaphysics, method
mis	worse, badly	mischief, misadventure, mistake
ob, of, op	toward, against, face-to-face	object, obnoxious, occupy, oppose
par, para	beside, near, faulty	paradox, parasite, parody
per	through, thoroughly	perceive, permit, perpetrate, persuade
peri	around, near, beside	perimeter, peripheral
pre	before, in front of	precept, precede, prediction, predominant, pregnant
pro	earlier, before, forward	proclivity, pronounce, propose
re	back, backwards	recant, recount, recur
se	aside, away	secede, seclude, sever

Prefix or Suffix	What It Means	Example
syl, sym, syn	united, together with, same	synonym, sympathy, syllogism
tra, trans	beyond, across, through	transact, traverse, transport
un	not	unable, undeniable, undone

Word Charge

Even when you don't know the exact meaning of a word, you may still get a sense of the general *feel* of the word; specifically, whether it carries a positive or negative charge. Sometimes you'll be able to recognize the charge of an unfamiliar word by comparing it to similar words you do know. Consider, for example, the word *morbific*. You may not know what this means, but you do know that words like *morbid*, *morgue*, and *mortuary* all have negative connotations, and for a good reason: They all deal with death. You could reasonably infer therefore that *morbific* carries a negative charge and look for something positive and cheerful among the choices as your opposite. In fact, *morbific* means "causing disease," so something life-affirming along the lines of *healthful* would do the trick. If, on the other hand, you can't nail down a precise definition of a word yet sense it has a positive aura, then you can narrow the choices down to those that sound negative.

DON'T GET STUCK IN NEUTRAL

Some words don't feel positive or negative, in which case they may be neutral. You won't see any neutral words as the featured word in an Antonym question since it's difficult to form an opposite of a word that doesn't lean in a particular direction. However, you may come across neutral words in the choices and can eliminate those off the bat since nothing that's neutral can be the opposite of the original word. What's the opposite of *statue*, or *computer*, or *turquoise*? There are no genuine opposites for these words, so they can't be correct.

Parts of Speech

Sometimes the test makers throw a curveball by using words with multiple meanings. Say you come to an Antonym question based on the word *compound*. This can be a noun meaning "a cluster of homes," as in "the Smith clan retreated to their family compound." As a noun, it can also mean "a chemical substance formed by two or more elements." *Compound* can also be an adjective meaning "something composed of multiple parts," like a compound sentence or a compound fracture. Then again, *compound* can be used as a verb, meaning "to combine to form a whole," or, in a different sense, to "intensify" or "complicate," as in "Jordan will compound his problems at work if he misses Thursday's meeting." *Compound* is clearly a complicated word with many possible meanings—how are you supposed to know which one is being tested?

One clue is the part of speech of the answer choices. If the choices are nouns, then the noun form of the stem word is the definition you should seek, since the part of speech of the choices must match that of the original word. If you're unsure of what form of the word they're after, take a quick look at choice **A** to see if it's a noun, verb, or adjective. You need not look any further than that, since all the choices will be the same part of speech. If you don't know the word in choice **A**, or it too can take various forms, then scan for an unambiguous word among the choices that you do know and note its part of speech. Check out how the choices help to clear up the ambiguity in our *compound* example:

COMPOUND:

- ○ relinquish
- ○ renounce
- ○ simplify
- ○ dismiss
- ○ amplify

The choices are verbs, which means we should focus on the verb forms of the capitalized word. We saw above that *compound* could mean to "complicate," which leads us to *simplify*, choice **C**, as the opposite. The choices provide the clue we need to help us zero in on the intended meaning of the original word, bringing us one step closer to the correct answer.

Traps

Even when you know the word, that doesn't guarantee the question will be cake. Remember the test makers' caveat: The questions may test "fine shades of meaning." What this means is that you will often come across wrong choices that come close to being the opposite of the original but are one small and subtle step removed. Such choices often seem reasonably related to the word in question, and may even lean in the opposite direction, but they don't make it all the way there. Take, for example, the word *permeate*. One definition is "to pass through or seep into," as in "the aroma permeated the second story window." An example of a trap for this question is *solid*. A *solid* may be an object that's difficult or impossible to permeate, but *solid* itself is not the opposite of *permeate*. The words are related in a negative sort of way, but not negatively enough to be opposites.

Here's a full example. See if you can not only get the right answer, but also figure out which choice is rigged as a trap.

TOXIN:

- ○ damage
- ○ health
- ○ inoculation
- ○ fragrance
- ○ antidote

Actually, there are two traps here, as the test makers hit you with a one-two punch in **B** and **C** hoping to waylay you before you make it to correct choice **E**. A *toxin* is a poison, and the opposite of poison is *antidote*, a substance that counteracts a poison. But **B** and **C** are sure tempting, because toxins are heavily associated with sickness and *health* is the opposite of sickness, while an *inoculation* is meant to *prevent* sickness. *Health* and *inoculation* both stand in contrast to *toxin* in some sense but don't qualify as actual opposites. That's what makes them traps. And speaking of antidotes, the only antidote to falling for such traps is a very careful consideration of each choice. Stay on the lookout for how the test makers manipulate the "shades of meaning" they warn you about in the directions. When you fall for traps in practice questions, analyze what sets the correct choice apart from the trap so you'll be less likely to make the same kind of mistake again.

That takes care of the fundamentals, so let's now turn our attention to a methodical process for attacking the nine or so Antonym questions you'll see on test day.

ANTONYM STEP METHOD

Antonym questions can take the least time of all the Verbal question types, if you know the meaning of the word in the question stem. The method for this best-case scenario is simple and to the point. We'll talk later about how to go about it when you're stumped by the stem word, but when you know it, follow these steps:

Step 1: **Simplify the Word.**

Step 2: **Predict an Opposite.**

Step 3: **Match Your Prediction to the Answer Choices.**

Here are the basics of each step.

Step 1: Simplify the Word. Even if you know the meaning of the word in question, that doesn't mean it's in its most user-friendly form. Since you'll be trying to make your own prediction in Step 2, it makes sense to work with the easiest form of the word you can think of. If the original word is already easy for you, then there's no need to simplify it. No doubt you can work with a word like *greedy* as is, and trying to simplify it may be more trouble than it's worth. However, it probably pays to turn a word like *relinquish* into *give up* before trying to think of potential opposites.

Step 2: Predict an Opposite. When you're comfortable with the word in question or a simplified synonym for it, try to come up with an opposite of your own before looking at the answer choices. If you go to the choices immediately, they may distract you from your understanding of the word or cause you to lose your train of thought. You're less likely to go off track if you have a notion in mind before you hit the choices. Remember that positively charged words will have negatively charged antonyms, and vice versa. Your prediction need not be elegant, nor should you expect to find your exact prediction among the choices. The important thing is to come up with a notion that will represent the essence of the right choice so you'll recognize it when you see it.

Step 3: Match Your Prediction to the Answer Choices. When you have a prediction in mind, scan the choices for it. Optimally, you'll breeze by the imposters until you come across one that matches your idea. Even then, you should quickly check the other choices to make sure there's not a stronger opposite. And sometimes you'll still have to work a bit harder for the point. Even if you know the meaning of the stem word and have a viable prediction at your fingertips, you still may need to employ some of the fundamentals discussed earlier, or other strategies discussed below, to eliminate wrong choices before settling on a choice.

Guided Practice

We'll demonstrate the basic step method with the following example.

SUPERFLUOUS:

- ⬭ derogatory
- ⬭ random
- ⬭ indispensable
- ⬭ intellectual
- ⬭ obstinate

Step 1: Simplify the Word. It may not be the toughest word you'll see on the test, so let's assume you know what *superfluous* means. Still, it could use a bit of translation for our purposes, so let's simplify: Something *superfluous* is something that's "more than required," "not essential," or "unnecessary." Any of these notions would do, so let's carry them with us into Step 2.

Step 2: Predict an Opposite. The opposite of something that's "more than required," "not essential," or "unnecessary" is something that's "required," "essential," or "necessary." Any of these words would make for a fine prediction.

Step 3: Match Your Prediction to the Answer Choices. With our predictions in mind, *indispensable* should jump out, since something indispensable is something one can't do without; that is, something required, essential, or necessary. **C** means the same as our prediction and is therefore correct.

But let's say you had some initial trouble with the word *indispensable*. Referring back to our section on word prefixes, suffixes, and roots, you can still make a proper guess at it. Note that the word is formed from the word *dispense*. You probably do know that *dispense* means "to get rid of." The prefix *in* means "not" or "without," so something *indispensable* is something that cannot be gotten rid of, which brings us back to *necessary*. It also brings us to our next section, which contains strategies to help you when you're not so sure of the tested word.

Tame the Tough Stuff

Mercurial? Phlegmatic? Parsimonious? Come on, virtually no one knows every word the test makers dig up for GRE Antonym questions, especially those lurking in the deep end of the question pool. And some, like the ones starting this paragraph, are simply beyond the pale if you didn't happen to memorize them. But that doesn't mean you still can't use a bit of strategy to tilt the odds in your favor. We've already discussed in the fundamentals section how word components, parts of speech, and word charges can provide clues to the meaning of unfamiliar words. We also provided examples of the kinds of traps the test makers like to set for the unwary. Here are a few more tips that may help you power through even when you're stumped at first by the word in question.

- Relate the Word to Words You Know

- Create a Context

Relate the Word to Words You Know

Let's jump right in with an example. Say you came across this word in an Antonym question: *metamorphose*. That's a scary bit of language, isn't it? But notice how you can alter it just a tad to come up with the similar-sounding word *metamorphosis*, which you likely remember from high school biology as the process by which a caterpillar changes into a butterfly. The operative word is *change*, and in fact, to *metamorphose* means "to change the nature of" or "to transform." The opposite will therefore be something along the lines of *remain unaltered, maintain,* or *preserve.*

Try another example: *alleviate.* You may know its meaning, but if you don't, you might notice that the root *lev* shows up in altered forms in words like *relieve* and *relief,* suggesting that *alleviate* might mean something like *make better.* It also wouldn't hurt if you were familiar with the pain reliever "Aleve." Is it likely that a company would name a pain reliever after something bad or harmful? No. The point is that words have associations with other words, and you can use word associations to help you get in the ballpark of the definitions of words you don't know.

Create a Context

While an unfamiliar word may bring other words to mind, even better is if it triggers a phrase or sentence based on a common usage of that word. For example, you may not know the word *surrogate* if you encounter it in isolation, but you may have heard the phrase "surrogate mother" applied to a woman who carries someone else's child. You can infer from this context that *surrogate* means someone who helps someone else, but it would be better to be as specific as possible: A *surrogate* is someone who *acts in place of someone else—a substitute.* An antonym for this might be *original* or *principal.* These may not be precise opposites, but remember, your job is to choose the word most nearly opposite in meaning to the word in question.

Let's try creating contexts for *veto* and *annulment*. If you aren't able to precisely define *veto*, you may still recognize its most common use, as in "The president vetoed the bill." If you know what a presidential veto is, then you can deduce that to veto means "to reject." It can also be used as a noun, being the rejection itself, as in "The president's veto was scorned by the opposing party." In this case, context can help you get a jump on the word, but you'd still benefit from checking the choices to see which part of speech the test makers are after.

As for the second example, what comes to mind when you hear the word *annul*? Marriages, of course—at least ones being called off. By itself the word *annulment* may elude you, but if you think of an annulled marriage, definitions like "cancellation" or "termination" should spring to mind.

PRACTICE PROBLEMS

Let's now try a few examples based on what you've learned.

<u>Directions</u>: Each question consists of a word printed in capital letters, followed by five words or phrases. Choose the word or phrase that is most nearly <u>opposite</u> in meaning to the word in capital letters.

Since some of the questions require you to distinguish fine shades of meaning, be sure to consider all of the choices before deciding which one is best.

1. BRAZEN:

    ○ profound
    ○ devilish
    ○ reticent
    ○ courteous
    ○ distressed

2. SANCTIFICATION:

    ○ religiosity
    ○ atheism
    ○ prescription
    ○ salutation
    ○ desecration

3. INTERMINABLE:

- ⟲ returnable
- ⟲ finite
- ⟲ lengthy
- ⟲ justifiable
- ⟲ luxurious

4. VARIEGATED:

- ⟲ subliminal
- ⟲ dazzling
- ⟲ bland
- ⟲ uniform
- ⟲ magnanimous

5. SOUND:

- ⟲ perplexing
- ⟲ judicious
- ⟲ deafening
- ⟲ long forgotten
- ⟲ ill-conceived

Guided Explanations

1. **C**

Step 1: Simplify the Word. *Brazen* means "bold," "loud," and "cocky"—it describes someone who's really in your face.

Step 2: Predict an Opposite. The opposite of someone who's loud and in your face is someone who's quiet or shy. Let's go with that as our prediction.

Step 3: Match Your Prediction to the Answer Choices. If you know that *reticent* means "quiet and reserved," then you'd scan right to **C** and pick up the point. But even if you didn't know that word, no other word matches our prediction, so you'd be left with **C** anyway. The next closest choice, the trap if you will, is *courteous*. While a quiet or shy person *may* be courteous, he or she may not be. *Reticent* better expresses the opposite of *brazen*, so **C** is correct.

2. **E**

Step 1: Simplify the Word. The word *sanctification* is difficult, but perhaps you benefited from an understanding of the word root *sanct*, which means *holy*. Or maybe you went the word association route: *Sanctify* and *sanction* mean "to bless or allow," so the word has a positive charge in any case. Even if you don't fully grasp the stem word, you can get a sense of its meaning from its root and a sense of its charge from words that sound similar.

Step 2: Predict an Opposite. If you know that *sanctification* means "dedication" or "blessing," a prediction like *violation* or *destruction* might spring to mind.

Step 3: Match Your Prediction to the Answer Choices. Choice **E**, *desecration* (meaning "defilement" or "vandalism"), comes closest to the predictions above. If you had to rely mainly on the positive charge of the stem word, then you could at least have determined that the answer must be negatively charged, allowing you to eliminate **D**, *salutation* (meaning "greeting" or "salute"), as too positive. *Prescription*, whether it refers to a recommendation or to medicine, is too neutral to serve as an opposite, so you can chop **C** on that count. Choices **A** and **B** are both traps, seeming to relate in some meaningful way to the religious aspect of *sanctification*. *Religiosity* is just what it sounds like—the quality of being religious—so it's actually in line with the stem word, if not a precise synonym. *Atheism* seems to go against the religious notion of sanctification but doesn't qualify as a full-fledged opposite. We need something that actively defies the spirit of consecration or dedication, and *desecration* best fits the bill.

3.　　**B**

Step 1: Simplify the Word. If you had trouble with the meaning of *interminable*, analyzing its components or placing it in a context may have helped you out. First the components: The word root *term* often designates some sort of ending, as in *termination* and "the *terminal* phase of the project." If nothing else, you may have heard about someone who was terminated from his job, meaning fired. The prefix *in* denotes "not" or "without," so *interminable* means "without end." Perhaps a sentence got you there instead: Have you ever heard someone (or yourself) say, "That lecture/plane ride/sermon/holiday dinner with the relatives was *interminable*? It's an emphatic way of saying the darn thing seemed to go on forever, and ever, and ever. . . . Maybe you just knew the word, or maybe you used some clues like these. Either way, our best simplification is *endless*.

Step 2: Predict an Opposite. The opposite of something that's *endless* is something that's *limited* or *restricted*, so let's go with those as our predictions.

Step 3: Match Your Prediction to the Answer Choices. *Finite* is a synonym for *limited* or *restricted* and is therefore the best antonym of the bunch. Something that's *finite* ends; something that's *interminable* doesn't. Incidentally, don't worry that in the sentence we constructed in Step 1 the *interminable* events (plane ride, holiday dinner, etc.) technically *do* have endings. We used a figure of speech—a valid form of context—to get closer to the definition, which is fine as long as we remember that the actual definition may be more precise.

4. **D**

Step 1: Simplify the Word. If you know the word *variegated*, then good for you!—you're surely in the minority. If not, then possibly you saw in that word the beginnings of other words you *do* know like *varied* and *variety*. True to form, *variegated* has a related meaning: "diversified" and "diverse," particularly in terms of appearance. We can go with "varied looking" as our simplification.

Step 2: Predict an Opposite. The opposite of something that is "varied looking" is an appearance that is standardized, homogenous, the same. We'll keep those ideas in mind as we hit the choices.

Step 3: Match Your Prediction to the Answer Choices. The prefix *uni* means one, so *uniform* means "having one form or appearance." That's the best antonym of the bunch, so **D** is correct. The closest trap choice is probably *bland* (**C**), but just because something isn't varied in appearance doesn't necessarily make it bland. *Dazzling* (**B**) has a similar kind of tenuous connection to *variegated*, although if anything it belongs in the same camp so is even further from qualifying as an opposite. *Subliminal* (**A**) means "unconscious" or "hidden," which has no obvious connection one way or the other to *variegated*. *Magnanimous*, choice **E**, means "generous" or "high-minded," which also has nothing to do with variety or appearance.

---

5. **E**

Step 1: Simplify the Word. Simplify a simple word like *sound*? No need to, right? Wrong. You may have assumed that *sound* is being used here as a noun, as in the thing that happens when you accidentally knock over Aunt Mabel's thousand-dollar crystal bowl (besides a whuppin'). If you went down that path, you wouldn't find anything quite resembling an opposite among the choices, although a trap is laid in that direction, as you'll see below. Here's where it helps to remember that the test makers like to use *secondary* meanings of common words to shake things up a bit. If you used our technique of noticing the part of speech of the answer choices, you'd see that they're not nouns but adjectives, which means that the noun form of *sound*—the kind of sound you hear—is not the meaning in play here. What does *sound* mean when used as an adjective? Try creating some context: You've no doubt heard about a *sound* argument—in fact, you yourself are charged with creating a *sound* argument in another section of the GRE. In this context, *sound* means "well thought-out" or "logical."

Step 2: Predict an Opposite. Once we nail down the correct form of the word, predicting an opposite isn't very difficult. The opposite of *logical* is *illogical*, so looking for something along those lines will be our plan of attack in Step 3.

Step 3: Match Your Prediction to the Answer Choices. *Ill-conceived,* meaning "badly thought-out," closely captures the essence of *illogical*, so **E** gets the point.

There are a few nasty traps lurking in this one, so let's have a look at them. While an illogical argument may be *perplexing* ("confusing, hard to understand"), it need not be, nor does something perplexing necessarily need to be illogical. So choice **A** is one step removed from being a viable opposite. **C**, meanwhile, seems to play off the more common definition of sound as something we hear, yet we still wouldn't say that the opposite of *sound* is *deafening*. The opposite of *sound* may be *silence*, and some genius coined the well-known phrase "the silence was deafening," but this is all too far afield to get the point, especially when **E** is pretty much dead on. In case you're wondering, one definition of *judicious* is "well thought-out," so **B** is actually synonymous with *sound*, while long forgotten, choice **D**, has no connection to *sound* at all.

Chapter 10

Analogies

In this question type, you're given two words that are related in some way, and it is your job to find the pair of words among the choices that exhibits the same relationship. Knowing the words in the original pair is a great first step, but if that's all there was to it, this question type would be called "Definitions" instead of "Analogies." An element of logic is also involved, since you need to reason out the link between the words in the original to determine the choice containing the parallel relationship. In this chapter, we'll teach you all about the kinds of relationships you're likely to see.

It's likely that you'll see roughly seven Analogy questions on your test interspersed throughout the Verbal section. The easiest way to wrap your mind around the concept of GRE Analogies is to see an example, so let's get right to our X-ray.

ANALOGY X-RAY

Here is what a typical Analogy question looks like:

Directions: In this question, a related pair of words or phrases is followed by five pairs of words or phrases. Select the pair that best expresses a relationship similar to that expressed in the original pair.

IMPLICIT : STATED ::

○ straightforward : pithy
○ urgent : imperative
○ harsh : bright
○ exotic : commonplace
○ cheap : devoted

Borrowing a term from the directions, we'll call the capitalized pair in the question the "original," and we'll dub the answer we seek the "match." We'll come back to this specific question later on, but first let's take a quick look at the directions so you'll never have to bother with them again.

The key word here is *relationship*. The original pair absolutely must have a relationship that will be mimicked in the correct match. Finding the connection between the two words of the original pair will therefore be at the heart of our strategy for this question type. As you'll see, some choices will contain pairs with weak or even nonexistent relationships, and you'll get practice dismissing these right off the bat.

ANALOGY FUNDAMENTALS

There are three fundamentals that are integral to mastering GRE Analogies:

- Vocabulary

- Analogy Types

- Weak Links

Vocabulary

The same thing we told you about Antonyms in the previous chapter applies here: The better your vocabulary, the better you'll do on Analogy questions. As you'll see, the first and best line of attack for these kinds of questions is to know what both words in the original mean and to use your understanding of the words to determine the connection between them. You will most likely come across some questions containing unfamiliar words (especially if you've answered many Verbal questions correctly, landing you in the deep end of the question pool), and we'll show you ways to improve your odds on those. But the most surefire method simply starts with knowing the words, so improving your vocabulary pays big dividends in this part of the test. You *are* studying our list of 400 words in the tear-out chart we provided, right? If not, get to it, and begin or continue working with the other vocabulary-enhancement strategies you learned about in the previous chapter.

Analogy Types

Now, the English language is vast, containing a near infinite number of possible connections between words. Luckily for you, the GRE test makers don't seem to know that. They rely on a fairly manageable number of common connections when constructing Analogy questions. There's no way to predict every single connection they may come up with, but here are eight major types of analogies to get you started:

1. Category

2. Attribute

3. Action

4. Function

5. Composition

6. Cause and Effect

7. Degree

8. Meaning

As we analyze the common connections found in the following analogy types, we'll suggest ways to generalize those connections into generic "templates" that will make it easier for you to test the choices. You'll see what we mean in our first type of analogy, which is called Category.

Category

In Category analogies, one word in the original pair names a category into which the other word typically fits. Here are some examples:

> a CANAL is a type of WATERWAY
>
> a SOLILOQUY is a type of SPEECH
>
> a NIGHTMARE is a type of DREAM

Notice in that last one that we can be even more specific regarding the connection: A nightmare is a *bad* type of dream. We'll talk more about narrowing the connection when necessary later on in this chapter.

Once you've determined the connection between the words in the original pair, creating a "template" to generalize the connection will make your life easier when it comes to searching for the match among the choices. We'll use Xs and Ys to form our templates. The common all-purpose template for Category analogies is:

> X is a type of Y

Whenever you can be more specific in your template—for example, as in the case of the nightmare/dream example—do so.

Attribute

In Attribute analogies, one word describes an integral characteristic of the other word. In easier questions, the characteristic is fairly obvious; in difficult questions, it's more subtle. Check out the following examples:

a DICTATOR has POWER

a NEOPHYTE is INEXPERIENCED

a JOKE contains HUMOR

In each case, the noun in the first word of the pair wouldn't be that thing without the attribute in the second word; for example, we couldn't call someone a *neophyte* if he or she wasn't *inexperienced*. Here's the basic Attribute template to use, to be modified depending on the specifics of the word pair in question:

X is characterized by Y

Notice that an analogy can also be based around the idea that one of the words is NOT characterized by the attribute stated in the other word. If we changed INEXPERIENCED in the second example above to EXPERIENCED, the template would become "X is NOT characterized by Y." The *form* of the relationship is not altered if we introduce a negative; it still falls into the Attribute category. The same goes for the other analogy types in this section as well.

Action

Action analogies relate something to what that thing or being typically does. Here's a simple example:

a SURGEON performs SURGERY

Here's a harder one:

a PREVARICATOR (*liar*) creates a FABRICATION (*lie, untruth*)

In both of the examples above, one noun relates to another noun, connected by an action verb (*performs, creates*). You might see a noun/verb Action pairing instead:

SURGEON : OPERATE

PREVARICATOR : LIE

An Action analogy can also be formed from an adjective/noun pair:

DISGRUNTLED : COMPLAIN

The connection in this one is that a person who is *disgruntled* is likely to *complain*.

So depending on the parts of speech of the words in the original, your Action template might look something like these, with the appropriate verb substituted for *does* depending on the situation:

X does Y

a person or thing that is X does Y

Function

Function analogies are similar to Action analogies, but in this case the function of one word is to perform some action on the other word. For example:

the purpose of a CHAINSAW is to cut down TREES

This represents a noun/noun pairing, so a good template would be:

the purpose of X is to do something to Y

Notice the difference between that example and this one:

the purpose of a HOMILY is to EDIFY

This one pairs a noun, *homily* (sermon, lecture), with a verb, *edify* (instruct). A good template for this would be:

the purpose of X is to Y

Composition

In Composition analogies, one word describes something made up of the other word. One word may be the predominant building block of the other, such as in the following examples:

a PARAGRAPH is composed of SENTENCES

a MOLECULE is composed of ELEMENTS

a THEOREM is composed of POSTULATES

Another possibility is that the smaller entity is part of the larger, but not the only or predominant part:

a PETAL is part of a FLOWER (although the flower
is not composed entirely of petals)

In such cases, if you can further define *what part of* one word the other word is, even better:

a GARRET is the top story of a DOMICILE

So when you think some form of composition characterizes a particular analogy, look to use some form of the following templates:

X is composed of Y

Y is a part of X

Cause and Effect

A Cause and Effect analogy works just like it sounds: One word in the pair is the cause, and the other is the effect. That means that one word is an action, result, or situation that the other word creates or stops. For example, in noun/noun Cause and Effect analogies, one of the nouns is an object that causes or stops the other noun:

a BANDAGE stops the flow of BLOOD

Template-wise, we can think about it that specifically or, if that's too narrow to match a choice, could generalize it a bit as well:

X stops the flow of Y

or:

X causes Y to stop doing something

In verb/adjective Cause and Effect analogies, the verb describes an action and the adjective describes the effect of that action:

to ABRIDGE something is to make it CONDENSED

Our template for this one could sound like:

to do X causes something to be Y

Notice that Cause and Effect analogies can work in two directions: One word can cause something to happen or cause it *not* to happen. Either way, there's a causal element at work.

Degree

In a Degree analogy, one word is a stronger version of the other. An effective word to express this relationship is *very*, as in the following examples:

to be METICULOUS is to be very CAREFUL

to be ARID is to be very DRY

to be EMACIATED is to be very SLIM

The most basic template to use for degree analogies is therefore:

X is very Y

There are other ways to express variances in degree other than using the word *very*. Anything that indicates a similarity in meanings differing only in intensity will do. The words you use to connect the dots and create a template will depend on the words in question. Here are a few other examples of degree relationships:

a POKE is weaker than a PUNCH

(X is a weaker form of Y)

a MURMUR is lower than a SHOUT

(X is a lower form of Y)

EUPHORIA is an extreme form of HAPPINESS

(X is an extreme form of Y)

Meaning

Linking the meaning of one word with that of another may be the most straight-forward connection you can create—maybe they mean exactly the same thing, or maybe they're opposites. Of course, just because the idea behind synonyms and antonyms is easy to understand doesn't mean the test makers won't toughen things up by throwing in some killer vocab. In any case, you may come across a pair of words that have the same definition and are also similar in both degree and connotation. For example:

something PERMEABLE is always PENETRABLE

Or in template form:

X is always Y

Using "is always" as opposed to just "is" when creating your template will help ensure that you're representing the synonym connection correctly.

Two variations on the synonym theme occur when two words generally mean the same thing but differ in *degree* or *connotation*. We just dealt with degree in the previous category, so let's take a look at connotation, which has to do with the general aura surrounding a word or concept. Consider the following pair:

QUESTION : INTERROGATE

You may be thinking these are pure synonyms since they do basically mean the same thing. However, *interrogate* has a bit of a negative connotation; it conjures up images of a suspect being grilled in a back room of a police station or a wit-ness being harangued by a lawyer at a trial. To *interrogate* is to *question* but with a slight hint of implied pressure. You might *question* your chemistry professor about why a solution turned bright orange, but you probably wouldn't *interro-gate* her on the matter. If the test makers were looking for a genuine synonym for *question*, they would go with something along the lines of *inquire*. If this QUESTION : INTERROGATE pair showed up on the GRE, the matching pair would also contain a similar element of connotation in its relationship.

Moving to the other side of *meaning*, the original may contain words that are opposites. As you know, Antonym questions appear as a distinct question type in the Verbal section, but don't be surprised if an Antonym pair makes a cameo among the Analogy questions too. Here's an example:

something LUCID is never CONFUSING

THE
GRE

And here's a simple template for it:

X is never Y

"Is not" is not the strongest template you can use here. Use "is never" to express the full opposition between the words.

So there you have it—eight of the most common connections that you'll see among word pairs in Analogy questions. These are by no means the only possible relationships tested, but they'll get you on your way. As you practice, take note of any other kinds of relationships you come across, and treat them the same way as we did above: Connect the dots between the words in the original, and then use that connection to form a general template that you'll use to test the choices.

Now let's move on to our next fundamental, which will help you to narrow down the answer choices.

Weak Links

Since the whole point of Analogy questions is to find the choice that best mimics the connection between the words in the original pair, it stands to reason that there must be a strong and definable link between those words. That means that a definite connection must also link the words in the correct choice. Some choices, however, fail to meet this standard. Learn to be very discerning when connecting the dots; some relationships that seem reasonable at first glance don't hold up to closer inspection. For example, consider the relationship of the following words to the word *basement*:

underground

dank

room

They all seem to relate, but only the first and third would legitimately appear in a dictionary definition of basement: *Underground* is *where* it is, and *room* is *what* it is. A basement *might* be dank, but nothing says it must be. Similarly, the word *yellow* wouldn't show up in the dictionary definition of the word *shirt*, although certainly many shirts in the world are yellow. The bottom line is that some choices in Analogies contain words that are weakly linked, or not linked at all, and these choices cannot be correct.

Let's get some practice chopping choices with weak links. Suppose you were presented with this analogy:

?????? : ?????? ::

○ diatribe : speech
○ assistant : prophecy
○ hunger : dinner
○ curmudgeon : discount
○ sage : wisdom

An original pair composed entirely of question marks might make this question seem impossible, but don't despair—you can still cut a few Weak Link answer choices. Is there a clear relationship between *assistant* and *prophecy*? Nope, so cut **B**. *Curmudgeon* and *discount*? Well, a *curmudgeon* might be unlikely to give someone a *discount*, but that's not the kind of definite relationship the GRE requires, so eliminate **D**. You may have even deemed *hunger* and *dinner* copasetic, since you certainly can eat *dinner* to alleviate *hunger*. Again, however, this is not the kind of relationship the GRE requires—the link must be stronger and more precise. So even with no idea of the original words, we'd be able to chop **B**, **C**, and **D** as weak links. Contrast the imprecision of those relationships with the strength of the connections in **A** and **E**: A *diatribe* is a form of *speech*, and a *sage* is characterized by *wisdom*—fine examples of our Category and Attribute connections, respectively. At the very least you could narrow the choices down to these two, and take your chances with an educated guess.

Okay, now that we have our fundamentals in place, let's talk about a framework for employing them. Which is to say, it's time to spell out our Analogy step method.

ANALOGY STEP METHOD

Here's our step method to solve Analogies. If you don't know the meanings of the words in the original pair, don't worry: Later we provide tips for how to deal with questions containing unfamiliar vocabulary. For now, here's what to do:

Step 1: Connect the Dots.

Step 2: Create a Template.

Step 3: Make the Match.

Step 4 (if necessary): Narrow the Connection.

Let's take a closer look at each step.

Step 1: Connect the Dots. The first step is to seek out the link between the words in the original pair. We demonstrated this for the eight major Analogy categories discussed in the previous section, and you should seek out similar kinds of links no matter what form the relationship between the words takes. Remember, there will always be a strong and defined connection in the question stem's original pair, and it's your job to recognize it.

Step 2: Create a Template. As we demonstrated earlier, the *form* of the original relationship is the important thing, so it's helpful to represent the connection you deduced in Step 1 as sentences substituting Xs and Ys for the words in the original pair.

Step 3: Make the Match. Now plug the choices into your template to see which one forms a logical relationship that mirrors the relationship of the words in the original. Be careful to substitute words in the proper order. For example, if your template goes from the second word back to the first (such as "Y is an extreme

form of X"), then make sure to read the choices into your template in that order as well. You can save time by immediately chopping choices containing weak links, as you learned to do in the fundamentals section above.

If you know the words in the original pair and you use this method, you should have your answer by the end of Step 3. However, it's unrealistic to expect this blue-sky scenario to play out for every question you face, so we've provided an additional step to use if you get stuck.

Step 4 (if necessary): Narrow the Connection. If you know the words in the original pair and perform steps 1–3, yet more than one choice still seems workable, it is possible that the connection you formed in Step 1 and generalized in Step 2 is too broad, causing more than one choice to fit its parameters. That's a clear sign that you didn't go far enough, so narrow the connection to weed out the imposters. We'll demonstrate how to do this in the following section, but first we'll employ the method in its most straightforward form.

Guided Practice

Let's test-drive the steps on a practice Analogy question. We'll consider this one a best-case scenario in which you know the meanings of the words, which means we'll have our answer by the end of Step 3. You'll recognize the following question as our X-ray example from earlier in the chapter. Try it now using Steps 1–3 of our method.

IMPLICIT : STATED ::

- straightforward : pithy
- urgent : imperative
- harsh : bright
- exotic : commonplace
- cheap : devoted

Step 1: Connect the Dots. How would you explain the meaning of *implicit* in terms of the word *stated*? *Implicit* means "implied" or "unspoken," so the original words are opposites, illustrated by the connection sentence "something *implicit* is never *stated*." This sentence captures the essential relationship between the words in the original pair and tells us we're dealing with a Meaning analogy.

Step 2: Create a Template. Generalizing from the connection sentence above yields "something X is never Y."

Step 3: Make the Match. We can go out on a limb to forge a link between *harsh* and *bright*, and between *cheap* and *devoted*, but our "Weak Links" fundamental reminds us that going out on a limb is not what GRE Analogy questions are all about. So let's chop **C** and **E** right off the bat. *Straightforward* and *pithy* aren't too closely related, but you may have found them close enough to test against our template: Something *straightforward* is never *pithy* ("brief")? Nope, that doesn't make sense. Something straightforward is more likely to be pithy than lengthy, but the connection is too vague in any case to pass GRE muster, so eliminate **A**. **B** serves up a pair of words that are closer to synonyms than antonyms, since something *urgent* can be said to be *imperative*. **D** is left, and it fits our template perfectly: Something *exotic* is never *commonplace*.

At this point you would click **D** and move on to the next question. If you know the meanings of the words in the original, and have no problem finding the match, then steps 1–3 are all you'll need. However, as mentioned above, sometimes you'll understand the original pair yet still be left with more than one choice standing at the end of Step 3. That's where Step 4 comes into play. We'll give you an example:

BRAIN : SKULL ::

- ○ soldier : fortress
- ○ foot : boot
- ○ turtle : shell
- ○ memory : calculation
- ○ clay : pottery

Step 1: Connect the Dots. The original fits into the Function category, as the purpose of the skull is to protect the brain.

Step 2: Create a Template. It's reasonable to generalize the connection from Step 1 as "the purpose of Y is to protect X."

Step 3: Make the Match. Scanning the choices, we can get rid of **D** on Weak Link grounds since we'd have to struggle to form a solid link between *memory* and *calculation*: Maybe someone with a good memory doesn't need to make calculations? Maybe someone with a good memory remembers how to make complex calculations? Who knows? Who cares? Just toss. But the others seem reasonable enough to test. A *fortress* protects a *soldier*, so **A**'s looking good. Uh-oh: A *boot* can be said to protect a *foot*, and a *shell* does protect a *turtle*, so we've got three answers that potentially fit. At least **E** is out: *clay* can be used to make *pottery*, but no one would say that pottery protects clay. But with **A**, **B**, and **C** still in the running, we'll have to move on to Step 4.

Step 4: Narrow the Connection. We need to make our connection more specific. *What kind of* protection does the *skull* afford the *brain*? Natural, biological protection—and that's enough to propel **C** into the winner's circle. When faced with more than one choice that fits your template, making the connection more specific will help the correct choice stand out.

If Step 4 still doesn't get you all the way home, then you'll need to take an educated guess. The following section contains tips that will help you narrow down the choices even when you don't know all of the words in a question.

Tame the Tough Stuff

Just as we presented ways to bluff your way closer to right answers in difficult Antonym questions, we'll now teach you ways to outmaneuver Analogy questions containing words you've never heard of. The goal is to eliminate as many choices as possible to put the odds in your favor so you can take your best guess.

We've already covered one good elimination strategy when we taught you to chop choices with Weak Links, a strategy that applies across the board whether you're having trouble with vocabulary or not. Two other helpful techniques are:

1. Work Backward

2. Follow the Charge

Work Backward

Let's say you got this difficult analogy and you didn't know the word *paean*:

> JOY : PAEAN ::
>
> ○ music : tempo
> ○ jeopardy : knoll
> ○ sorrow : dirge
> ○ water : peninsula
> ○ dregs : society

We can't effectively connect the dots between words if we don't know one of them, but we can work backward from the answer choices to create a connection for each of those, seeing if a viable relationship reveals itself in the process. What we mean by "viable relationship" is a link that *could* possibly apply to the original pair, even though we don't know one of those words. This is doable because we do know what *joy* means, and there are only so many reasonable ways we can link the concept of *joy* to another word.

Here's how it works: For **A**, *tempo* is the speed of *music*. Does it seem likely that *paean* (or any word) could mean "the speed of *joy*?" Not likely—the GRE test makers aren't particularly poetic, so eliminate **A**. No GRE-worthy connection exists for **B**, so we can chop this choice for containing a weak link. In **C**, *dirge* is a difficult word. If you're not sure what it means, it's dangerous to eliminate it, so we'll keep **C** for now. In **D**, a *peninsula* is surrounded on three sides by *water*. Is it likely that a *paean* is surrounded on three sides by *joy*? Not really, so eliminate **D**. Finally, *dregs* are the bottom of *society*. Could *joy* be the bottom of anything? Doubtful, so let's get rid of **E**. That leaves **C**. **C** is the best guess, even if one of its words is a complete mystery. If you knew the meaning of *paean*, you could have created the connection, "A *paean* is a song of *joy*." Similarly, "A *dirge* is a song of *sorrow*," which confirms that **C** is in fact correct. Working backward, you could have arrived at **C** even without knowing a word in both the original and the correct choice. At the very least, you could have narrowed the choices down to increase your odds if you had to guess.

Another way to work backward is to notice when two choices contain pairs of words whose relationships are functionally identical. For example, if one choice contains a pair of words that are synonyms, and another choice does as well, then neither can be the answer since there would be no way to select one over the other. Then, even if you didn't know one or both words in the original pair, at least you'd know they can't be synonyms, and you'd also be able to narrow the choices down. You'll see an example of this strategy at work in the practice set at the end of the chapter.

Follow the Charge

We discussed word charge in the Antonyms chapter and reiterated this strategy earlier in our discussion of Meaning analogies where we defined *connotation* as "the general *aura* surrounding a word or concept." We can think of these auras as positive and negative *charges* that can help you get a feel for words even if you don't know their precise meanings. This feeling can lead you in the right direction and put you in a better position if you have to venture a guess. Let's look at an example.

MALEDICTION : BLESSING ::

- paleontology : dinosaur
- malingerer : bureaucrat
- anxiety : panic
- anathema : intelligentsia
- dissonance : harmony

Though *malediction* is a tough word, you may still know that it means something negative because the prefix *mal* in front of a word means "bad" or "badly." You can also think of words beginning with *mal* that you do know—*malfunction, malnourished,* and so on—to help you recognize the negative aura surrounding *malediction*. *Blessing*, on the other hand, is clearly positive, so the stem words have opposite charges. That means that the words in the correct match will also be opposite in charge. Let's test them out with that in mind.

The words in **A** are pretty neutral, so cut. In **B**, *malingerer* has the same negative charge as *malediction*, but *bureaucrat* is not really strongly positive or negative. Notice also that the first word in **B** contains the same prefix as *malediction* in the original, a possible trap. **C** has *two* negative words, so it's out. This leaves **D** and **E**, and if you got it down to these two choices by following the word charges, that's a victory—you'd have a fifty-fifty chance of getting the point even though you weren't sure of all the words. The correct answer, by the way, is **E**: *Dissonance* ("disagreement," "conflict," or "a harsh sound") is never in *harmony*, just as a *malediction* ("curse") is never a *blessing*.

PRACTICE PROBLEMS

Okay, it's time to apply what you've learned to an Analogies practice set. If your vocabulary is smokin' and you can power through these using only Steps 1–3 of our step method, fantastic. If you need some of the extra ammunition we've provided to get you through, that's fine too—whatever gets the point. Don't forget to thoroughly review the explanations that follow the set.

> <u>Directions</u>: In each of the following questions, a related pair of words or phrases is followed by five pairs of words or phrases. Select the pair that best expresses a relationship similar to that expressed in the original pair.

1. ICONOCLAST : CONVENTION ::

   ○ tailor : robe
   ○ sycophant : passion
   ○ pariah : friendship
   ○ anarchist : government
   ○ firefighter : safety

2. ANGUISH : EMOTION ::

   ○ frenetic : fascination
   ○ money : compensation
   ○ data : dossier
   ○ cabbage : vegetable
   ○ burning : sensation

3. COVERT : SURREPTITIOUS ::

   ○ passive : forward
   ○ sociable : affable
   ○ causal : remorseful
   ○ taciturn : auspicious
   ○ outmoded : contemporary

4. GLUTTON : WILLPOWER ::

   ○ charlatan : hoax
   ○ traitor : fidelity
   ○ platoon : squad
   ○ savant : gumption
   ○ coward : courage

5. PROPAGANDA : OPINION ::

- ○ sermon : morality
- ○ existentialism : philosophy
- ○ newspaper : editorial
- ○ desiccant : moisture
- ○ institution : assignment

Guided Explanations

---

1. **D**

Step 1: Connect the Dots. An *iconoclast* is a person who attacks traditional ideas, so we have an Action relationship in this pair: An *iconoclast* opposes *convention*. Notice that we could term this an Attribute analogy, in the sense that defying convention is inherent in being an iconoclast. Don't get hung up on the terminology—the Analogy types we discussed are meant to make it easier to recognize the patterns that show up on the test, and they may overlap in some cases.

Step 2: Create a Template. "X opposes Y" is a straightforward generalization of the connection we uncovered.

Step 3: Make the Match. A *tailor* may *create* or *modify* a robe but wouldn't *oppose* one, so eliminate **A**. *Sycophant* is a hard word, so let's keep **B** on the table while we see what else we have to work with. A *pariah* is a recluse or an outsider, but not necessarily by choice. It therefore doesn't work to say that a *pariah* opposes *friendship* in the same way that an *iconoclast* opposes *convention*, so we can cross off **C** as close but no cigar. **D** matches perfectly, however: An *anarchist* opposes *government* as part of his or her nature in the same way as the *iconoclast's* nature is to oppose *convention*. As for **E**, *firefighter* and *safety* are too closely related to fit our template.

You should feel confident enough about **D** to select it and move on, without even worrying about the choice we skipped. It's actually nice to not have to worry about a difficult word like *sycophant* in **B**. Having confidence in a choice that works is another way to get around difficult vocabulary words, both in Analogy and Antonym questions. In case you were wondering, a *sycophant* is a person who tries to win favor through flattery, so the relationship between that word and *passion* is fairly ambiguous. If you did know the meaning of *sycophant*, you could have chopped **B** from the get-go as a weak link.

---

2. **E**

Step 1: Connect the Dots. This one may not seem too difficult at first glance, but sometimes the seeming simplicity of a relationship between the words of the

original pair may cause you to jump at a connection that's too broad. *Anguish* is a type of *emotion*, so that may have been the gist of the connection you formed.

Step 2: Create a Template. We saw in Step 1 that the words fall into the Category type, so you may have settled on "X is a type of Y" for your template.

Step 3: Make the Match. We can quickly chop **A** as a Weak Link choice, since there's no strong or obvious connection between *frenetic* ("chaotic," "hectic") and *fascination*. And our template helps us axe **C**, since *data* may be contained in a *dossier* ("report," "database") but can't be said to be a *type* of dossier. But that's where we run into trouble, since **B**, **D**, and **E** all fit our template perfectly. That means we'll have to move on to Step 4—which is, after all, why it's there.

Step 4: Narrow the Connection. We know the connection we formed in Step 1 and generalized in Step 2 is too broad because it encompasses three different choices. We'll therefore need to get more specific. *Anguish* is not just any old kind of *emotion*; it's an intense and unpleasant type of emotion. Does that help? You bet: While some people—children especially—might argue that *cabbage* is an intense and unpleasant type of vegetable, the GRE test makers would never go with such a loose connection for the right answer to an Analogy question, so **D** is incorrect. And of course there's a better choice that's spot on anyway: *Burning* is an intense and unpleasant *sensation* in the same way that *anguish* is an intense and unpleasant *emotion*. *Money*, for most people, is a pleasant form of *compensation*, so **B** doesn't fit our narrowed parameters. All it took was narrowing the connection a bit to find the right answer. Select **E** and move on.

---

3.   **B**

Step 1: Connect the Dots. To demonstrate some of the other strategies presented in this chapter, let's assume that you have some trouble with the words in this question. If you don't know the meaning of *covert* and/or *surreptitious*, you can't very well form a connection, can you? But as we've demonstrated, all is not lost, so let's see how we might sneak around this temporary setback.

Step 2: Create a Template. Since we're assuming we don't know the words, we have nothing to form a template, so we'll get right to Step 3.

Step 3: Make the Match. Let's use our "Work Backward" strategy to see if we can eliminate some choices or deduce anything about the relationship in the original pair. *Casual* and *remorseful* aren't particularly difficult words, so perhaps you noticed that there's no solid connection between being *informal/relaxed* and being *sad*. So we can chop **C** as a weak link, immediately shifting the odds in our favor. Now, perhaps you noticed something interesting about the pairs in **A** and **E**: They both contain antonyms. Being *passive* is the opposite of being *forward*, and being *outmoded* ("obsolete," "out-of-date," "passé") is the opposite of being *contemporary* ("fashionable," "current," "modern"). Since **A** and **E** contain the same exact kind of relationship, neither can be correct since we'd have no way to choose between them. That means that we can eliminate **A** and **E**, and also tells us that the words in the original pair can't be antonyms.

We've deduced that **A**, **C**, and **E** are all unlikely to be correct. At this point you may know the words in **B** and **D** sufficiently well to choose between them; if not, then it's a toss-up between those as you take your best guess. Notice that even if you don't know what *covert*, *surreptitious*, *affable*, *taciturn*, or *auspicious* means, you can still use a bit of strategy to give yourself a fifty-fifty chance—not bad if you crashed and burned on the vocabulary front.

In case you're wondering, **B** is correct because *covert* and *surreptitious* are synonyms, both meaning "secret" or "stealthy." *Sociable* and *affable* are synonyms as well, both meaning "friendly" or "outgoing." As for **D**, *taciturn* means "quiet" or "introverted" and thus has no direct connection to *auspicious*, which means "favorable" or "promising."

Don't get us wrong—knowing the vocab is clearly the most effective way to go, but most test takers encounter words they don't know at some point on Analogy questions, and it's helpful to have a few techniques at your disposal to help you narrow the field to make an informed guess. If you found yourself baffled at some of the words in this one, then a guess between **B** and **D** would be pretty good under the circumstances.

4.   **E**

We'll demonstrate this one from both directions: first as if you're good with the vocab, and then working backward from the choices in case you had some trouble.

Step 1: Connect the Dots. A *glutton* is someone who eats or drinks to excess, and if you knew that, you'd have little trouble connecting the dots: A *glutton* lacks *willpower*, which is a fine example of an Attribute analogy stated in the negative.

Step 2: Create a Template. "An X lacks Y" is a fine template for the connection from Step 1; so without further ado, let's make the match.

Step 3: Make the Match. A *coward* lacks *courage*. This fits the template perfectly. The only other choice that fits the template at all is **B**: a *traitor* lacks *fidelity*. However, faced with these two possibilities, **E** is the better choice because just like the original, it speaks to a lack of a personal quality leading to the degradation of the individual lacking that quality. In contrast, the traitor lacks fidelity *to another person or cause,* not to himself or herself, so the match isn't as complete. **E** gets the point.

Working Backward

In the best-case scenario, an Analogy question need not be any more difficult than this—if, of course, you know the meaning of the words in question. If you didn't know the words here, then your encounter with question 4 might have gone a little something like this—

"Glutton? *What's that? Who knows . . . Wait—I do know what* willpower *means; that's what I use to stop myself from eating all that chocolate. I can't form a connection, but let me see if I can work backward from the choices . . .*"

This line of thinking is right on the mark, making the best of a difficult situation. Beginning with **A**, a *charlatan* perpetrates a *hoax*. Even if you didn't know what *glutton* means, is it likely that a *glutton* perpetrates a *willpower*? Um . . . no. As for **B**, a *traitor* lacks *fidelity* (loyalty), and the unknown *glutton* could lack *willpower* (something many of us lack), so we'll hold on to that one for now. Choice **C** serves up a Composition-type connection: A *platoon* is made up of *squads*. Can anything be made up of *willpower*? Doesn't sound likely, so eliminate **C**. In **D**, a *savant* is a really smart person, which has nothing directly to do with *gumption* ("guts," "bravery"), so we'll chop that one as a weak link. (Remember: No choice that contains words ambiguously related to each other can be correct in an Analogy question.) That leaves **E**: A *coward* lacks *courage*, and we decided earlier that the unknown word could possibly lack *willpower*, so **E** could logically work. So even if you were hazy on the meaning of *glutton*, you could still use the strategies we've discussed to narrow down the choices to **B** and **E**. As we saw in our first explanation to this one, **E** is the choice that works best.

---

5.   **A**

Step 1: Connect the Dots. It's likely that you know the meaning of the words in the original, so let's work forward from those. The pair is a good example of a Function relationship, as the purpose of *propaganda* is to influence *opinion*.

Step 2: Create a Template. We can replace the specifics with X and Y to form this template: "The purpose of X is to influence Y."

Step 3: Make the Match. A fits the template, as it's appropriate to say that the purpose of a *sermon* is to influence *morality*. But let's check to see if anything better comes along. *Existentialism* is a type of *philosophy*, so **B** exhibits a different relationship than that of the original pair. Be careful of **C**: *Newspaper* and *propaganda* sound related in some way, as does *opinion* and *editorial*. Sometimes the test makers get tricky and try to fool you into selecting a choice with words that remind you of the words in the original, but the connection between the words in **C** doesn't mimic the connection of the original pair: A *newspaper* may contain an *editorial*, but we wouldn't say that the *purpose* of a newspaper is to influence editorials. **D** is closer, since its words do fall into the Function category: The purpose of a *desiccant* ("drying agent") is to remove *moisture*. If instead of using the word *influence* in your template, your template says "the purpose of X is to do something to Y," then **D** might look as good as **A**, and you'd need to employ Step 4 of our method to narrow the connection. But as it stands, **A** is right in line with the template we formed in Step 2, while **D** is not, so we can eliminate **D** as close but not a perfect match. **E** is easier to discard; it's a Weak Link choice since there's no direct connection between *institution* and *assignment*.

Part III

THE ESSAY SECTION

Gameplan

Once again we provide you with a game plan to maximize your study time. Here's what you'll see in the following chapters:

- **Meet GRE Essays.** This chapter provides an overview of the Essay section, including how it's scored and details about the requirements of each of the two essays. We also provide the writing strategies you'll need to tackle these essays successfully.

- **The Issue Essay.** First we'll familiarize you with the basics of the Issue Essay, including the prompt, the directions, and the grading system. Then we'll get right down to an effective method for writing a "6" essay.

- **The Argument Essay.** As with the Issue Essay, we'll explain everything you need to know about this essay type, as well as provide a step method that will help you write a "6" Argument essay. In both chapters, we'll take a look at two sample essays, a "6" and a "3," dissected for your reading pleasure.

MEET GRE ESSAYS
Grad Schools and GRE Essays

Chapter 11

Meet GRE Essays

Although you'll see this section first on test day, we're covering it last for two reasons: We wanted to get your confidence up before tackling this portion of the test, the one that strikes fear into the hearts of even the most fearless test takers. After all, this section requires you to write not one but two essays under pretty severe time constraints. But we're here to say, *Fear not, friends*. The Essay section is as beatable as any other section on the GRE.

The second reason we're covering this section last is because many of the concepts you got under your belt in the Verbal section, and particularly in the Reading Comprehension chapter, will be very helpful here. Good readers make good writers—and if you've got the Verbal question types down, as we hope you do, you'll be much better prepared to embark upon the writing challenges of the GRE essays. Let's begin.

You're required to write two essays in 75 minutes: an "Issue" essay and an "Argument" essay. For the Issue essay, you'll be given two statements presenting two different issues, officially known as the *topics*, and you'll have 45 minutes to write a cogent, coherent essay detailing your perspective on one of them. You get to choose which of the two topics you'd like to write about. For the Argument essay, you'll be given a short argument, also known as the *topic*, and 30 minutes to write a cogent, coherent, argumentative essay critiquing the given argument. Both essays require you to make *arguments*, despite their different names. We describe the essay types in more detail below.

You'll type the two essays using the most rudimentary software program you've ever seen. Think Fred Flintstone with a couple of rocks. This word-processing program does let you type, cut, paste, and undo, but you won't have a spell-checker, a grammar-checker, or even the ability to use fancy fonts such as bold or italics, nor does the software recognize keyboard shortcuts.

GRAD SCHOOLS AND GRE ESSAYS

Historically, admissions committees haven't given much weight to the Essay section. Even graduate programs for which essay writing is crucial tended to de-emphasize GRE essay scores. It's not that these programs didn't care about your writing ability—far from it—but they typically used your *application* essays to assess this ability.

But increasingly, grad schools have begun relying on the GRE essays to make high-stakes decisions about admissions and funding. Not only will most admissions committees look at your Essay score, but they'll likely also be *reading* your essays.

That said, the Essay section is neither the time nor the place to be sarcastic or controversial. It's not the place to espouse random views about life or death or hot fudge sundaes. Save all that for your blog. The Essay section is your chance to show admissions committees and essay graders that you can thoughtfully and articulately construct two written argumentative essays in 75 minutes. You may include evidence from your personal life, but only such evidence that's relevant to the topic. On test day, you'll want to be clear and direct and always follow the directions. Now let's see how your essays will be graded.

SCORING

In a word, GRE essays are scored *quickly*. Essay graders are instructed to spend no more than three minutes reading an essay before giving it a score from "0" (awful) to "6" (awesome—the highest possible grade) in half-point increments. Just three minutes!

Every essay is actually read by at least two graders, who each assign the essay a score. If these scores differ by more than one point—an essay gets a "3" and a "5," for example—the essay will be read by another grader. The final score for one particular essay is an average of these individual scores. You'll receive a single score for the Essay section: an average of the scores you received on the Issue and Argument essays.

For example, say your Issue essay receives a "4" and a "5" from the two graders. Your Issue essay score would be a "4.5." If your Argument essay gets a "6" and a "6," you'd receive a "6" for the Argument essay. The graders will then average your two scores: $\frac{(4.5+6)}{2} = 5.25$ Your final score, however, would be "5.5", since the test makers round up to the nearest half point. That's the only number reported for the Essay section. Your 0-to-6 Essay score is completely independent from, and has no impact on, either your Math or Verbal score.

The 0-to-6 Scale

Let's take a look at the 0-to-6 score in more detail. GRE essay graders are told to grade *holistically*. That is, although the graders are looking for specific elements in your essays, no element is assigned a particular weight. The score you receive is based on an overall impression of your essay. That's great news: It means that you can make a few mistakes and still get a good score.

The graders must refer to a set-in-stone list of criteria when evaluating each essay and deciding what grade ("0"–"6") it deserves. The following chart is our explanation of the grading criteria that the test makers give the graders.

By the way, you might recognize these criteria from the SAT—the criteria used to grade the essays are essentially the same. What's different is the level of writing. Later, we'll analyze a couple of different essays to show you the difference between essays that receive so-so scores and essays that receive great scores, in the chapters on the Issue and Argument essays.

SCORE	DESCRIPTION OF ESSAY
6	A "6" essay is *superior* and demonstrates a *strong and consistent* command of the language throughout the entire essay, with at most a few small errors. A "6" essay: • shows a firm grasp of critical thinking and takes a powerful and interesting position on the topic • supports and develops its position with appropriate and insightful examples, arguments, and evidence • is tightly organized and focused, with a smooth and coherent progression of ideas • demonstrates a facility with language through the use of descriptive and appropriate vocabulary • uses intelligent variation in sentence structure • contains, at most, a few errors in grammar, spelling, and punctuation
5	A "5" essay is *strong* and demonstrates a *generally consistent* command of language throughout the entire essay, with no more than a few significant flaws and errors. A "5" essay: • shows well-developed critical-thinking skills by taking a solid position on the topic • supports and develops its position on the topic with appropriate examples, arguments, and evidence • is organized and focused and features a coherent progression of ideas • demonstrates competence with language throughout by using appropriate vocabulary • uses varied sentence structure • contains few errors in grammar, spelling, and punctuation

SCORE	DESCRIPTION OF ESSAY
4	A "4" essay is *competent* and demonstrates a *basic* command of the language throughout the entire essay. A "4" essay: • shows adequate critical-thinking skills by taking a position on the topic and supporting that position with generally appropriate examples, arguments, and evidence • is mostly organized and focused, with a progression of ideas that is mostly coherent • demonstrates inconsistent facility with language and uses mostly appropriate vocabulary • uses some variation in sentence structure • contains some errors in grammar, spelling, and punctuation
3	A "3" essay shows *developing competence* and contains one or more of the following: • some critical-thinking skills, as demonstrated by its position on the topic • inadequate support or development of its position based on deficiencies in examples, arguments, or evidence presented • lapses in organization and focus, including ideas that are not always coherent • a capacity for competent use of language, with occasional use of vague or inappropriate vocabulary • only minor variation in sentence structure • a variety of errors in grammar, spelling, and punctuation
2	A "2" essay is *seriously flawed* and demonstrates a *poor* command of the language throughout the entire essay. A "2" essay contains one or more of the following: • poor critical-thinking skills as shown by an inconsistent or unclear position on the topic • insufficient support for the position on the topic as a result of faulty or nonexistent examples, arguments, and evidence • weak organization and focus, including ideas that are frequently incoherent • poor language skills through use of limited or wrong vocabulary • errors in sentence structure • errors in grammar, spelling, punctuation, and other rules of writing that make the meaning hard to understand

SCORE	DESCRIPTION OF ESSAY
1	A "1" essay is *profoundly flawed* and demonstrates a *very poor* command of the language throughout the entire essay. A "1" essay contains one or more of the following: • no position on the topic or almost no support or development of the position • poor organization and focus that makes the essay incoherent • numerous vocabulary errors • fundamental errors in sentence structure • errors in grammar, spelling, and punctuation that make parts of the essay unintelligible
0	Essays written on a topic other than the one assigned will receive a score of 0.

GRE ESSAY TYPES

You'll write two essays on test day, an Issue essay and an Argument essay. We go into more detail about these essays, and decode their directions, in the following chapters. But here's a brief glimpse of what each essay entails.

The Issue Essay

Technically, this essay is called "Present Your Perspective on an Issue." The Issue essay topic gives you a broad statement or quotation about some aspect of life. It's your job to agree or disagree with this statement or quotation and present your reasons for doing so. These reasons can come from your life, your studies, current events, literature, history, and just about any other source you can think of. The topic is broad enough that no right or wrong answer exists. But you do need to pick a side and stick to it. You'll be limited to just 45 minutes.

The Argument Essay

The test makers call this essay "Analyze an Argument." In contrast to the Issue essay topic, the Argument essay topic presents a specific argument, making a case for one side of an issue. Your job is to analyze the validity of the argument; whether you agree with its conclusion is irrelevant. Your reasons and evidence should come directly from the argument itself. The test makers want to know whether you can assess an argument based on its conclusions and assumptions. You've got 30 minutes for the Argument essay.

GENERAL ESSAY STRATEGIES

To write two "6" essays on the GRE in the time allotted, you need to work fast. You won't have weeks, days, or even hours to ponder the topics and gradually craft your ideas into a masterpiece. Instead, you have to get in, give the essay graders exactly what they want, and get out. To do that, you need to have a firm essay-writing strategy in place and a solid grasp of the fundamentals of GRE essay writing before you sit down to take the test. Here they are:

- **Organization:** The "Three-Act Essay"

- **Effective Writing Elements:** The "Cast of Characters"

Now let's see how they work.

Organization: The "Three-Act Essay"

As you write your essays, keep in mind your purpose and your audience: Your purpose is to get a high score, and your audience is the GRE essay graders. Remember too that all the graders expect from you is that you write two strong first drafts; they don't expect the kind of carefully crafted prose and arguments found in polished work.

The most successful essays on the GRE follow a set formula, which we refer to as the three-act essay. Many of you will be already familiar with this formula from years of writing five-paragraph essays in high school and college:

Act	Also Known As	Number of Paragraphs	Purpose
I	Introduction	One	Set the stage
II	Body paragraphs	Three	Tell the story
III	Conclusion	One	Wrap it up

In the same way that a three-act play tells a story, a three-act essay begins by setting the stage for the argument to come (Act I), then makes the argument over three body paragraphs (Act II) using reasons and evidence, and finally concludes by wrapping up the argument (Act III). You'll use this structure, with a few modifications, for both the Issue and the Argument essays.

Let's see how the three-act essay structure works by practicing with an Issue essay topic:

"We can learn more from conflicts than we can from agreements."

Act I: Set the Stage

Quite literally, the first act of a play sets the stage for the drama to follow. It grabs the audience's attention, introduces key plot elements and characters, and prepares the audience for the rest of the play. Act I of your GRE essay (aka your first paragraph, or the introduction) accomplishes virtually the same tasks.

Act I of your GRE essays should include the following:

- **The Thesis Statement:** Your position on the topic

- **The Summary:** Your preview of the points you will discuss

To accomplish these goals, you need at least four sentences in your introduction. These sentences need to convey your thesis statement and the overall structure of your essay to the grader. The thesis statement is usually one sentence, and each of the three points you'll discuss in the body paragraphs also gets at least one sentence.

The Thesis Statement. The thesis statement should be the first sentence of your essay. It summarizes your position on the topic and grabs the reader's attention by clearly explaining what the essay's going to argue.

Take a look at the following thesis statement:

> Although agreements have value, the juxtaposition of different ideas in a conflict inevitably leads to more significant progress and evolution.

This thesis statement clearly takes a stand on the issue presented by the topic. It's fluid but not fancy. It's grammatically correct but doesn't include clause after clause or comma after comma. It uses a few big words *(juxtaposition, significant, inevitably)*, but the words aren't so big that you'd need a dictionary to understand them.

The Summary. After the thesis statement, the rest of your introduction should summarize the three points that will form your body paragraphs. This summary lets the essay graders know how you'll structure your essay. You need to explain and describe your three points to show how they fit into your argument. Make sure to give each main point its own sentence. Here's an example:

> Although agreements have value, the juxtaposition of different ideas in a conflict inevitably leads to more significant progress and evolution. What scientific progress would we have, for example, if it weren't for intellectual debate? None—intellectual debate leads to scientific progress. The reformation of outdated political ideas and concepts is also marked by struggle. Finally, in the words of Friedrich Nietzsche, "What doesn't kill us makes us stronger." This quotation captures the sentiment that personal growth arises from conflict.

These short sentences have summarized the three main points persuasively and effectively, and the paragraph includes a quotation from a famous German philosopher to boot. The paragraph is organized and focused, and it presents three thoughtful examples. It also includes sentence variety, as well as active verbs to demonstrate the facility of language essay graders want to see in a "6" essay. Also, as you will see, the intro paragraph (Act I) presents its points in the same order that they appear in Act II.

Act II: Tell the Story

This is where things get interesting, because it's here, in your three body paragraphs, that you'll actually make the essay's argument. These paragraphs provide clear, thoughtful evidence for your thesis by explaining your examples. The directions for both the Issue and Argument essays say it loud and clear: *Organize, develop, and express your ideas* and *Support your critique with relevant reasons and examples.* Act II is where you'll do all of this.

As such, each of your three Act II paragraphs should include:

- **The Topic Sentence:** The thesis statement of the paragraph

- **The Evidence:** The specific, concrete facts, phenomena, events, quotes, or situations that support your overarching thesis statement

---

The Topic Sentence. Each body paragraph should begin with a topic sentence. It might help to imagine your body paragraphs as three mini-arguments, each with its own thesis statement, examples, and explanations. Taken together, these mini-arguments add up to form your essay's main argument. The thesis statement of your body paragraph is the topic sentence, or the first sentence of your paragraph. Here you'll explain what the paragraph's about and how it links to your essay's main argument. Let's look at an example:

> First, historically, scientific progress has been inspired by conflicts of ideas.

This topic sentence succinctly summarizes the paragraph's point: Scientific progress is a great example of the benefits of conflict (which supports the essay's main claim about conflict from Act I). The word *first* shows focus and organization; it also shows a progression of ideas, because *first* lets us know that other paragraphs will follow.

The Evidence. Each Act II paragraph must provide evidence to make the essay graders believe your thesis; this evidence forms the backbone of your argument. The essay graders want to see that you're capable of making a logical argument in both the Issue and Argument essays. Good reasons make readers believe in your argument. You'll need several sentences in each body paragraph to develop your examples and provide evidence for that paragraph's claim. For now we're just going to show you one Act II paragraph. As we continue through the essay chapters, you'll see several more. Your GRE essays should have three body paragraphs.

First, historically, scientific progress has been inspired by conflicts of ideas. In the sixteenth century, for example, a great debate arose because Copernicus vehemently challenged the notion that the earth is the center of the solar system. Although he paid a price both socially and politically for this remonstration, Copernicus disabused a long-held belief, much to the chagrin of the Catholic Church and to other astronomers of his day. Because of this conflict, humankind eventually gained a new understanding of astronomy.

This paragraph uses the specific, astute example of Copernicus and his work on the solar system to prove its position: Copernicus's ideas caused lots of problems back in the day, but ultimately his theories proved correct and thus advanced our understanding of astronomy.

Act III: Wrap It Up

We've all been to a play or movie that leaves its audience hanging. Maybe it did so to entice you to watch the sequel, or maybe it was one of those movies that's deliberately confusing and ambiguous so that you can think about it for days afterward. Regardless of your feelings about such plays and movies, leaving essay graders hanging is a great way to lose a few points on your essay score. Do not go all arty and forget to include a conclusion in your essay.

Act III, the fifth and final paragraph of your essay, should summarize and broaden the points you made in Act II. Your conclusion should be a few sentences long and finish your argument. Act III of your GRE essay should:

- **Recap** your essay

- **Expand** your position

Recap. The recap is a summary of what you've already argued. As in the thesis statement, the recap should be straightforward, bold, and declarative. Here's a recap example:

> Clearly, conflict has been responsible for several upward surges of humankind in diverse respects. In the areas of science, politics, and individual character, progress requires struggle.

Expand. The last two or three sentences of the essay should take the ideas you just recapped and push them a little further. One of the best ways to push your argument further is to look to the future and think about what would happen if the position that you've taken in your essay could be applied on a broader scale or to a broader field, such as politics or art. Take a look at these sentences:

> Rather than avoiding conflict at all costs, we should accept conflict as a necessary—and beneficial—part of the human condition, whether the conflicts arise among scholars or states. Conflict permits true transformation and growth.

The essay discussed scholars in its first Act II paragraph about Copernicus. Although the essay hasn't discussed the relative pros and cons of conflicts that arise among countries in our essay, it implies that the argument would hold for such a discussion. (Would it? Sure . . . look at the way the United Nations rose from the ashes of World War II.) And that's what you want to do when you expand your position: Imply how your argument could apply to another field or situation.

ACT III wraps up the entire GRE essay. It says to your essay grader, "I hope you enjoyed the show."

Effective Writing Elements: The "Cast of Characters"

Characters bring a play to life and make it worth watching. Similarly, a great GRE essay needs interesting, effective writing elements to make it worth reading. We call these elements characters to keep with our three-act essay idea, but it doesn't matter what you call them. All that matters is that you include these elements in your GRE essays:

- An Argument

- Evidence

- Varied Sentence Structure

- Facility with Language

These are, quite literally, the stars of your play. Don't even think about writing your GRE essays without them.

An Argument

This one's a biggie: The test makers want to see your ability to develop an argument in both the Issue and the Argument essays. On that note, your argument must be related to the topic. You cannot freestyle your way into the grader's good graces; you must address the topics given to you. Save the creativity for the way you develop and support your examples.

To make an argument, you need to take a stand and then provide and develop enough evidence to support it. Your thesis statement lets readers know where you stand and what you're going to argue. Take a look again at the thesis statement we've been using throughout this section:

> Although agreements have value, the juxtaposition of different ideas in a conflict inevitably leads to more significant progress and evolution.

We're saying that when it comes to making progress, conflicts are more helpful than agreements. So, on the issue of whether we learn more from conflicts or agreements, we're coming down firmly on the side of conflicts. Now we'll spend the rest of the essay developing examples that support that stand.

Evidence

To write a "6" essay, you've got to load it up with thoughtful examples—or evidence that shows why your argument is sound. In the Issue essay, your examples can come from any source, including personal experience, academic knowledge, and current events. In the Argument essay, however, your evidence will come from the argument topic provided by the test makers. Not to worry: In the upcoming chapters, we'll discuss the five steps to a "6" Issue essay and the five steps to a "6" Argument essay.

Let's say you're trying to think of examples to support the position that "struggle is a required element for progress." Perhaps you come up with the example of scientific progress. Okay. That's a potentially great example. To actually make it great, though, you have to be able to say more than just "Conflict leads to scientific progress." You need to be specific: Give dates; mention specific people, theories, or facts.

Just as bricks hold up a building, such detailed facts support an argument. There are literally dozens of good, potential examples for every position you might choose. Your job is to choose examples that prove your essay's argument. The test makers instruct their graders to look for "appropriate and insightful examples," which demonstrate a "powerful and interesting position on the topic."

For instance, knowing that Copernicus was part of the debate about the solar system is a good start, but it's not enough to prove the essay's main argument *(the juxtaposition of different ideas in a conflict inevitably leads to more significant progress and evolution)*. How did Copernicus or the conflict surrounding his ideas lead to progress? This is where the detail comes in:

> In the sixteenth century, for example, a great debate arose because Copernicus vehemently challenged the notion that the earth is the center of the solar system. Although he paid a price both socially and politically for this remonstration, Copernicus disabused a long-held belief, much to the chagrin of the Catholic Church and other astronomers of his day.

This example demonstrates a thorough understanding of the controversy surrounding Copernicus. It provides dates and a broad outline of the ideas that led to the controversy. It shows thought and careful consideration, and it helps prove the essay's main argument.

To prove the position that *conflict leads to progress,* you might choose one example from science, politics, and personal experience. Here are three examples that you might choose from those areas:

- **Science.** Copernicus's challenge to the idea that the earth was the center of the solar system

- **Politics.** The abolition of slavery

- **Personal experience.** Hardships leading to personal growth

---

A broad array of reasons and support provides a more solid and defensible position than three examples drawn from personal experience or from just one or two areas. If you derive relevant points from diverse examples, your Act II will be nothing short of a "6"—that is, if you also include the other two writing elements that round out our Cast of Characters.

Varied Sentence Structure

Take a look at the following paragraph:

> Sentence structure is very important. Sentence structure, if appropriately varied, can keep your readers engaged and help make your essay exciting and easier to read. Sentence structure, if it is monotonous and unchanging, can make your essay sound boring and unsophisticated. Sentence structure is important on the GRE essay. Sentence structure is also important in essays you write for school.

Are you crying yet? That's because every sentence not only started in the same way but also all had the same straight-ahead plodding rhythm. *Sentence structure is . . . Sentence structure can . . .* That's about as original as roses on Valentine's Day.

Now take a look at the sample Act II paragraph on Copernicus. Notice how the various sentences start differently and also have different internal rhythms.

> Historically, scientific progress has been inspired by conflicts of ideas. In the sixteenth century, for example, a great debate arose because Copernicus vehemently challenged the notion that the earth is the center of the solar system. Although he paid a price both socially and politically for this remonstration, Copernicus disabused a long-held belief, much to the chagrin of the Catholic Church and other astronomers of his day. Because of this conflict, humankind eventually gained a new understanding of astronomy.

These variations in sentence structure keep the writing vibrant and interesting. As you write your essay, focus on changing the structure of your sentences. You don't have to invert every clause, but you should be careful not to let a few sentences in a row follow the same exact structure. You've got to mix it up. Here's the boring first paragraph of this section rewritten with varied sentence structure:

> Sentence structure is very important. Varying the structure of your sentences keeps your reader engaged; it also makes your writing easier—and more exciting—to read. Monotonous, repetitive sentence structure can make your essay sound boring and unsophisticated. Practice mixing up your sentence structure on the essays for the GRE, but don't forget to also vary your sentence structure on the application essays you write for graduate school!

Much easier to read and far less repetitive, right? Right.

Keep It Simple. Sometimes test takers think writing long complicated sentences will impress professors. Maybe, but it won't impress GRE essay graders. Be varied in your sentence structure, but also remember to make sure your sentences make sense. Complex sentences can be difficult to understand, and your GRE essays should be as clear and easy to read as possible.

We could fill an entire book with rules about creating simple and succinct prose. Instead, here are two handy rules to simplify the sentences that you write on test day:

1. Never write a sentence that contains more than three commas. Try to avoid sentences with more than two commas (unless you need to include a list).

2. Never write a sentence that takes up more than three lines on the screen.

Those rules are certainly not foolproof, but abiding by them will keep you from filling your essays with overly complex sentences. Ultimately, these rules will make your essays easier to understand, which will please your essay graders and, hopefully, help you get a higher score.

Transitions. Transitions let readers understand the flow of your argument. They're words, phrases, and sentences that take readers gently by the hand, leading them through your essay. Here are some different kinds of transitions you can use to spice up your sentence structure:

- **Showing contrast.** Katie likes pink nail polish. *In contrast*, she thinks red nail polish looks trashy.

- **Elaborating.** I love going to the movies. *Even more than that*, I love eating popcorn and candy in the dark while I'm there.

- **Providing an example.** If you save up your money, you can afford pricey items. *For example*, Patrick saved up his allowance and eventually purchased a sports car.

- **Showing results.** Manuel ingested nothing but soda and burgers every day for a month. *As a result*, he gained ten pounds.

- **Showing sequence.** The police arrested Bob at the party. *Soon after*, his college applications were all rejected, and eventually Bob drifted into a life of crime.

Your first Act II paragraph probably dives right into its thesis statement, but the second and third Act II paragraphs need transitions. The simplest way to build these transitions is to use words like *first* and *second*. That means you'll essentially number your three Act II paragraphs as *first*, *second*, and *third* or *finally*.

A slightly more sophisticated way to build transitions is to choose examples from different sources, such as from politics and personal experience. If the first paragraph is about a political instance of learning from failure and the second concerns a personal encounter with conflict from your own experience, make that fact your transition: *As in politics, conflict leads to personal growth. For example, once I . . .*

But you also want to use transitions within paragraphs as a way of varying your sentence structure and aiding the logical flow of your ideas.

Facility with Language

As the chart at the beginning of this chapter indicates, a "6" essay "demonstrates a facility with language through the use of descriptive and appropriate vocabulary." However, that does not mean that you have to use tons of sophisticated vocabulary words to score well. *Don't submit to a compulsion to evidence your estimable and irrepressible loquaciousness in an endeavor to astonish your future academic compatriots into acknowledging the vital, indisputable, and inevitable advisability of acceding to your fervent desire to obtain entrance to their graduate-level institution.*

In other words, avoid sentences like that—it sounds pretentious and increases the risk that you and your logic will get lost in the wordiness. Use language that's appropriate to make your case. Avoid overly complex sentences, and don't get carried away with flowery embellishments. You don't have enough time to create the next Great American Masterpiece, but you do have enough time to construct clear and persuasive essays. Use the vocabulary you have to the fullest, but don't try to squeeze in big words that you may not know how to use correctly.

Let's look again at the paragraph about scientific progress:

> First, historically, scientific progress has been inspired by conflicts of ideas. In the sixteenth century, for example, a great debate arose because Copernicus vehemently challenged the notion that the earth is the center of the solar system. Although he paid a price both socially and politically for this remonstration, Copernicus disabused a long-held belief, much to the chagrin of the Catholic Church and other astronomers of his day. Because of this conflict, humankind eventually gained a new understanding of astronomy.

This paragraph is a great illustration of how to use words effectively. Both *remonstration* and *disabused* are advanced words, and, more important, they're used appropriately. Sophisticated vocabulary used in the proper context is what makes for excellent word choice.

Compelling Word Choice. Here's a suggested list of some words that you may want to use as you write your GRE essays. These words can be effective and impressive-sounding synonyms for words you probably already know.

Use . . .	Instead of . . .
albeit (adv.)	even if
connote (v.)	mean
conversely (adv.)	but
corroborate (v.)	support or strengthen
depict (v.)	show
dire (adj.)	urgent
emblematic (adj.)	an example of, symbolic
hence (adv.)	so
heretofore (adv.)	until now
highlight (v.)	show
implication (n.)	suggestion
majestic (adj.)	great
paramount (adj.)	important
symbolize (v.)	demonstrate

Proper Grammar and Spelling. A few grammar or spelling mistakes sprinkled throughout your essay will not destroy your score. The test makers understand that you're bound to make minor mistakes in a rushed 30- or even 45-minute essay.

Although essay graders will sympathetically ignore a few mistakes here and there, they definitely will not ignore *patterns* of errors. If a grader sees that your punctuation is consistently wrong, that your spelling of familiar words is often incorrect, or that you write run-on sentences again and again, your score will suffer.

In other words, you should proof your essays. It's better to spend another thirty seconds or so to change a word or a sentence than to potentially lose points for having too many errors.

Quotations. One way to distinguish your essay from the sea of thousands of similar essays is to include a relevant quote. Prior to test day, memorize a handful of widely applicable quotes from a source, such as *Bartlett's Familiar Quotations*, on big topics such as love, success, and life. Then, when you're writing the essays, look for an opportunity to include one of these quotes.

Limit yourself to one quote per essay. After all, it's supposed to be your essay, so it shouldn't seem like you're merely regurgitating the words of others. Because people tend to remember first and last impressions best, try if you can to place your quote in either the introduction or the conclusion of your essay.

A quotation isn't necessary to get a "6," but it may help add spice and flavor to your prose.

Okay, one last important note before we get to our in-depth treatment of the individual GRE essay types in the following two chapters.

EVERYONE IN THE POOL!

The interesting thing about the GRE essay topics is that they're already published on the Internet. No, not on some illegal downloading site, but on ETS's GRE site itself, at www.gre.org/pracmats. Crazy, you say? Who ever heard of any test writer giving out the questions in advance?

Well, before you get carried away with your good fortune, realize that there are more than 200 Issue and 200 Argument topics in the pool—far too many to prepare responses for in advance. However, the good news is that scanning through the list of topics will give you an excellent idea of the types of issues and arguments you'll face on test day. Moreover, you'll have more than enough material to practice on after you've taken in all the strategies and techniques in this Analytical Writing section of the book.

Now that you have your Analytical Writing foundation in place, turn to the next chapter for the lowdown on the Issue essay.

Chapter 12

The Issue Essay

On test day, you'll have 45 minutes to plan, draft, and proofread what the test makers call the "Present Your Perspective on an Issue" essay. The test makers will always give you two broad proclamations or thoughts about life, known as the "topics." You might even see a quotation from a real person or a made-up statement. You'll choose one topic, and your essay will analyze your position on this issue. In this chapter, we'll show you how to write a "6" Issue essay, using the three-act essay structure and the cast of characters you learned about in the previous chapter.

ISSUE ESSAY X-RAY

Here's a sample Issue essay topic, including directions, like the one you'll see on test day:

Directions: You will have a choice between two Issue topics. Each topic will appear as a brief quotation that states or implies an issue of general interest. Read each topic carefully; then decide on which topic you could write a more effective and well-reasoned response.

You will have 45 minutes to plan and compose a response that presents your perspective on the topic you select. A response on any topic will receive a score of zero. You are free to accept, reject, or qualify the claim made in the topic you selected, as long as the ideas you present are clearly relevant to the topic. Support your views with reasons and examples drawn from such areas as your reading, experience, observations, or academic studies.

GRE readers, who are college and university faculty, will read your response and evaluate its overall quality, based on how well you

- consider the complexities and implications of the issue

- organize, develop, and express your ideas about the issue

- support your ideas with relevant reasons and examples

- control the elements of standard written English

You may want to take a few minutes to think about the issue you have chosen and to plan a response before you begin writing. Be sure to develop your ideas fully and organize them coherently, but leave time to reread what you have written and make any revisions that you think are necessary.

Present your perspective on the issue below, using relevant reasons and/or examples to support your views.

"Environment determines personality."

The directions are fairly straightforward, so if you spend a few minutes getting the gist of them now you won't have to bother with them on test day. Essentially, you're given a choice of Issue topics and need to select one of them to discuss. The test makers are not looking for a right or wrong answer, and they don't care what position you take on the issue. What they do care about is whether your essay demonstrates careful consideration of the issue, a well-reasoned argument, and strong command of language.

Essay graders want to see that you're able to think about the complexities of a given issue by making an argument, supporting that argument with thoughtful examples, and communicating your ideas articulately. You're given the freedom to accept (agree with), reject (disagree with), and even qualify the claim made in the topic, which means you're allowed to restrict the issue to parameters of your own choosing as long as your argument remains relevant to the topic. They want you to pull your examples from diverse areas, including your studies, personal experience, and reading, and they want your essay to be organized and coherent. Finally, the essay graders will be grading your essay holistically, looking at your essay's "overall quality," so a few grammar or spelling errors won't hurt you.

ISSUE ESSAY STEP METHOD

Now that you're clear about what the essay graders are looking for, it's time to see how to use our essay step method and the three-act essay structure to write a "6" Issue essay, using our sample topic and directions.

With so much to do in so little time, you need a precise plan for the 45 minutes allotted for the Issue essay. Here are five strategic steps, along with the amount of time you should spend on each one on test day:

Step 1:	Understand the Topic and Take a Stand.	2 minutes
Step 2:	Brainstorm Examples.	5–7 minutes
Step 3:	Create an Outline.	4–6 minutes
Step 4:	Write the Essay.	25 minutes
Step 5:	Proof the Essay.	5 minutes
Total		45 minutes

Step 1: Understand the Topic and Take a Stand (2 minutes). The first thing you must do before you can even think about your essay is read the topic very carefully. Let's use our sample topic about conflicts from the previous chapter:

> "We can learn more from conflicts than we can from agreements."

Before you move those fingers across the keyboard, make sure you understand the topic thoroughly. To do that, you should:

- **Rephrase the topic.** Fighting and disagreeing can teach us more stuff than just agreeing can. Okay, so it's not elegant, but who cares? All that matters is that you've put the topic into your own words so it's clear to you.

- **Take a stand.** We've decided to agree with the topic: Yes, we can learn more from disagreements and conflicts. Remember that there's no right or wrong position, so just pick the position that seems easier to write about. Go with your gut.

That's it. One step down, four more to go.

Step 2: Brainstorm Examples (5–7 minutes). Once you've chosen your position, you need to figure out why you feel that way and present examples that will support your case. Plenty of test takers will succumb to the temptation to plunge straight from Step 1 into writing the essay Step 4). Bad idea. Skipping the brainstorming session will leave you with an opinion on the topic but with no clearly thought-out examples to prove your point. You'll write the first thing that comes to mind, and your essay will probably derail somewhere around Act II. Don't succumb to temptation and skip this step.

At first glance, brainstorming seems simple. You just close your eyes, scrunch up your face, and THINK REALLY HARD until you come up with some examples. But in practice, brainstorming while staring at a blank page under time pressure can be intimidating and frustrating. To make brainstorming less daunting and more productive, we've got three ideas:

- Brainstorm by Category

- Prepare Ahead of Time

- Use the Best Three

Brainstorm by Category. The best examples you can generate to support your Issue essay topic will come from a variety of sources such as science, history, politics, art, literature, business, and personal experience. So, brainstorm a list split up by category. Here's the list we brainstormed for the topic "We can learn more from conflicts than we can from agreements."

Current events	Failure of 9/11 security led to the creation of Homeland Security
Science	Copernicus challenged incorrect theory, led to correct theory
History	Challenge of status quo led to abolition of slavery
Politics	Democrats vs. Republican, bipartisanship
Art	Can't think of one
Literature	Can't think of one
Personal experience	Hardship leads to growth
Business	Competition in computers . . . Lower prices and better technology

Prepare Ahead of Time. If you want to put in the time, you could also do some brainstorming ahead of time. You can actually prepare examples for each of the eight categories we've listed above in our chart. You could, for instance, read up on various scientists, learning about their beliefs, their conflicts with current theories, and the impact of their discoveries (positive and negative) and memorize dates, events, and other facts.

Obviously, the trouble with preparing ahead is that you run the risk of getting stuck with a topic that doesn't allow you to use your prepared examples. But since the GRE essay topics are so broad, it's likely that you'll be able to massage at least some of your examples to fit.

You can also use the published topics on the GRE website to give you ideas of what kinds of preplanned examples might apply to the types of issues in the topic pool. You'll notice that there's a great deal of overlap in the pool; for example, numerous Issue topics deal with the nature and implications of modern technology. Great! If you want to prepare ahead of time, researching the history of technology and some theories concerning it could pay off. Even if your Issue topic does not specifically concern technology, you may still be able to squeeze your tech examples in there somewhere, as long as they're relevant; if it's too much of a stretch, the graders will know. You can do the same regarding some broadly applicable quotations and some well-known historical events.

Use the Best Three. No matter which method you use to generate examples, you'll still need to choose your best three. These examples will form the heart of your essay's body paragraphs. As you go through your brainstormed and/or pre-prepared examples to decide, keep these three questions in mind:

- Which examples let you go into the most detail?

- Which examples will give your essay the broadest range?

- Which examples are not controversial?

The first two reasons are pretty straightforward: *Detail* and *diversity* in your examples will help you write the strongest essay. The last question about whether your examples are controversial is a little subtler. Staying away from very controversial examples ensures that you won't accidentally offend or annoy your essay grader, who might then be more inclined to lower your grade.

Once you've chosen your three examples to develop, head to Step 3: outlining.

Step 3: Create an Outline (4–6 minutes). It's also tempting to skip this step. Many students hate outlining as much as they hate brainstorming. We're here to encourage you to embrace the outline. Love the outline! Live the outline! At the very least, write the outline!

The GRE essay rewards the conformity found in the three-act essay. You need an intro (Act I), three substantive body paragraphs (Act II), and a conclusion (Act III). The advantage of writing an outline is that the outline forces you to adhere to the formula. It also lets you double-check or rework your examples as necessary. Here's a summary of the template we learned about in the previous chapter:

Act	Purpose	Description
I	Set the stage	Thesis statement: Three examples: 1. 2. 3.
II	Tell the story	Topic sentence for example 1: Explanation for example 1:
		Topic sentence for example 2: Explanation for example 2:
		Topic sentence for example 3: Explanation for example 3:
III	Wrap it up	Recap thesis: Expand your position:

Memorize this table now so that you'll be able to quickly fill in the blanks on test day. And as you fill in the blanks, remember that conveying your ideas *to yourself* is what clearly matters at this stage. Your outline need not be articulate or even comprehensible to anyone other than you. Nobody will ever see it, so don't worry about whether it's even legible to others. All you need to do is make sure that your outline contains the essential raw material that will become your essay's thesis statement, topic sentences, supporting evidence, and concluding statement.

Here's a sample outline we've written based on the topic and examples we have already discussed:

Act	Purpose	Description
I	Set the stage	Thesis statement: Struggle is a required element for progress Three examples: 1. Copernicus/solar system 2. abolition of slavery 3. hardship
II	Tell the story	Topic sentence for example 1: Copernicus challenged common belief about solar system Explanation for example 1: Paid price politically and socially. Worth it because corrected an error
		Topic sentence for example 2: Challenge of status quo led to abolition of slavery in U.S. Explanation for example 2: Allowed freedom and contributions of entire population
		Topic sentence for example 3: Personal hardships lead to growth. Explanation for example 3: No hardships—spoiled, immature individuals. Perspective, character, insight come from struggles
III	Wrap it up	Recap thesis: Struggle beneficial in virtually every area Expand your position: Shouldn't avoid it, should seek it out

Notice how in the example above we write in a note-taking style. Feel free to write just enough to convey to yourself what you need to be able to follow during the actual writing of your essay. Once you have the outline down on paper, writing the essay becomes more a job of polishing language and ideas than creating them from scratch.

Step 4: Write the Essay (25 minutes). Writing the essay means filling out your ideas by following your outline and plugging in what's missing. That should add up to only about ten more sentences than what you've jotted down in your outline. Your outline should already contain a basic version of your thesis statement, ideas for the topic sentences for each of your three examples, and a conclusion statement that ties everything together.

Do not break from your outline. Never pause for a digression or drop in a fact or detail that's not entirely relevant to your essay's thesis statement. Remember, you're writing a three-act essay, not a four-act essay, and certainly not everything you could possibly say about the topic.

As you write, keep the "cast of characters" fresh in your mind (see chapter 11 for a full explanation of these fundamental writing elements):

- An Argument

- Evidence

- Varied Sentence Structure

- Facility with Language

Don't forget to vary your sentence structure, and make sure that every sentence in the essay serves the greater goal of proving your thesis statement, as well as the more immediate purpose of building on the supporting examples you present in the intro and in each Act II paragraph's topic sentence. Finally, be clear in your language, but don't forget to use a few well-placed vocabulary words that you definitely know how to use correctly.

If you're running out of time before finishing your three acts, don't panic. There's still hope of getting an okay score. Here's what you should do: Drop one of your example paragraphs. You can still get a decent score, possibly a "4" or "5," with just two, especially if they're really, really good. Three examples is definitely the strongest and safest way to go, but if you can't get through three, take your two best examples and go with them. Just be sure to include an introduction and a conclusion in both of your GRE essays.

Step 5: Proof the Essay (5 minutes). Proofing your essay means reading through your finished essay to correct mistakes. Use whatever time you have left after completing Step 4 to proof your essay. Read over your essay and search for rough writing, bad transitions, grammatical errors, repetitive sentence structure, and all that "cast of characters" stuff.

If you're running out of time and you have to skip a step, proofing is the step to drop. Proofing is important, but it's the only one of the five steps to a "6" that isn't absolutely crucial.

Now let's take a look at a successful GRE Issue essay.

A SAMPLE "6" ISSUE ESSAY

We're about to present you with an example of a complete GRE Issue essay. It's based strictly on our template and the outline we built in Step 3. We'll analyze it based on the essay graders' criteria. Below is our sample Issue essay topic, which is designed to be as close as possible to an essay topic that might appear on the GRE.

Our sample topic presents you with a big idea and then asks you to explain your view and back it up with concrete reasons that show why your view is the right one. On the actual exam, you might see a quotation from a famous person, a question, or a statement like ours. No matter what the topic looks like, every Issue essay question will require you to take a position and defend it with examples. And remember, you'll have a choice between two topics, so spend some time determining which one will be easier for you to write about.

Here's the sample Issue essay topic again:

"We can learn more from conflicts than we can from agreements."

As you read the essay below, note that we've marked certain sentences and paragraphs to illustrate where and how the essay conforms to our template. Use the info in brackets as a reminder of what your own Issue essay needs to include.

Although agreements have value, the juxtaposition of different ideas in a conflict inevitably leads to more significant progress and evolution. [THESIS] What scientific progress would we have, for example, if it weren't for intellectual debate? None— intellectual debate leads to scientific progress. [EXAMPLE 1] The reformation of outdated political ideas and concepts is also marked by struggle. [EXAMPLE 2] Finally, in the words of Friedrich Nietzsche, "What doesn't kill us makes us stronger." This quotation captures the sentiment that personal growth arises from conflict. [EXAMPLE 3]

First, historically, scientific progress has been inspired by conflicts of ideas. [TOPIC SENTENCE FOR EXAMPLE 1] In the sixteenth century, for example, a great debate arose because Copernicus vehemently challenged the notion that the earth is the center of the solar system. Although he paid a price both socially and politically for this remonstration, Copernicus disabused a long-held belief, much to the chagrin of the Catholic Church and other astronomers of his day. Because of this conflict, humankind eventually gained a new understanding of astronomy. [THREE SENTENCES THAT DEVELOP & SUPPORT EXAMPLE 1]

Second, sociohistorical evolution rarely comes about without turmoil and unrest. [TOPIC SENTENCE FOR EXAMPLE 2] For example, prior to the 1860s in the United States, it was legally acceptable to enslave other human beings and to view them as "property" with few rights. This view led several states to secede from the Union, which, in turn, led to the Civil War, a violent conflict that threatened to destroy the nation. After the war, though, slavery was abolished, and the Fourteenth Amendment to the Constitution essentially made discrimination on the basis of race illegal. As a result, the United States grew stronger as a nation. To advance takes constant questioning of the status quo. [FIVE SENTENCES THAT DEVELOP & SUPPORT EXAMPLE 2]

Third, conflict can lead to personal growth. [TOPIC SENTENCE FOR EXAMPLE 3] Adversity helps make us stronger. People who have not known some type of conflict or difficulty tend to be immature and spoiled. Americans so believe this sentiment about adversity that they have institutionalized it as an oft-repeated saying: If at first you don't succeed, try, try again. This saying emphasizes the way overcoming difficulty helps us grow as individuals: Each time we fail, we must pick ourselves up and try again. We shouldn't expect life to be easy. Sometimes the value of struggle is in the struggle, meaning that such conflicts, whether internal or external, give us perspective and insight. [SIX SENTENCES THAT DEVELOP & SUPPORT EXAMPLE 3]

Clearly, conflict has been responsible for several upward surges of humankind in diverse respects. In the areas of science, history, and individual character, progress requires struggle. [RECAPS THESIS] Rather than avoiding conflict at all costs, we should accept conflict as a necessary—and beneficial—part of the human condition, whether the conflicts arise among scholars or states. [EXPANDS THE POSITION] Conflict permits true transformation and growth.

Why This Essay Deserves a "6"

First, we need to assess whether this essay has the proper three-act structure, as well as the cast of characters that makes for a great Issue essay. Here they are, just to refresh your memory:

- An Argument

- Evidence

- Varied Sentence Structure

- Facility with Language

The organization of the essay follows our template perfectly, both at the paragraph level (topic sentences and development sentences) and at the overall essay level (intro, an action-packed Act II, a strong conclusion). It effectively argues that conflict is necessary to human advancement. It uses three examples from a very diverse array of disciplines—from science to politics to personal growth—to make the argument, and it never veers from using these examples to support the thesis statement's position. The essay takes a very strong and clear stance on the topic in the first sentence and sticks to it from start to finish.

Sentence structure varies often, making the entire essay more interesting and engaging to the grader. Note, though, how two sentences in paragraph 3 both use colons to link independent clauses. Your sentence structure doesn't have to be super-fancy each and every time. A little repetition in terms of grammar or sentence patterns won't hurt your score. The word choice is effective and appropriate. Our writer doesn't take risks with unfamiliar vocabulary but instead chooses a few out-of-the-ordinary words such as *juxtaposition, sentiment, vehemently,* and *institutionalized.* The quotation from Nietzsche adds some spice. No significant grammar errors disrupt the overall excellence of this Issue essay.

A Note on Length

Our sample essay is twenty-seven sentences long. However, a "6" essay is not based on the particular length of the essay but instead on the quality of the writing and adherence to ETS's grading criteria. Strong essays will vary in length depending on how the arguments are presented and the language and vocabulary that the writer employs. So don't worry too much about length. If you follow our step method, you'll write a strong essay that will satisfy the essay graders.

Here's a quick-reference chart that takes a closer look at this "6" essay based on the ETS evaluation criteria for graders and on the standards set forth in our Issue essay template.

ETS CRITERIA	YES OR NO?
Responds to the issue	YES
Develops a position on the issue through the use of incisive reasons and persuasive example	YES
Ideas are conveyed clearly and articulately	YES
Maintains proper focus on the issue and is well organized	YES
Demonstrates proficiency, fluency, and maturity in its use of sentence structure, vocabulary, and idioms	YES
Demonstrates an excellent command of the elements of standard written English, including grammar, word usage, spelling, and punctuation—but may contain minor flaws in these areas	YES
OUR CRITERIA	YES OR NO?
Uses the three-act essay structure	YES
Thesis statement in first sentence of paragraph 1	YES
Three examples that support the thesis listed in paragraph 1, in the order in which they're discussed in essay	YES
Topic sentence for example 1 in paragraph 2	YES
Development sentences to support example 1	YES
Topic sentence for example 2 in paragraph 3	YES
Development sentences to support example 2	YES
Topic sentence for example 3 in paragraph 4	YES
Development sentences to support example 3	YES
Conclusion (paragraph 5) rephrases thesis	YES
Conclusion (paragraph 5) expands position	YES

A SAMPLE "3" ISSUE ESSAY

Now that you know what to do for the Issue essay, here's what *not* to do. In fact, here's what can happen if you don't write a three-act essay or include the necessary cast of characters. The following essay would receive a "3" on the test:

> While we can learn a little from agreements, we can learn more from conflicts than we can from agreements. When you have conflicts you are often fighting over different opinions or ideas. If you have agreements you just agree and there is little to talk about or discuss. History provides many examples of conflicts and learning from conflicts. Just think about any war. War is a conflict where two sides want two different things. If we didn't want two different things, there would be agreement and we would never learn.

> Another example is when you fight with your family. You want one thing and they want another. You just never learn if you want the same thing. Conflicts teach you how to compromise and work things out. If you agree there is no need to compromise. Everything is to easy that way. You also learn from conflicts because you have to try and convince people that youre way is the right way and that their way is the wrong way. You must use skills you don't need to when you just agree. When there is conflict there is also learning. When there is agreement no one learns.

> In conclusion, then, agreement have less value than conflict. Many examples show this, and there are certainly many others. It's clear that we can learn from conflicts and arguments with the right perspective.

Why This Essay Deserves a "3"

Okay, this essay's pretty bad. But let's see exactly why it would receive a mediocre score. Thinking about what this essay does poorly will help you concentrate on avoiding these mistakes on your own GRE essays.

To begin with, it doesn't demonstrate thoughtful organization or include a stellar cast of characters. The argument—*that conflict is better than agreement*—never really gets off the ground. It contains only two examples (one about war and the other about family), but neither is developed. The writer could have strengthened the essay by talking about one specific war or one specific fight. Its organization is only fair, as it combines the introduction and first example into a single paragraph.

There are no transitions between paragraphs or sentences. Although the grammar and spelling are not horrible, this essay does contain at least a few errors (*conflcits, to easy; youre,* and *agreement have*). The sentence structure is repetitive. Note how many sentences in the second paragraph begin with *You*. The word choice is more like that of a third grader than a college graduate.

So, how does this poor essay stack up against the official ETS criteria and our checklist? Not very well. This essay misses the mark in almost every respect. Every "no" in the chart represents yet another weakness of this particular essay. Remember: To get a "6," you need to answer "yes" to most or all criteria.

ETS CRITERIA	YES OR NO?
Responds to the issue	YES
Develops a position on the issue through the use of incisive reasons and persuasive examples	NO
Ideas are conveyed clearly and articulately	NO
Maintains proper focus on the issue and is well organized	NO
Demonstrates proficiency, fluency, and maturity in its use of sentence structure, vocabulary, and idioms	NO
Demonstrates an excellent command of the elements of standard written English, including grammar, word usage, spelling, and punctuation—but may contain minor flaws in these areas	NO
OUR CRITERIA	**YES OR NO?**
Uses the three-act essay structure	NO
Thesis statement in first sentence of paragraph 1	YES
Three examples that support the thesis listed in paragraph 1, in the order in which they're discussed in essay	NO
Topic sentence for example 1 in paragraph 2	YES
Development sentences to support example 1	NO
Topic sentence for example 2 in paragraph 3	NO
Development sentences to support example 2	NO
Topic sentence for example 3 in paragraph 4	NO
Development sentences to support example 3	NO
Conclusion (paragraph 5) rephrases thesis	YES
Conclusion (paragraph 5) expands position	NO

Chapter 13

The Argument Essay

The test makers call this essay "Analyze an Argument," because that's exactly what they want you to do. You'll be given 30 minutes to plan, draft, and proof-read an essay about an argumentative passage, known as the "topic." Argument essay topics always give you a brief argumentative paragraph, which will include a conclusion and at least two premises. Your job is to analyze the validity of the argument. Our job is to ensure you know how to respond to a GRE argument and support your analysis with relevant examples—in other words, produce a "6" Argument essay.

ARGUMENT ESSAY X-RAY

Here's a sample Argument topic with the actual directions you'll see on the GRE:

<u>Directions</u>: You will have 30 minutes to plan and write a critique of an argument presented in the form of a short passage. A critique of any other argument will receive a score of zero.

Analyze the line of reasoning in the argument. Be sure to consider what, if any, questionable assumptions underlie the thinking and, if evidence is cited, how well it supports the conclusion.

You can also discuss what sort of evidence would strengthen or refute the argument, what changes in the argument would make it more logically sound, and what additional information might help you better evaluate its conclusion. *Note that you are NOT being asked to present your views on the subject.*

GRE readers, who are college and university faculty, will read your critique and evaluate its overall quality, based on how well you

- identify and analyze important features of the argument

- organize, develop, and express your critique of the argument

- support your critique with relevant reasons and examples

- control the elements of standard written English

Before you begin writing, you may want to take a few minutes to evaluate the argument and to plan a response. Be sure to develop your ideas fully and organize them coherently, but leave time to reread what you have written and make any revisions that you think are necessary.

Discuss how well reasoned you find this argument.

> Global warming has not and will not have the disastrous consequences predicted by the scientific community. Although experts claim that temperatures have risen dramatically, with detrimental effects, these claims are largely exaggerated. For example, the mean global temperature has only risen 0.4 degrees Fahrenheit in twenty-five years. Further, Arctic sea ice has decreased less than 0.3 percent since 1996, indicating that the polar ice caps have not melted significantly. Thus, we need not take any measures to reverse the alleged effects of global warming.

You're asked to analyze the "line of reasoning in the argument," and fortunately, the test makers go on to spell out exactly what they mean by that. The first key feature they mention is "questionable assumptions that underlie the argument." We'll talk more about "assumptions" below, but essentially they're looking to see whether you recognize things the argument writer takes for granted—that is, doesn't state explicitly—and are required for the argument to be valid.

But you are also given another related task, which concerns evaluating how well the evidence supports the conclusion. Notice that you're given free rein to mess with the argument—that is, to say what changes you would suggest to make the argument better or to state what kinds of evidence might blow it to pieces. You can even go as far as discussing *extra* information you would need to better evaluate the conclusion.

In a nutshell, then, there's a lot of leeway as to the ground you can cover. However, do not expect the argument to be airtight; you can't get away with writing "It's all good—I'm cool with it." Regardless of the topic, the Argument essay will always ask you to analyze the given argument, talking about what's good and not so good about the argument's conclusion, premises, and assumptions. There will always be a possibility for legitimate and cogent analysis based on the argumentative components highlighted in the directions.

Since the Argument essay tests not only your ability to write but also your ability to analyze arguments, we'll spend the next section explaining how to identify the conclusion, premises, and assumptions behind any argument. We'll then provide you with a step method that shows you how to apply these essential concepts to a GRE argument.

ARGUMENT FUNDAMENTALS

To write an effective Argument essay, you'll need to first understand the essential components of an argument. Here's a quick breakdown of an argument's three parts:

- **Conclusion:** What the argument's arguing

- **Premise(s):** How it's making that argument

- **Assumption(s):** What's unstated yet required by the argument

The Argument essay requires you to be an expert at identifying these three main parts and knowing how they work together. Regardless of the topic, the Argument essay will always ask you to evaluate the given argument and to highlight what's good and not so good about the argument's conclusion, premises, and assumptions.

Every single argument, whether on the GRE or in life, has a conclusion and at least one premise to support it. Many real-life arguments contain multiple premises and at least one assumption. The argument topic you'll see on the GRE will consist of a conclusion backed up by at least two premises and will most likely contain one or more central assumptions.

Conclusion

The conclusion of an argument is the author's point. The conclusion may or may not be explicitly stated in the argument, but it's always what the author is trying to prove or suggest.

Here are a few words and phrases that indicate a conclusion is coming:

- As a result

- Clearly

- Consequently

- Hence

- In conclusion

- In short

- It follows that

- So

- The point is

- Therefore

- Thus

Not every argument will contain one of these words, but most probably will. This brings us to a great rule of thumb for identifying conclusions:

The conclusion is often the first or last sentence of an argument.

Consider the following sample Argument essay topic:

> Studies show that as we've become more technically advanced, our health has deteriorated rapidly. Heart disease, cancer, diabetes, and virtually every major ailment are far more common today than they were thirty years ago. The primary reason for this deterioration is the sedentary lifestyle associated with today's high-tech jobs. Clearly, our health will continue to decline as long as we persist in our technological advances.

So, what's the conclusion, or point, of this argument? The word *clearly* in the final sentence might have tipped you off that the conclusion was coming, or the sentence's placement might have clued you in. Either way, the assertion that "our health will continue to decline as long as we persist in our technological advances" is what the author of this argument is trying to prove. We'll use this topic as the basis for the sample Argument essay we'll write later in this chapter.

Premises

The premises of an argument are the facts or beliefs used to support the conclusion. They are always stated. In other words, premises are the stated reasons for the author's point. Think of premises as evidence—they're the reasons that lead to the topic. After you've identified the conclusion of an argument, the premises are often whatever's left in the paragraph.

Paraphrasing Premises

In our sample Argument essay topic, the premises are everything except the last sentence of the argument:

> Studies show that as we've become more technically advanced, our health has deteriorated rapidly. Heart disease, cancer, diabetes, and virtually every major ailment are far more common today than they were thirty years ago. The primary reason for this deterioration is the sedentary lifestyle associated with today's high-tech jobs.

To ensure that you really understand the premises, try to translate them into your own words. This is a great way to help simplify what could be a complicated, confusing argument. It might help to jot down a few notes on your scratch paper.

The table below shows our paraphrase of this argument topic's premises.

Premise	Our Paraphrase
1. Studies show that as we've become more technically advanced, our health has deteriorated rapidly.	Our health has declined as tech has advanced
2. Heart disease, cancer, diabetes, and virtually every major ailment are far more common today than they were thirty years ago.	Health significantly worse than 30 yrs ago; disease widespread
3. The primary reason for this deterioration is the sedentary lifestyle associated with today's high-tech jobs.	Health bad b/c people w/high-tech jobs don't exercise regularly

That's it. Don't waste time trying to craft beautifully written premises. Just write them in your own words, quick and dirty. Anything goes, as long as it helps you understand how the author is attempting to support the conclusion.

You probably noticed that our sample topic has three premises, which is pretty standard on the GRE. On test day, you might see as few as one premise or as many as four, but usually you'll get something in between.

Remember too that premises are always stated. This is in sharp contrast to assumptions, the last piece of the argument puzzle, which we'll discuss next.

Assumptions

Assumptions are additional beliefs the author must have in order to reach the conclusion. They are the bridge between the premises and the conclusion. Assumptions are never stated. And because they're not stated, assumptions are usually the hardest part of an argument to identify. On all but the simplest arguments, you'll have to stop and think about what else is necessary to reach the author's conclusion. Here's a tip:

Assumptions usually concern anything mentioned in the premises but not in the conclusion, or anything mentioned in the conclusion but not in the premises.

Think about this for a second, and it should make sense. Assumptions link the premises and the conclusion, so you need to pay attention to what is mentioned in the conclusion and what is mentioned in the premises. How the author moves from one part of the argument to the other almost always involves the assumptions, or the link between the two parts.

Identifying Assumptions

Identifying assumptions requires you to really think about the argument. You should constantly be asking yourself, "What else besides what is actually written must the author believe to reach the conclusion? How are the parts related? What's the link?" Let's see how this works, first in the context of our sample argument from the X-ray and then using the sample Argument essay topic discussed earlier in this section. Here again for your consideration is the X-ray topic. See if you can pick out any unstated yet necessary premises.

> Global warming has not and will not have the disastrous consequences predicted by the scientific community. Although experts claim that temperatures have risen dramatically, with detrimental effects, these claims are largely exaggerated. For example, the mean global temperature has only risen 0.4 degrees Fahrenheit in twenty-five years. Further, Arctic sea ice has decreased less than 0.3 percent since 1996, indicating that the polar ice caps have not melted significantly. Thus, we need not take any measures to reverse the alleged effects of global warming.

Okay, how'd you make out? The conclusion is the last sentence: *We need not take any measures to reverse the alleged effects of global warming.* Everything else in the topic is a premise. The argument assumes that an increase in temperature of 0.4 degrees and a reduction in Artic sea ice of 0.3 percent are insignificant. Although these numbers may sound small, it's very possible that they represent significant effects. Furthermore, the argument assumes that temperatures and sea ice will rise or decline at the same steady rate, and it discounts the idea that there could be a dramatic increase in global temperatures or a dramatic decrease in Arctic sea ice as a result of global warming. To make the unequivocal assertion that no anti–global warming measures need be taken, the argument assumes that what holds for the present will also hold for the future. A "6"-caliber essay written on this topic would need to point out and discuss these assumptions.

Now try the same for the sample topic discussed earlier:

> Studies show that as we've become more technically advanced, our health has deteriorated rapidly. Heart disease, cancer, diabetes, and virtually every major ailment are far more common today than they were thirty years ago. The primary reason for this deterioration is the sedentary lifestyle associated with today's high-tech jobs. Clearly, our health will continue to decline as long as we persist in our technological advances.

The conclusion of the argument (*Clearly, our health will continue to decline as long as we persist in our technological advances*) is the only point in the argument that talks about the future. Interesting. The premises just talk about the past and the present (disease is more widespread now; people with high-tech jobs don't exercise as much). So, the link between the premises and the conclusion must somehow connect the premises about the past and present with this conclusion about the future. One assumption that makes this connection is this:

Past and present trends are indicative of the future.

In other words, by thinking about how the past differs from the present in some respect, we might be able to come to some conclusions about the future. So, what are some other assumptions? Again, we need to think about what the author is really saying: We have high-tech jobs, so we don't exercise, and so we get sick—and as technology has increased, our health has deteriorated.

So far, so good. But couldn't there be other factors that influence our health? Considering these other factors leads to a couple more assumptions:

Advances in medicine won't counteract the effect of a sedentary lifestyle.

Aha! Medicine helps us get better when we're sick, but the author of this argument assumes that medicine or advances in health care won't be able to fix the lack of exercise that comes with high-tech jobs.

Diet is not as important as exercise in determining health.

This argument assumes that lack of exercise trumps all other considerations, including a good diet. According to the author's assumptions, then, even a good diet won't be enough to counterbalance the sedentary lifestyle that comes with a high-tech job. These assumptions will form the backbone of our Argument essay, which we'll construct using our step method.

ARGUMENT ESSAY STEP METHOD

As with the Issue essay, there are five steps to scoring a "6" on the Argument essay. Here's a preview, along with the amount of time you should spend on each step on test day.

Step 1:	Understand the Topic and Find its Conclusion.	1 minute
Step 2:	Identify the Topic's Assumptions.	5 minutes
Step 3:	Create an Outline.	4–6 minutes
Step 4:	Write the Essay.	15 minutes
Step 5:	Proof the Essay.	3 minutes
Total		30 minutes

Now let's go through each step in slow motion.

Step 1: Understand the Topic and Find Its Conclusion (1 minute). The first thing you must do before you can even think about your essay is read the argument topic very carefully. Let's look at our sample again.

> Studies show that as we've become more technically advanced, our health has deteriorated rapidly. Heart disease, cancer, diabetes, and virtually every major ailment are far more common today than they were thirty years ago. The primary reason for this deterioration is the sedentary lifestyle associated with today's high-tech jobs. Clearly, our health will continue to decline as long as we persist in our technological advances.

As you read the argument topic, ask yourself, "What's the author's point?" This will help you identify the topic's conclusion. As we previously discussed, look for the conclusion in the first or last sentence. Here the conclusion is the last sentence: *Clearly, our health will continue to decline as long as we persist in our technological advances.*

Figuring out the conclusion will help you with Step 2, identifying the topic's assumptions.

Step 2: Identify the Topic's Assumptions (5 minutes). The assumptions you identify will provide the foundation for the three reasons you employ for why or why not the argument's conclusion works.

As we discussed earlier, assumptions are additional beliefs the author must have to reach the conclusion. Assumptions are never stated; you'll have to read between the lines to figure them out. As you read the argument, ask yourself, "What else must the author believe? What's stated in the premises but not the conclusion? What's stated in the conclusion but not the premises?" The answer to these questions will lead you to the assumptions. Coming up with assumptions can be time consuming, and you don't want to waste time thinking of more assumptions than you have to. Just pick three, which you'll then discuss in the three Act II body paragraphs.

We came up with these assumptions:

1. Past and present trends are indicative of the future.

2. Advances in medicine won't counteract the effect of a sedentary lifestyle.

3. Diet is not as important as exercise in determining health.

Could we have thought of others? Yup, we sure could have. But you have just 30 minutes to craft and write the Argument essay, so choosing three ensures you have what you need to craft your essay.

You can and should use the topics in the argument pool of the GRE website to practice spotting the kinds of assumptions these arguments contain. Practice with these sample topics by weeding out their assumptions and then thinking through how you would exploit those assumptions in your essay. For example, you might show how the assumption you noticed is questionable, thus weakening the argument; or, conversely, you may come up with a specific instance in which the assumption doesn't apply, thus highlighting a circumstance in which the argument is more valid.

Step 3: Create an Outline (4–6 minutes). Don't forget that the essay graders reward conformity. Use our three-act Argument essay template to create a map of your essay that will please the essay graders. You need an intro (Act I), three hearty body paragraphs (Act II), and a conclusion (Act III). Creating an outline reinforces this structure, makes sure you conform to this structure, and helps you organize your essay appropriately before you begin writing. Here's a summary of our template before we begin.

Act	Purpose	Description
I	Set the stage	Thesis statement: Three examples: 1. 2. 3.
II	Tell the story	Topic sentence for example 1: Explanation for example 1: --- Topic sentence for example 2: Explanation for example 2: --- Topic sentence for example 3: Explanation for example 3:
III	Wrap it up	Recap thesis: Expand your position:

Get familiar with this template now so that you don't even need to think about it come test day. It will just be automatic. As you fill in the outline, remember that what matters is that you convey your ideas clearly to yourself. Don't worry about being articulate or even comprehensible to anyone other than you. Just make sure that you've got down the raw material that will become your thesis statement, topic sentences, and concluding statement when you write your essay.

Here's a sample outline we've written based on the topic and assumptions we've already discussed.

Act	Purpose	Description
I	Set the stage	Thesis statement & topic's conclusion: Argument weakened by three unstated assumptions; argument claims that our health will continue to decline as long as we persist in our technological advances. Three reasons: 1. medical advances 2. diet vs. exercise 3. past/present → future
II	Tell the story	Topic sentence for reason 1: Assumes advances in medicine won't counteract effect of sedentary lifestyle Analysis of reason 1: Consider implications if this weren't true: Medicine could advance as high-tech does. If so, might have more effect than exercise; could be good
		Topic sentence for reason 2: Assumes diet not as important as exercise in determining health Analysis of reason 2: Consider implications if this weren't true: Diet could improve as exercise declines. If diet is determining factor, health won't decline
		Topic sentence for reason 3: Assumes past and present trends indicative of the future Analysis of reason 3: Consider implications if this weren't true: Even though tech. has improved and health has declined so far, this doesn't necessarily mean anything about future; example of how tech has improved???
III	Wrap it up	Recap thesis: Conc (health in jeopardy) relies on these three questionable assumptions; argument doesn't really work Expand your position: Author needs to address these issues to strengthen the argument and more evidence

We wrote our outline in a note-taking style, using abbreviations. When we couldn't think of an example for the third paragraph of Act II, we wrote *???* to remind ourselves to think of something later. Feel free to do the same on your own outline. Write just enough in the outline to remind yourself of what you want to write in the essay. If it helps you to write in complete sentences, great— do that. But don't feel obligated, since no one but you will ever see your outline.

Developing the Reasons. As you can see from our template, each Act II paragraph identifies and analyzes an assumption that underlies the topic's conclusion. Your critique of these three assumptions forms the basis of the argument set forth in your thesis statement. Each paragraph will need to carefully consider what would happen to the argument's conclusion if the assumption under discussion were false.

We might have also chosen to structure our essay around additional information that would be necessary to evaluate the argument's validity or specific restricted contexts in which the argument might carry more weight. When outlining your response, try to settle on points that will be easiest for you to defend.

Step 4: Write the Essay (15 minutes). Once you have the outline down, the essay naturally flows from there. All you'll need to do is flesh out your ideas. If you've written a thorough outline according to our template, you only need to add about ten more sentences. After all, your outline should already contain a basic version of the argument's conclusion, rough topic sentences for the three supporting reasons you will develop, and a conclusion that wraps it up.

As you write, remember your old friends, the cast of characters (see chapter 11 for a full explanation of these fundamental writing elements):

- An Argument

- Evidence

- Varied Sentence Structure

- Facility with Language

It should be pretty clear by now that the argument you make in your Argument essay should be related to the topic's conclusion. Basically, you'll be arguing that either the conclusion works or it doesn't work. Your thoughts during the crucial Step 2 will form the backbone of your essay's Act II. Make sure that every sentence in the essay serves the greater goal of showing how your thesis depends on each reason you develop and analyze.

Remember that your evidence will come from your understanding of the argument's assumptions. Unlike the Issue essay, which is based on examples you think up, the Argument essay relies on evidence taken directly from the topic given by the test makers. In our sample essay, we're arguing that the conclusion is weakened by its three unstated assumptions.

Try to jazz up your writing with varied sentence structure and a few polysyllabic words. Instead of writing sentences that rely on the subject-verb, subject-verb pattern, try to shake things up by using a mix of dependent and independent clauses. Now's not the time to experiment with semicolons or fancy vocab, though. Use only the words and punctuation that you absolutely know how to use correctly. Above all, state your points clearly and coherently: Making an articulate argument is the surest way of demonstrating your facility with language to the essay graders.

Don't panic if you start to run out of time. Ignore the clock, take a deep breath, and say "So long" to the third Act II paragraph. You can still get a pretty good score with a strong Act I, two Act II paragraphs, and a thoughtful Act III. Three Act II paragraphs is definitely the strongest and safest way to go, but if you just can't get through three, take your two best assumptions and go with them. Just be sure to include an introduction and a conclusion in both essays you write for the GRE.

Step 5: Proof the Essay (3 minutes). Proofing your essay means reading it over one last time to fix typos, correct grammar errors, check spelling, and just make sure that everything looks okay. If you don't have a full three minutes after you've finished writing the essay (Step 4), spend whatever time you do have left proofing. Read over your essay and search for rough writing, bad transitions, grammatical errors, repetitive sentence structure, and all that stuff that often spells the difference between a score of "4" and a score of "6."

That said, if you run out of time, skip this step. The test makers instruct the essay graders to look for patterns of errors, so the occasional misspelled word or awkward turn of phrase won't kill you.

A SAMPLE "6" ARGUMENT ESSAY

Below is our sample argument topic, which we've been working with throughout this chapter:

> Studies show that, as we've become more technically advanced, our health has deteriorated rapidly. Heart disease, cancer, diabetes, and virtually every major ailment are far more common today than they were thirty years ago. The primary reason for this deterioration is the sedentary lifestyle associated with today's high-tech jobs. Clearly, our health will continue to decline as long as we persist in our technological advances.

As you read the sample response, notice how we've marked certain sentences and paragraphs to illustrate where and how the essay conforms to our template. The info in brackets should remind you of what your own Argument essay needs to include.

> The conclusion of this argument, "Clearly, our health will continue to decline as long as we persist in our technological advances," rests weakly on three primary assumptions. [THESIS STATEMENT & TOPIC'S CONCLUSION] First, it assumes that advances in medicine will not counteract the detrimental effects of a lack of exercise. [REASON 1] Second, it requires the tacit belief that the effect of a proper

diet on health is insignificant in comparison to the effects of a sedentary lifestyle. [REASON 2] Finally, it presumes that whatever holds true for the past and present will also hold true for the future. [REASON 3]

The argument assumes that the positive effects of regular exercise on health override any positive effects resulting from advances in medicine. [TOPIC SENTENCE FOR REASON 1] As society becomes increasingly high tech, we might plausibly argue that medicine will similarly develop and advance. Nonetheless, the validity of the author's argument depends on the idea that medicine will not advance as rapidly as technology or, at the very least, on the idea that any advance in medicine will have a relatively insignificant effect on health, compared to the effects of regular exercise. But what might happen if medicine progresses such that health care can counteract the effects of a sedentary lifestyle? Might we imagine a pill or procedure that could easily and effectively combat heart disease, diabetes, and other diseases linked to lack of exercise? If this occurs, whether our lives become more sedentary as a result of technology will not matter when it comes to our health, because medicine will offset the negative effects of a lack of exercise. [FIVE SENTENCES THAT DEVELOP & ANALYZE REASON 1]

Similarly, the argument's conclusion depends on the assumption that improvements in diet will not prevent or stave off the decline in wellness that results from working at a high-tech job. [TOPIC SENTENCE FOR REASON 2] Whether it's reasonable to expect our diets to improve as technology advances is irrelevant to this argument; the fact remains that the author assumes that diet has little to no impact on the general well-being of a person who gets no exercise. Yet a healthy diet could negate the effects of a sedentary lifestyle. In fact, if a good diet could be shown to improve one's health, then it would be unreasonable to conclude that a sedentary lifestyle automatically leads to poor health and increased disease in everyone. There would be no easy way to show such a correlation between exercise and health. Indeed, a sedentary lifestyle coupled with a good diet might lead to good health. [FIVE SENTENCES THAT DEVELOP & ANALYZE REASON 2]

The most significant assumption made by the author to arrive at the conclusion is that the past and present are reliable indicators of the future. [TOPIC SENTENCE FOR REASON 3] Specifically, the author assumes that since our overall health has declined as technology has improved, this pattern will continue. Such an assumption is unwarranted; many trends reverse direction entirely or eventually cease. For example, the rapid rise and success of high-tech companies in the late '90s eventually came to a screeching halt, almost without warning. If the trend toward technological advancements and the sedentary lifestyles with which they are associated came to a similar halt, it would be illogical to conclude that our health would also continue to decline. [FOUR SENTENCES THAT DEVELOP & ANALYZE REASON 3]

In sum, this argument relies heavily on its assumptions, perhaps too heavily. Denying any one of these assumptions results in a weakened or, in some cases, invalid conclusion. Nevertheless, the conclusion that our health is in jeopardy may in fact be true, despite its not being proven with the premises given and assumptions made by the author. [RECAP] To strengthen the argument, the author would need to not only address these three assumptions but also to more firmly establish a link between deteriorating health and technological advances. In the words of Hippocrates, "A wise man should consider that health is the greatest of human blessings." An argument conclusively linking rising technology to failing health would be a strong argument indeed. [EXPANDS POSITION]

Why This Essay Deserves a "6"

Now we'll take a look at what makes this essay so deserving of a "6." First, we need to assess whether this essay contains proper structure, as well as the cast of characters needed for a "6" Argument essay. Here they are again:

- An Argument

- Evidence

- Varied Sentence Structure

- Facility with Language

The essay is definitely organized, with all three assumptions clearly stated in Act I and analyzed in Act II. The analyses in Act II certainly show how the implications of the assumptions might make the conclusion invalid. Finally, Act III states the essay's thesis and explains what the author could do differently to strengthen the topic's argument. This essay also features all the characters. Argument? Yup—this essay argues that although the topic's conclusion might be true, the assumptions made by the author diminish the strength of the author's conclusion. Reasons and evidence? Yes and yes. This essay clearly discusses the three unstated assumptions that weaken the argument.

Also, the essay has varied sentence structure: a semicolon here, beginning with a gerund there, and linking ideas using *if . . . then* and *but . . . also* constructions. Our writer does not take risks with unfamiliar vocabulary but instead chooses a few out-of-the-ordinary words such as *tacit*, *detrimental*, and *presumes*. No significant grammar errors disrupt the fluidity. The essay concludes with a well-placed quote. You may have noticed that the quote isn't precisely the same as the original, albeit translated, version. That's okay. The essay graders are sympathetic to the fact that you only have 30 minutes for each essay—and the quote just adds spice.

A Note on Length

Our sample essay is twenty-six sentences long. As we noted in the previous chapter, a "6" essay is not based on the particular length of the essay but instead on the quality of the writing and adherence to ETS's grading criteria.

Now let's look at our essay from the point of view of an essay grader by taking a look at the ETS evaluation criteria for graders and the criteria for our Argument essay template.

ETS CRITERIA	YES OR NO?
Responds to the argument given in the topic	YES
Identifies the key features of the argument and analyzes each one in a thoughtful manner	YES
Supports each point of critique with insightful examples and analysis	YES
Develops its ideas in a clear, organized manner, with appropriate transitions to help connect ideas together	YES
Demonstrates proficiency, fluency, and maturity in its use of sentence structure, vocabulary, and idioms	YES
Demonstrates an excellent command of the elements of standard written English, including grammar, word usage, spelling, and punctuation—but may contain minor flaws in these areas	YES
OUR CRITERIA	**YES OR NO?**
Uses the three-act essay structure	YES
States conclusion in first sentence of paragraph 1	YES
Three reasons that support the thesis listed in paragraph 1, in the order in which they're discussed in essay	YES
Topic sentence for reason 1 in paragraph 2	YES
Development sentences to analyze reason 1	YES
Topic sentence for reason 2 in paragraph 3	YES
Development sentences to analyze reason 2	YES
Topic sentence for reason 3 in paragraph 4	YES
Development sentences to analyze reason 3	YES
Conclusion (paragraph 5) rephrases thesis	YES
Conclusion (paragraph 5) expands position	YES

A SAMPLE "3" ARGUMENT ESSAY

What happens if you don't follow our Argument essay template or if you forget about the cast of characters? You get a mediocre score. Don't even think about arguing with that conclusion. See what we mean by taking a look at this essay, which would receive a "3" on the exam. We've included it to show you what *not* to do on test day.

> There are several reasons for the authors statement that the primary reason for our deteriorating health is the "sedentary lifestyle associated with today's high-tech jobs," and that "our health will continue to decline as long as we persist in our technological advances."

While the author states that "studies show that, as we've become more technically advanced, our health has deteriorated rapidly. Heart disease, cancer, diabetes, and virtually every major ailment are far more common today than they were 30 years ago," no evidence is presented that this link is relevant. While it is possible that their is a connection between technolgy and poor health, the author doesn't support it. The author doesn't say that there are many other things that could contribute to increases in health problems besides a sedentary lifestyle. In addition, the author states that "studies show," but does not mention the numberr or kinds of those studies.

Finally, while the statement that health has deteriorated over time may be true, the author says that the lifestyle associated with "today's high tech jobs" is responsible but does not back it up. Without presenting more information and studies, the author's claim can be easily disproven.

Why This Essay Deserves a "3"

Oof. Not so hot, this essay. Its so-so argument, mediocre organization, and long-winded second paragraph cost this essay points. This essay only includes two assumptions, and the second one is hardly developed. Plus the conclusion is tacked onto the third paragraph. Our writer hasn't even clearly identified the assumptions underlying the topic's argument. Although the vocabulary is passable, the frequent typos are a distraction. First, the essay loses major points for not including a great cast of characters. Finally, quoting the topic does not count as including a quotation.

But let's look at it compared to the ETS criteria and to our criteria. How do you think it's going to measure up?

ETS CRITERIA	YES OR NO?
Responds to the argument given in the topic	YES
Identifies the key features of the argument and analyzes each one in a thoughtful manner	NO
Supports each point of critique with insightful examples and analysis	NO
Develops its ideas in a clear, organized manner, with appropriate transitions to help connect ideas together	NO
Demonstrates proficiency, fluency, and maturity in its use of sentence structure, vocabulary, and idioms	YES
Demonstrates an excellent command of the elements of standard written English, including grammar, word usage, spelling, and punctuation—but may contain minor flaws in these areas	NO
OUR CRITERIA	**YES OR NO?**
Uses the three-act essay structure	NO
States conclusion in first sentence of paragraph 1	YES
Three reasons that support the thesis listed in paragraph 1, in the order in which they're discussed in essay	NO
Topic sentence for reason 1 in paragraph 2	YES
Development sentences to analyze reason 1	YES
Topic sentence for reason 2 in paragraph 3	YES
Development sentences to analyze reason 2	NO
Topic sentence for reason 3 in paragraph 4	NO
Development sentences to analyze reason 3	NO
Conclusion (paragraph 5) rephrases thesis	NO
Conclusion (paragraph 5) expands position	NO

Part IV

GRE PRACTICE

Practicing with Practice Tests

Studying practice tests is a powerful test-prep tool for the GRE. That's why we give you free access to additional practice tests online. Below we explain, step by step, exactly how to do it yourself.

CONTROL YOUR ENVIRONMENT

You should do everything in your power to make every practice test you take feel like the real GRE. As the GRE is a computer-based test, your online practice will better prepare you for the real thing. However, the practice test in this book is a very good starting point.

- **Take a timed test.** Don't give yourself any extra time. Be as strict as the proctor who will be administering the test. If you have to go to the bathroom, let the clock keep running. That's what'll happen on test day.

- **Take the test in a single sitting.** Training yourself to endure roughly four hours of test-taking is part of your preparation.

- **Take the test without distractions.** Don't take the practice test in a room with lots of people walking through it. Go to a library, your bedroom, an empty classroom—anywhere quiet.

Simulating the real GRE experience as closely as possible during your study time will ensure that there will be no surprises to distract you on test day. Understanding what you're in for will give you the focus and calm you'll need to reach your target score. Don't forget to get online and take our free practice test to better simulate the computer-based test-taking experience.

SCORE YOUR PRACTICE TEST

After you take your practice test, score it and see how you did. However, when you do your scoring, don't just tally up the number of questions you answered correctly. As part of your scoring, you should also keep a list of every question you got wrong and every question you skipped. This list will be your guide when you study your test.

If you're missing lots of easy questions, be careful of careless mistakes. It's great if you're missing only the hardest questions, but make sure to review the relevant content and techniques, and watch for distractors and traps.

The test makers will score your real test by using an algorithm to convert your raw score into your scaled score (a number between 200 and 800). Our practice test comes with a chart that shows you how to translate your raw scores on the Math and Verbal sections into scaled scores.

STUDY YOUR PRACTICE TEST

After grading your test, you should have a list of the questions you answered incorrectly or skipped. Studying your test involves using this list and examining each question you answered incorrectly, figuring out why you got the question wrong and understanding what you could have done to get the question right.

The practice tests in our book and online were specifically designed to help you study. Each question is categorized by its question type, such as Problem Solving; and by its specific content, such as circles; and by its difficulty level. Here's what you'll see:

1. **A**
Quantitative Comparisons: Linear Equations, Square Roots *Rating:* Easy

The answers also provide full explanations of each question so you can identity and focus on your specific weakness.

Why'd You Get It Wrong?

As you study your practice tests, you need to pay particular attention to the questions you answered incorrectly. There are three reasons why you might have gotten an individual question wrong:

1. You didn't know the concept being tested.

2. You guessed blindly, without eliminating any answer choices.

3. You knew the answer but made a careless error.

You should know which of these reasons applies to each question you got wrong. Once you figure out why you got a question wrong, you need to figure out what you could have done to get the question right.

Reason 1: Lack of Knowledge. A question answered incorrectly for reason 1 pinpoints a weakness in your knowledge. Discovering this kind of error gives you the opportunity to fill the void in your knowledge base and eliminate future errors on the same question type.

For example, if the question you got wrong refers to factoring quadratics, don't just work out how to factor that one quadratic; take the chance to go over the fundamental techniques that allow you to factor all quadratics.

Remember, you will not see a question exactly like the question you got wrong. But you probably will see a question that covers the same topic as the practice question. For that reason, when you get a question wrong, don't just figure out the right answer to the question. Study the broader topic that the question tests.

Reason 2: Guessing Ineffectively. If you guessed wrong, review your guessing strategy. By thinking in a critical way about the decisions you made while taking the practice test, you can train yourself to make quicker, more decisive, and better decisions.

Did you guess intelligently? Did you eliminate answers you knew were wrong? Could you have eliminated more answers? If yes, why didn't you? Remember: If you can eliminate even one of the answer choices, you've increased your odds of getting the question right.

If you took a guess and chose the incorrect answer, don't let that discourage you from guessing. The GRE is mostly a multiple-choice test, which means the answer is right there in front of you. If you eliminated at least one answer, you followed the right strategy by guessing even if you got the question wrong. Review the answer choices for every question, even those you answered correctly. Figuring out why certain answer choices are wrong will help you identify other wrong answers on future questions.

Reason 3: Carelessness. Here it might be tempting to say to yourself, "Oh, I made a careless error," and assure yourself you won't do that again. Unacceptable! You made that careless mistake for a reason, and you should figure out why. Getting a question wrong because you didn't know the answer reveals a weakness in your knowledge about the test. Making a careless mistake represents a weakness in your test-taking method.

To overcome this weakness, you need to approach it in the same critical way you would approach a lack of knowledge. Study your mistake. Retrace your thought process on the problem and pinpoint the origin of your carelessness: Were you rushing? If you pin down your mistake, you are much less likely to repeat it.

GRE
Practice Test

GRE PRACTICE TEST ANSWER SHEET

SECTION 2

1. ○ ○ ○ ○ ○	8. ○ ○ ○ ○ ○	15. ○ ○ ○ ○ ○	22. ○ ○ ○ ○ ○
2. ○ ○ ○ ○ ○	9. ○ ○ ○ ○ ○	16. ○ ○ ○ ○ ○	23. ○ ○ ○ ○ ○
3. ○ ○ ○ ○ ○	10. ○ ○ ○ ○ ○	17. ○ ○ ○ ○ ○	24. ○ ○ ○ ○ ○
4. ○ ○ ○ ○ ○	11. ○ ○ ○ ○ ○	18. ○ ○ ○ ○ ○	25. ○ ○ ○ ○ ○
5. ○ ○ ○ ○ ○	12. ○ ○ ○ ○ ○	19. ○ ○ ○ ○ ○	26. ○ ○ ○ ○ ○
6. ○ ○ ○ ○ ○	13. ○ ○ ○ ○ ○	20. ○ ○ ○ ○ ○	27. ○ ○ ○ ○ ○
7. ○ ○ ○ ○ ○	14. ○ ○ ○ ○ ○	21. ○ ○ ○ ○ ○	28. ○ ○ ○ ○ ○

SECTION 3

1. ○ ○ ○ ○ ○	9. ○ ○ ○ ○ ○	17. ○ ○ ○ ○ ○	25. ○ ○ ○ ○ ○
2. ○ ○ ○ ○ ○	10. ○ ○ ○ ○ ○	18. ○ ○ ○ ○ ○	26. ○ ○ ○ ○ ○
3. ○ ○ ○ ○ ○	11. ○ ○ ○ ○ ○	19. ○ ○ ○ ○ ○	27. ○ ○ ○ ○ ○
4. ○ ○ ○ ○ ○	12. ○ ○ ○ ○ ○	20. ○ ○ ○ ○ ○	28. ○ ○ ○ ○ ○
5. ○ ○ ○ ○ ○	13. ○ ○ ○ ○ ○	21. ○ ○ ○ ○ ○	29. ○ ○ ○ ○ ○
6. ○ ○ ○ ○ ○	14. ○ ○ ○ ○ ○	22. ○ ○ ○ ○ ○	30. ○ ○ ○ ○ ○
7. ○ ○ ○ ○ ○	15. ○ ○ ○ ○ ○	23. ○ ○ ○ ○ ○	
8. ○ ○ ○ ○ ○	16. ○ ○ ○ ○ ○	24. ○ ○ ○ ○ ○	

SECTION 1

Analytical Writing

PRESENT YOUR PERSPECTIVE ON AN ISSUE

Time—45 minutes

Directions: You will have a choice between two Issue topics. Each topic will appear as a brief quotation that states or implies an issue of general interest. Read each topic carefully; then decide on which topic you could write a more effective and well-reasoned response.

You will have 45 minutes to plan and compose a response that presents your perspective on the topic you select. A response on any topic will receive a score of zero. You are free to accept, reject, or qualify the claim made in the topic you selected, as long as the ideas you present are clearly relevant to the topic you select. Support your views with reasons and examples drawn from such areas as your reading, experience, observations, or academic studies.

GRE readers, who are college and university faculty, will read your response and evaluate its overall quality, based on how well you do the following:

• consider the complexities and implications of the issue

• organize, develop, and express your ideas on the issue

• support your ideas with relevant reasons and examples

• control the elements of standard written English

You may want to take a few minutes to think about the issue and to plan a response before you begin writing. Be sure to develop your ideas fully and organize them coherently, but leave time to reread what you have written and make any revisions that you think are necessary.

Present your perspective on one of the issues below, using relevant reasons and/or examples to support your views.

TOPIC 1:

> "The proliferation, portability, and increasing speed of electronic communication devices have increased the value of discourse among those who regularly communicate via these devices."

TOPIC 2:

> "The value of a person's education can best be measured by what profession it allows that person to pursue."

SECTION 1

Analytical Writing

ANALYZE AN ARGUMENT

Time—30 minutes

Directions: You will have 30 minutes to plan and write a critique of an argument presented in the form of a short passage. A critique of any other argument will receive a score of zero.

Analyze the line of reasoning in the argument. Be sure to consider what, if any, questionable assumptions underlie the thinking and, if evidence is cited, how well it supports the conclusion.

You can also discuss what sort of evidence would strengthen or refute the argument, what changes in the argument would make it more logically sound, and what additional information might help you better evaluate its conclusion. Note that you are NOT being asked to present your views on the subject.

GRE readers, who are college and university faculty, will read your critique and evaluate its overall quality, based on how well you

- identify and analyze important features of the argument

- organize, develop, and express your critique of the argument

- support your critique with relevant reasons and examples

- control the elements of standard written English

Before you begin writing, you may want to take a few minutes to evaluate the argument and plan a response. Be sure to develop your ideas fully and organize them coherently, but leave time to reread what you have written and make any revisions that you think are necessary.

Discuss how well reasoned you find this argument.

More than half of those who use the gym at Park East, a luxury high-rise in New York City, support the idea of gym improvements. The owners have pledged to direct building maintenance funds according to the wishes of the majority of building residents. Moreover, the gym received nearly double the number of average monthly visits three months ago in early January immediately following the installation of five new weight and aerobic machines, demonstrating the link between improvements and the facility's popularity. In addition, numerous health studies have conclusively shown that people who exercise lead fitter and healthier lives than people who do not. It is therefore clear that the owners of Park East have been negligent in their management of the building and should make immediate improvements to the building's gym.

SECTION 2

QUANTITATIVE

Time—45 minutes

28 Questions

<u>Numbers</u>: All numbers used are real numbers.

<u>Figures</u>: Position of points, angles, regions, etc., can be assumed to be in the order shown; and angle measurements can be assumed to be positive.

Lines shown as straight can be assumed to be straight.

Figures can be assumed to lie in a plane unless otherwise stated.

Figures that accompany questions are intended to provide information useful in answering the questions. However, unless a note states that a figure is drawn to scale you should solve these problems NOT by estimating sizes by sight or by measurement, but by using your knowledge of mathematics.

<u>Directions for Quantitative Comparison Questions</u>: These questions consist of two quantities, one in Column A and one in Column B. You are to compare the quantity in Column A with the quantity in Column B and decide whether:

A if the quantity in Column A is greater;

B if the quantity in Column B is greater;

C if the two quantities are equal;

D if the relationship cannot be determined from the information given.

<u>Note</u>: Since there are only four choices, NEVER MARK (E).

<u>Common Information</u>: In a question, there may be additional information, centered above the two columns, that concerns one or both of the quantities to be compared. A symbol that appears in both columns represents the same thing in Column A as it does in Column B.

<u>Directions for Multiple-Choice Questions</u>: These questions have five answer choices. For each of these questions, select the best of the answer choices given.

$$2x^2 = 6$$

1.

Column A	Column B
x	$\sqrt{3}$

○ The quantity in Column A is greater.
○ The quantity in Column B is greater.
○ The two quantities are equal.
○ The relationship cannot be determined from the information given.

2.

Column A	Column B
$\dfrac{9}{14}$	$\dfrac{52}{87}$

○ The quantity in Column A is greater.
○ The quantity in Column B is greater.
○ The two quantities are equal.
○ The relationship cannot be determined from the information given.

$$i = 3t, \quad j = 2k, \quad k = \frac{3}{2}t$$

3.
Column A	Column B
i	j

○ The quantity in Column A is greater.
○ The quantity in Column B is greater.
○ The two quantities are equal.
○ The relationship cannot be determined from the information given.

4.
Column A	Column B
$(1347 - 1517)(496 - 208)$	$(167 - 270)(672 - 856)$

○ The quantity in Column A is greater.
○ The quantity in Column B is greater.
○ The two quantities are equal.
○ The relationship cannot be determined from the information given.

5. Solve for x if $-4x + 7 > 2x - 7$.

○ $x > \dfrac{7}{3}$

○ $x < \dfrac{3}{7}$

○ $x < \dfrac{7}{3}$

○ $x > \dfrac{3}{7}$

○ $x > \dfrac{11}{13}$

Questions 6–7 refer to the following graph.

University C: Total Student Expenses

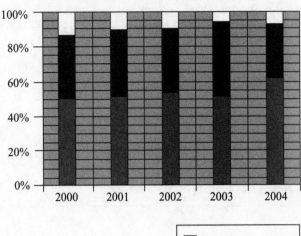

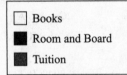

6. Approximately what percentage of total student expenses in 2001 was spent on room and board?

○ 10%
○ 35%
○ 55%
○ 85%
○ 90%

7. If tuition in 2003 was $10,800, which of the following is the closest approximation of the student expense for books that year?

○ $775
○ $1,275
○ $1,950
○ $3,225
○ $21,600

8. If b blocks of cement cost d dollars, how many cents will x blocks of cement cost at the same rate?

- ○ $\dfrac{xd}{b}$

- ○ $100xbd$

- ○ $\dfrac{xbd}{10}$

- ○ $100\dfrac{xd}{b}$

- ○ $100\dfrac{xb}{d}$

9.

Column A	Column B
53% of 1,505,000	73% of 985,000

- ○ The quantity in Column A is greater.
- ○ The quantity in Column B is greater.
- ○ The two quantities are equal.
- ○ The relationship cannot be determined from the information given.

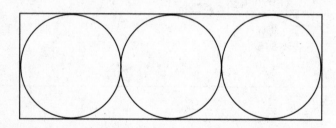

10. If the area of each of the three identical circles inscribed in the rectangle above is 25π, what is the perimeter of the rectangle?

- ○ 30
- ○ 40
- ○ 75
- ○ 80
- ○ 300

The sales tax in County C is 9% for non-food items and 3% for food items. Customer X buys $120 in non-food items and $50 in food items in County C. Customer Y buys $100 in non-food items and $70 in food items in County C.

11.

Column A	Column B
The sales tax paid by customer X	The sales tax paid by customer Y

- ○ The quantity in Column A is greater.
- ○ The quantity in Column B is greater.
- ○ The two quantities are equal.
- ○ The relationship cannot be determined from the information given.

$$3m + n = -5$$
$$m + 3n = 5$$

12.

Column A	Column B
m	n

- ○ The quantity in Column A is greater.
- ○ The quantity in Column B is greater.
- ○ The two quantities are equal.
- ○ The relationship cannot be determined from the information given.

A school has allotted exactly three hours to crush trash bags full of aluminum cans for the school's annual recycling drive. It takes Donna 15 minutes to crush one trash bag.

13.

Column A	Column B
The number of people working at Donna's rate needed to assist Donna to crush 180 bags in the allotted time	The number of bags that Donna can crush in 3.75 hours

- ○ The quantity in Column A is greater.
- ○ The quantity in Column B is greater.
- ○ The two quantities are equal.
- ○ The relationship cannot be determined from the information given.

14. If $36a + 24 = \dfrac{a}{2} + 3(a+4)$, then $a =$

○ $\dfrac{11}{17}$

○ $\dfrac{-24}{65}$

○ $\dfrac{-7}{3}$

○ $\dfrac{19}{57}$

○ $\dfrac{-40}{7}$

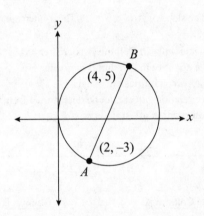

15. If $\overline{AB}$ is a diameter of the circle, the y-coordinate of the circle's center subtracted from the x-coordinate of the circle's center is equal to

   I. twice the y-coordinate of the circle's center
   II. half the product of the coordinates of the circle's center
   III. one less than the x-coordinate of the circle's center

○ I only
○ III only
○ I and III only
○ II and III only
○ I, II, and III

16.
Column A	Column B
$3x^3 + 9$	$4x^2 + 6$

○ The quantity in Column A is greater.
○ The quantity in Column B is greater.
○ The two quantities are equal.
○ The relationship cannot be determined from the information given.

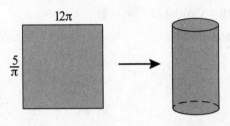

17. If the rectangle in the figure is rolled into a cylinder so that the edges of length $\dfrac{5}{\pi}$ touch, what is the volume of the cylinder?

○ 60
○ 60π
○ 100
○ 100π
○ 180

18.
Column A	Column B
The average degree measure of the five interior angles of an irregular pentagon	The sum of two interior angles of an isosceles right triangle

○ The quantity in Column A is greater.
○ The quantity in Column B is greater.
○ The two quantities are equal.
○ The relationship cannot be determined from the information given.

19. If the mean of a and b is 10 and the mean of c and d is 12, what is the mean of the set $\{a, b, c, d, 26\}$?

   ○ 13
   ○ 14
   ○ 15
   ○ 16
   ○ 17

22. A clothes designer must choose 3 of 10 possible fabrics and 2 of 4 possible styles for a single outfit. What is the total number of different outfits that the designer can create given these requirements?

   ○ 6
   ○ 38
   ○ 120
   ○ 575
   ○ 720

Questions 20–21 refer to the following graph.

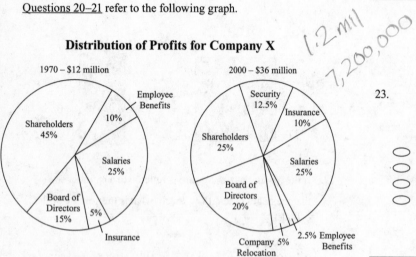

Distribution of Profits for Company X

1.2 mil
7,200,000

$\overline{AB}$ is the line defined by $x = \dfrac{3}{2}y - 1$

23.   Column A   Column B

   The slope of $\overline{AB}$ The x-intercept of $\overline{AB}$

   ○ The quantity in Column A is greater.
   ○ The quantity in Column B is greater.
   ○ The two quantities are equal.
   ○ The relationship cannot be determined from the information given.

20. In 2000, Company X added security costs and company relocation to its profit distribution. These expenses were taken out of employee benefits. What was the percentage decrease in employee benefits from 1970 to 2000?

   ○ 7.5%
   ○ 17.5%
   ○ 25%
   ○ 33.3%
   ○ 35%

24.   Column A   Column B
       $8^{10} + 8^{12}$ 65×8^{10}

   ○ The quantity in Column A is greater.
   ○ The quantity in Column B is greater.
   ○ The two quantities are equal.
   ○ The relationship cannot be determined from the information given.

21. The board of directors consisted of eight people in both 1970 and 2000. If the board members divide their share of the profit equally each year, then how much greater was a board member's share of the profits in 2000 compared to that same board member's share of the profits in 1970?

   ○ $225,000
   ○ $675,000
   ○ $900,000
   ○ $1,200,000
   ○ $1,800,000

25. If $3\left|\dfrac{x+2}{3}\right| = y^2 - 1$, which of the following is a possible solution for x expressed in terms of y?

   ○ $-y^2 - 1$
   ○ $y^2 - 1$
   ○ $-y^2 + 1$
   ○ $-y^2 - 3$
   ○ $y^2 + 1$

Data set K: 10, –7.5, 70, –0.5, 0, 23, –25, 2

Data set L: 1, 27, –5, 52, 2, –5, 2, –41, 12

26.

Column A	Column B
The median of data set K	The mode of data set L

○ The quantity in Column A is greater.
○ The quantity in Column B is greater.
○ The two quantities are equal.
○ The relationship cannot be determined from the information given.

---

27. If $x@y = xy - yx$, which of the following values of x and y result in a negative value of $x@y$?

I. $x = 8, y = 2$
II. $x = 0, y = 8$
III. $x = -5, y = 7$

○ I only
○ II only
○ I and II only
○ I and III only
○ I, II, and III

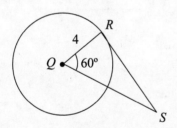

RS is tangent to circle Q.

28.

Column A	Column B
The perimeter of triangle QRS	The circumference of circle Q

○ The quantity in Column A is greater.
○ The quantity in Column B is greater.
○ The two quantities are equal.
○ The relationship cannot be determined from the information given.

SECTION 3

VERBAL

Time—30 minutes

30 Questions

<u>Directions for Sentence Completion Questions</u>: These sentences have one or two blanks, each blank indicating that something has been omitted. Beneath the sentence are five words or sets of words. Choose the word or set of words from each blank that best fits the meaning of the sentence as a whole.

<u>Directions for Antonym Questions</u>: These questions consist of a word printed in capital letters, followed by five words or phrases. Choose the word or phrase that is most nearly opposite in meaning to the word in capital letters.

Since some of the questions require you to distinguish fine shades of meaning, be sure to consider all of the choices before deciding which one is best.

<u>Directions for Analogy Questions</u>: In these questions, a related pair of words or phrases is followed by five pairs of words or phrases. Select the pair that best expresses a relationship similar to that expressed in the original pair.

<u>Directions for Reading Comprehension Questions</u>: Each passage in this group is followed by questions based on its content. After reading a passage, choose the best answer to each question. Answer all questions following a passage on the basis of what is stated or implied in the passage.

1. The famously concise Hemingway once accepted a challenge to showcase his _____ literary style by telling a story in just six words.

   ○ bellicose
   ○ bombastic
   ○ garrulous
   ○ terse
   ○ histrionic

2. INTENTIONAL :

   ○ disputable
   ○ illogical
   ○ deliberate
   ○ desirable
   ○ accidental

3. DISTANCE : METER ::

   ○ race : runner
   ○ volume : liter
   ○ exhaustion : mile
   ○ time : hourglass
   ○ heat : summer

4. CRITICAL :

   ○ stable
   ○ understated
   ○ grave
   ○ significant
   ○ noteworthy

5. PALETTE : PAINTER ::

   ○ trial : lawyer
   ○ barber : scissors
   ○ fuel : automobile
   ○ saddle : jockey
   ○ tapestry : weaver

6. Although invasive nonindigenous species certainly have the potential to be ecologically disastrous, the majority are fairly _____ .

   ○ innocuous
   ○ mercurial
   ○ pervasive
   ○ precarious
   ○ recalcitrant

7. INDULGENT :

   ○ reckless
   ○ flexible
   ○ stringent
   ○ transitory
   ○ sadistic

8. AMBIVALENT : ENERGIZED ::

   ○ enticing : beguiling
   ○ bored : enthralled
   ○ forsaken : understood
   ○ irreligious : devout
   ○ derogatory : furious

9. DISPARAGE :

- ○ jettison
- ○ solidify
- ○ eulogize
- ○ convene
- ○ undulate

10. Whereas some critical evaluations of Steinbeck's 1952 epic East of Eden evidenced only mild _____ , the reaction of many residents of his hometown of Salinas, California, who were depicted unflatteringly in the novel, bordered on outright _____ .

- ○ appreciation . . commendation
- ○ censure . . approbation
- ○ denigration . . bewilderment
- ○ criticism . . condemnation
- ○ acceptance . . rejection

Questions 11–12 refer to the following passage.

When the division of labor has been once thoroughly established, it is but a very small part of a person's wants that the produce of his own labor can supply. He supplies the far greater part of them by exchanging
5   that surplus part of the produce of his own labor, which is over and above his own consumption, for such parts of the productions of other people's labor as he has occasion for. Every person thus lives by exchanging, or by becoming in some measure a
10   merchant, and the society itself grows to be what is properly a commercial society.

But when the division of labor first began to take place, this power of exchanging must frequently have been very much clogged and embarrassed in
15   its operations. One person, we shall suppose, has more of a certain commodity than he himself has occasion for, while another has less. The former consequently would be glad to dispose of, and the latter to purchase, a part of this superfluity. But if
20   this latter should chance to have nothing that the former stands in need of, no exchange can be made between them.

11. What is the purpose of the statement made in the final sentence of the first paragraph?

- ○ It illustrates a step in the development of an economic system.
- ○ It summarizes the main point of the passage.
- ○ It points out a disadvantage of living in a commercial society.
- ○ It demonstrates the means by which individuals produce more goods than they need to sustain themselves.
- ○ It contradicts a statement made earlier in the passage.

12. The passage supports all of the following statements EXCEPT:

- ○ Barter is a component of a commercial society.
- ○ Before the division of labor was established, people produced a greater percentage of the items needed to satisfy their individual needs.
- ○ In a commercial society, the majority of a person's labor produces goods that he or she will consume.
- ○ Differences in supply and demand have in some cases hindered economic transactions.
- ○ Producing more of an item than one can use is not necessarily a disadvantage.

13. SAGACITY :

- ○ illogicality
- ○ dispensability
- ○ irreverence
- ○ timelessness
- ○ prudence

14. EXPLANATION : BEWILDER ::

- ○ summary : belabor
- ○ gesture : agitate
- ○ inauguration : commence
- ○ demagogue : modernize
- ○ epilogue : conclude

15. The toppling of the leader during the revolution was largely fueled by the ire of _____ industrial workers, who refused to work under such harsh conditions.

- ○ quixotic
- ○ recalcitrant
- ○ erudite
- ○ disparate
- ○ facetious

Changed habits produce an inherited effect, as in the period of the flowering of plants when transported from one climate to another. With animals the increased use or disuse of parts has had a more
5   marked influence; thus, we find in the domestic duck that the bones of the wing weigh less and the bones of the leg more, in proportion to the whole skeleton, than do the same bones in the wild duck. This change may be safely attributed to the domestic duck
10   flying much less, and walking more, than its wild parents. The great and inherited development of the udders in cows and goats in countries where they are habitually milked, in comparison with these organs in other countries, is probably another instance of
15   the effects of use. Not one of our domestic animals can be named that has not in some country drooping ears; and the view that has been suggested that the drooping is due to disuse of the muscles of the ear, from the animals being seldom much alarmed,
20   seems probable.

16. Which of the following statements is supported by the passage?

   I. An organism's traits are affected by its behavior.
   II. The same species may exhibit different characteristics in different environments.
   III. Animals evolve more rapidly than plants.

   ○ I only
   ○ II only
   ○ I and II only
   ○ I and III only
   ○ I, II, and III

17. Which of the following would be the most appropriate title for the passage?

   ○ "The History of Evolutionary Theory"
   ○ "A Comparative Study of Animal Species"
   ○ "Environmental Influences on Duck Weight Distribution"
   ○ "The Development of Animal Characteristics"
   ○ "Effects of Use and Disuse on Animal Traits"

18. INIMITABLE :

   ○ desperate
   ○ redundant
   ○ obstinate
   ○ universal
   ○ delusional

19. EMBEZZLEMENT : TRANSGRESSION ::

   ○ cruelty : tyranny
   ○ banishment : exile
   ○ desert : irrigation
   ○ psychosis : disorder
   ○ oscillation : decisiveness

Questions 20–23 refer to the following passage.

While clear-cut guidelines exist to delineate and adjudicate blatant cases of copyright infringement, the legal implications of appropriating copyrighted materials into new forms of art and social
5   commentary are much less clearly defined. In such cases, the Fair Use provision of Article 107 of U.S. copyright law can provide some guidance. Fair use provides an exception to copyright restrictions, allowing one to copy, publish, or distribute without
10   permission partial (or in some cases even entire) copyrighted works for purposes such as criticism, comment, news reporting, teaching, scholarship, or research.

Not surprisingly, copyright holders have difficulty
15   condoning any unlicensed use of their works. Fair use proponents counter that to prevent artists and critics from freely reusing cultural sounds, objects, and iconography would flout basic democratic principles, stifle creativity, and lead to cultural
20   stagnation. Such restrictions, they believe, would severely limit the opportunity to engage those who create and consume mainstream culture in meaningful dialogue.

Judges generally consider four factors when
25   evaluating fair use claims. The first is the purpose and character of the use, such as whether the product incorporating the material will be used in a nonprofit, educational, or commercial environment. Within this category, judges look favorably on
30   "transformative" uses, those involving radical alterations of the material's original intent. The second consideration is the nature of the work used. For example, judges generally favor the fair use of nonfiction over fiction, and of scholarly works
35   for which quoting is expected. The third factor

concerns the amount used; the lower the proportion
of the original whole, the more likely fair use will
be granted. However, the more central the used
portion is to the spirit of the original work, the lower
40 the chance of a fair use ruling. The fourth factor
considers the effect on the value of the original;
that is, the extent to which the new product will
directly compete with the copyrighted work in the
marketplace.

45 There are no hard-line rules regarding how and in
what proportion judges apply the four factors to fair
use determinations. Moreover, fair use is not an
affirmative protection—like, for example, the right
to public assembly—but rather a defense that one
50 can appeal to only after a charge has been brought.
Individuals averse to the pressure and expense of
legal confrontations often decide not to invoke their
fair use privilege, essentially constituting a form
of self-censorship. Capitalizing on this hesitancy,
55 many well-funded copyright holders have launched
aggressive attacks on fair use attempts through
near-automatic issuances of cease-and-desist
letters, regardless of legal merit. Nonetheless, fair
use provides a necessary restraint on otherwise
60 unbounded copyright privileges and remains a
powerful legal instrument should artists and social
commentators choose to invoke it.

20. The author's primary purpose in the passage is to

○ discourage copyright holders from erecting
    unwarranted and illegal obstacles to necessary forms
    of cultural innovation
○ delineate the mechanisms of a legal provision and
    encourage its utilization
○ outline a way in which artists and social commentators
    can reuse cultural sounds, objects, and iconography
    while avoiding all accusations of copyright
    infringement
○ explain the four factors that judges generally consider
    when evaluating fair use claims
○ show how copyright holders attempt to discourage
    people from exploiting a loophole in copyright law

21. With respect to the prospect of the successful employment
of the fair use defense, the author of the passage can most
accurately be described as

○ mildly perplexed
○ exceedingly assured
○ brazenly defiant
○ cynically suspicious
○ cautiously optimistic

22. According to the passage, self-censorship results when

○ politicians who would otherwise criticize the behavior
    of well-funded copyright holders choose not to do so
    for fear of losing political support
○ artists and social commentators who would otherwise
    appropriate cultural objects to create new works
    choose not to do so for fear of legal repercussions
○ lawyers choose not to advise clients as to their fair use
    privileges because they are wary of entangling their
    clients in protracted and costly litigation
○ artists and social commentators choose not to explore
    certain subjects because there is no way to do those
    subjects justice without appropriating cultural
    materials
○ artists and social commentators refuse to make fair use
    a subject of their works for fear of being embroiled in
    legal confrontations

23. The author mentions the right to public assembly (lines
48–49) primarily to

○ suggest that two kinds of legal protection that differ in
    one respect are similar in another respect
○ distinguish laws with hard-line interpretations from
    those with more flexible interpretations
○ establish that appealing to affirmative protections is
    preferable to reacting to lawsuits only after charges
    have been brought
○ provide an example of a right that can be defended only
    after one has been accused of breaking the law
○ illustrate by means of contrast a limitation in the fair
    use provision

24. King Charles II of England was known to surround himself with a merry gang of _____ , whose raucous and often illicit behavior exemplified the _____ that came to define the libertine philosophy of seventeenth- and eighteenth-century Europe.

- ⬭ misanthropes . . fallacy
- ⬭ ascetics . . chicanery
- ⬭ miscreants . . turpitude
- ⬭ reprobates . . decorum
- ⬭ renegades . . determination

25. APPROPRIATE :

- ⬭ glamorize
- ⬭ repurpose
- ⬭ hallucinate
- ⬭ ameliorate
- ⬭ jettison

26. PERFIDY : STEADFAST ::

- ⬭ energy : dynamic
- ⬭ jubilance : melancholy
- ⬭ haughtiness : domestic
- ⬭ sorrow : penitent
- ⬭ impudence : snubbed

27. UNFLEDGED :

- ⬭ seditious
- ⬭ mature
- ⬭ ravenous
- ⬭ parsimonious
- ⬭ malleable

28. OBSESSION : PREDILECTION ::

- ⬭ gravity : condition
- ⬭ fire : inferno
- ⬭ capillary : vein
- ⬭ torrent : sprinkle
- ⬭ courtship: sentimentality

29. REDOUBTABLE :

- ⬭ indubitable
- ⬭ querulous
- ⬭ farcical
- ⬭ cylindrical
- ⬭ microscopic

30. The range of Gothic architecture extends from the severely _____ lines of the Basilica of Mary Magdalene in southern France to the intricately _____ ornamentation of Italy's Cathedral of Siena.

- ⬭ unconventional . . esoteric
- ⬭ decadent . . lavish
- ⬭ stark . . unadorned
- ⬭ celestial . . rigorous
- ⬭ austere . . florid

Answers
&
Guided
Explanations

ANSWER KEY

SECTION 2 (Quantitative)

1. D	8. D	15. C	22. E
2. A	9. A	16. D	23. A
3. C	10. D	17. E	24. C
4. B	11. A	18. D	25. A
5. C	12. B	19. B	26. D
6. B	13. B	20. C	27. E
7. B	14. B	21. B	28. B

SECTION 3 (Verbal)

1. D	9. C	17. E	25. E
2. E	10. D	18. D	26. B
3. B	11. A	19. D	27. B
4. A	12. C	20. B	28. D
5. D	13. A	21. E	29. C
6. A	14. A	22. B	30. E
7. C	15. B	23. E	
8. B	16. C	24. C	

Calculating Your Score

You can add up the number of questions you got right on the two sections and covert it to a 200–800 score using the table below. Keep in mind that this score is just a rough estimate. The only completely accurate predictors of your current scoring level are the scoring scales provided with official GRE materials, so make sure you practice with them in the week or two before the test to gauge where you stand.

Quantitative		Verbal	
Raw Score	Scaled Score	Raw Score	Scaled Score
28	800	30	800
27	780	29	780
26	760	28	760
25	740	27	740
24	720	26	720
23	700	25	700
22	680	24	680
21	660	23	660
20	640	22	640
19	620	21	620
18	600	20	600
17	580	19	580
16	560	18	560
15	540	17	540
14	520	16	520
13	500	15	500
12	480	14	480
11	460	13	460
10	440	12	440
9	420	11	420
8	400	10	400
7	380	9	380
6	360	8	360
5	320	7	340
4	300	6	320
0–3	200	5	300
		0–4	200

SECTION 1

A "6" Issue Essay

> "The value of a person's education can best be measured
> by what profession it allows that person to pursue."

The real value inherent in a good education is not simply the professional training it provides, but instead the opportunity it creates for self-knowledge, lifelong learning, and intellectual curiosity. First, education gives us the opportunity to understand ourselves on a deeper level. Second, a solid education helps us grow by instilling the longing to continue learning throughout our lives. Finally, a good education has value because it sparks our intellectual curiosity.

A well-rounded education lays the foundation for knowing oneself. Indeed, both the development of self-knowledge and the recognition of our talents and gifts are nurtured through a good education. Through exposure to particular texts, philosophies, music, and works of art, our frame of reference is expanded. In my own experience as an undergraduate, I had difficulty deciding on a specific course of study and eventual career path since many subjects interested me. After pursuing a general liberal arts curriculum during my first year of college, including courses in history, philosophy, and math, I discovered that my enjoyment of literature illuminated other branches of knowledge for me, so I chose to major in English. Hester Prynne's adultery in puritan New England in The Scarlet Letter, for example, or the Joad family's hardships as they sought a better life in the promised land of California in The Grapes of Wrath gave me a better understanding of historical events as revealed through the literature of these time periods—and instilled in me the desire to go to graduate school in English. With a more specific vocational goal in mind, I doubt I would have followed this path and might not have enjoyed its various twists and turns leading to more acute self-knowledge along the way.

We might also consider the true value of education in terms of how motivated students are to continue its pursuit after programs are concluded and degrees are bestowed. Lifelong learning results when the seeds of knowledge, carefully planted during our formative years, fully germinate in the years following formal schooling. Although Benjamin Franklin received little formal education, his remarkable learning and contributions to many diverse fields, including science, politics, and philosophy, extended far into his adult life, making him a seminal figure in early American history. His avid reading and passion for learning endured throughout his lifetime, and he became well known for his achievements as a diplomat, abolitionist, and inventor. Despite his lack of higher education, Franklin rose to great prominence through his own lifelong, passionate commitment to learning.

Curiosity about many areas of study and the serendipitous quest for new knowledge are also hallmarks of an excellent education. An education that simply drives one toward a profession prevents the student from truly engaging with the material at hand. One intriguing passage from a book or several measures of an especially beautiful piece of music could lead a student to contemplate further study of similar works, if that student sees education as an experience, rather than as a means to an end. Education may result in a more profound interest in a related subject. Exposure to the field of sociology allowed me to analyze literature from a new perspective. After reading Erich Fromm's Escape From Freedom, for example, I couldn't help but notice that his recurrent theme of human isolation as a product of modernity was also reflected in the literature of this period, such as Eliot's "The Hollow Man," Fitzgerald's The Great Gatsby, and Hemingway's The Sun Also Rises. Intellectual curiosity led Albert Einstein, who dropped out of school at an early age, to develop revolutionary scientific theories, including his seminal theory of relativity.

Although a good education provides a vital framework for most professions, its value cannot be measured solely by a single tangible outcome. Education is not exclusively the attainment of degrees and credentials; moreover, it should not be deemed successful or unsuccessful on the basis of one's eventual career. The true value of an excellent education is more abstract and offers the recipient opportunities that continue well beyond his or her academic training. Through the understanding of oneself, the inclination toward lifelong learning, and an ever-evolving intellectual curiosity, a fine education prepares us to be better human beings and enjoy a richer, more meaningful existence.

Discussion

The charts below evaluate this sample essay according to the ETS criteria for graders and the standards set forth in our Issue essay template.

ETS CRITERIA	YES OR NO?
Responds to the issue	YES
Develops a position on the issue through the use of incisive reasons and persuasive examples	YES
Ideas are conveyed clearly and articulately	YES
Maintains proper focus on the issue and is well organized	YES
Demonstrates proficiency, fluency, and maturity in its use of sentence structure, vocabulary, and idioms	YES
Demonstrates an excellent command of the elements of standard written English, including grammar, word usage, spelling, and punctuation—but may contain minor flaws in these areas	YES
OUR CRITERIA	**YES OR NO?**
Uses the three-act essay structure	YES
Thesis statement in first sentence of paragraph 1	YES
Three examples that support the thesis listed in paragraph 1, in order in which they're discussed in essay	YES
Topic sentence for example 1 in paragraph 2	YES
Development sentences to support example 1	YES
Topic sentence for example 2 in paragraph 3	YES
Development sentences to support example 2	YES
Topic sentence for example 3 in paragraph 4	YES
Development sentences to support example 3	YES
Conclusion (paragraph 5) rephrases thesis	YES
Conclusion (paragraph 5) expands position	YES

THE
GRE

Let's take a closer look at the essay based on the four necessary Issue essay elements: argument, evidence, varied sentence structure, and facility with language.

Argument. In this essay, the author must take a position on the following premise: "The value of a person's education can best be measured by what profession it allows that person to pursue." In the introductory paragraph, the author takes a clear position that disagrees with this conclusion. She proceeds to offer several concrete reasons for this disagreement. She argues that education is best measured instead through increased self-knowledge, continuing lifelong education, and the development of intellectual curiosity.

This essay follows the three-act formula. First, the introduction (Act 1) clearly introduces the topic. The first sentence directly states the essay's thesis: "The real value inherent in a good education is not simply the professional training it provides, but instead the opportunity it creates for self-knowledge, lifelong learning, and intellectual curiosity." Each body paragraph (Act II) begins with a topic sentence reflecting the order of subtopics introduced in the thesis statement. At the conclusion of the essay (Act III), a restatement of the thesis and the three major points complete the essay.

Evidence. To support her claim that the real value of a person's education is "the opportunity it creates for self-knowledge, lifelong learning, and intellectual curiosity," the author takes examples from personal experience, the biographies of notable figures from philosophy and science, and important literary and scholarly works. Her evidence comes from a diverse array of sources.

The topic sentence of each body paragraph clearly outlines the evidence to be discussed. The author doesn't just state her ideas, however. She develops each piece of evidence, showing exactly how it ties back to the paragraph's topic sentence and to her essay's overarching claim about education. For example, in the second paragraph, she draws on her own life to make the point that education "lays the foundation for knowing oneself." She includes specific details about the literary works she read as an English major to demonstrate exactly how these works gave her a better understanding not only of history but also of her own scholarly interests, and she makes it clear that she didn't go to college with the intended goal of either majoring in English or going to graduate school. The final sentence of the paragraph directly invokes her essay's thesis: She values her education precisely because it gave her the freedom to pursue different academic subjects, including English. As a result of this freedom, she now intends to pursue further study in that field. Her "lifelong learning" and "intellectual curiosity" points are similarly supported by specific examples in paragraphs 3 and 4.

Varied Sentence Structure. This author's English major has paid off: She writes well, making her argument using a mix of simple subject-verb and complex, multi-clause sentences. She anchors the fourth paragraph, for example, with a brief statement: "Exposure to the field of sociology allowed me to analyze literature from a new perspective." At the same time, however, she's not afraid to begin sentences with long introductory phrases, as in this sentence from the second paragraph: "After pursuing a general liberal arts curriculum during my first year of college, including courses in history, philosophy, and math, I discovered that my enjoyment of literature illuminated other branches of knowledge for me, so I chose to major in English." The relationship among the clauses in this example is clear, because the author links her ideas using commas and the coordinating conjunction so. In the third paragraph, she traces a metaphor across several sentences to show how "seeds of knowledge, carefully planted" will eventually "fully germinate" in adulthood.

Facility with Language. The author is careful with her vocabulary throughout the essay. She uses advanced words when possible. This helps her enhance the overall quality of the essay, clarify her position on the topic, and prove her mastery of language. In her introductory paragraph, for instance, she mentions how education "sparks our intellectual curiosity." Later, in the fourth paragraph, she mentions the "serendipitous quest" that a good education can instigate for the student. In the concluding paragraph, she restates her position that the true value of an education cannot be measured by a "tangible outcome." This restatement reinforces both her point of view on the issue and her expertise with language.

You may have noticed that the author didn't italicize or underline the book titles she mentioned in her essay. That's because the GRE's essay-writing software won't let you use any fancy formatting, so don't worry about losing points for not italicizing or underlining words on test day.

THE
GRE

A "6" Argument Essay

> More than half of those who use the gym at Park East, a luxury high-rise in New York City, support the idea of gym improvements. The owners have pledged to direct building maintenance funds according to the wishes of the majority of building residents. Moreover, the gym received nearly double the number of average monthly visits three months ago in early January immediately following the installation of five new weight and aerobic machines, demonstrating the link between improvements and the facility's popularity. In addition, numerous health studies have conclusively shown that people who exercise lead fitter and healthier lives than people who do not. It is therefore clear that the owners of Park East have been negligent in their management of the building and should make immediate improvements to the building's gym.

The conclusion of this argument—that Park East owners have been negligent and should make gym improvements—is questionable because it relies on several shaky assumptions. First, it assumes that the group that makes up "most of the gym's users" also represents "the majority of building residents." Second, it assumes that users frequented the gym in January directly because of the newly installed equipment. Finally, it assumes an incorrect definition of what constitutes negligence.

The first of the argument's suspect assumptions is the idea that the views of "most of those who use the gym" reflect the views of "the majority of building residents." This assumption is questionable, because the argument never explains the relationship between "those who use the gym" and the entire population of the building. While the high rise's owners have pledged to direct building maintenance funds according to the wishes of the majority of building residents, and while more than half of gym users may indeed be favorable toward the idea of gym improvements, the argument does not provide any evidence that this group makes up a majority of building residents. Therefore, the majority of the building's residents might very well not support gym improvements, in which case the author's conclusion would be severely weakened.

The second of the argument's shaky assumptions is the idea that the gym experienced more use in January as a direct result of the new gym equipment. In fact, usage could have been spurred by factors unrelated to the additional equipment, including predictable New Year's resolutions by residents to lose weight or improve their cardiovascular health. Or perhaps the weather had been particularly severe in the winter month of January, causing individuals who usually get their exercise outside to work out indoors. In light of these alternative possibilities, the argument does not sufficiently demonstrate a link between the improvements and the increase in the gym's popularity that the author cites.

Finally, there is no evidence for the conclusion that the owners of Park East have been negligent in their management of the building. Negligence, in the strict definition of the term, implies a blatant inattention to a matter that would result in foreseeable harm or injury. Failing to put salt on an icy patch in front of the building, or failing to repair a broken window in the building's lobby that contains protruding jagged shards of glass, would both constitute negligence. Forcing building residents to forego the possible benefits derived from a gymnasium's improvement, on the other hand, does not constitute negligence. The gym is an amenity, which has, in fact, not been neglected as of late: The author of the argument himself admits that the gym was improved as recently as three months ago.

Because three of the argument's main assumptions are questionable, the author's conclusion about the imperative of gym improvements is also called into question. To strengthen his argument, the author might provide statistics gathered from polling all the residents, not just those who are currently using the gym. If most of the building residents do support gym improvements and have demanded them for some time, the author's conclusion would be bolstered. Moreover, the argument would be improved if the author downgraded the charge of negligence to a more qualified assertion that further gym improvements may be warranted.

Discussion

The charts below evaluate this sample essay according to the ETS criteria for graders and the standards set forth in our Argument essay template.

ETS CRITERIA	YES OR NO?
Responds to the argument given in the topic	YES
Identifies the key features of the argument and analyzes each one in a thoughtful manner	YES
Supports each point of critique with insightful examples and analysis	YES
Develops its ideas in a clear, organized manner, with appropriate transitions to help connect ideas together	YES
Demonstrates proficiency, fluency, and maturity in its use of sentence structure, vocabulary, and idioms	YES
Demonstrates an excellent command of the elements of standard written English, including grammar, word usage, spelling, and punctuation—but may contain minor flaws in these areas	YES
OUR CRITERIA	YES OR NO?
Uses the three-act essay structure	YES
States conclusion in first sentence of paragraph 1	YES
Three reasons that support the thesis listed in paragraph 1, in the order in which they're discussed in essay	YES
Topic sentence for reason 1 in paragraph 2	YES
Development sentences to analyze reason 1	YES
Topic sentence for reason 2 in paragraph 3	YES
Development sentences to analyze reason 2	YES
Topic sentence for reason 3 in paragraph 4	YES
Development sentences to analyze reason 3	YES
Conclusion (paragraph 5) rephrases thesis	YES
Conclusion (paragraph 5) expands position	YES

THE
GRE

Let's take a closer look at the essay based on the four necessary Argument essay elements: argument, evidence, varied sentence structure, and facility with language.

Argument. This essay takes a clear position regarding problems with the argument presented in the prompt. The essay author finds that the prompt's conclusion is based on three faulty assumptions. These assumptions are mentioned in the introductory paragraph (Act I) and described in detail in the three body paragraphs (Act II). The author then restates her thesis clearly and expands her position by suggesting ways to strengthen the argument in the concluding paragraph (Act III).

Evidence. In Act II, the author presents detailed evidence through each of the three body paragraphs. These paragraphs explain the faulty assumptions in the test prompt argument one by one. First, in paragraph 2, the author explains the problem with the prompt's assumption about "residents' views." In paragraph 3, she questions an assumption about gym use, pointing out that gym use might not have increased because of new equipment. Finally, in paragraph 4, the essay author defines negligence in a way that suggests that the argument author's charge against Park East's owners is overblown. This paragraph ends with the assertion that the argument author undermines his own charge of negligence.

Varied Sentence Structure. This essay presents an interesting mix of sentence structures. It combines shorter sentences with more complex constructions throughout. But the essay also uses different grammatical constructions, rather than relying on the standard subject-verb. The use of em dashes in the very first sentence shows the author's strong writing ability, as do the smooth integration of direct quotes from the topic and the use of a colon to signal a definition in the final sentence of the fourth paragraph. The author also relies on dependent clauses to clarify and provide more explanation to the ideas asserted by her independent clauses, as in this sentence: "Or perhaps the weather had been particularly severe in the winter month of January, causing individuals who usually get their exercise outside to work out indoors." Overall, the essay has a nice rhythm and reads well.

Facility with Language. To show readers her facility with language, the author makes a concerted effort to include unusual and advanced words where appropriate. In the fourth paragraph, she not only defines the word *negligence* but also uses *implies*, *blatant*, and *foreseeable* for added pizzazz. Elsewhere in the essay, she drops in *spurred*, *cardiovascular*, *protruding*, and *imperative*. Finally, in her concluding paragraph, she states that the prompt's conclusion "would be *bolstered*." Unique vocabulary choices and combinations make the prose more vibrant and interesting.

Essay Score

Now that you've seen sample "6" essays, it's time to evaluate your own work. Use the following scoring chart to assess your two essays on the 0-to-6 scale. A "6" essay would meet all of the criteria, a "4" essay would meet some of the criteria, and a "0" essay would meet none of the criteria. Be honest!

Your final score on this section on this section is the average of these two scores. For example, a "5" on the Issue essay and a "6" on the Argument essay will result in a final score of "5.5."

Issue Essay: _____

ETS CRITERIA	YES OR NO?
Responds to the issue	
Develops a position on the issue through the use of incisive reasons and persuasive example	
Ideas are conveyed clearly and articulately	
Maintains proper focus on the issue and is well organized	
Demonstrates proficiency, fluency, and maturity in its use of sentence structure, vocabulary, and idioms	
Demonstrates an excellent command of the elements of standard written English, including grammar, word usage, spelling, and punctuation—but may contain minor flaws in these areas	
OUR CRITERIA	**YES OR NO?**
Uses the three-act essay structure	
Thesis statement in first sentence of paragraph 1	
Three examples that support the thesis listed in paragraph 1, in the order in which they're discussed in essay	
Topic sentence for example 1 in paragraph 2	
Development sentences to support example 1	
Topic sentence for example 2 in paragraph 3	
Development sentences to support example 2	
Topic sentence for example 3 in paragraph 4	
Development sentences to support example 3	
Conclusion (paragraph 5) rephrases thesis	
Conclusion (paragraph 5) expands position	

THE
GRE

Argument Essay: _____

ETS CRITERIA	YES OR NO?
Responds to the argument given in the topic	
Identifies the key features of the argument and analyzes each one in a thoughtful manner	
Supports each point of critique with insightful reasons and examples	
Develops its ideas in a clear, organized manner, with appropriate transitions to help connect ideas together	
Demonstrates proficiency, fluency, and maturity in its use of sentence structure, vocabulary, and idioms	
Demonstrates an excellent command of the elements of standard written English, including grammar, word usage, spelling, and punctuation—but may contain minor flaws in these areas	
OUR CRITERIA	**YES OR NO?**
Uses the three-act essay structure	
States conclusion in first sentence of paragraph 1	
Three reasons that support the thesis listed in paragraph 1, in the order in which they're discussed in essay	
Topic sentence for reason 1 in paragraph 2	
Development sentences to analyze reason 1	
Topic sentence for reason 2 in paragraph 3	
Development sentences to analyze reason 2	
Topic sentence for reason 3 in paragraph 4	
Development sentences to analyze reason 3	
Conclusion (paragraph 5) rephrases thesis	
Conclusion (paragraph 5) expands position	

Essay Score: _____ + _____ ÷ 2 = _____

               Issue Essay   Argument Essay

SECTION 2

Quantitative

1. **D**
Quantitative Comparisons: Linear Equations, Square Roots   *Rating:* Easy

Step 1: Get the Specs. The question is in classic disguised Problem Solving form. It contains an equation as additional information, a variable to solve for in Column A, and a number to compare your solution to in Column B.

Step 2: Plan the Attack. Since it's basically a Problem Solving question, we'll just go ahead and solve the equation and then compare what we get to the number in Column B.

Step 3: Mine the Math. To solve linear equations, we need to isolate the variable. We'll also need to remember that when a number squared is set equal to another number, there will be both a negative and positive solution since two positive numbers multiplied together yield a positive number and two negative numbers multiplied together also yield a positive number.

Step 4: Make the Comparison. Divide both sides by 2 to get $x^2 = 3$. Taking the square root of both sides, x is equal to $\sqrt{3}$ because $\sqrt{3} \times \sqrt{3} = 3$, but x is also equal to $-\sqrt{3}$ since $-\sqrt{3} \times -\sqrt{3} = 3$. Columns A and B are equal in the first case, but Column B is greater in the second case, so the answer is **D**.

2. **A**
Quantitative Comparisons: Fractions, Magic X   *Rating:* Easy

Step 1: Get the Specs. There's no additional information, and only numbers involved, so we know the answer can't be **D**. That's about all there is to notice at this point.

Step 2: Plan the Attack. We're dealing with a fraction comparison problem, so the Magic X should do us just fine.

Step 3: Mine the Math. When we cross multiply fractions diagonally and up, the greater product will emerge over the greater fraction. This is the essence of our Magic X technique.

Step 4: Make the Comparison. Multiplying 87 by 9 gives us 783 to write over the fraction in Column A. Multiplying 14 by 52 gives us 728 to write over the fraction in Column B. The product over Column A is bigger, so the fraction in Column A is larger than the fraction in Column B. **A** is correct.

3. **C**

Quantitative Comparisons: Substitution, Mirroring   *Rating:* Easy

Step 1: Get the Specs. We're given three separate equations as additional information, but there's no need to panic. The columns contain two of the three variables, so we need to see how these variables relate based on the additional information given.

Step 2: Plan the Attack. Variable i is defined strictly in terms of t, while j is defined in terms of k. That's one step removed from what we need, since we're called upon to compare i to j. Luckily, k is defined in terms of t, so we'll be able to compare i to j if we rewrite j in terms of t. That is, we'll employ our Mirroring technique to make j look more like i.

Step 3: Mine the Math. The math involves a simple substitution. If a variable that's set equal to a certain value appears in another equation, we can substitute that variable's defined value into that second equation in place of the variable itself.

Step 4: Make the Comparison. Substituting $\frac{3}{2}t$ for k in the second equation gives $j = (2)\frac{3}{2}t$. Canceling the 2s yields $j = 3t$. Since i also equals $3t$, the columns are equal and **C** is correct.

4. **B**

Quantitative Comparisons: Positive vs. Negative Numbers   *Rating:* Easy

Step 1: Get the Specs. Here's one of those problems that looks fairly nightmarish, since it appears to involve some heavy-duty calculations. However, that should be your first clue that there's probably a shortcut. Also notice that since only numbers are involved, the answer must be **A**, **B**, or **C**.

Step 2: Plan the Attack. You may have been tempted to buckle down and crunch through the math, but remember that the GRE never presents you with such complicated computations without also making possible a more elegant solution. So we'll hold off on the number crunching until we take a better look at these numbers to see whether some cleverness might help us out.

Step 3: Mine the Math. One of our QC shortcuts involves checking to see whether the quantity in one column is negative while the other is positive. If so, it doesn't matter what the *actual* values are, since all positive numbers are greater than all negative numbers. Here, three rules for positive and negative numbers come into play: A number subtracted from another number smaller than itself yields a negative number; a negative number multiplied by a positive number yields a negative number; and the product of two negative numbers is positive.

Step 4: Make the Comparison. In Column A, 1347 is less than 1517, so 1347 – 1517 is negative. However, 496 – 208 is positive, so we know the product of the two parentheses in Column A must be negative even without doing the math. Using the same logic on Column B, we find that both parentheses yield a negative number, so their product will be positive. We can therefore conclude with certainty that Column B is greater than Column A. **B** is correct.

5. **C**

Problem Solving: Inequalities   *Rating:* Easy

Step 1: Get the Specs. The > symbol tells us we're in inequalities territory, and while these can be tough, this one appears fairly straightforward.

Step 2: Plan the Attack. There's no reason not to just apply what we know about inequalities to solve the problem in the usual way.

Step 3: Mine the Math. We solve inequalities the same as we solve standard equations, except we have to be ever aware of the Inequality Exception: Multiplying or dividing both sides of an inequality by a negative number requires flipping the direction of the inequality. Let's have at it.

Step 4: Power Through. Here's the inequality given in the problem:

$$-4x + 7 > 2x - 7$$

Subtract 7 from both sides:

$$-4x > 2x - 14$$

Next, subtract $2x$ from both sides to isolate the x term on the left:

$$-6x > -14$$

Now divide both sides by $-6x$, and remember to flip the inequality sign since we're dividing both sides by a negative number:

$$x < \frac{14}{6}$$

Reducing the fraction gives us $x < \frac{7}{3}$, choice **C**. Notice that incorrect choice **A** is waiting in the wings to tempt those who forget to switch the sign.

6. **B**

Data Interpretation: Multipart Bar Graphs, Eyeballing   *Rating:* Easy

Step 1: Get the Specs. This multipart bar graph depicts the three components of total student expenses at a university. Five consecutive years are identified on the bottom of the graph, and the percentage of each expense is represented by the percentages on the left-hand side. Notice that the percentages jump by increments of 20%, with four subdivisions within each. That means each box moving up the scale represents 5%. Note the colors used for each expense—white for books, black for room and board, and gray for tuition—and you're all set.

Step 2: Grill the Interrogator. We're looking for the approximate percentage of total expenses spent on room and board in 2001, which means we need to focus on the black portion of the second column.

Step 3: Gather the Data. If you remember from the Data Interpretation chapter how to read multipart bar graphs, you won't be fooled by choice **E**. We're not looking for the number corresponding to the *top* of the room and board bar, which is around 90%, but rather the difference between that number and the place in the graph where the room and board bar *starts*—a little more than 50%.

Eyeballing the graph, we see that the 2001 room and board expense goes from a little over 50% to a little under 90%, for a total of just under 40%. Choice **B**, 35%, is closest to this approximation, and gets the point.

Step 4: Power Through. No need—we're already done. In most Data Interpretation questions, you will need to perform some calculations, but in the easiest ones, like this one, eyeballing the graph or graphs is all that's required.

7.　**B**
Data Interpretation: Multipart Bar Graphs,
Double Eyeballing, Approximating, Percentages　　　　　　*Rating:* Medium

Step 1: Get the Specs. We got the specs before tackling the previous question, so we'll move right to Step 2.

Step 2: Grill the Interrogator. This time we're given an actual figure for 2003 tuition and asked to approximate the book cost that year. Unlike the last question, this one requires a multistep process. We have to do the same kind of eye-balling, but this time to approximate two percentages. We need to do some calculating as well, based on those eyeballed percentages and the $10,800 figure given.

Step 3: Gather the Data. If 2003 tuition was $10,800, we can approximate how much total expenses were that year if we know the percentage of total costs that tuition constituted that year. Once we calculate the total figure, we'll be able to figure out roughly how much was spent on books, but only if we know the book percentage that year too. Those are the data we need, so let's eyeball:

The 2003 tuition bar begins at the bottom of the graph and goes up to what looks to be a little more than 50%, which is an easy number to work with, so we'll keep it. The 2003 books bar ends at the top of the graph and begins just under 95%, so we can approximate that as a little more than 5%. That's all we need, so let's go to Step 4 and crunch the numbers.

Step 4: Power Through. If $10,800 was the tuition cost in 2003, and tuition costs came to a little more than 50% of the total, then we can estimate the total at just under double $10,800. Multiplying $10,800 by 2 gives us $21,600, so let's round down to $21,000 to make our lives easier. (Note that it's also rounded in the right direction.) Now, if the total student cost that year was around $21,000, and a little more than 5% of that went for books, we can just multiply that out.

You can use your scratch paper or take this shortcut: It's always easy to find 10% of a number—just move the decimal one place to the left. Since 10% of $21,000 is $2,100, 5% of $21,000 must be half of that, or $1,050. That's our book cost approximation, and we're sticking with it. Choice **B**, $1,275, comes closest. And for those keeping track at home, it all makes sense, since the actual book percentage is a bit higher than 5%, so we'd expect the real 2003 book cost to come out a little above our estimate.

8. **D**

Problem Solving: Ratios, Making Up Numbers   *Rating:* Medium

Step 1: Get the Specs. We've got three variables in the question and some nasty looking combinations of them in the choices. The phrase "at the same rate" tells us that some sort of ratio is in play, and the whole thing has a word problem feel to it. That's a pretty solid jump on the question, so let's get to Step 2.

Step 2: Plan the Attack. Questions with difficult algebraic expressions in the choices are good candidates for our "making up numbers" alternative approach, so that's just what we'll do: Make up some numbers, see where they lead, and find the choice that matches the value we get.

Step 3: Mine the Math. It pays to remember that the units of a problem must be kept consistent throughout. Here, that's important because information is provided in terms of both dollars and cents, so you have to make sure to convert where appropriate. Also, a ratio is a fraction, and if the same ratio applies to different scenarios, we can set those fractions equal to each other.

Step 4: Power Through. Let's use the easiest numbers we can think of, outside of 0 and 1 (which tend to wreak havoc in these kinds of problems). Letting $b = 2$, $d = 3$, and $x = 4$ gives the problem a much better real-world feel: "If 2 blocks of cement cost 3 dollars, how many cents will 4 blocks of cement cost at the same rate?" Let's set up a simple equivalency ratio and solve it first in dollars and then convert to cents:

$$\frac{2 \text{ blocks}}{3 \text{ dollars}} = \frac{4 \text{ blocks}}{a \text{ dollars}}$$

You can solve the equation by cross multiplying or by seeing that doubling the number of blocks from 2 to 4 results in doubling the number of dollars from 3 to 6. Since the question asks for the number of cents required, we should now convert the 6 dollars to 600 cents. That's the value that emerges from the numbers we made up. Now all we have to do is see which of the choices comes out to 600 when we plug in 2 for b, 3 for d, and 4 for x. Let's try them:

A: $\frac{xd}{b} = \frac{4 \times 3}{2} = 6$. This one looks good only if you forget to convert dollars to cents. Otherwise, no-go.

B: $100xbd = 100 \times 4 \times 2 \times 3 = 2{,}400$. This choice is *too* big.

C: $\frac{xbd}{10} = \frac{4 \times 2 \times 3}{10} = 2.4$. This choice is *too* small.

D: $100\frac{xd}{b} = 100 \times \frac{4 \times 3}{2} = 100 \times 6 = 600$. This choice is *just right*! We have a winner. Just for the record:

E: $100\frac{xb}{d} = 100\frac{4 \times 2}{3} = 100 \times \frac{8}{3} =$ not 600, whichever way you slice it.

(We hope you noticed the *Goldilocks* reference in choices **B** through **D**.)

9.   **A**

Quantitative Comparisons: Percentages, Approximating   *Rating:* Medium

Step 1: Get the Specs. There are no variables, so choice **D** is out of the question. The size of the numbers also suggests that we look for a shortcut before we attempt to perform such large calculations.

Step 2: Plan the Attack. Percentage problems containing huge numbers literally scream for approximations, so that's the tack we'll take. The fact that the percentages in the columns hover close to 50% and 75% is another clue that approximating is the way to go.

Step 3: Mine the Math. Recognizing that 50% is equal to one-half and that 75% is equal to three-quarters are the main tidbits to draw on from your reservoir of math knowledge.

Step 4: Make the Comparison. Since 53% is more than 50%, and 1,505,000 is more than 1.5 million, the quantity in Column A must be greater than half of 1.5 million, or 750,000. On the other hand, the quantity in Column B must be less than 750,000, since three-quarters (75%) of 1 million equals 750,000, and the actual percentage given is 73% (less than three-quarters) of a number less than 1 million. So approximating the quantities allows us to determine that the quantity in Column A exceeds 750,000, while the quantity in Column B falls short of that number. Choice **A** is therefore correct.

10.   **D**

Problem Solving: Circles, Rectangles, Mish-Mashes   *Rating:* Medium

Step 1: Get the Specs. A nifty little circle/rectangle mish-mash picture comes along with this geometry question, so we may need to employ some creative visualization to see how a part of one shape tells us what we need to know about the other. Mish-mashes are by definition multiple-concept questions, since we need to draw on our knowledge of multiple geometric shapes.

Step 2: Plan the Attack. There's no alternative approach to use here, so we'll just apply what we know about circles and rectangles to get the information we need to solve the problem.

Step 3: Mine the Math. We covered all the relevant particulars back in Math 101, so we hope you were paying attention. Here are the geometry math concepts we'll need here: The area of a circle is πr^2, where r is the radius. The diameter of a circle is twice its radius, $2r$. The perimeter of a rectangle equals the sum of its sides.

Step 4: Power Through. Did you see the relationship between the three circles and the rectangle's perimeter? The width of the rectangle is equal to the diameter of each circle, while the length of the rectangle equals the diameter of the first circle + the diameter of the second circle + the diameter of the third circle. So if we find the diameter of the circles (all equal, since the circles are identical), then we can find the rectangle's perimeter.

Start with what we know: The area of each circle is 25π. Plugging that into our area formula, we get:

$$\text{area} = \pi r^2$$

$$25\pi = \pi r^2$$

$$25 = r^2$$

$$r = 5$$

If the radius of each circle is 5, then the diameter is 10. The width of the rectangle is therefore 10, and its length is 10 + 10 + 10 = 30. The rectangle therefore has two sides of width 10 and two sides of length 30. The perimeter is therefore 10 + 10 + 30 + 30 = 80, choice **D**.

Some traps are scattered among the choices: If you mistakenly used the radius instead of the diameter to calculate the perimeter, you'd have come up with 40, choice **B**. And if you accidentally multiplied the rectangle's length by the width (i.e., found its area), you'd have arrived at 300, choice **E**.

11.   **A**
Quantitative Comparisons: Percentages,
Basic Deductive Reasoning   *Rating:* Medium

Step 1: Get the Specs. This one comes with a bit of a story, giving it the feel of a word problem. It's the story of the taxes resulting from two customers' purchases. The customers are named X and Y, but be careful—they're not variables. In fact, this one concerns numbers only, so **D** can't be correct.

Step 2: Plan the Attack. Once again, we have a choice between crunching the numbers and looking for a shortcut. Let's see if a good look at the numbers in the problem can help us out. Worse comes to worst, we can calculate the percentages if we have to, but using math logic is preferable when possible.

Step 3: Mine the Math. We're dealing with percentages, so there's not much to say mathwise other than the basic principle that to calculate a percentage of a raw number, multiply the number by the percentage. In this case, however, we won't actually perform the multiplication, since we'll use deductive reasoning to make the comparison.

Step 4: Make the Comparison. The key is to notice that the two customers spent the same amount, and that customer X spent more money than customer Y on the item type with the higher tax, non-food items. If they spent the same amount, but X spent more money on the higher-taxed items, then X must have paid more sales tax than Y. Math logic, in the form of basic deductive reasoning, leads us to choice **A**.

12.   **B**
Quantitative Comparisons: Simultaneous Equations   *Rating:* Medium

Step 1: Get the Specs. We're given two equations with two variables and asked to compare the variables. There's not much else to notice, so on to Step 2.

Step 2: Plan the Attack. This is essentially a Problem Solving question in disguise, as we have to solve the equations to compare m and n. No fancy shortcuts here—we'll just try to determine values for the variables so we can see how they relate.

Step 3: Mine the Math. When there are an equal number of variables and equations, it's possible to solve for the variables. Here, we have two variables and two equations, so we can solve for both m and n, which means **D** can't be correct. We can use either of the two solving methods from our Math 101 arsenal: solving for one variable in one equation and substituting what we get into the other equation or combining the simultaneous equations to make one variable drop out, thus enabling us to solve for the other variable and then substitute that value into either original equation to solve for the variable that dropped out. We'll go with the latter. We may need to manipulate one equation to get it into the form we want, which is fine, as long as we obey the Golden Rule of Algebra: Do the same thing to both sides of the equation.

Step 4: Make the Comparison. Multiplying the second equation by –3 gives $-3m - 9n = -15$. The system of equations is now:

$$3m + n = -5$$

$$-3m - 9n = -15$$

We like this form because it causes m to drop out when we combine the equations. The $3m$ and $-3m$ cancel out; the n and $-9n$ combine to form $-8n$; and the –5 and –15 combine to –20. We're therefore left with $-8n = -20$. Dividing both sides by –8 gives us $n = \frac{20}{8}$, which simplifies to $n = \frac{5}{2}$. Plugging in $\frac{5}{2}$ for n in the first equation gives us: $3m + \frac{5}{2} = -5$. We need to subtract $\frac{5}{2}$ from both sides to isolate the m, which means there will be a negative number (–7.5) on the other side of the equation. Without bothering to finish the solution, we now can see that m will be negative. Since n is positive, n is greater than m, and **B** is correct.

13.   **B**

Quantitative Comparisons: Work Word Problem,
Double-Column Calculations

Rating: Medium

Step 1: Get the Specs. Looks like a word problem . . . Smells like a word problem . . . It is a word problem! And a work word problem at that, one of those pesky questions that concerns how fast things get done, how much time is spent doing them, and so on.

Step 2: Plan the Attack. We have no choice in this one but to bear down and work through the problem in each column.

Step 3: Mine the Math. Luckily we have our handy work formula to guide us: **rate × time = units produced** (or in this case, trash bags crushed). That's about all we need to know; the rest is execution.

Step 4: Make the Comparison. Superman may leap a building in a single bound, but Donna can crush a single bag of aluminum cans in 15 minutes, or a quarter of an hour. Plugging into our work formula gives us:

$$\text{rate} \times \frac{1}{4}\text{hour} = 1 \text{ bag}$$

Multiplying both sides by 4:

$$\text{rate} = 4 \text{ bags per hour}$$

We can use this rate to figure out the quantity in Column B:

$$4 \text{ bags per hour} \times 3.75 \text{ hours} = 4 \times 3\frac{3}{4} = 4 \times \frac{15}{4} = 15$$

So 15 is the quantity in Column B. As for Column A, we'll need to plug into the work formula again. If people are crushing bags at a rate of 4 bags per hour, crushing 180 bags will take:

$$4 \text{ bags per hour} \times x \text{ hours } = 180 \text{ bags}$$
$$x = \frac{180}{4} = 45 \text{ hours}$$

So we have 45 people-hours worth of work, but only 3 hours to crush bags. What would you do in this situation? That's right—get help! Dividing 45 by 3 tells us that 15 people are needed to get the job done in the time allotted for bag crushing. If you got to this point and recognized this answer as the same 15 we came up with for Column B, and you selected choice **C**, the quantities are equal, bzzzzz!!!—no point for you. Column A is looking for the number of people needed to *assist* Donna in crushing 180 bags in 3 hours, so Column A is actually 14, one less than Column B. So **B** is correct. This question provides an excellent example of how it's possible to do everything right only to lose out at the very end if you don't read carefully.

14.   **B**

Problem Solving: Linear Equations   *Rating:* Medium

Step 1: Get the Specs. We're faced with a somewhat complicated-looking equation, but there's only one variable, which makes things a bit simpler.

Step 2: Plan the Attack. Our attack will be fairly straightforward; not much to do except jump right in and solve via a standard application of math concepts.

Step 3: Mine the Math. We'll make use of many of our equation-solving tricks: multiplying to eliminate fractions, distributing across parentheses, combining like terms, and of course, the granddaddy of all equation rules, isolating the variable to solve for it.

Step 4: Power Through. Here's the equation we're up against:

$$36a + 24 = \frac{a}{2} + 3(a+4)$$

First, eliminate the fraction by multiplying each term by 2. This gives:

$$72a + 48 = a + 6(a + 4)$$

Now use the distributive law to simplify the right-hand side:

$$72a + 48 = a + 6a + 24$$

Combine like terms on the right-hand side by adding the a terms together:

$$72a + 48 = 7a + 24$$

Subtract $7a$ from both sides:

$$65a + 48 = 24$$

Subtract 48 from both sides:

$$65a = -24$$

Finally, divide both sides by 65:

$$a = \frac{-24}{65}$$

That's choice **B**. Many steps, but all of them manageable.

15.　**C**

Problem Solving: Coordinate Geometry, Midpoints　　　　　　　*Rating:* Medium

Step 1: Get the Specs. This one features a circle lying in the coordinate plane, with two defined points connected by a diameter of the circle. The other main thing to notice up front is that the question is in Roman numeral format.

Step 2: Plan the Attack. Roman numeral questions are like three mini-questions in one, in that we have to test each of three statements individually to see which ones are part of the correct choice. There are no values to work backward from, or variables in the choices that would suggest making up numbers, so let's take the standard head-on approach and perform the calculations necessary to test the choices.

Step 3: Mine the Math. Since the midpoint of a line cuts the line exactly in half, the midpoint of a circle's diameter must lie at the circle's center. The x- and y-coordinates of the midpoint of a line in the coordinate plane are the averages of the x- and y-coordinates of the line's endpoints.

Step 4: Power Through. The concepts in Step 3 above will help us to find the coordinates of the circle's center, but from there we'll still have to perform some simple math and correctly interpret the wording of the choices before we can pick up the point.

First things first. Let's use the midpoint formula to find the average of the end-points of the diameter:

$$\text{midpoint} = \frac{x_1 + x_2}{2}, \frac{y_1 + y_2}{2}$$

$$= \frac{4+2}{2}, \frac{5+-3}{2}$$

$$= \frac{6}{2}, \frac{2}{2}$$

$$= (3,1)$$

Phase 1 complete—the circle's center has an *x*-coordinate of 3 and a *y*-coordinate of 1. Now we have to follow the rest of the question's instructions and subtract the *y*-coordinate from the *x*-coordinate: 3 − 1 = 2. Now let's see which Roman numeral statements come out to 2:

I: Twice the *y*-coordinate is 2 × 1 = 2, so statement I works out, meaning we can take choices **B** and **D** off the table.

II: The product of the coordinates of the circle's center is 3 × 1 = 3, and half of that is $\frac{3}{2}$, which isn't equal to 2. This statement would work out to 2 if it said *sum* instead of *product*, another reminder that the Math section tests your ability to read carefully. So we have to ditch statement II, which means the answer will be **A** or **C**, depending on whether statement III pans out.

(Note that we're checking the **A** through **E** choices as we go along, because in some Roman numeral questions it's possible via the process of elimination to determine the answer without having to check the third Roman numeral statement. Here that didn't work out, but it's good test-taking strategy nonetheless.)

III: The *x*-coordinate of the circle's center is 3, and 1 less than that is equal to 2. So III is in, and **C** is our final answer.

16.   **D**
Quantitative Comparisons: Square Roots, Cube Roots, FONZ   *Rating:* Medium

Step 1: Get the Specs. There's no extra info gracing this QC, so we'll focus all our attention on the expressions in the columns. The fact that there are no restrictions placed on the expressions will factor into how we go about it. And speaking of which, let's plan the attack.

Step 2: Plan the Attack. Testing some numbers should shed light on how these two expressions stack up, so it looks like an excellent opportunity to break out our FONZ technique. We'll begin, as always, with the easier numbers represented in our acronym—One and Zero—and move on to Negatives and Fractions as necessary.

Step 3: Mine the Math. If we get to the stage of testing negative numbers, it will pay to recall that a negative number squared turns positive, but a negative number cubed remains negative.

Step 4: Make the Comparison. Let's plug the number 1 into the expressions and see what happens:

$$\text{Column A: } (3)(1)^3 + 9 = (3)(1) + 9 = 12$$

$$\text{Column B: } (4)(1)^2 + 6 = (4)(1) + 6 = 10$$

If our strategy was called "O" instead of "FONZ," Column A would be the winner. Let's see what happens when we plug our Z, 0, into the expressions:

$$\text{Column A: } (3)(0)^3 + 9 = (3)(0) + 9 = 9$$

$$\text{Column B: } (4)(0)^2 + 6 = (4)(0) + 6 = 6$$

Column A is still looking good, but we haven't proven anything until we test the other kinds of numbers in our acronym. Let's try a negative—an easy one like –1:

$$\text{Column A: } (3)(-1)^3 + 9 = (3)(-1) + 9 = 6$$

$$\text{Column B: } (4)(-1)^2 + 6 = (4)(1) + 6 = 10$$

And there we have it—the shoe is on the other foot, except that there are no shoes or feet here. But there are different relationships depending on the kinds of numbers we plug into the two expressions, which means the correct answer is **D**.

17.   **E**

Problem Solving: Right Circular Cylinders, Mish-Mashes   *Rating:* Medium

Step 1: Get the Specs. The question indicates that a rectangle is to be rolled into a cylinder, and the figure helpfully shows how this is to be done. It's a mish-mash question since we need to use a measurement from the rectangle to calculate a property of the cylinder, namely its volume.

Step 2: Plan the Attack. This one calls for a standard application of math concepts, and one concept in particular comes to the fore: the volume of a right circular cylinder. We'll pick that up in Step 3.

Step 3: Mine the Math. A right circular cylinder has a circular base, so the volume of a right circular cylinder is equal to the area of the circular base times the height, or $\pi r2h$. We'll also need to call on our knowledge of circles to help us determine the radius: circumference $= 2\pi r$.

Step 4: Power Through. We need to grab the numbers from the rectangle and plug them into their proper place in the cylinder volume formula. When the rectangle is rolled as shown, the top part labeled 12π becomes the circumference of the cylinder. Plugging that number into the circumference formula yields:

$$12\pi = 2\pi r$$
$$12 = 2r$$
$$r = 6$$

The height of the cylinder corresponds to the other side of the rectangle, $\frac{5}{\pi}$. We now have all the values we need to plug into the cylinder volume formula:

$$
\begin{aligned}
\text{volume} &= \pi r^2 h \\
&= \pi (6)^2 \left(\frac{5}{\pi} \right) \\
&= 36\pi \left(\frac{5}{\pi} \right) \\
&= 36 \times 5 = 180
\end{aligned}
$$

E is correct.

18.　**D**
Quantitative Comparisons: Polygons, Triangles, Missing Info　　*Rating:* Medium

Step 1: Get the Specs. This QC features independent blurbs in the columns, and nothing else.

Step 2: Plan the Attack. We'll have to evaluate each scenario to see if we can come up with numbers to compare.

Step 3: Mine the Math. There are a few facts we need to know about polygons and triangles to sink our teeth into this one. First, the interior angles of any polygon add up to $(n-2)180°$, where n is the number of sides of the polygon. Moreover, we need to know that a pentagon has five sides. (It may help to think of the Pentagon in Washington, D.C. And just think: If the architects who designed that building decided on two extra sides, Americans would get reports from the "Heptagon" every time a new war broke out. One fewer side, and news anchors would report on statements made by "anonymous Quadrilateral officials." How embarrassing!) Regarding Column B, an isosceles right triangle contains one 90° angle and two 45° angles.

Step 4: Make the Comparison. Plugging a pentagon's five sides into the polygon interior angle formula, we find that the interior angles of the polygon in question total to $(5-2)180° = 540°$. In an irregular polygon, the angles aren't equal, but the average degree measure per angle can be calculated by simply dividing 540 by 5 to get 108.

Is this bigger, smaller, or equal to the quantity in Column B? Turns out we can't tell, because of a classic case of *missing info*. We recalled from Math 101 that an isosceles right triangle contains one 90° angle and two 45° angles, but we can't find the sum of two of those angles since *we're not told which two*. If you assumed they meant the two equal 45° angles, you'd total those to 90° and select choice **A** since 108 is larger than 90. If, instead, you added 90° to one of the 45° angles, you'd get 135° and accordingly choose **B**. Only if you noticed that either sum could fit the description in Column B would you realize that there's not enough information to make a comparison. That means **D** is correct.

19. **B**
Problem Solving: Mean, Working Backward   *Rating:* Medium

Step 1: Get the Specs. The problem concerns the data analysis topic *mean*, which is basically a fancy way of saying *average*. A quick glance also reveals that the choices are simple numbers in ascending order, which influences our plan of attack. And speaking of which . . .

Step 2: Plan the Attack. You can approach this one head-on if you prefer, but we'll work backward from the choices to give you more practice with that technique.

Step 3: Mine the Math. The formula for arithmetic mean is:

$$\text{mean} = \frac{\text{sum of terms}}{\text{number of terms}}$$

An important corollary of this formula, derived from cross multiplying its terms, is that the mean times the number of terms equals the sum of the terms. This corollary is the concept that will get us through this question.

Step 4: Power Through. When working backward from the choices, we start with choice **C** to speed our work. There are five terms in set $\{a, b, c, d, 26\}$, so if 15 (choice **C**) is the mean of this set of terms, the sum of the set must be $15 \times 5 = 75$. Since one of the terms is known to be 26, the other four terms—a, b, c, and d—must total to $75 - 26 = 49$. But that doesn't jibe with the other information in the question. If the mean of a and b is 10, then the sum of those two terms is $2 \times 10 = 20$. Likewise, the sum of c and d must be $2 \times 12 = 24$. So a, b, c, and d must total to $20 + 24 = 44$, but we got 49 for their total when we tried 15 as the overall mean. So **C** is too big, which means **D** and **E** must be too big as well. Let's try **B**.

If the mean of all five terms is 14, then the sum of all five is $14 \times 5 = 70$, and subtracting out the 26 term, the sum of a, b, c, and d would be $70 - 26 = 44$. That does match the sum of those terms we calculated above, so **B** is correct.

You may have found it easier to work forward on this problem instead of backward—that's a matter of personal preference. But it's still important that you understand the mechanics of working backward so that you'll have this alternative approach at the ready should you need it on test day.

20. **C**
Data Interpretation: Circle Graphs, Percent Decrease   *Rating:* Medium

Step 1: Get the Specs. This Data Interpretation set consists of two circle graphs indicating the various ways in which a company's profits are divvied up. (They should have dedicated some money to a name-change campaign. "Company X" is pretty boring.) The major thing to notice off the bat is that we're given totals for the two years in question, which means we'll probably be doing some percentage calculations along the way. And although overall profits increased, that doesn't necessarily mean the actual amounts in every category increased also—that depends on the percentages. Another thing to notice is that two new categories appear in the 2000 graph that aren't there in 1970. But for the most part, these circle graphs are fairly standard, so let's see what we're asked to do with them.

Step 2: Grill the Interrogator. Well, now we know where the money for the two new initiatives came from in 2000: It got taken out of employee benefits. Ain't that always the way!—make the little guy pay. Notice that the board of directors voted themselves a nifty 5% boost from 1970 to 2000. Interesting . . . Anyway, we're not here to comment on the social inequities of corporate policy; if you're taking the GRE to get your masters in political economy, you can take up this issue when you get to grad school. We just need to determine the percentage decrease in employee benefits from 1970 to 2000, so let's gather the data we need to figure that out.

Step 3: Gather the Data.

$$\text{Percent decrease} = \frac{\text{difference between the two numbers}}{\text{greater of the two numbers}} = 100\%$$

The problem is, we don't have the two numbers yet, only the employee benefits percentage of total profits for each year: 10% in 1970 and 2.5% in 2000. We also know that the total pie was $12 million in 1970 and $36 million in 2000, so we have all the data we need and we're good to go.

Step 4: Power Through. The dollar value of employee benefits in 1970 came to 10% of $12 million, or $1.2 million. The dollar value of employee benefits in 2000 came to 2.5% of $36 million, which you can use your scratch paper to calculate as $900,000. (You might have also employed the shortcut we used on an earlier DI problem, taking 10% of $36 million to get $3.6 million, halving that to get a 5% figure of $1.8 million, and halving that again to get a 2.5% figure of $900,000.) Now that we have the actual dollar amounts, we can plug them into the percent decrease formula:

$$\frac{\$1,200,000 - \$900,000}{\$1,200,000} \times 100\% = \frac{\$300,000}{\$1,200,000} \times 100\%$$
$$= \frac{1}{4} \times 100\%$$
$$= 25\%$$

That's choice **C**.

21. **B**

Data Interpretation: Circle Graphs, Percentages   *Rating:* Medium

Step 1: Get the Specs. We scoped out the specs in the previous question, so we'll head right to Step 2.

Step 2: Grill the Interrogator. The question instructs us to focus our attention on the board of directors and provides some additional information about that group that we'll need to use in our solution. Special attention should be paid to the fact that the question concerns the board members' actual share of the profits, which we'll need to calculate in each year.

THE
GRE

Step 3: Gather the Data. To compare the board members' take in 1970 and their take in 2000, we need to first find their respective percentages from those years and bounce those figures off of the total profits. Not so tough—these figures are all indicated clearly in the graphs. In 1970, the board of directors took a 15% cut of $12 million, and in 2000 the board took a 20% cut of $36 million. Add to that the fact there were eight board members each year, and we're ready to solve.

Step 4: Power Through. We definitely have a multistep problem on our hands, but no one step is unusually difficult. The board got 15% of $12 million in 1970, so we multiply those to get $1.8 million. Dividing by 8 board members gives us $225,000 per member. In 2000, the board got 20% of $36 million, or $7.2 million. Dividing by the 8 board members yields $900,000 per member. The increase in an individual board member's take from 1970 to 2000 is therefore $900,000 – $225,000 = $675,000, choice **B**. Inflation, you know.

22.   **E**

Problem Solving: Combinations   *Rating:* Difficult

Step 1: Get the Specs. The lingo should alert you immediately to what you're up against: Choosing 3 of 10 of one thing, and 2 of 4 of another, indicates that this is a permutation or combination problem. The question is, *which is it?* We'll settle that matter in Step 3 when we dig down into our Math 101 stock-pile of useful math information. The other feature you may have noticed at first glance is that we're dealing with a *multiple* permutation/combination problem, since there are *two* aspects of the prospective outfit (fabric and style) under consideration.

Step 2: Plan the Attack. Permutation and combination problems require little more than crunching through a formula, so our modus operandi will be to plug the numbers in and solve. Of course, you have to *know* the formula to use, so the battle in this one is pretty much won or lost in Step 3.

Step 3: Mine the Math. The key to determining whether to use the combination or permutation formula is figuring out *whether or not order is significant*. In a race or ranking, clearly order matters. But in an *outfit?* Does anyone look at an outfit and say "Hey, that outfit has some wool, and after that it has some polyester"? No, of course not. If it has both, it has both—it doesn't contain one before the other. Same for style. So order doesn't matter in this case. Order is significant in permutations but not in combinations, so we're in combination territory. The combination formula is:

$$_nC_r = \frac{n!}{(n-r)!r!}$$

where unordered subgroups of size r are selected from a set of size n. A factorial (!) following a number represents the product of all the numbers up to and including that number. To solve a problem containing multiple permutations or combinations, calculate each one individually and multiply the results.

Step 4: Power Through. If you know what permutations and combinations are, how to determine which to use in which circumstances, and even know each formula and how to solve them, then the rest is definitely doable. As we said above, the battle in this question takes place primarily in Step 3. If you know all the concepts discussed in the previous step, the rest is little more than the kind of number crunching we practiced in the permutation/combination section of Math 101. Here goes:

Fabric Combinations

$$_{10}C_3 = \frac{10!}{(10-3)!3!}$$

$$= \frac{10!}{7!3!}$$

$$= \frac{10 \times 9 \times 8 \times 7!}{7!3!}$$

$$= \frac{10 \times 9 \times 8}{3 \times 2 \times 1} = \frac{720}{6} = 120$$

Style Combinations

$$_4C_2 = \frac{4!}{(4-2)!2!}$$

$$= \frac{4!}{2!2!}$$

$$= \frac{4 \times 3 \times 2!}{2!2!}$$

$$= \frac{4 \times 3}{2 \times 1} = \frac{12}{2} = 6$$

Multiplying the individual results gives 120 × 6 = 720, choice **E**. Trap choices **A** and **C** contain the individual results, 6 and 120, while choice **B** may be there to catch anyone who took a guess by adding 3 × 10 to 2 × 4, thus coming up with 30 + 8 = 38. Not a bad guess if you had no idea how to go about this—but wrong. The GRE generally doesn't reward guessing. If you don't know how to do a problem, the odds aren't great that you'll get it right accidentally.

23.　**A**
Quantitative Comparisons: Coordinate Geometry,
Slope, Intercepts   *Rating:* Difficult

Step 1: Get the Specs. We're given the formula for a line and asked to compare the slope and *x*-intercept of that line. Sounds like another Problem Solving challenge in disguise. Given the formula for the line, we have no reason to believe that it's impossible to figure out the line's slope and *x*-intercept, so we should at least scratch choice **D** from contention right off the bat.

Step 2: Plan the Attack. We're going to have to face this one head-on and figure out the things it's asking us to determine. In other words, we'll treat it like the kind of Problem Solving question it really is.

Step 3: Mine the Math. The formula for the equation of a line in the coordinate plane is $y = mx + b$, where m is the slope of the line and b is the y-intercept.

Since the x-intercept is the value of x where the line crosses the x-axis, to find the x-intercept, set $y = 0$.

Step 4: Make the Comparison. The given equation is not yet in the $y = mx + b$ format, so we'll need to play with it until it is. That means isolating the y term on one side and getting the x term and constant on the other. Here's how:

$$x = \frac{3}{2}y - 1$$

$$x - \frac{3}{2}y = -1$$

$$-\frac{3}{2}y = x - 1$$

Now we need to get rid of the $-\frac{3}{2}$ in front of y to get the y alone, so multiply both sides by $-\frac{2}{3}$:

$$y = \frac{2}{3}x + \frac{2}{3}$$

Now the equation is in the proper form, and we can see from it that the slope is the number before the x, $\frac{2}{3}$, and the y-intercept is the constant, also $\frac{2}{3}$. If you misread the question and thought you were asked to compare these two quantities, you'd choose **C** at this point, thinking the columns are equal. However, the question asks for the x-intercept, not the y-intercept, so we have to set $y = 0$ in any of our equations to find this last piece of the puzzle. The original equation makes for the simplest calculation:

$$x = \frac{3}{2}y - 1$$

$$x = \frac{3}{2}(0) - 1$$

$$x = -1$$

So the slope is $\frac{2}{3}$ and the x-intercept is -1, which means Column A trumps Column B, and choice **A** is correct.

24.   **C**

Quantitative Comparisons: Exponents, Mirroring   *Rating:* Difficult

Step 1: Get the Specs. This QC has no additional information, so we'll focus on the expressions in the columns. The problem concerns exponents, so we'll need to scour our arsenal of math concepts to dig out what we know about that arithmetic subject.

Step 2: Plan the Attack. Of course there's no way to calculate the actual values here—they're simply too large. But we can try to make the columns resemble each other, which means that Mirroring is the best way to go.

Step 3: Mine the Math. The Product Rule of exponents states that to multiply exponential terms containing the same base, add the exponents together. A corollary of this rule is that to factor exponential terms, subtract the exponents. That's precisely what we'll do in Step 4.

Step 4: Make the Comparison. In Column A, 8^{10} can be factored from both terms. Factoring 8^{10} from 8^{10} yields 1, since 1 always results when we factor a number from itself. If you prefer to use the subtraction method, it comes out the same: $8^{10} - 8^{10} = 8^{10-10} = 8^0 = 1$. Factoring 8^{10} from the second term in Column A, 8^{12}, yields $8^{12} - 8^{10} = 8^{12-10} = 8^2$. So the expression in Column A factors to this: $8^{10}(1 + 8^2)$. Simplifying the parentheses gives $8^{10}(1 + 64)$, which is $8^{10} \times 65$. Now we can see that the two columns are equal, and **C** is correct.

25.   **A**

Problem Solving: Absolute Value   *Rating:* Difficult

Step 1: Get the Specs. The absolute value bars are the most striking feature of this problem, but if you read carefully, you'll notice a hint that suggests how you'll need to go about this. The question asks for a *possible* solution for x, which implies that there may be more than one. Even if you forgot the mechanics of absolute value, the question itself reminds you that you may need to investigate more than one scenario.

Step 2: Plan the Attack. We'll meet the challenge head-on and methodically work through the steps of solving the equation.

Step 3: Mine the Math. The main thing to recall is that we need to find both positive and negative solutions for algebraic equations containing absolute value bars, since negative values within the absolute value bars turn positive when the bars are removed.

Step 4: Power Through. The concept highlighted in Step 3 tells us that to get rid of the absolute value bars and isolate x in terms of y, we need to solve the equation twice: once with the right-hand side as written and again after negating the expression on the right. Of course, if we find a solution among the choices that works after the first round, we'll stop there. Here's the original equation:

$$3\left|\frac{x+2}{3}\right| = y^2 - 1$$

First isolate the expression within the absolute value brackets by dividing both sides by 3:

$$\left|\frac{x+2}{3}\right| = \frac{y^2 - 1}{3}$$

Next, solve for x as if the expression within absolute value bars were positive. That means we'll get rid of the bars and leave the right-hand side as is:

$$\frac{x+2}{3} = \frac{y^2 - 1}{3}$$

Multiply both sides of the equation by 3:

$$x + 2 = y^2 - 1$$

Subtract 2 from both sides:

$$x = y^2 - 3$$

So one solution for x in terms of y is $y^2 - 3$. That's not one of the choices, so we'll find the other solution by solving for x as if the expression within absolute value bars were negative. That means we'll get rid of the bars and make the right-hand side negative:

$$\frac{x + 2}{3} = -\frac{y^2 - 1}{3}$$

Multiply both sides of the equation by 3:

$$x + 2 = -(y^2 - 1)$$

Distribute the negative sign on the right side of the equation:

$$x + 2 = -y^2 + 1$$

Subtract 2 from both sides:

$$x = -y^2 - 1$$

So another solution for x in terms of y is $-y^2 - 1$, which, thankfully, does appear in choice **A**.

26. **D**

Quantitative Comparisons: Median, Mode   *Rating:* Difficult

Step 1: Get the Specs. We're presented with two data sets and asked for the median of one and the mode of the other. There are no variables in the problem, so it may appear at first glance that choice **D** is out of contention. However, as you'll see, a particularity of the mode function throws all that to the wind.

Step 2: Plan the Attack. This is essentially disguised Problem Solving, Double-Column Calculations style, as we have no choice but to work out each mini-problem and compare the results.

Step 3: Mine the Math. The *median* of a group of numbers is the middle term when the numbers are written in either ascending or descending order or the *mean (average) of the two middle numbers* if the total number of terms in the data set is even. The *mode* of a group of numbers is the number that occurs most frequently. A data set may include more than one mode.

Step 4: Make the Comparison. Data set K has eight terms, an even number, so the median of the set will be the average of its two middle terms. To see which ones fall in the middle, put the terms in ascending order:

$$-25, -7.5, -0.5, 0, 2, 10, 23, 70$$

The middle two terms are happily 0 and 2—happily, because it's easy to see that their average is 1. (With more difficult numbers, we'd simply add them and divide by 2.) So the quantity in Column A boils down to 1.

The mode of data set L is simply the number that appears the most, and here we have a tie between −5 and 2, each of which occurs twice. So set L has two modes: −5 and 2. Since −5 is less than 1, but 2 is greater than 1, the exact relationship between the columns can't be determined. **D** is correct.

Be careful with mode! Test takers tend to forget that more than one mode is possible, since other statistical descriptors such as mean and median always boil down to a single number. The test makers are known to exploit nuances like this when constructing difficult questions.

27.   **E**
Problem Solving: Made-Up Symbols, Exponents,
Positive vs. Negative Numbers   *Rating:* Difficult

Step 1: Get the Specs. Here's another Roman numeral question, this one containing a made-up symbol involving exponents. We're given the definition of the symbol and then asked to determine which set of values yields a negative number.

Step 2: Plan the Attack. First we'll make sure we understand the symbol's definition; then we'll plug in the numbers from the Roman numeral statements and perform the calculations to see which ones come out negative.

Step 3: Mine the Math. An important bit of exponent theory that comes into play here is that when the bases of exponential terms differ, those terms can't be combined. That means we'll need to work out each term individually and see where that leads. Two other exponent concepts are relevant: For any number x, $x^0 = 1$, and $x^{-y} = \dfrac{1}{x^y}$.

Step 4: Power Through. Before plugging anything in, let's get a handle on the made-up symbol. Here's the definition: $x@y = x^y - y^x$. That simply means that when we're given a number before and a number after an @ sign, we should raise the first number to the power of the second number and subtract from that the value of the second number raised to the power of the first number. If it sounds confusing, it should be clearer when we plug in the numbers, so let's consider the Roman numerals, one at a time:

I. $x = 8$, $y = 2$

$$x^y - y^x = 8^2 - 2^8 = 64 - 2^8$$

You shouldn't have to multiply out 2^8 to see that that number is bigger than 64, which means the expression in I resolves to a negative number. If you did multiply it—or, better yet, memorized it from the table we provided in Math 101—you'd see that $2^8 = 256$, confirming that $64 - 256$ is negative. We're looking for negative results, so Roman numeral I must be included in the correct answer, which means **B** is out.

II. $x = 0, y = 8$

$$x^y - y^x = 0^8 - 8^0 = 0 - 1 = -1$$

This one comes out negative, so II must be included as well, which means neither **A** nor **D** can be correct.

III. $x = -5, y = 7$

$$x^y - y^x = -5^7 - 7^{-5} = -5^7 - \frac{1}{7^5}$$

In this case, the first term, -5^7 is negative since a negative number raised to an odd exponent will remain negative. In addition, it will be a very *large* negative number—the negative of the product of seven 5s. Meanwhile, the second term, 1 divided by 7^5, is a very small fraction which will make -5^7 a little more negative when subtracted from it. So plugging these values into the made-up symbol expression yields a number way less than 0. Statement III therefore makes the cut as well, meaning **E** is the correct answer.

28.   **B**
Quantitative Comparisons: Circles, Triangles,
Tangent Lines, Mish-Mashes   *Rating:* Difficult

Step 1: Get the Specs. In this one, a circle overlaps with a triangle, so we have a mish-mash problem. It's a difficult problem because it requires that you know the rules of circles, triangles, and tangent lines. Luckily we covered all that in Math 101, so let's get to it.

Step 2: Plan the Attack. This is another disguised Problem Solving question, so again we'll work out each problem individually. However, since we're dealing with a mish-mash, we'll be careful to note any overlapping parts of the diagram that may figure in our calculations.

Step 3: Mine the Math. Here are the math concepts you need to draw from your Math 101 reservoir to answer this question: A circle is named after its center point. A line drawn from the center to the edge of a circle is the radius. A radius whose endpoint is the intersection point of the tangent line and the circle is perpendicular to the tangent line. Perpendicular lines form a 90° angle. A triangle has 180°. The sides of a 30–60–90 triangle are in the ratio of $1:\sqrt{3}:2$. The perimeter of a triangle equals the sum of its sides. The circumference of a circle equals $2\pi r$, where r is the radius. π is equal to approximately 3.14.

Wow, that's a lot to know! This would certainly fall into the category of "Multiple-Concept" questions. All of the little steps involved are what make the difficult questions so difficult. However, not one of the math concepts above is particularly complicated in itself, so if you know these things, the question really isn't so terrible. Let's put all of this knowledge to work and solve the problem.

Step 4: Make the Comparison. Since the circle is defined as "circle Q," point Q must be the center and QR must therefore be a radius of length 4. Tangent line RS must therefore be perpendicular to QR, forming a 90° angle where they meet. Since angle RQS is given as 60°, triangle QRS must be a 30-60-90 right triangle with angle RSQ clocking in at 30°. Side QR is opposite this 30° angle, so it must correspond to the 1 in the $1:\sqrt{3}:2$ ratio of the triangle's sides. Since QR is 4, RS, the side opposite the 60° angle, must be $4\sqrt{3}$, and QS, the hypotenuse, must be twice QR, or 8. That brings the perimeter of triangle QRS to $4 + 4\sqrt{3} + 8$, or $12 + 4\sqrt{3}$.

The circumference of circle Q is a bit easier, since we know the radius is 4. Plugging into the circumference formula gives us:

$$c = 2\pi r = 2\pi 4 = 8\pi$$

In an easier problem we'd be done by now, having calculated the quantities in both columns. But in this one, even the final comparison is complicated. What's bigger, $12 + 4\sqrt{3}$ or 8π? We need to perform one final step to find out. Since $\sqrt{3}$ is less than 2, $4\sqrt{3}$ is less than 8, which means $12 + 4\sqrt{3}$ is smaller than 20. Similarly, since π is equal to approximately 3.14, 8π must be larger than 24.

Finally, after a good deal of math, we have the problem right where we want it: A number larger than 24 is bigger than a number smaller than 20, so **B** is correct for this final question of the section.

Sure, this one was tough. But remember—*they only get this tough if you're doing really well.* So rather than dreading a question on this level, you should be working toward seeing as many of them as you can.

SECTION 3

Verbal

1. **D**
Sentence Completions: Definition   *Rating:* Easy

Step 1: Find the Keywords. The main keyword is concise, which presumably describes the style that Hemingway attempted to show off in his six-word story.

Step 2: Look for Road Signs. There are no obvious road signs that indicate that the author is attempting to veer off in some new direction, so we can assume that this is a simple Definition type of sentence.

Step 3: Make a Prediction. The keyword *concise*, combined with the amazing six-word story, strongly suggests that the literary style in question is one of brevity, saying things in very few words. So something on the order of *brief* or *to the point* should do the trick.

Step 4: Compare Your Answer(s) to the Answer Choices. Of the answers given, *terse* fits the bill, since terse is a synonym of *concise*, and in Definition sentences, we're looking above all for synonyms for the keywords we find. *Garrulous* means "talkative," and *histrionic* means "exaggerated." These two distractors are antonyms of *concise* and thus derail the author's meaning.

Step 5: Plug It In. Plugging *terse* back into the original sentence confirms that **D** is correct.

In case you were wondering, here's Hemingway's story: "For sale: baby shoes, never worn." Rumor has it that Hemingway himself declared this his greatest work.

2.   **E**

Antonyms: Common Usage   *Rating:* Easy

Step 1: Simplify the Word. *Intentional* means "on purpose." We'll go with this common use of the word.

Step 2: Predict an Opposite. The opposite of something that's done on purpose is something that's *not* done on purpose; using the word itself, we can even say *unintentional*. You really don't need anything fancier than that, especially in the first few Antonym questions at the beginning of the Verbal section that will most likely consist of common words with straightforward definitions.

Step 3: Match Your Prediction to the Answer Choices. Something that's not done on purpose, or that's unintentional, can be said to be *accidental*, choice **E**. *Deliberate*, choice **C**, is a synonym for *intentional*, while *illogical* (**B**) may be the most enticing trap. However, something that's not done on purpose need not be illogical.

3.   **B**

Analogies: Composition   *Rating:* Easy

Step 1: Connect the Dots. *Distance* is composed of and measured in meters, so we have a Composition type Analogy on our hands.

Step 2: Create a Template. "X is composed of and measured in Y" is a straightforward generalization of this connection.

Step 3: Make the Match. *Volume* is composed of and measured in liters, so **B** exhibits the same relationship as the original pair. (You may have noticed that correct choice **B** rhymes with the original pair, but you certainly shouldn't expect *that* to happen all too often. Poetry is not the test makers' forte.) There's no need to go on to Step 4 and narrow the connection if the connection you determine initially gets you all the way there. Try to knock out easier Analogy questions in three steps, especially those near the beginning of the section.

4.   **A**

Antonyms: Multiple Meanings, Create a Context   *Rating:* Easy

Step 1: Simplify the Word. *Critical* is a word with multiple meanings, so we'll need to be careful. It can mean "important," as in "the mission is critical." It can also mean "very serious," as in "the patient is in critical condition." So we'll keep these two different contexts in mind as we go forward.

Step 2: Predict an Opposite. The opposite of *important is unimportan*t, or *trivial.* For the opposite of *very serious* we'll just go with *not serious.* Let's see whether either of these possibilities emerges in the choices.

Step 3: Match Your Prediction to the Answer Choices. *Grave*, choice **C**, is a synonym for our very serious prediction, so we can ditch that, while *significant*, choice **D**, is a synonym for our prediction *important. Noteworthy* and *understated* don't have any obvious relation to critical, leaving *stable*, choice **A**. And if we recall the health context we invoked earlier, the opposite of a patient who's in *critical* condition is a patient who's *stable*, so choice **A** is the best of the bunch.

5.   **D**

Analogies: Action   *Rating:* Easy

Step 1: Connect the Dots. A *painter* uses a *palette* as part of his or her work, so this one takes the form of an Action analogy.

Step 2: Create a Template. Make sure you get the order in your template right; there's a trap among the choices that tests whether you do. A fine template is "a Y uses X as part of his job." Let's use that to make our match.

Step 3: Make the Match. "A *jockey* uses a *saddle* as part of his job" fits the template perfectly, so **D** is correct. Notice that if we omitted "as part of his job" from the template, **C** would have looked tempting too, as an automobile *does* use fuel. In that case, we'd narrow the choices down to **C** and **D** and would have to proceed to Step 4, Narrow the Connection, to distinguish between them.

As for the others, a *lawyer* participates in a *trial* but doesn't *use* a trial as a tool of the trade in the same way that a *painter* uses a *palette*. **B** bollixes up the order; switch *barber* and *scissors* and we'd have a match. In **E**, a *weaver* may create a *tapestry*, but we wouldn't say a *weaver* uses a *tapestry*.

6.   **A**

Sentence Completions: Contrast   *Rating:* Medium

Step 1: Find the Keywords. The keywords are *nonindigenous* species, the subject of the sentence, and potential to be *ecologically disastrous*, which presumably is a description of those species. However, we can't fully get our hands around the sentence's logic until we take its road sign into account.

Step 2: Look for Road Signs. *Although* is one of the most common road signs, and it signals that a change of direction will take place. This road sign tells us we're dealing with a Contrast sentence type.

Step 3: Make a Prediction. The Contrast sentence structure tells us that the characteristic of the species under consideration will be the opposite of disastrous. We can therefore predict that the author means to tell us that the majority of these species are actually fairly harmless, or something along those lines.

Step 4: Compare Your Answer(s) to the Answer Choices. *Innocuous*, choice **A**, means "inoffensive" or "harmless," and provides the best completion here. The sentence doesn't suggest anything about how many plants there are or whether these plants are hearty or fragile, so *pervasive* and *precarious*, tempting wrong choices, don't work.

Step 5: Plug It In. Plugging *innocuous* back into the original sentence confirms that **A** is correct.

7. **C**

Antonyms: Relate the Word to Words You Know,
Create a Context   *Rating:* Medium

Step 1: Simplify the Word. *Indulgent* is formed from the word *indulge*, which means to "spoil," "pamper," or "coddle." A familiar context might be the *indulgent* parent who caters to his or her child's every whim. So to be *indulgent* is to be *lenient* or *tolerant*.

Step 2: Predict an Opposite. The opposite of someone who's *lenient* or *tolerant* is someone who's strict, inflexible, or domineering. Think of the opposite of an *indulgent* parent and you'll get an idea of what we're looking for.

Step 3: Match Your Prediction to the Answer Choices. *Stringent*, choice **C**, means "strict" or "severe" and works fine as the opposite we seek. *Flexible* (**B**) is closer to a synonym than an antonym of indulgent, and **E**, *sadistic*, goes too far. Someone may be strict, tough, and even domineering, yet not be cruel or vicious.

8. **B**

Analogies: Meaning, Weak Links   *Rating:* Medium

Step 1: Connect the Dots. Someone who is *ambivalent* is indifferent, noncommittal, or hesitant and is therefore the opposite of one who is *energized*. So the words in the original pair have nearly opposite meanings.

Step 2: Create a Template. We'll try "X is the opposite of Y" as our template.

Step 3: Make the Match. **C** and **E** fall by the wayside fairly quickly if you recognize that the words in these pairs contain no obvious internal relationship; that is, that they're weak links. **A** is next to go, since *enticing* and *beguiling* are synonyms, and we're looking for opposites. However, both **B** and **D** make the cut because *bored* is the opposite of *enthralled*, and *irreligious* is the opposite of *devout*. How are we going to decide? By invoking Step 4, of course—that's what it's there for.

Step 4: Narrow the Connection. Viewing the words in the original pair as opposites is not enough to help us decide between **B** and **D**, so we need to narrow the connection. *Ambivalent* and *energized* represent reactions to life, situations, or events. *Bored* and *enthralled* qualify as similar general kinds of reactions to our surroundings. *Irreligious* and *devout*, however, are opposite worldviews with respect to one specific domain: religion. Narrowing the connection to "X is the opposite reaction of Y pertaining to any situation or event" helps us differentiate the two contenders and see that **B** edges out **D** by a nose. It's not the most elegant formulation, but it'll do.

9. **C**

Antonyms: Create a Context   *Rating:* Medium

Step 1: Simplify the Word. Maybe you simply know that *disparage* means to "ridicule" or "mock," or maybe creating a context helped you out, such as "he made disparaging remarks."

Step 2: Predict an Opposite. One opposite of "to ridicule" or "to mock" is "to praise." Keep it simple heading into Step 3. You don't need to be a psychic and predict the exact answer the test makers wrote; you just need to get into the ballpark so you'll recognize the correct choice when you see it.

Step 3: Match Your Prediction to the Answer Choices. With *praise* in mind as a prediction, *eulogize* should jump off the page at you (or off the screen during the real test). *Eulogize* means to "praise," "extol," and "rave about," definitions you may be familiar with from funeral eulogies, a ceremony in which someone speaks favorably of the deceased. To *disparage* is to speak badly about someone or something. To *eulogize*, or praise, is a fine opposite.

10. **D**

Sentence Completions: Amplification   *Rating:* Medium

Step 1: Find the Keywords. The keywords in this one are not obvious, but they are there. The words *only mild* serve as a description of the *reaction* to a book described in the first blank, while *bordered on outright* prefaces the reaction described in the second blank. Moreover, *critical evaluations* pertains to the first reaction, while people *depicted unflatteringly in the novel* relates to the second.

Step 2: Look for Road Signs. *Whereas* is the sentence's major road sign and signals that while the first reaction was like one thing, the second reaction was like something else. Combining this road sign with the keywords uncovered in Step 1 reveals that the sentence contains an Amplification structure: A mild form of reaction in the first blank turns into something stronger in the second.

Step 3: Make a Prediction. It doesn't sound like the hometown folks are all too pleased with their unflattering portrayal at the hands of Steinbeck, so the second blank may be the easier one to approach. Their reaction would be negative, so we need a negative word at the end like *anger* or *hostility*. The Amplification structure suggests that the first blank will also contain a negative appraisal from the critical evaluators, but something milder than the reaction of the outraged townspeople.

Step 4: Compare Your Answer(s) to the Answer Choices. The pair of words in choice **D** correctly solidifies the sentence's structure. The logic of the sentence

THE
GRE

supports a reaction that builds from *mild criticism* to *outright condemnation*. *Commendation* and *approbation* both mean "praise" or "approval," certainly not something that's likely to come from Steinbeck's pissed-off neighbors. That allows us to eliminate choices **A** and **B**. *Bewilderment* is too weak, as these people seem more angry than surprised. Moreover, *denigration* ("scorn," "vilification") is too strong to be matched with mild in the first blank, so **C** has numerous problems. **E** is tricky but doesn't fit the Amplification structure, since to up the ante after only *mild acceptance*, the sentence would have to end with *a real lot of acceptance*, which it doesn't, nor would that kind of positive reception make sense in this context coming from residents who were made to look foolish.

Step 5: Plug It In. Plugging in the pair in choice **D** creates a logical and coherent sentence.

11.   **A**

Reading Comprehension: Detail Purpose   *Rating:* Medium

Step 1: Skim and Outline. We trust you've skimmed the passage and jotted down brief notes on its major points and themes. Let's get right to the question in Step 2.

Step 2: Read the Question and Search for Triggers. This one's a Detail Purpose question that's interested in the function that the final sentence of the first paragraph serves. Our trigger words are *purpose* and *final sentence of the first paragraph*.

Step 3: Locate Relevant Information and Make a Prediction. We know right where to look but should make sure we understand the sentence in its proper context. The sentence is "Every person thus lives by exchanging, or by becoming in some measure a merchant, and the society itself grows to be what is properly a commercial society." This relates back to the fact that once division of labor has set in, people produce more of their own special product than they themselves can consume, but not enough of everything else they need, which they must get from other people. This creates a situation that requires exchange and leads to what we know as a commercial society. The author tells us this, therefore, to explain how division of labor ultimately leads to commercialism.

Step 4: Match Your Prediction to the Answer Choices. Choice **A** states our prediction above in general terms. The *economic system* it refers to is the commercial system, and the *step* is the process of exchange detailed in the sentence under consideration.

As for the other choices:

B: The sentence in question doesn't qualify as the passage's main point because it doesn't take into account the information in paragraph 2.

C: No disadvantages are mentioned or alluded to in the sentence in question. The author merely states how the commercial system he's discussing came to be. If anything, the sentence presents the *advantages* of each person becoming a kind of merchant to exchange what he has for what he needs.

D: The sentence doesn't go into the actual specifics of the production process.

E: The statements in the first paragraph lead seamlessly to the description put forth in its final sentence, so no contradictory elements exist within that paragraph.

12.   **C**

Reading Comprehension: Implied Information   *Rating:* Medium

Step 1: Skim and Outline. You took care of this before working through the first question in the set, so it's on to Step 2.

Step 2: Read the Question and Search for Triggers. The word *supports* tells us we're dealing with an Implied Information question, and the word *EXCEPT* tells us that we need to select the one choice that's *not* suggested by the information in the passage.

Step 3: Locate Relevant Information and Make a Prediction. Since there are no specific trigger words that tell us which information is tested, or where in the passage to look, we'll move right to the choices and test them out, one by one.

A: The sentence we analyzed in the previous question speaks to the truth of the statement in **A**: According to the author, the exchange made possible and necessary by the division of labor helps society grow into what is properly deemed a commercial society.

B is inferable, since the passage suggests that only once the division of labor was established did people supply only a small part of their own wants, making the exchange discussed later in the paragraph necessary. If that's the case, then it's reasonable to believe that before the division of labor came into being, people supplied more of their own wants themselves.

C contradicts the idea that individuals in a commercial society produce only a small part of the things they themselves need, thus making it necessary to exchange with others. Since we're looking for the statement that's not inferable, C is correct.

D is inferable from the statement "this power of exchanging must frequently have been very much clogged and embarrassed in its operations." The author suggests that transactions have been hindered when differences existed between what some people had to offer and what other people wanted to acquire.

E is inferable because the whole passage is structured to lead to the conclusion that producing more of a product than a person himself can consume may be just fine, because in a commercial society, such a person can often exchange his product with others to get the things he needs.

13.   **A**

Antonyms: Relate the Word to Words You Know   *Rating:* Medium

Step 1: Simplify the Word. *Sagacity* is a tough word if you don't know it, but you can use one of our "tough stuff" Antonym techniques and relate it to a word you may know: *sage*. A *sage* is a wise and learned person, and accordingly, *sagacity* means "wisdom," "level-headedness," and "shrewdness and clarity in thought."

Step 2: Predict an Opposite. Opposites of *wisdom* and *shrewd clear thinking* are *unintelligence*, *stupidity*, and *absurdity*. We'll look for something along those lines among the choices.

Step 3: Match Your Prediction to the Answer Choices. Something that's unintelligent, stupid, or absurd can be said to be illogical, so *illogicality*, choice **A**, works as a reasonable antonym for *sagacity*. **C** is a trap. Someone who has *sagacity*—a sage or religious leader, for instance—may be *revered* ("respected," "worshipped"), but the opposite of sagacity is not the opposite of reverence, *irreverence*. **C** has that "one step removed" feel of tricky Antonym traps. *Prudence*, choice **E**, is more of a synonym than an antonym of *sagacity*.

14. **A**

Analogies: Function, Weak Links, Identical Relationships   *Rating:* Medium

Step 1: Connect the Dots. The function of an *explanation* is to do the opposite of *bewilder*—it's to *clarify*. So we have a Function analogy on our hands, except the function is stated in the negative. That's the key element to express in our template.

Step 2: Create a Template. Here's a template that suitably expresses the element of negativity noted in the connection above: "The function of X is to do the *opposite* of Y." Let's see how far that gets us.

Step 3: Make the Match. Choice **A** contains the same relationship as the original pair: The function of a *summary* is the opposite of *belaboring* ("dwell on," "overstress")—it's to *simplify*. **B** and **D** contain weak links. If we don't know what kind of gesture **B** refers to, we can't know how that word relates to *agitate*. Similarly, a *demagogue* (leader who passionately appeals to emotion) may do many things, but where *modernize* fits into a demagogue's agenda is anyone's guess. (In fact, *agitate* relates better to *demagogue* than it does to *gesture*.)

As for the other two, **C** and **E** both contain pairs of words that describe positive functions: The purpose of an *inauguration* is to *commence* something, and the purpose of an *epilogue* is to *conclude* a book or a play. Both of these lack the opposite element contained in the original. Moreover, since **C** and **E** exhibit an identical relationship, neither can be correct since there's no way to distinguish between them.

15. **B**

Sentence Completions: Definition   *Rating:* Medium

Step 1: Find the Keywords. The keys to the sentence are the *toppling of the leader*, which was *fueled by the ire*—that is, "anger" or "displeasure"—of some people who *refused to work under such harsh conditions*.

Step 2: Look for Road Signs. There are no road signs to speak of, so we'll move right to Step 3.

Step 3: Make a Prediction. In the absence of road signs, this is a Definition sentence in which the missing word serves to define, or describe, the workers. What kind of workers would be *fueled by ire* to rise up and *topple* their leader over the issue of poor working conditions? Pissed-off ones, that's what kind. You may have come up with any prediction along the lines of *angry, fed up, defiant, irate,* and so on to match the mood of the revolutionary workers. Let's see which choice accords with these predictions.

Step 4: Compare Your Answer(s) to the Answer Choices. B is correct. *Recalcitrant* is an adjective describing a state of stubborn defiance and thus best completes the sentence. *Quixotic* ("idealistic"), *erudite* ("intelligent"), *disparate* ("different"), and *facetious* ("sarcastic") are all off the mark.

Step 5: Plug It In. The sentence flows and makes logical sense when we insert *recalcitrant* as the missing piece.

16. **C**

Reading Comprehension: Implied Information   *Rating:* Medium

Step 1: Skim and Outline. The first step is to skim and jot down the passage's most salient features. When that's taken care of, you're ready for Step 2.

Step 2: Read the Question and Search for Triggers. This one is a Roman numeral Implied Information question, so we'll jump right to the three statements to see which are supported by the passage.

I. This statement is supported by the sentences "Changed habits produce an inherited effect" and "With animals the increased use or disuse of parts has had a more marked influence."

II. This statement is supported by the phrase "development of the udders in cows and goats in countries where they are habitually milked, in comparison with these organs in other countries."

III. Although the effects of environment on animals is said to be more marked than on plants, this idea doesn't suggest anything regarding how rapidly this evolution occurs. This statement therefore goes to extremes and is not inferable from the passage.

I and II are inferable, III is not, so **C** is correct.

17. **E**

Reading Comprehension: Primary Purpose   *Rating:* Medium

Step 1: Skim and Outline. You've taken care of this step already, so let's move on to Step 2.

Step 2: Read the Question and Search for Triggers. Don't get tripped up by what this question asks. Since the title reflects the main reason the author wrote the passage, and foreshadows what it's primarily about, this is really a Primary Purpose question in disguise. There are no specific triggers because Primary Purpose questions concern the passage as a whole.

Step 3: Locate Relevant Information and Make a Prediction. The whole passage is relevant in this case, but hopefully you put some thought into the main thrust of the passage during your first skim through. The author is concerned with ways in which the use and disuse of plant and animal parts affect the way those parts develop. This thesis is set out in the first sentence in regard to plants but is then fleshed out with examples from the animal kingdom. From duck bone weight to drooping dog ears, the examples that follow do little more than elaborate on the use/disuse idea set forth in the first sentence. So your prediction for the title should have centered on this central idea of the effects of use and disuse on plant and animal parts, without getting overly influenced by the specific examples put forth which are there only to support the hypothesis.

Step 4: Match Your Prediction to the Answer Choices. Choice **E** captures the essence of this prediction, focusing on the passage's overall issue of how use and disuse affect animal traits. **A** and **B** both go far beyond the scope of the passage. The entire *history of evolutionary theory* is not discussed, and only very few traits of a very small number of species are mentioned—a far cry from a *comparative study*. Both choices also omit the passage's main focus on the effect of use and disuse, the same problem that plagues **D**. **C** is too narrow, since the passage discusses more than just the weight of ducks. Again, all of the specific examples exist to support a larger point.

18.   **D**

Antonyms: Prefixes, Relate the Word to Words You Know   *Rating:* Medium

Step 1: Simplify the Word. A more familiar word that resembles *inimitable* is *imitate*, but we also need to take the prefix in, meaning "not," into consideration. Combining the two, we can infer that something *inimitable* is something that cannot be imitated—something *unique*.

Step 2: Predict an Opposite. Possible opposites of *unique* are *usual* and *ordinary*. We'll take those with us into Step 3.

Step 3: Match Your Prediction to the Answer Choices. *Universal* is another way of saying "widespread," "ordinary," or "usual," so **D** provides the best antonym of *inimitable*. Something that can't be imitated is the opposite of something that exists across the board. *Redundant* ("unneeded," "superfluous"), choice **B**, is close, but no cigar. Something that's not unique is common or ordinary but not necessarily unnecessary.

19.   **D**

Analogies: Category   *Rating:* Medium

Step 1: Connect the Dots. *Embezzlement* is a form of fraud that involves the misappropriation of funds, so it is a type of *transgression*, or crime.

Step 2: Create a Template. We'll go with our standard Category template, namely "X is a type of Y."

Step 3: Make the Match. Choice **D** works: *Psychosis* is a type of *disorder*. As for the others: A *tyranny* may be characterized by *cruelty*, but we wouldn't properly say that *cruelty* is a type of *tyranny*, so **A** is wrong. In **B**, *banishment* and *exile* are pretty much the same, since anyone's who's banished is exiled, while anyone who's exiled is also banished. There's too much overlap between these two for this pair to fall into the Category type, in which one word is clearly a subset of the other. A *desert* lacks *irrigation* (**C**), which also isn't the relationship we seek, whereas *oscillation* and *decisiveness* seem to go in different directions: One who *oscillates* is *indecisive*. **E** therefore also fails to match our Category template.

20.   **B**
Reading Comprehension: Primary Purpose   *Rating:* Medium

Step 1: Skim and Outline. You should skim long passages for their most prominent features and ideas, even if you need to scroll down on the screen to see the whole passage. Once you've done that, and jotted down some notes on your scratch paper, you're ready to face the first question in the set.

Step 2: Read the Question and Search for Triggers. There are no triggers in this one because Primary Purpose questions concern the passage as a whole. So we'll move on to the next step to make a prediction.

Step 3: Locate Relevant Information and Make a Prediction. Up until the word *nonetheless* at the end of paragraph 4, we may have reasonably concluded that the author's purpose was to bore us to death with facts about fair use. And perhaps she accomplished this purpose, in any case. But her purpose takes a new turn in the final sentence of the passage where she advocates for the employment of fair use, despite the difficulties she cites. So we'd expect the correct choice to reflect this element of advocacy, and we should eliminate any choice that leaves this part out.

Step 4: Match Your Prediction to the Answer Choices. Choice **B** accords with this prediction and is correct. The author does spend much time telling us what the fair use provision is all about (*delineates the mechanisms . . .*), and then encourages artists and social commentators to use it (*encourage its utilization.*) As for the wrong choices:

A and **E** focus too heavily on copyright holders. The author doesn't write primarily to illuminate *their* motives or persuade *them* to not be so stringent but rather to rally those who would use their works for art and commentary to make use of a legal tool at their disposal. Nor is *loophole* the best word to describe fair use, but we need not quibble with that since **E** has a bigger problem in mistaking the main focus of the passage.

C and **D:** Considering the encouragement given to artists and social commentators in the passage's final sentence, ultimately the author is out to do more than merely "outline" or "explain." She writes also to urge people to act.

21.   **E**
Reading Comprehension: Tone, Style, or Attitude   *Rating:* Medium

Step 1: Skim and Outline. You've taken care of this step already, so we'll move on to Step 2.

Step 2: Read the Question and Search for Triggers. The trigger words are *author of the passage can be most accurately described as* . . . These words are significant because they tell us we're dealing with a Tone, Style, or Attitude question, which is to say we need to locate the author's opinion on the other trigger words in the question: *successful employment of the fair use defense.*

Step 3: Locate Relevant Information and Make a Prediction. The final sentence of the passage is the place to look, since it is there, and there alone, that we hear about the author's opinion on anything. The author says that the fair use provision is *necessary* and could be *powerful* if people go ahead and use it, despite potential obstacles (its ambiguity, the possibility of receiving cease-and-desist letters, etc.). So that sounds positive, but with qualifications, for after all, the author admits there's some serious opposition to using the provision. We'll look for a choice that's in line with these ideas.

Step 4: Match Your Prediction to the Answer Choices. Choice **E** is correct. Based on our thinking above, it's reasonable to say that the author is optimistic, but cautiously so.

A: There is no sense of confusion on the part of the author, who appears to have a firm grasp of the issues.

B takes the author's optimism to an unwarranted extreme, ignoring all of the obstacles and caveats the author documents regarding the application of fair use.

C: The author wouldn't qualify as *brazen* ("bold," "brash") or *defiant*. In fact, she barely surfaces at all until the final paragraph; not exactly a sign of audacity. She voices her opinion in a reasoned, qualified way. So **C**, like **B**, is too extreme.

D suggests a sense of paranoia not evident in any part of the passage. The author may be wary or cautious, but is neither *cynical* nor *suspicious* regarding the prospects of utilizing fair use.

22.   **B**

Reading Comprehension: Detail   *Rating:* Difficult

Step 1: Skim and Outline. Been there, done that, so move on to Step 2.

Step 2: Read the Question and Search for Triggers. Our trigger is *self-censorship*, which tells us the topic of this Detail question.

Step 3: Locate Relevant Information and Make a Prediction. The third sentence of paragraph 4 tells us what constitutes self-censorship: when individuals who fear legal confrontations consciously decide not to make use of their fair use privileges. The individuals referred to are inferably the people the author discusses throughout the passage who could and should utilize fair use—artists and social commentators who would like to appropriate cultural materials. We'll look for something among the choices that captures the essence of this thought.

Step 4: Match Your Prediction to the Answer Choices. Choice **B** provides the best paraphrase of the author's take on this issue. According to the author, self-censorship occurs when artists and social commentators choose not to appropriate cultural objects in the way they would wish, out of fear of legal repercussions.

Let's take a look at how the wrong choices go awry:

A: *Politicians*? They're irrelevant, so toss **A**.

C distorts the passage. We're told that individuals censor themselves by not invoking fair use because of fear of legal confrontations, not that *lawyers* are afraid of entangling clients in long and costly litigation. (And besides, aren't lawyers the ones who *like* long and costly litigation?)

D may be the result *after* the individuals in question have been scared off and have thus engaged in the self-censorship the author mentions, but choosing to ditch projects for lack of appropriated materials is not what the author means by self-censorship. Again, that involves failing to utilize fair use privileges.

E changes the idea of artists using fair use to produce their works into the idea of artists producing works *about* fair use. Be wary of such choices that distort the passage's ideas.

23.   **E**

Reading Comprehension: Detail Purpose   *Rating:* Difficult

Step 1: Skim and Outline. You've already skimmed and outlined, so move on to the final question of the set.

Step 2: Read the Question and Search for Triggers. Our triggers are *right to public assembly* and the very handy line reference, (lines 48–49).

Step 3: Locate Relevant Information and Make a Prediction. Locating the relevant info isn't tough, given the line reference, so unless this detail is fresh in your mind, it pays to head to the highlighted part of the passage to remind yourself what was said about the right to public assembly. The structure of the sentence in question suggests that the right to public assembly is intended to provide an example of something that fair use is *not*—specifically, an affirmative protection. So the author is using this example to present a contrast of sorts. That will suffice as our prediction, so let's see what the choices have to offer.

Step 4: Match Your Prediction to the Answer Choices. Choice **E** speaks of contrast, but we better make sure the rest of **E** pans out. Does the author use the contrast to point to a limitation in fair use? Yes; we can infer that from the way she describes fair use as a "defense that one can appeal to *only after a charge has been brought.*" That certainly doesn't sound as good as an *affirmative protection*, a law that directly allows people to do something such as assemble in public. **E** therefore pinpoints the purpose of this detail. As for the rest:

A: The author describes no similarity between fair use and the right to public assembly. Moreover, fair use is deemed a defense, not a protection, so this choice fails on that count as well.

B focuses on a different element of the passage, the distinction made early on between clearly defined laws and those with looser, more flexible interpretations.

C would be correct for a passage focusing on the advantages of affirmative protections over after-the-fact defenses, but that's not what we get here. The *right to public assembly* bit is provided to shed light on the applicability of fair use. It's not mentioned to help the author make a general argument for the superiority of one kind of legal vehicle over another.

D gets is backward: The right to public assembly is presented as an example of an affirmative protection. *Fair use* is defined as a right that can be defended only after a charge has been brought.

24.   **C**

Sentence Completions: Definition   *Rating:* Difficult

Step 1: Find the Keywords. The first blank is defined as a *merry gang*, while the phrase *raucous and often illicit behavior* holds the key to the second blank.

Step 2: Look for Road Signs. No road sign appears to send the sentence's logic off in a particular direction, so we can safely assume that the missing words relate in a definitional way to the keywords identified in Step 1.

Step 3: Make a Prediction. The first blank is a bit vaguer, since lots of nouns can accord with the phrase *merry gang*. The second blank is defined a bit more specifically: It must contain a word that's exemplified *by raucous and often illicit behavior*. Something along the lines of *wickedness*, *depravity*, or *debauchery* could work. We'll look to narrow the choices down to ones whose second word matches these predictions and then address this *merry gang* business after that.

Step 4: Compare Your Answer(s) to the Answer Choices. *Decorum* and *determination* are positive attributes that don't accord well at all with our predictions, so **D** and **E** are out. It also makes no sense to link a concept like debauchery with the word fallacy ("mistaken belief") so we'll knock off **A** as well.

As for the remainders, *depraved, raucous* behavior doesn't necessarily involve *chicanery* ("trickery," "deception"), but it does accord well with the word *turpitude*, meaning "extreme immorality." To verify, let's look at the first words of choices **B** and **C**. While we might properly define the king's depraved, merry gang as *miscreants* ("troublemakers," "scoundrels"), we wouldn't call them *ascetics* (people who renounce material comforts)—quite the opposite.

Step 5: Plug It In. A coherent and logical sentence emerges when we use the words in choice **C** to fill in the blanks.

25.   **E**

Antonyms: Multiple Meanings, Parts of Speech   *Rating:* Difficult

Step 1: Simplify the Word. The word *appropriate* may already seem simple enough to you, but that's a trap. If you see what appears to be an easy word toward the end of the Verbal section, especially if you think you've been doing fairly well up to that point, chances are an alternative meaning is in play. *Appropriate* is most commonly used as an adjective, meaning "fitting" or "suitable," as in "the principal took the appropriate action." But you'll notice that the choices in this question are all verbs, so in this case *to appropriate* means to take possession of and make use of something. For example, a government may appropriate funds for education, or a writer may appropriate quotations to use in his own work. (In fact, you even saw this concept of appropriation in the long Reading Comp passage on fair use a bit earlier in the section.)

Step 2: Predict an Opposite. The opposite of *taking* and *using* something is *discarding* and/or *not using* it. Let's see where this basic prediction leads.

Step 3: Match Your Prediction to the Answer Choices. *Jettison* (**E**) means "to throw away" or "get rid of" and is therefore the closest antonym of the bunch. *Repurpose* implies using something in some way, so **B** is closer to a synonym than an antonym. The other choices bear no relation to *appropriate*.

26. **B**
Analogies: Attribute   *Rating:* Difficult

Step 1: Connect the Dots. *Perfidy* means "treachery" or "betrayal," while *steadfast* means to be "loyal" or "trustworthy." So anyone who is *steadfast* will lack the attribute of *perfidy*.

Step 2: Create a Template. We'll go with our usual Attribute template, of course remembering to include the negative: "One who is Y is NOT characterized by X."

Step 3: Make the Match. The pair of words in **B** contains the same relationship: One who is *melancholy* ("sad") is not characterized by *jubilance* ("euphoria," "extreme happiness"). Choice **A** fits the Attribute mold but omits the negative: One who is *dynamic* IS characterized by *energy*, while **E** flirts with the same relationship but doesn't quite get there: One who is snubbed ("insulted," "slighted") might respond with *impudence* ("rudeness") but need not. In any case, we're looking for a negative relationship, so **E** fails on that count alone. Choices **C** and **D** contain weak links, as there is no discernible relationship between the words in these two pairs.

27. **B**
Antonyms: Relate the Word to Words You Know,
Create a Context   *Rating:* Difficult

Step 1: Simplify the Word. *Unfledged* is an uncommon word you simply don't hear every day, but there is a word like it that you may be more familiar with: full-*fledged*. Maybe you've heard a battle described as "a full-fledged assault," as in a full-blown, complete onslaught. Or maybe you've heard someone who has graduated into the full ranks of his or her profession described as a "full-fledged" doctor, lawyer, or what have you. In these contexts, the word suggests a sense of complete development, so something that's *unfledged*, in contrast, is something that's "undeveloped," raw," or "not fully formed."

THE
GRE

Step 2: Predict an Opposite. Since we actually went ahead and used the more common opposite of *unfledged* to lead us to its meaning, we only need to call to mind definitions of *full-fledged*: "fully developed," "ripe," "complete," "seasoned," and so on.

Step 3: Match Your Prediction to the Answer Choices. The word among the choices that accords with the predictions above is mature, choice **B**.

28.   **D**

Analogies: Degree   *Rating:* Difficult

Step 1: Connect the Dots. To highlight one of our more advanced Analogies strategies, we'll explain this one as if you didn't know the meaning of predilection—and hey, maybe that's even the case, since it *is* a tough, uncommon word. But you most likely do know what *obsession* means, so this is a good opportunity to work backward from the choices to establish some relationships and sniff out which ones may be likely or not for the original pair.

Step 2: Create a Template. No can do, since we're assuming we don't know what *predilection* means, so let's go right to the choices and see what kinds of relationships we can find.

A: *Gravity* describes the seriousness of a *condition*. Can *predilection* describe the seriousness of an *obsession*? Not impossible, but not likely; that just doesn't sound right, so we'll *jettison* (see question 25) **A** for now.

B: *Fire* and *inferno* are related in that one is an extreme form of the other. That's not out of the realm of possibility for *obsession* and *predilection*, so we'll keep **B** around and see what else we can find.

C: A *capillary* connects a vein to an artery. Might *predilection* connect *obsession* to something else? Probably not; *obsession* doesn't sound like the kind of thing you connect to. So let's add **C** to our "not promising" pile.

D: *Torrent* and *sprinkle*, like the pair in choice **B**, are related in terms of degree: A *torrent* ("deluge," "downpour") is an extreme form of a *sprinkle*. This relationship could work, so we'll hold on to **D**.

E: There's no noticeable logical relationship between *courtship* and *sentimentality*. It sounds as if they might be in the same ballpark: Maybe people who are in a courtship (period of wooing often with the intention of marriage) are sentimental—but maybe they're not. That's a bit too tenuous for the test makers' liking, so we'll chop **E** on the familiar grounds of *weak-link-ish-ness*.

So even without knowing the meaning of *predilection*, a little strategy can help us narrow things down to **B** and **D**; a fifty-fifty proposition. **D** wins out: A *predilection* is a "fondness" or "liking" for something, which means that the relationship in the original pair is one of Degree: *Obsession* is an extreme form of *predilection*, just as *torrent* is an extreme form of *sprinkle*. Incidentally, choice **B** also contains a Degree relationship—just in the wrong direction. In the original and in correct choice **D**, the milder form of the phenomenon is on the right, with the extreme form on the left. **B** has it the other way around.

29. **C**

Antonyms: Expand Your Vocabulary   *Rating:* Difficult

Step 1: Simplify the Word. This question serves as a reminder that the most indispensable asset when it comes to Antonyms is a large vocabulary. *Redoubtable*, for example, is deceptive, and for the most part not amenable to the strategies we've discussed. It contains the prefix *re* but has nothing to do with the notion of "backward," as this prefix often denotes ("replay," "repeat," "redundant," etc.). It also contains the word *doubt*, but its meaning has nothing to do with "uncertainty" or "skepticism." You simply need to know that *redoubtable* means "commanding," "formidable," "worthy of respect or honor," often in regard to a commanding figure as in "the redoubtable General Robert E. Lee."

Step 2: Predict an Opposite. The opposite of a *commanding* person *worthy of respect* is someone who's "ridiculous," "preposterous," "incompetent," or "embarrassing."

Step 3: Match Your Prediction to the Answer Choices. Our predictions lead us to *farcical*, choice **C**. Unlike *redoubtable*, *farcical* does contain a clue as to its meaning, the word *farce*, which means a "sham" or "mockery." *Cylindrical*, choice **D**, is one of those neutral-sounding words that's unlikely to be correct. What, after all, is the opposite of *cylindrical*? *Flat*? *Square*? It's too murky, so scratch choices like **D** that seem to have no clear opposite. So we can at least apply one technique in this one to narrow down the choices. Still, your best bet in tough Antonym questions is to have memorized as many difficult, uncommon vocabulary words as you can before taking the GRE. Use the word list we provide in the tear-out chart that comes with this book for starters, and then continue to build your vocabulary in any way you can.

30. **E**

Sentence Completions: Contrast   *Rating:* Difficult

Step 1: Find the Keywords. Gothic architecture is the sentence's topic, but the words just before and just after each blank are the keywords we need to focus on: *severely* (blank) *lines*; *intricately* (blank) *ornamentation*. We need to consider the sentence's road sign, however, to figure out what these things mean and how they relate.

Step 2: Look for Road Signs. Unlike simple single-word road signs, this one stretches throughout the sentence. It's contained in the formulation *range extends from* (blank 1) to (blank 2). This is an uncommon road sign, but to say that a range extends from one thing to another is to contrast those two things—in other words, to say that they lie on opposite extremes. Noting that the missing words must contrast makes this difficult Sentence Completion easier to handle.

Step 3: Make a Prediction. With this contrast sentence structure in mind, we can now infer that the author of the sentence means to tell us that on one hand Gothic architecture is characterized by lines that are *severely* (blank), while on the other hand it's noted for ornamentation that *intricately* (blank). *Intricate* is the easier word to deal with; it suggests that the ornamentation the author describes is *fancy*. This is contrasted with severe lines, which in this context we can just think of as "non-fancy." Remember, don't worry if the actual words you use for your predictions aren't complex or GRE-like—it's the *spirit* of your predictions that matters, and that will help you recognize correct choices.

Step 4: Compare Your Answer(s) to the Answer Choices. Searching for something along the lines of *fancy* ornamentation for the second blank may be the easier way to go. *Florid* means "ornate," "fancy," or "flowery," so makes for a good completion for the second blank. *Austere* ("plain," "stark"), *florid's* counterpart in choice **E**, fits the bill for "strict" or "non-fancy."

Step 5: Plug It In. The contrast is established and the sentence makes sense when **E** is added to the mix.

The Future of the GRE

The folks who create the GRE have big plans, but they're implementing them in small steps. In 2007, they planned a massive revision of the test, including a nonadaptive testing format and many new question types. They scrapped that plan at the last minute for what appears to be technical reasons. In its place, they announced a plan to introduce new question types little by little, first as unscored sample questions, and later, when enough data has been gathered, as full-fledged components of the test.

NEW QUESTION TYPES

As of this publication, ETS is trying out one new Math question type and one new Verbal question type on the computer-based GRE General Test. If you take the test on computer, you may see one of these question types, but not both. As this book goes to press, these new questions are unscored, but that will likely change at some point in the future. Therefore, be sure to go to www.gre.org for the latest information as your test date approaches.

Here's a brief look at these first new question types to debut on the GRE.

Math: Numeric Entry

This question type requires you to enter a numeric answer either into a single box, or into two boxes for answers in fraction form. The math in these questions is the same as that tested in the standard Problem Solving question type you've learned about in this book. The major difference is that the choices will be missing, and you'll have to enter your answer using the computer's mouse and keyboard. You'll need to pay careful attention to rounding instructions, and to the units required for the answer. For example, if you calculate an answer as 17.62 but they ask for the answer to be rounded to the nearest integer, you must enter 18 into the box to receive credit. Similarly, if a problem is worded in feet, but the word *yards* appears after the entry box, you must be sure to convert your answer into yards or you'll get the question wrong.

Here's an example of what a Numeric Entry question will look like if you come across one on your test:

1. Machine A builds 8 bolts in 4 hours, Machine B builds 3 bolts in 30 minutes, and Machine C takes apart 3 bolts in 1 hour. If all three machines operate simultaneously and independently, what will be the net gain in bolts after 10 hours?

Click on the answer box and type in a number. Backspace to erase.

In case you're wondering, the answer is 50. At the rates indicated, Machine A will add 20 bolts to the tally, Machine B will add 60, and Machine C will dismantle 30, for a net gain of 50 bolts.

Verbal: Text Completions

Text Completions are basically ramped-up versions of Sentence Completions. However, the differences are significant: Instead of consisting of a single sentence with one or two blanks, Text Completions are one to five sentences in length and contain either two or three blanks. Moreover, each blank comes with an *independent* list of three words or phrases to choose from to fill the blank. We say independent because unlike Sentence Completions, what you select for one blank does not influence what you choose for the others. Naturally, the words you select must work together to create a coherent sentence or short paragraph, and *all* of your selections must be correct to receive credit. In other words, there is no partial credit—you must answer each blank correctly to get the point.

An example will clarify what this new question type is all about. Try this one:

Directions: For each blank select one entry from the corresponding columns of choices. Fill all blanks in the way that best completes the text.

1. Colleagues knew FBI counterintelligence official Robert Philip Hanssen to be _____(i)_____ anti-communist, so it came as a great surprise to many when he was accused of spying for Russia for 15 years. As punishment for his _____(ii)_____, believed to be among the worst security _____(iii)_____ in the bureau's history, Hanssen was sentenced to life imprisonment.

Blank (i)	Blank (ii)	Blank (iii)
intermittently	perfidy	routines
fervently	prowess	strategies
moderately	insularity	breaches

The correct answers are *fervently*, *perfidy*, and *breaches*.

The information here is correct as of the date of publication. For more information, strategies, sample questions, and updates on plans for these and other new GRE question types, go to www.gre.org.

Top 15 GRE Test Day Tips

Hey, everyone and his grandmother has a Top Ten list of Test Day advice, so we figured we'd one-up 'em—actually, five-up 'em, to be precise. Here goes:

'TWAS THE NIGHT BEFORE GRE . . .

#15: Get it together. Pack up the day before so you don't have to go scrambling around in the morning. Get your admission ticket, ID, water, and nonsugar energy snack (for the break) all ready to go.

#14: Wind down. Runners don't run a full marathon the day *before*; they rest up for the big day. Avoid cramming the day before the test. Read a book, watch a movie, hang out with friends, whatever relaxes you—but make it an early night. And speaking of which . . .

#13: Get enough sleep. Don't get into bed at 7:00 just to stare at the ceiling, but do get to bed early enough to ensure you have enough sleep to be alert and energetic for Test Day.

#12: Set two alarms. You don't want to miss your testing appointment because your alarm was set for P.M. instead of A.M.—stranger things have happened. Also, one of your alarms should be battery-operated, just in case something crazy like a power outage occurs during the night. Unlikely, sure, but peace of mind will help you sleep better. Of course, if your appointment is scheduled for the afternoon, waking up on time shouldn't be an issue.

RISE AND SHINE . . .

#11: Eat normally. Sure, GRE day is special, but that doesn't mean you need to treat yourself to a special breakfast. Nerves can turn a huge bacon, egg and cheese omelet against you—especially if you don't usually eat that kind of thing. Eat what you normally eat for breakfast; not too much, not too little. If your test is in the afternoon, still make sure to eat something before it. Bring a nonsugar snack for the break. It's a long day, and you'll need the energy.

#10: Dress for success. One word: layers. If it's hot, take some off. If it's cold, leave them on. Comfort is key.

#9: Jump-start your brain. To employ the marathon analogy again (see #14), runners stretch before the big event to warm up. Likewise, it helps to do a bit of reading before the test to get your mind warmed up and stretch those brain cells into shape. We're not talking Plato or Shakespeare here. Articles from a well-written newspaper, magazine, or journal containing the same kind of sophisticated writing you'll see on the test will do.

PUT ON YOUR GAME FACE . . .

#8: Arrive early. Save fashionable lateness for your social life. Rushing around like a crazy person isn't the best way to start your GRE day. If the testing center is in unfamiliar territory, you may even wish to scout it out a week or two before just to be sure you know your way. One less thing to worry about couldn't hurt.

#7: Don't sweat the small stuff. Okay, so what if it's 9 billion degrees in the testing room and that obnoxious kid from high school is at the computer right next to you? If something potentially correctable is bothering you, by all means talk to a test site administrator, but if there's nothing you can do about it, let it go. Don't allow small annoyances to distract you from your mission.

#6: Gear up for a long haul. Some people arrive at the test center all revved up, bouncing off the walls—the big day is finally here! Slow down; you don't want to overheat and peak too soon. You'll get to the test site, endure the usual standardized testing bureaucratic technicalities, and then be shown to a computer. "Go time" isn't until you've completed the testing tutorial and the first Analytical Writing essay prompt appears on the screen. Which brings us to our tips for the final and most important phase of the testing experience . . .

GO TIME . . .

#5: Prepare for the worst. This is by no means to say you should go in with a negative attitude, but you need to be ready to start the test with Analytical Writing topics of absolutely no interest to you, followed by your less favorite multiple-choice section (since the Math and Verbal sections can appear in either order). If something like that happens, you'll be prepared; if it doesn't, you'll be relieved. Win-win.

#4: Keep your focus. Maybe the woman at the computer to the right of you will appear to breeze through her Issue essay in five minutes, while the guy to the left of you seems unaware that a test is even taking place. If you have a large enough group, chances are someone may even freak out and leave the room in tears. Assuming that this person isn't you, don't let it bother you. Stay focused on your objective and let the others take care of themselves.

#3: Choose your battles. No one question can hurt you significantly unless you spend all day on it. Keep moving throughout each section. If a question isn't working for you, guess and move on.

#2: Stick it out. There may come a time in the last section when you'll do anything to end your agony five minutes early. Hang in there and keep applying what you've learned. True champs finish strong.

AND THE #1 GRE TEST DAY TIP . . . RELAX. If you've worked hard and prepared conscientiously, take heart from the fact that you've done all you can do. True testing terror comes from being unprepared; conversely, proper preparation breeds confidence. Nerves are normal, but how you deal with them is up to you. Channel your adrenaline positively to give you the energy you need to maintain your focus all the way through. Also remember that while the GRE is surely important, *it's not the end of the world*. Put the event into perspective. Then do the best you can, which is the most you can ask of yourself.

FINAL THOUGHT

We began this book by telling you that the GRE is systematic, coachable, and conquerable. 431 pages later we hope you agree. We at SparkNotes wish you the best of luck on the GRE, and all possible success wherever that may lead. Thanks for allowing us to be part of your future.

THE
GRE

ABOUT THE AUTHORS

ERIC GOODMAN began his career in test preparation and instructional design soon after graduating from Cornell University. His numerous top-selling, critically acclaimed books and courses have helped tens of thousands of students master the LSAT, GMAT, GRE, and SAT. He has also authored online courses and innovative computer-based simulations in the fields of economics, corporate training, and e-commerce.

DAVID YOUNGHANS has taught the GRE for more than a decade. After working for two major test preparation companies, David founded Gorilla Test Prep. *SparkNotes Guide to the GRE Test* is the basis for Gorilla Test Prep's very successful GRE course. Before working in test preparation, David was a ski instructor for the disabled in Winter Park, Colorado. David holds a degree in mathematics and economics from Dartmouth College, where he was named Outstanding Tutor of the Year.

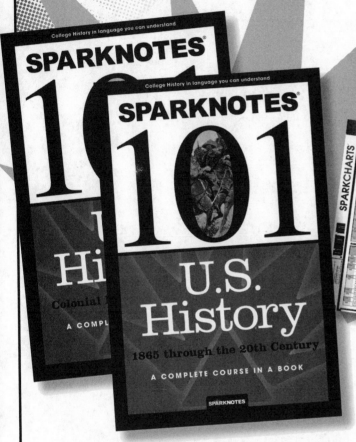

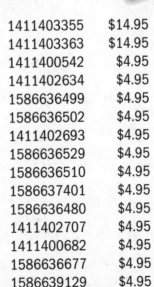

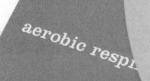